1

STORY BY
JUNICHI FUJISAKU

ART BY
YUKI YOSHIMOTO

BASED ON THE GHOST IN...

THE GHOST IN THE SHELL

攻殻機動隊

THE HUMAN ALGORITHM

CONTENTS

01 SECTION 9   003

02 UNDERCOVER   055

03 WHITE BEAR   097

04 STORMING   129

05 THE BEGINNING OF THINGS   157

06 NO MASTER NO LIFE   187

07 INVISIBLE ENEMIES   217

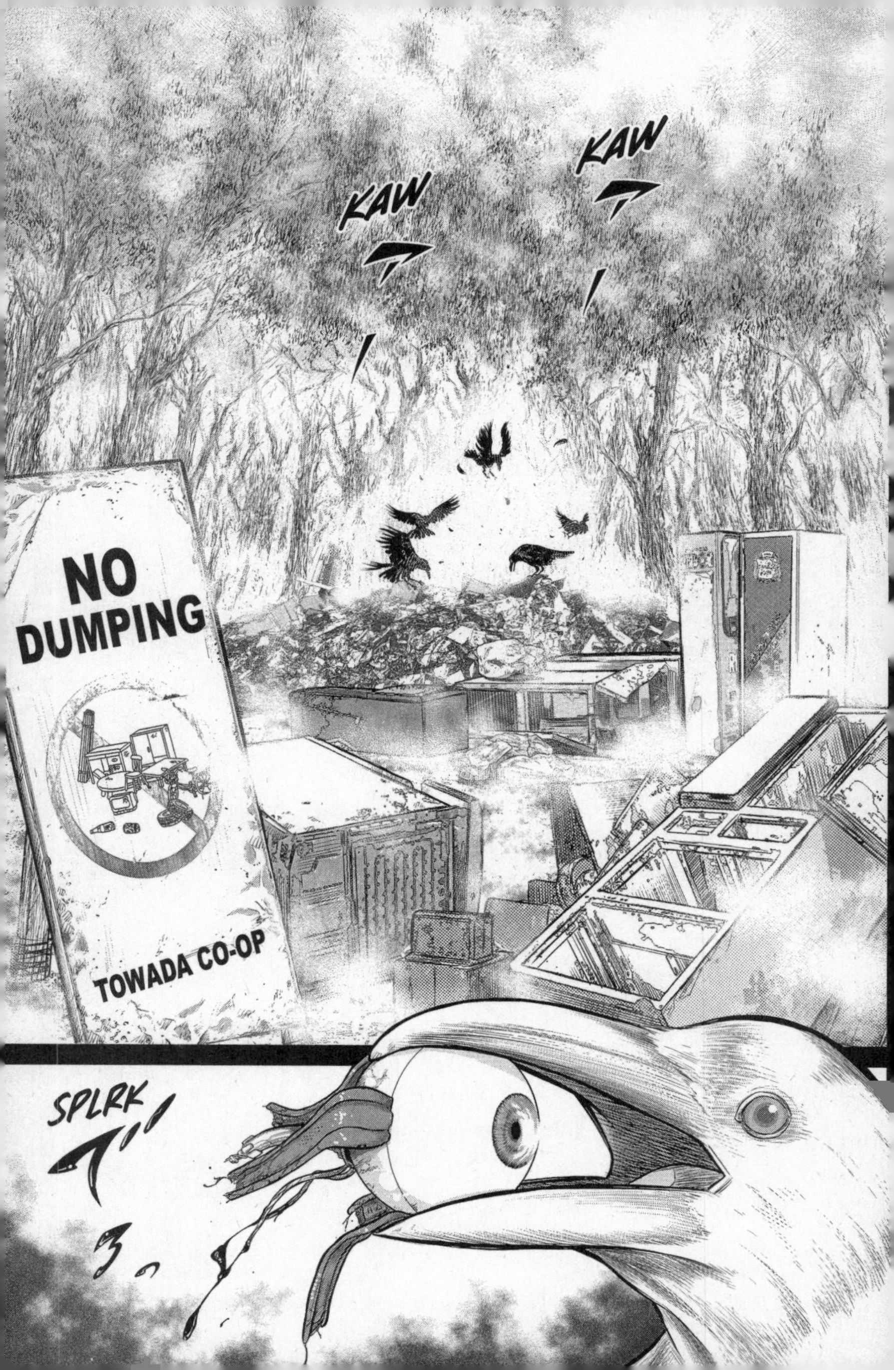
KAW
KAW
NO DUMPING
TOWADA CO-OP
SPLRK

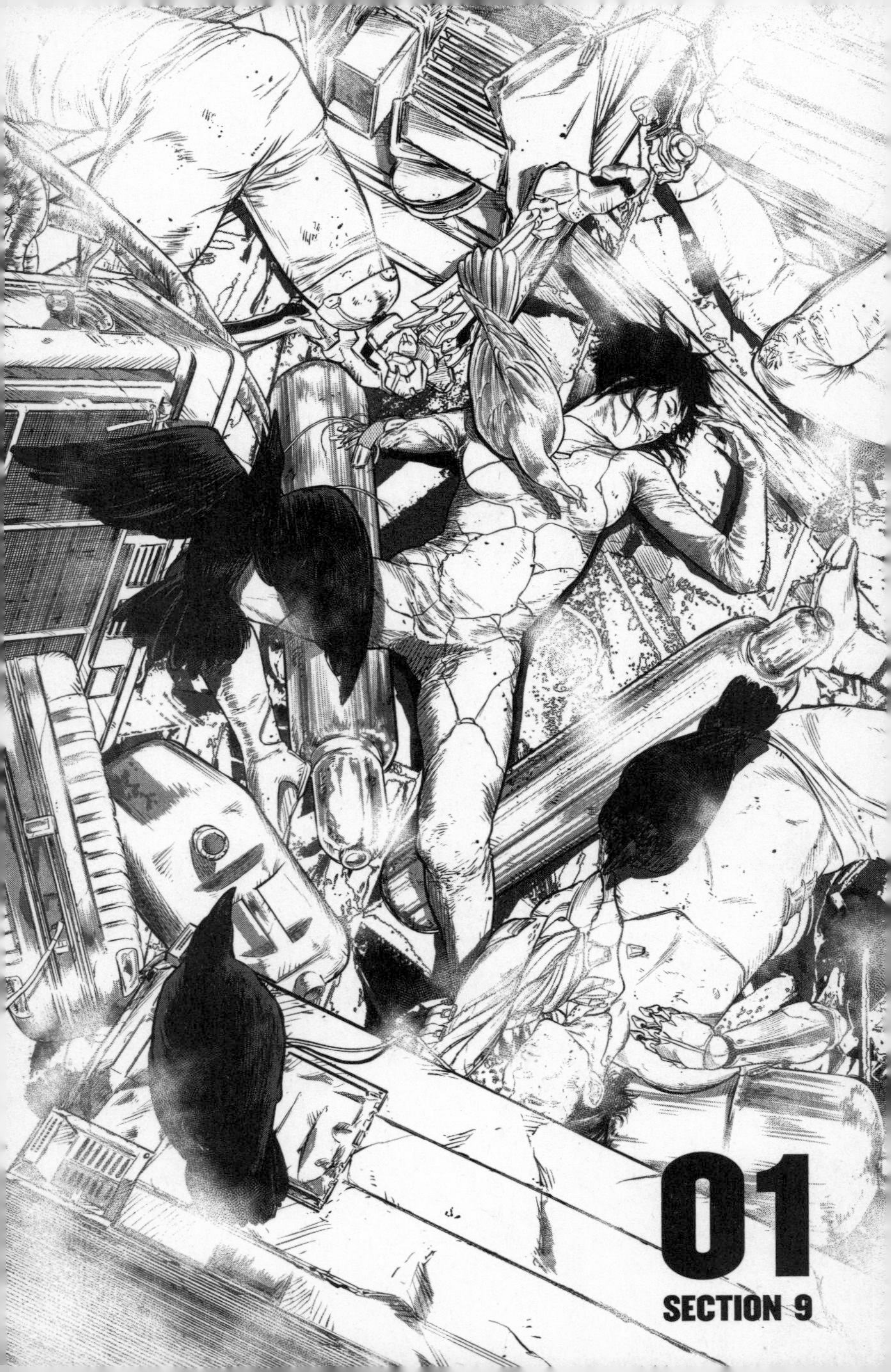
01
SECTION 9

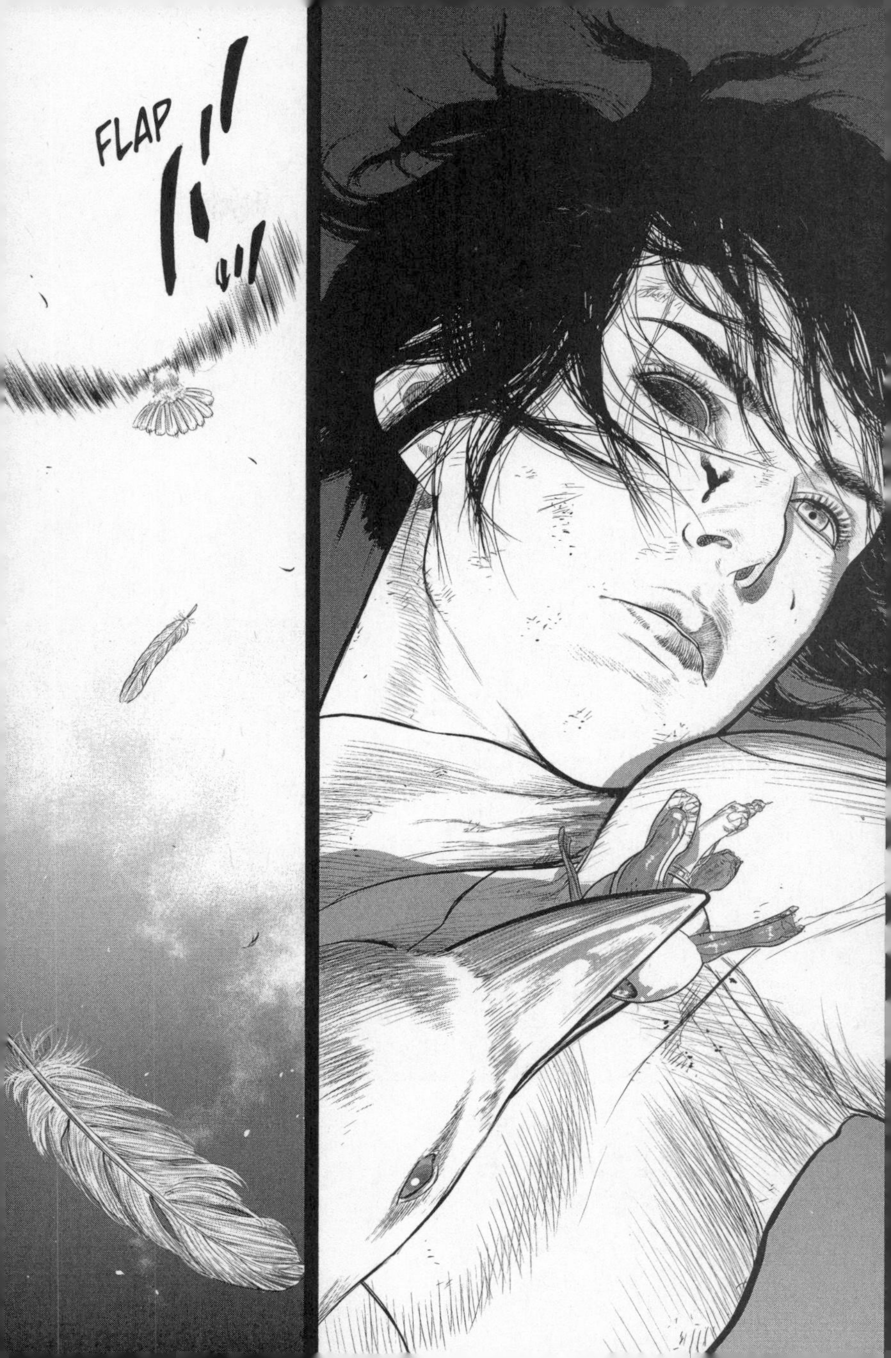
FLAP

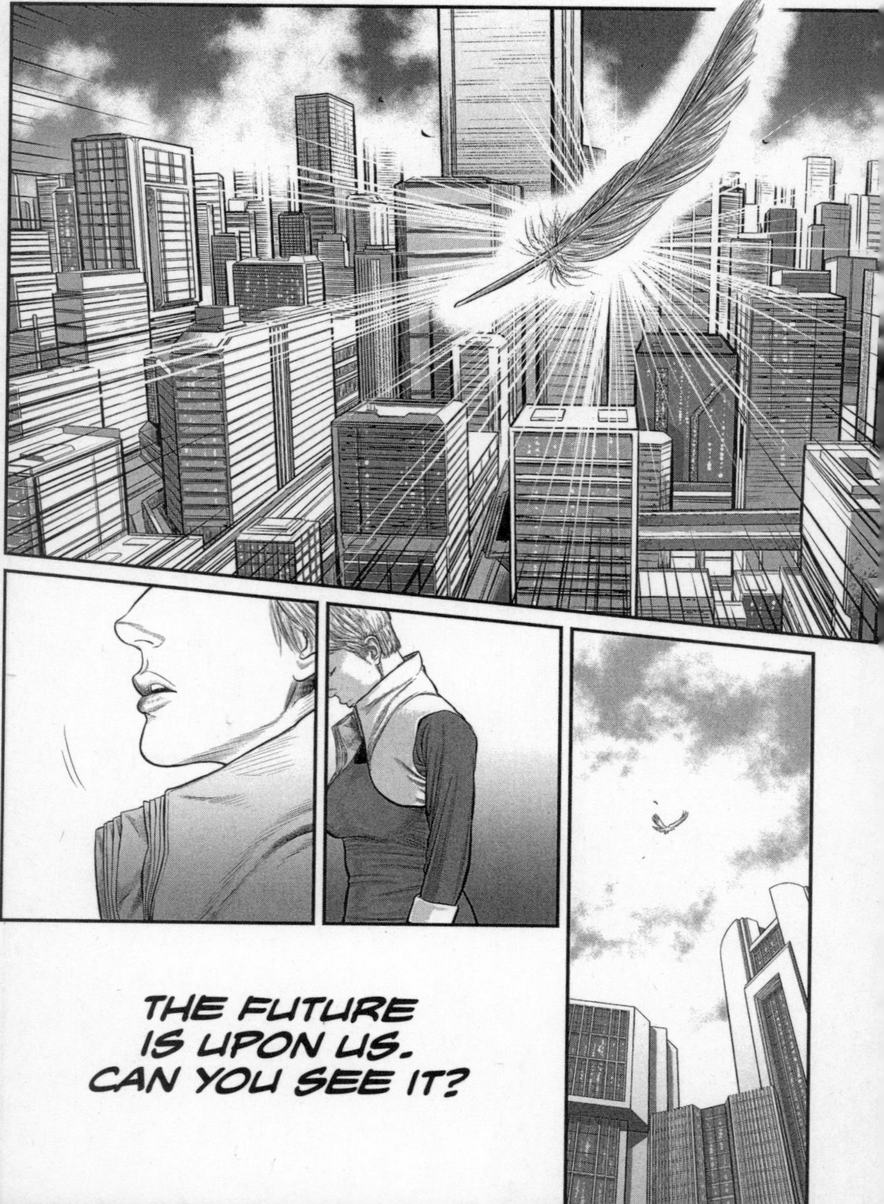
THE FUTURE
IS UPON US.
CAN YOU SEE IT?

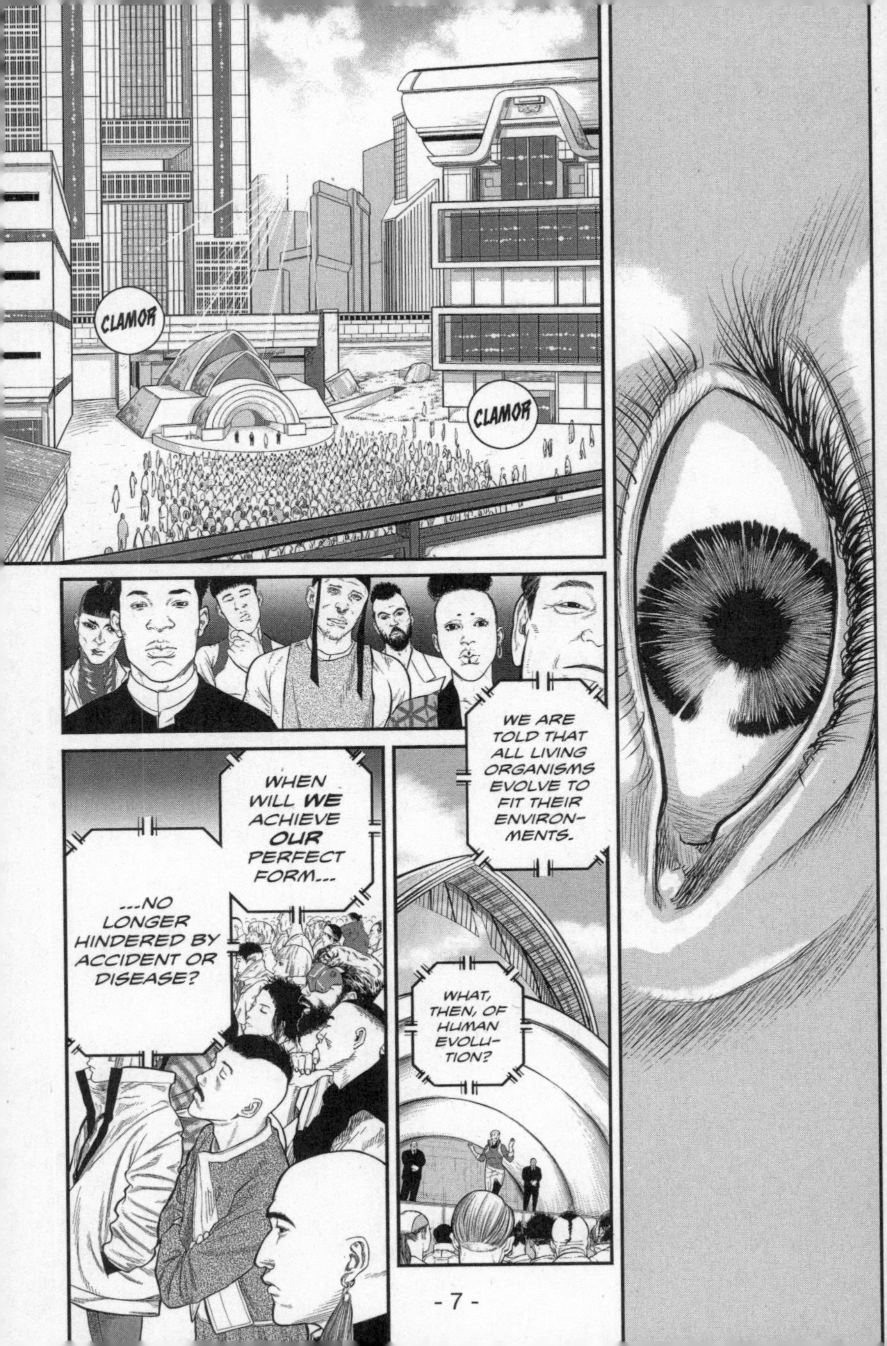
CLAMOR
CLAMOR
WE ARE TOLD THAT ALL LIVING ORGANISMS EVOLVE TO FIT THEIR ENVIRON-MENTS.
WHAT, THEN, OF HUMAN EVOLU-TION?
WHEN WILL **WE** ACHIEVE **OUR** PERFECT FORM...
...NO LONGER HINDERED BY ACCIDENT OR DISEASE?

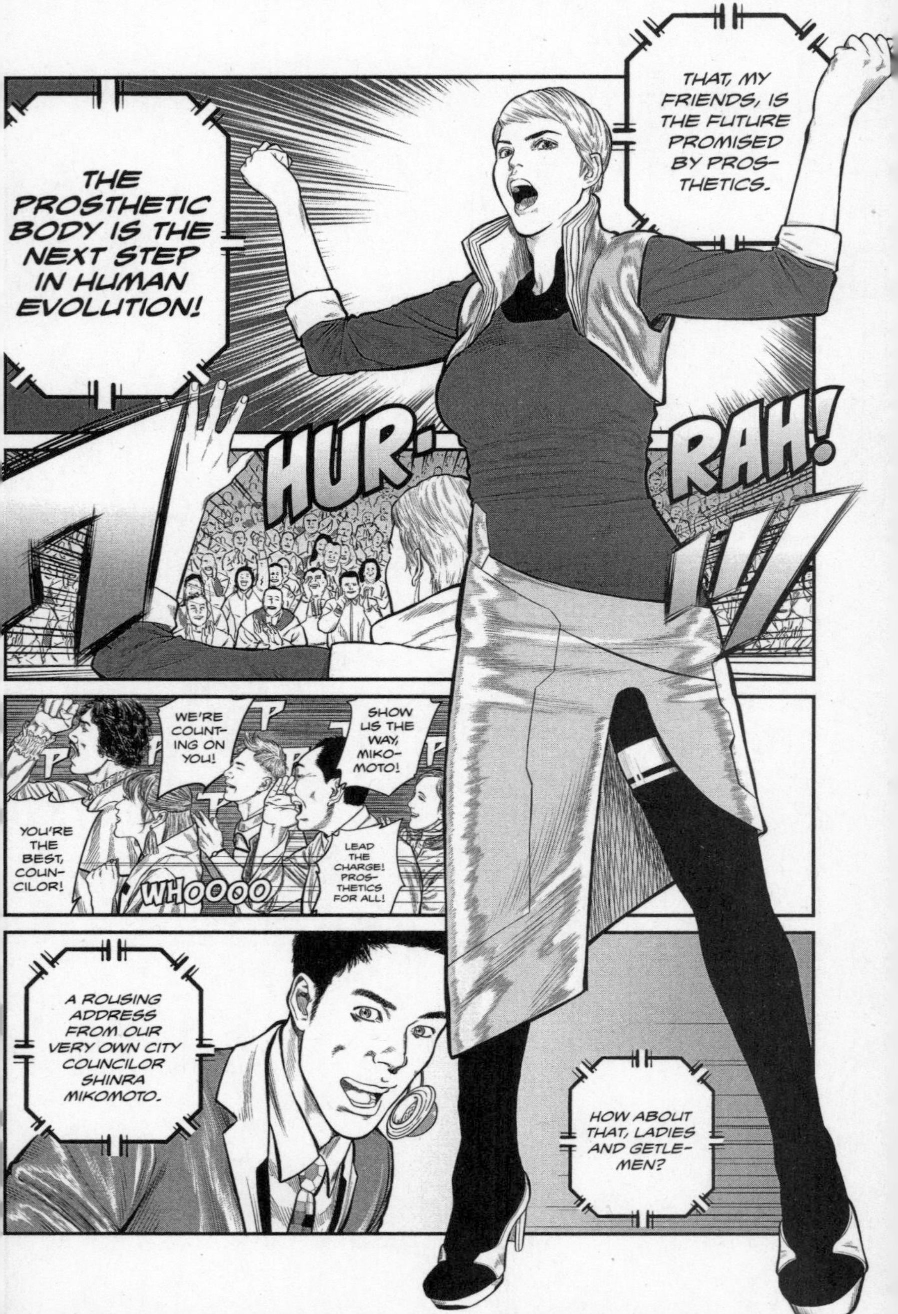
THAT, MY FRIENDS, IS THE FUTURE PROMISED BY PROS-THETICS.
THE PROSTHETIC BODY IS THE NEXT STEP IN HUMAN EVOLUTION!
HUR-RAH!
SHOW US THE WAY, MIKO-MOTO!
LEAD THE CHARGE! PROS-THETICS FOR ALL!
WE'RE COUNT-ING ON YOU!
WHOOOO
YOU'RE THE BEST, COUN-CILOR!
HOW ABOUT THAT, LADIES AND GETLE-MEN?
A ROUSING ADDRESS FROM OUR VERY OWN CITY COUNCILOR SHINRA MIKOMOTO.

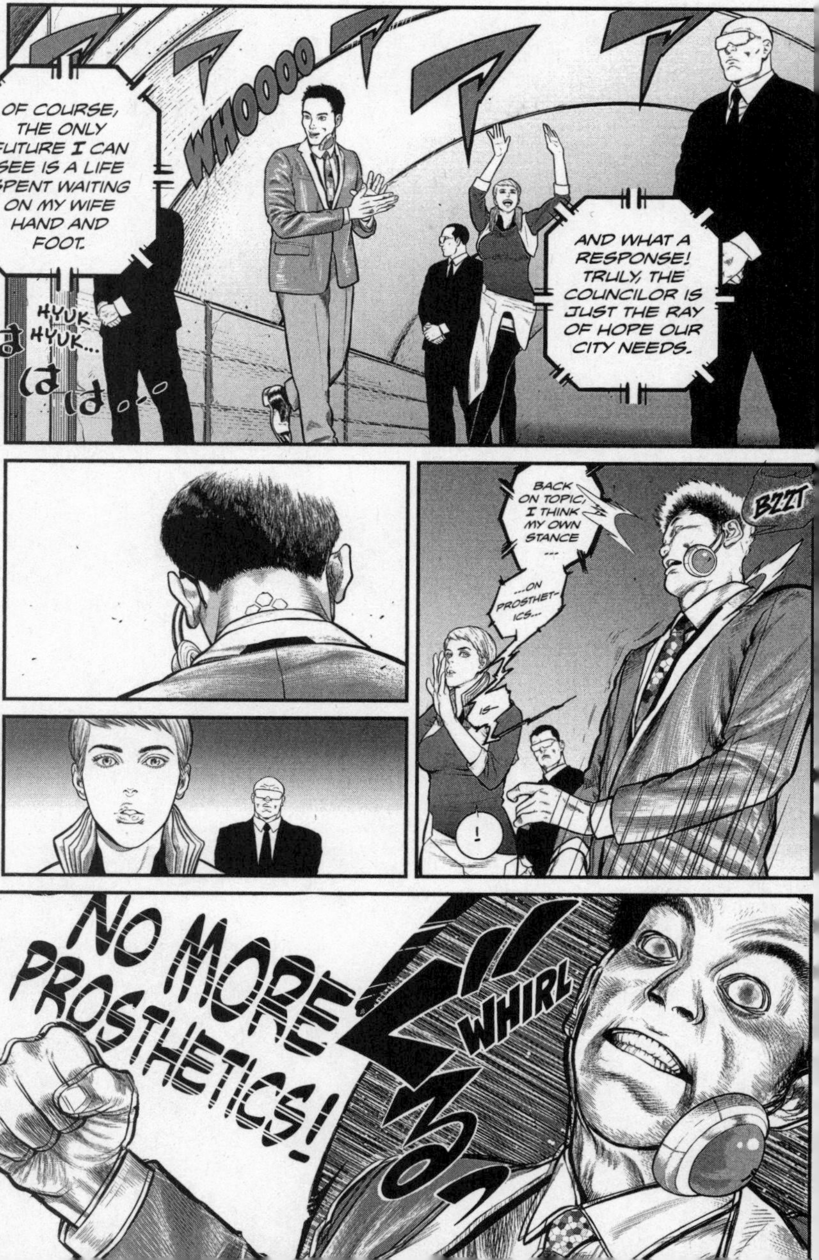
WHOOOO
OF COURSE, THE ONLY FUTURE I CAN SEE IS A LIFE SPENT WAITING ON MY WIFE HAND AND FOOT.
AND WHAT A RESPONSE! TRULY, THE COUNCILOR IS JUST THE RAY OF HOPE OUR CITY NEEDS.
HYUK HYUK...
ははは
BZZT
BACK ON TOPIC, I THINK MY OWN STANCE ---
...ON PROSTHETICS...
IS-
!
NO MORE PROSTHETICS!
WHIRL

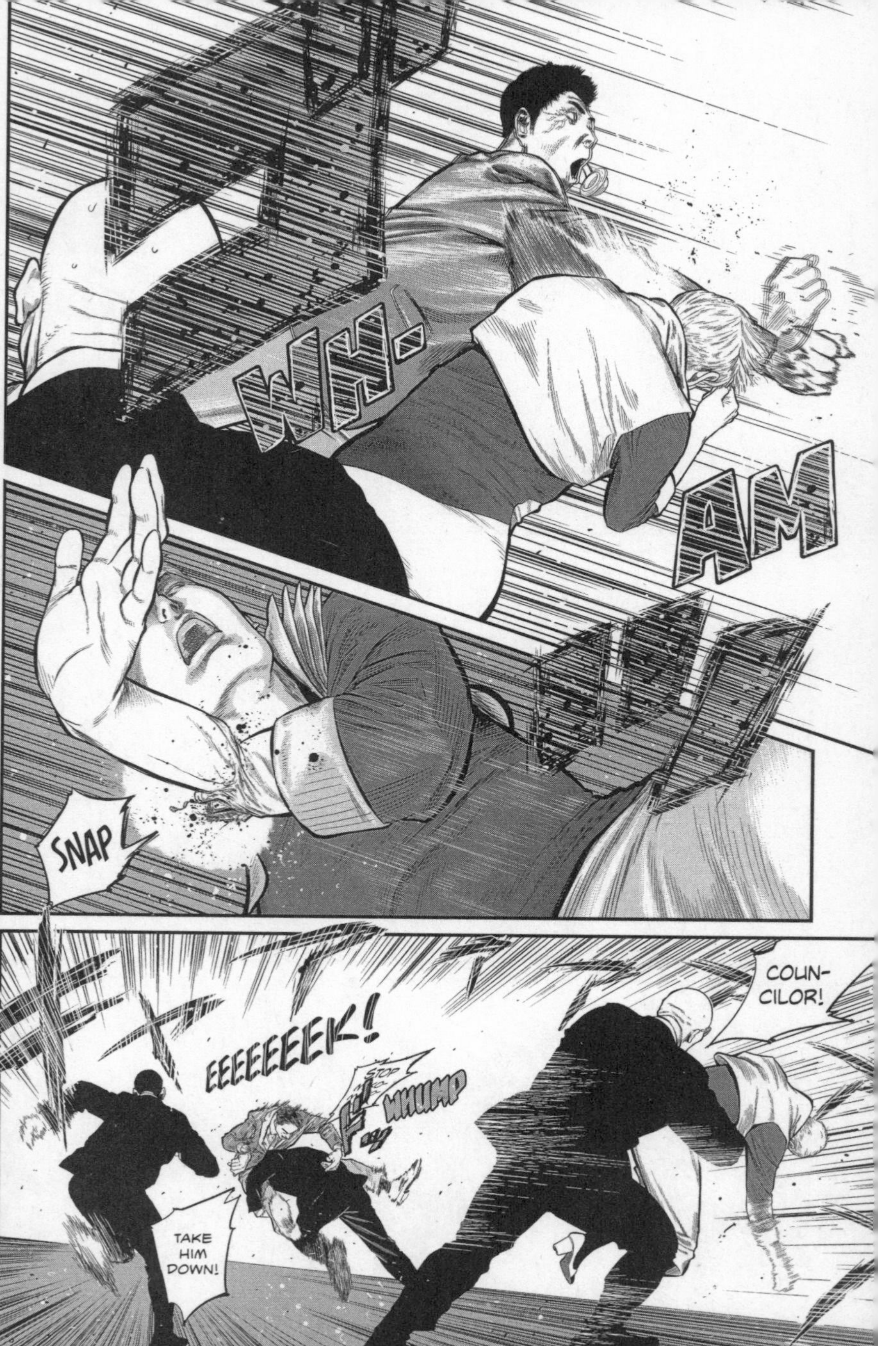
WH-
AM
SNAP
COUN-CILOR!
EEEEEEEK!
STOP
WHUMP
TAKE HIM DOWN!

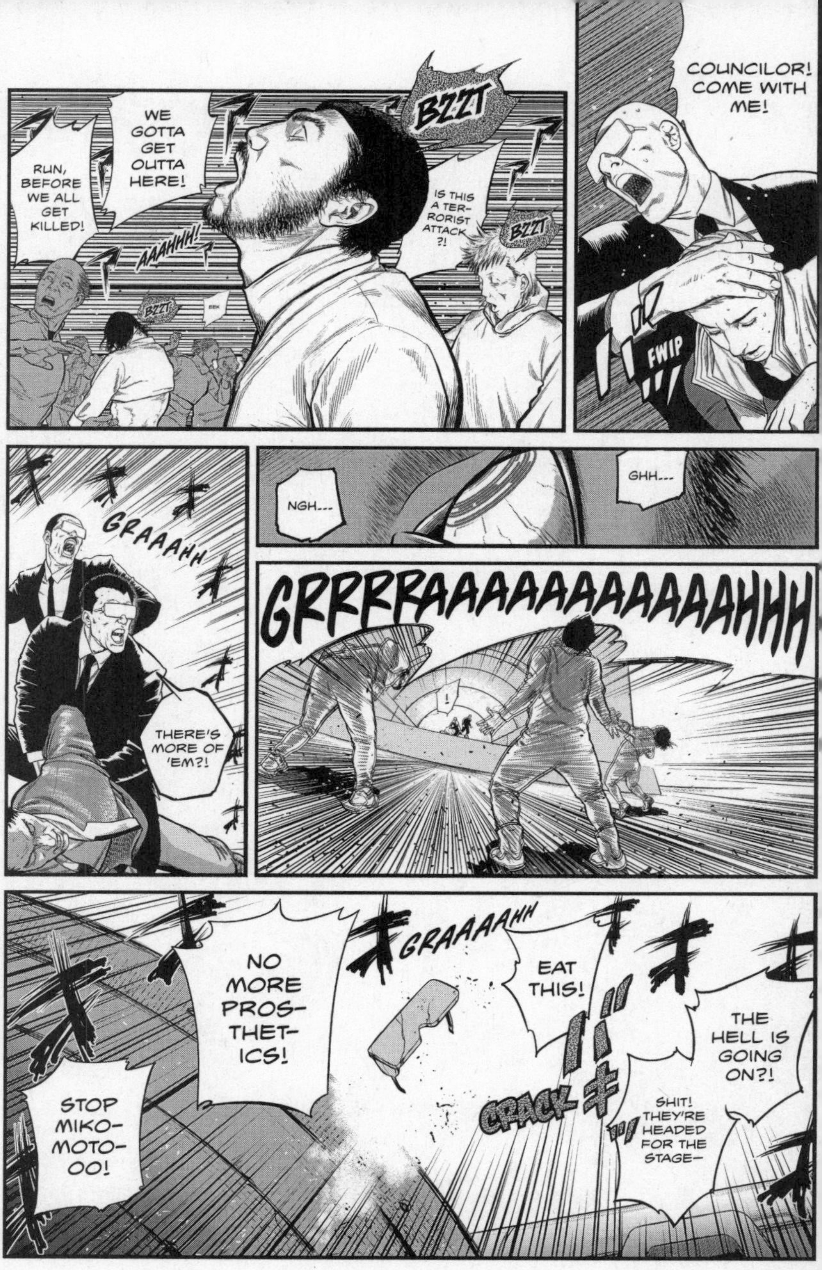
COUNCILOR! COME WITH ME!
FWIP
BZZT
IS THIS A TER-RORIST ATTACK ?!
BZZT
WE GOTTA GET OUTTA HERE!
RUN, BEFORE WE ALL GET KILLED!
AAAHHH!
BZZT
EEK
GHH...
NGH...
GRRRRAAAAAAAAAAAAHHH
!
GRAAAHH
THERE'S MORE OF 'EM?!
THE HELL IS GOING ON?!
SHIT! THEY'RE HEADED FOR THE STAGE—
EAT THIS!
CRACK
GRAAAAHH
NO MORE PROS-THET-ICS!
STOP MIKO-MOTO-OO!

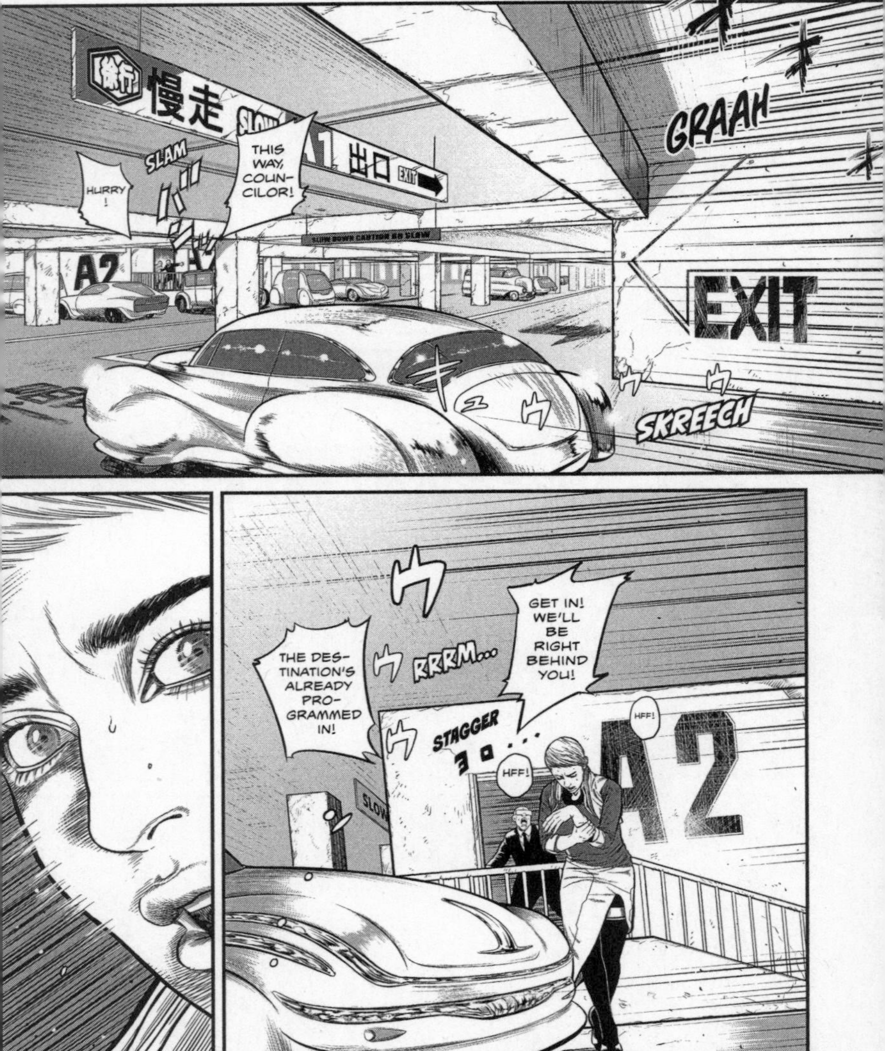
GRAAH
EXIT
SKREECH
出口 EXIT
THIS WAY, COUNCILOR!
慢走 SLOW
SLAM
HURRY!
A2
GET IN! WE'LL BE RIGHT BEHIND YOU!
RRRM...
THE DESTINATION'S ALREADY PROGRAMMED IN!
HFF!
A2
HFF!
STAGGER
SLOW

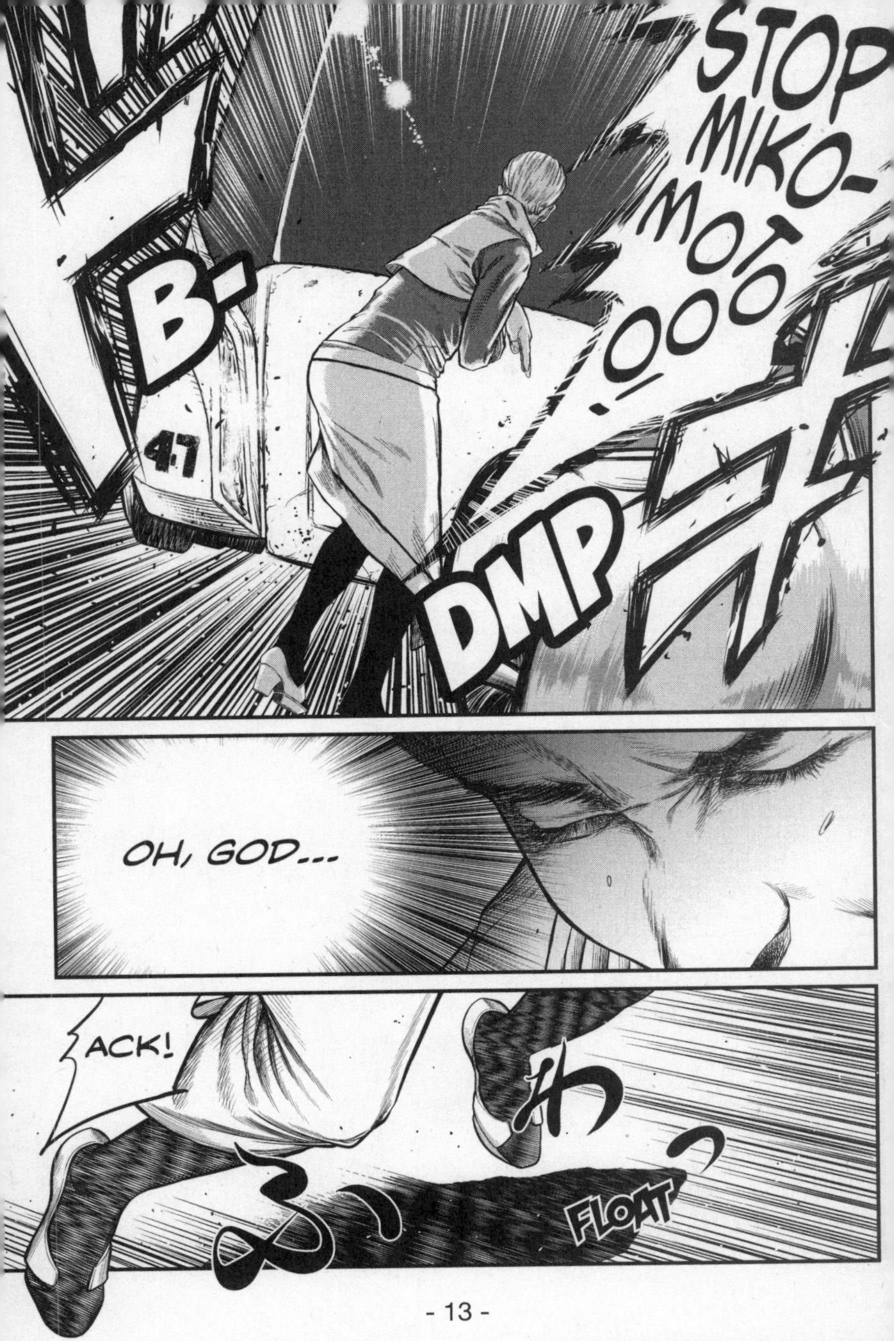
STOP MIKO-MOTOOOO
B-
DMP
OH, GOD...
ACK!
FLOAT

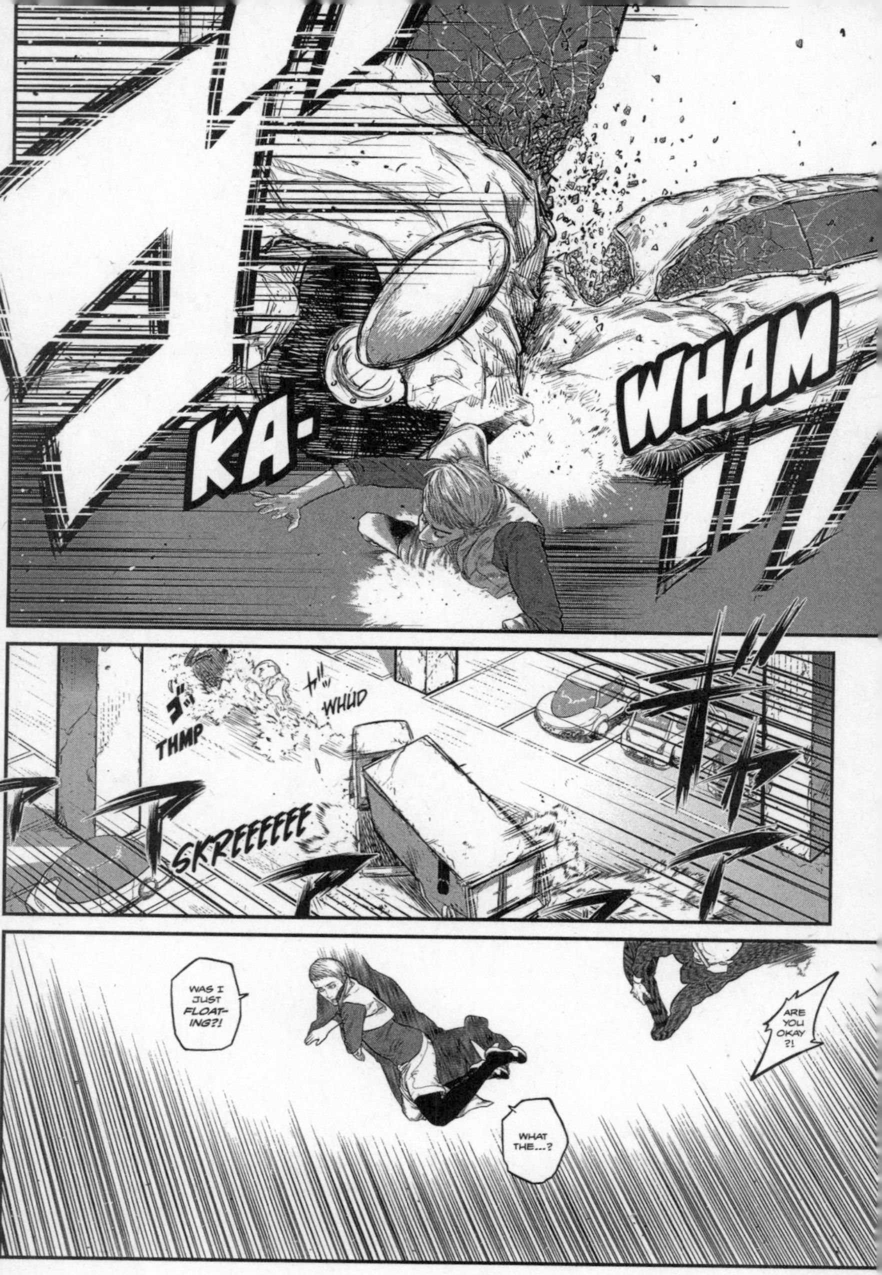
KA-WHAM
WHUD
THMP
SKREEEEEE
ARE YOU OKAY ?!
WAS I JUST FLOAT-ING?!
WHAT THE...?

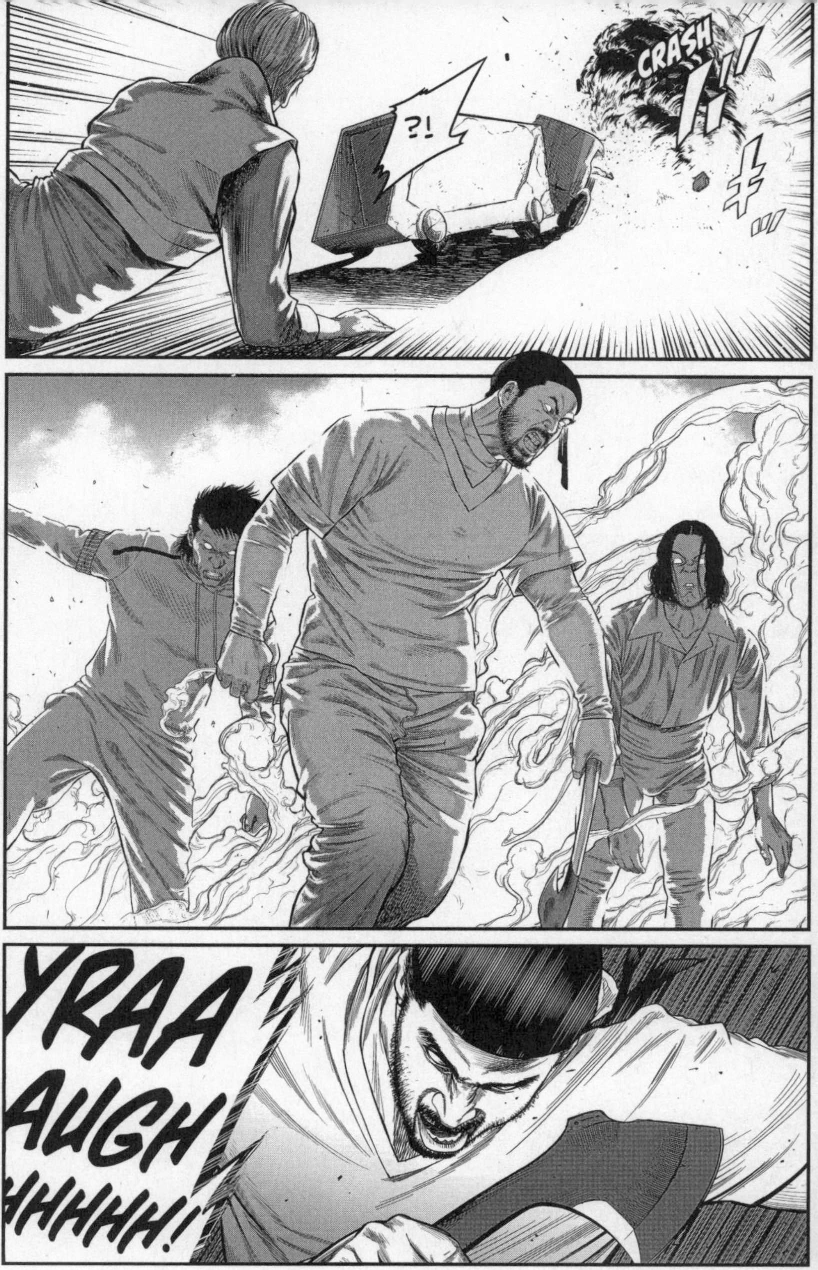
CRASH
?!
YRAA
AUGH
HHHHH!

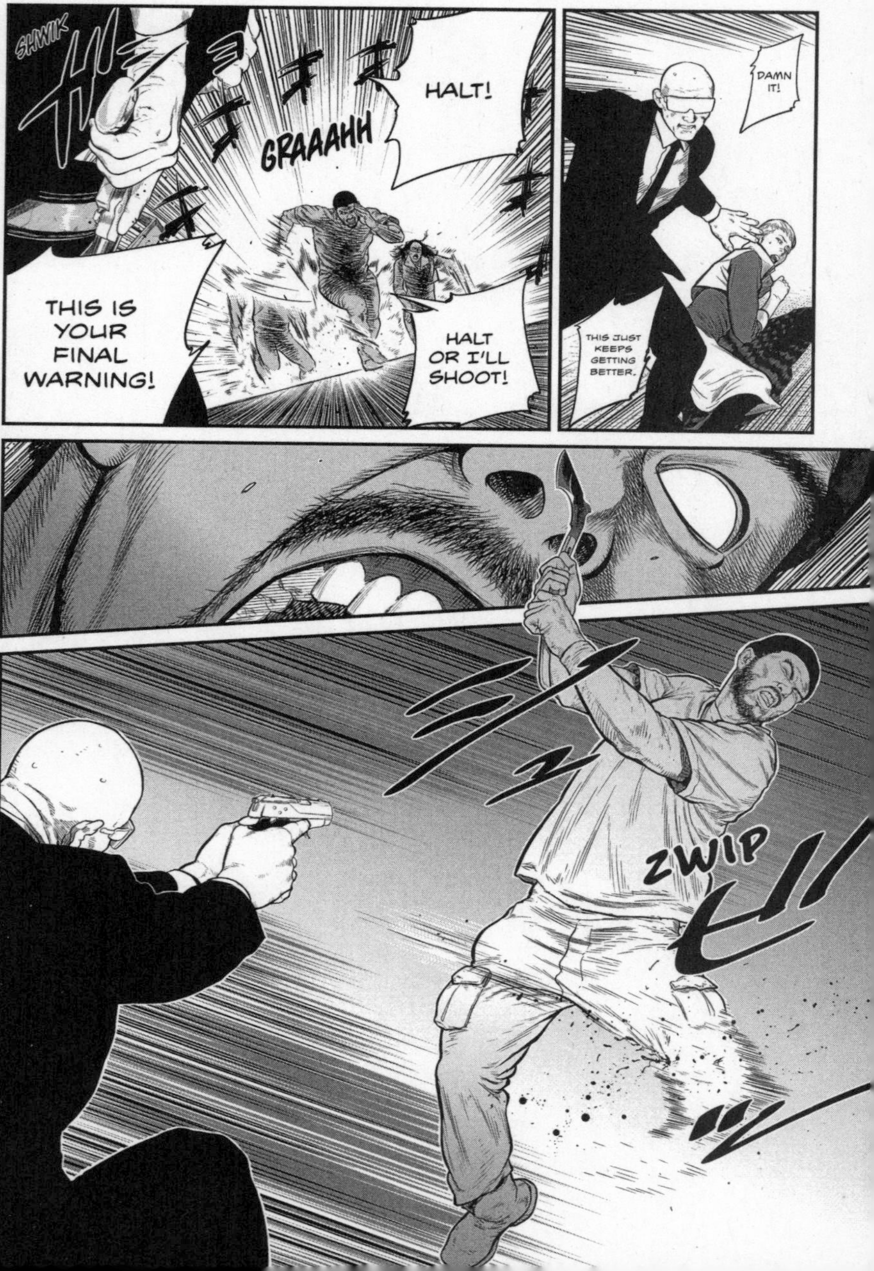
DAMN IT!
THIS JUST KEEPS GETTING BETTER.
HALT!
GRAAAHH
SHWIK
HALT OR I'LL SHOOT!
THIS IS YOUR FINAL WARNING!
ZWIP

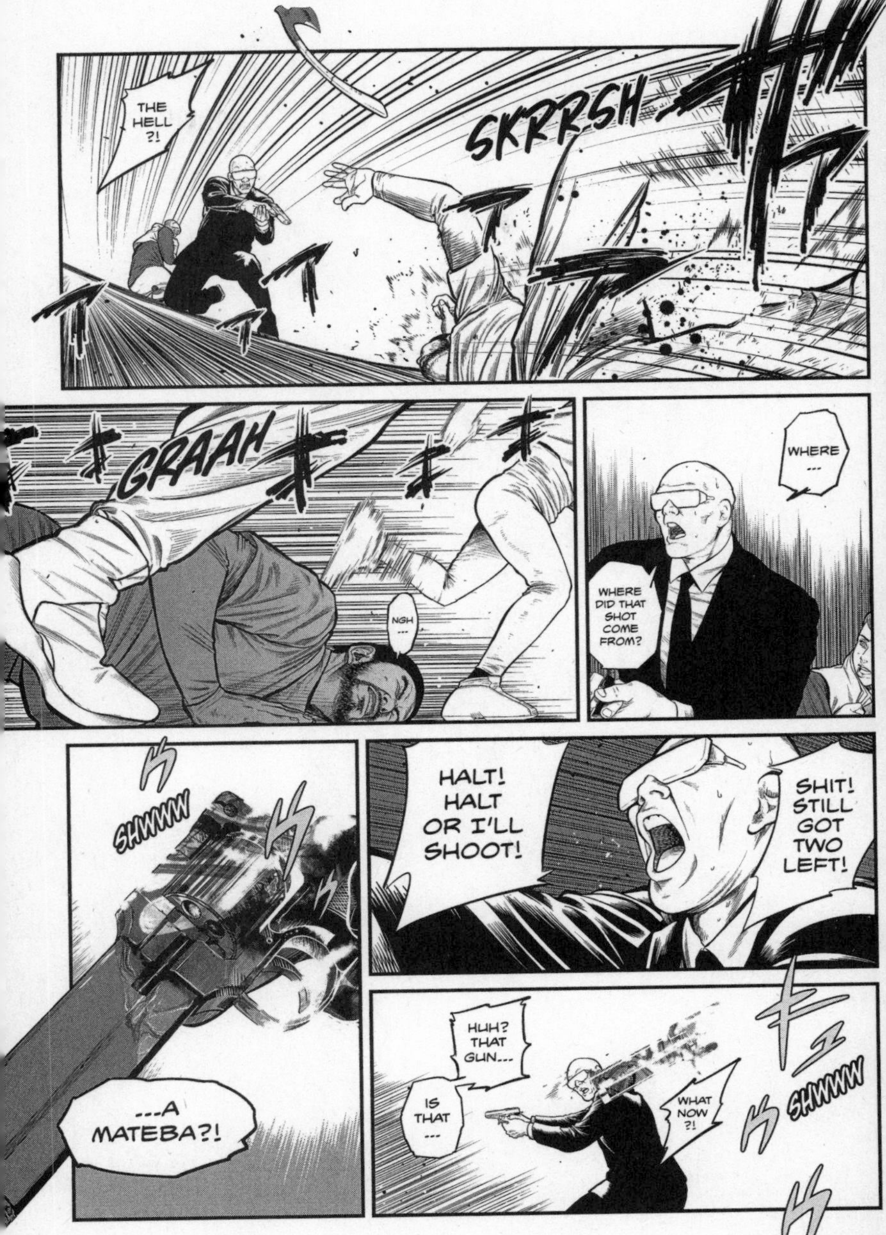
SKRRSH
THE HELL ?!
WHERE ---
WHERE DID THAT SHOT COME FROM?
GRAAH
NGH ---
SHIT! STILL GOT TWO LEFT!
HALT! HALT OR I'LL SHOOT!
SHWWW
WHAT NOW ?!
HUH? THAT GUN---
IS THAT ---
SHWWW
---A MATEBA?!

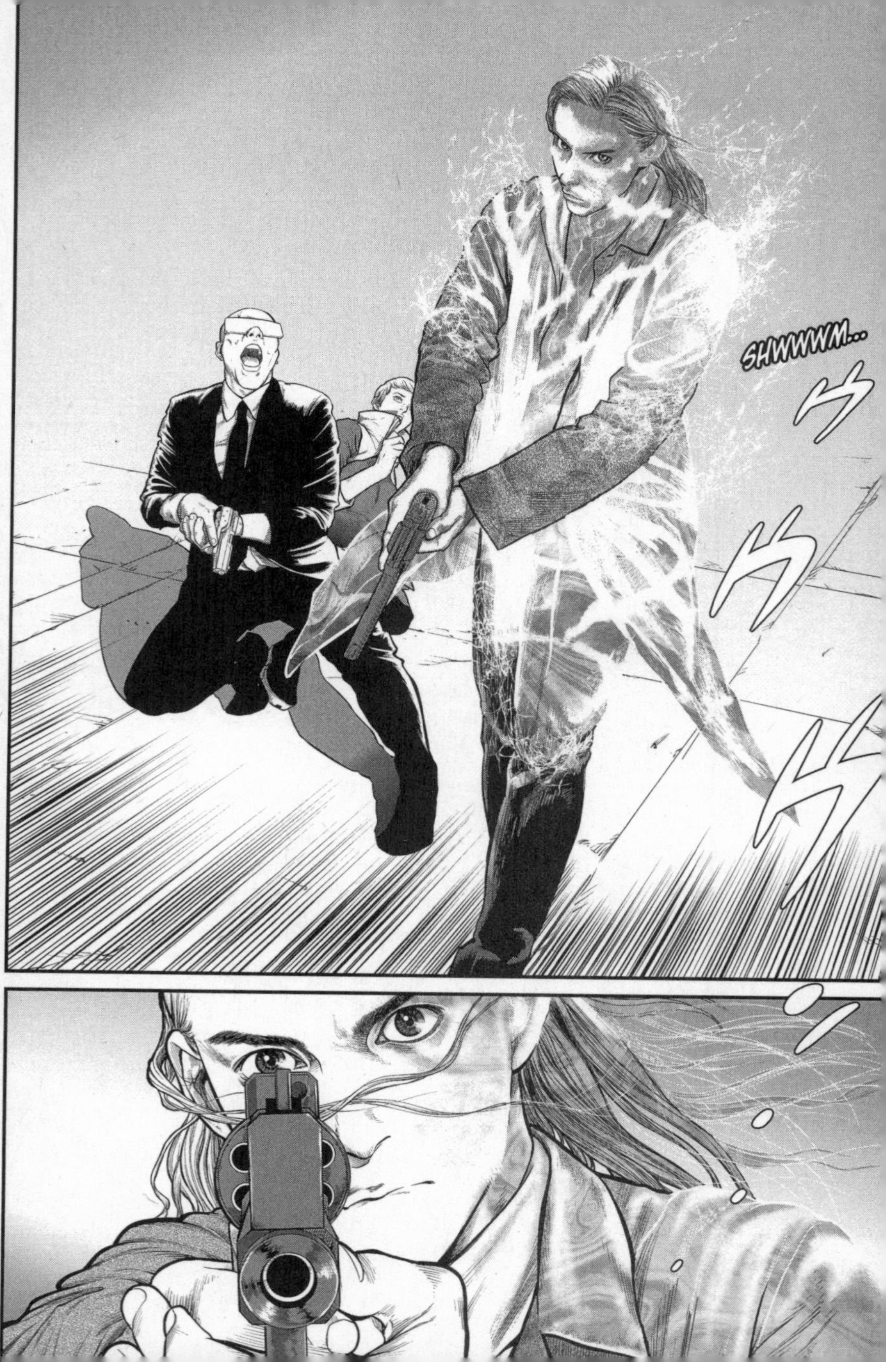
SHWWWM...

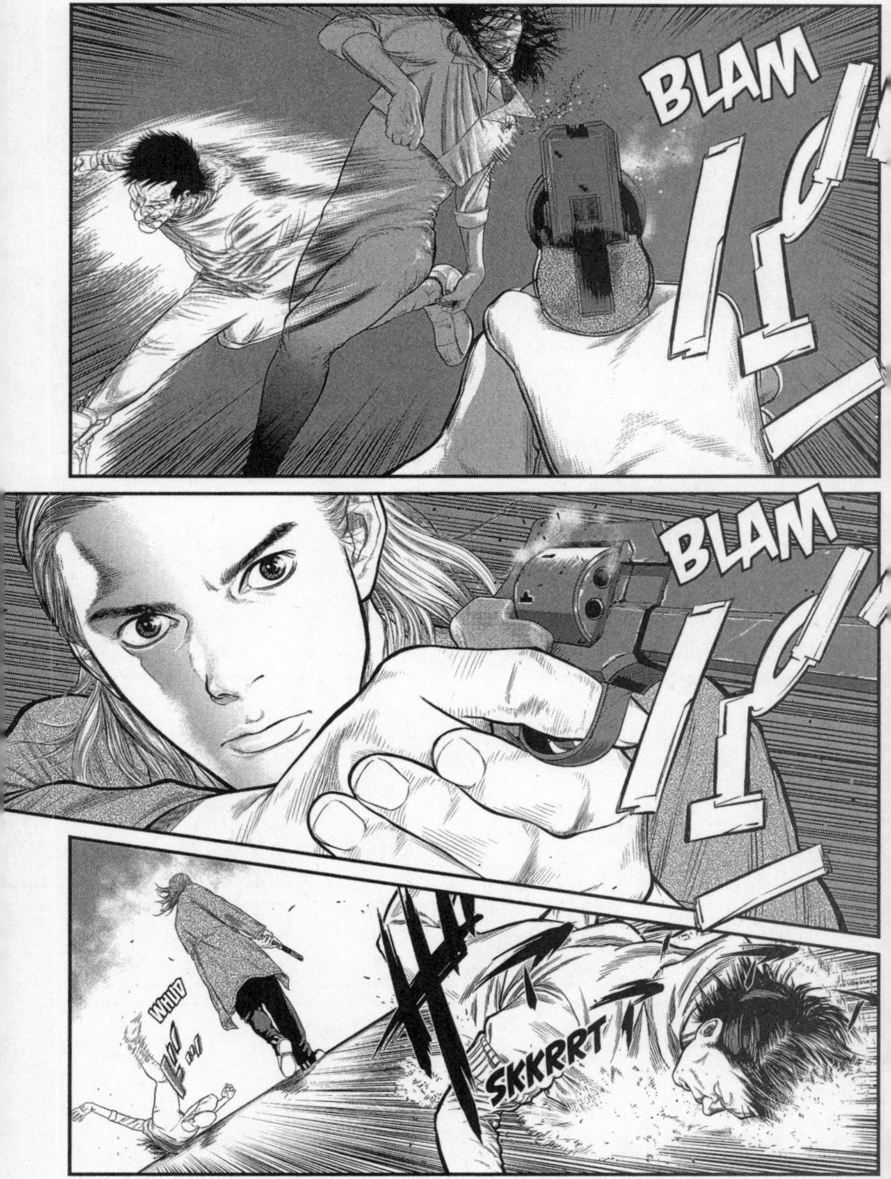
BLAM
BLAM
SK·KRRT
WHUD

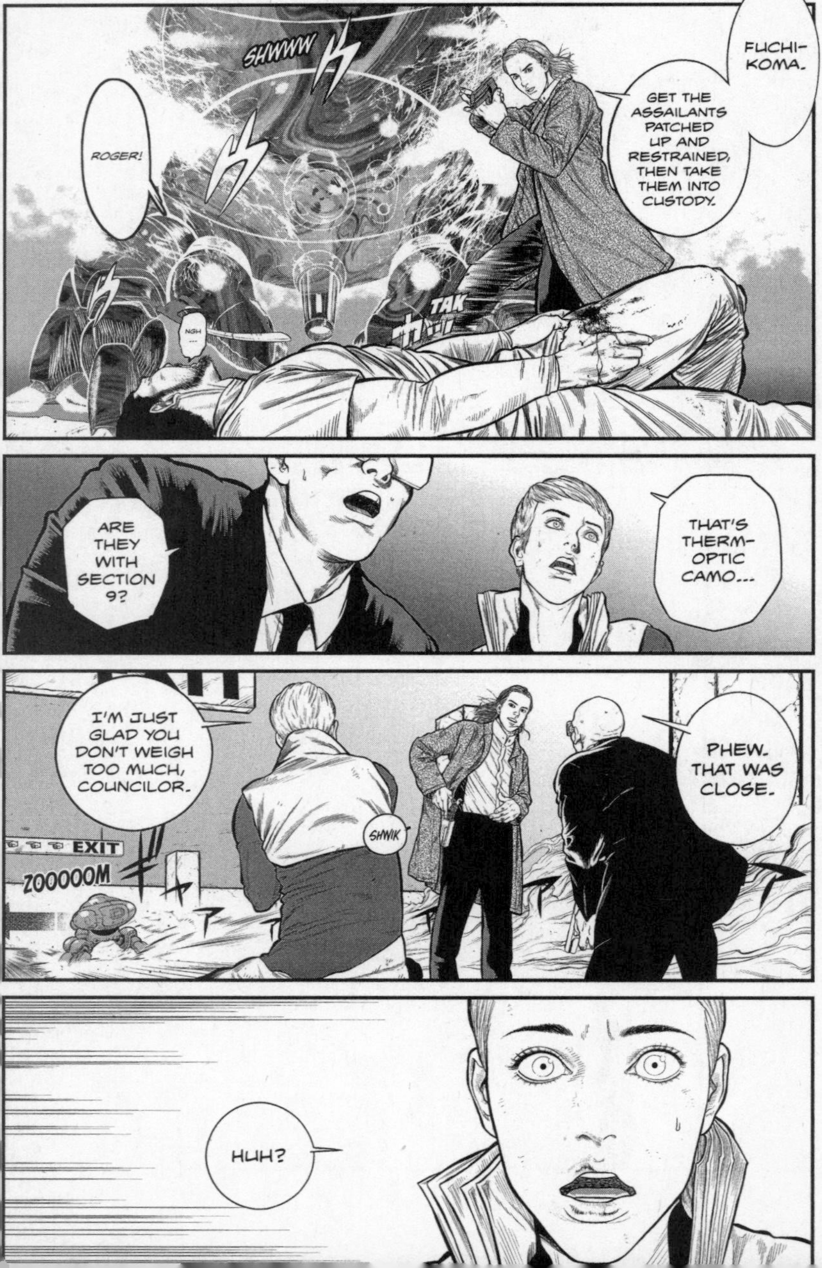
FUCHI-KOMA.
GET THE ASSAILANTS PATCHED UP AND RESTRAINED, THEN TAKE THEM INTO CUSTODY.
SHWWW
ROGER!
TAK
NGH...
THAT'S THERM-OPTIC CAMO...
ARE THEY WITH SECTION 9?
PHEW. THAT WAS CLOSE.
I'M JUST GLAD YOU DON'T WEIGH TOO MUCH, COUNCILOR.
SHWIK
EXIT
ZOOOOOM
HUH?

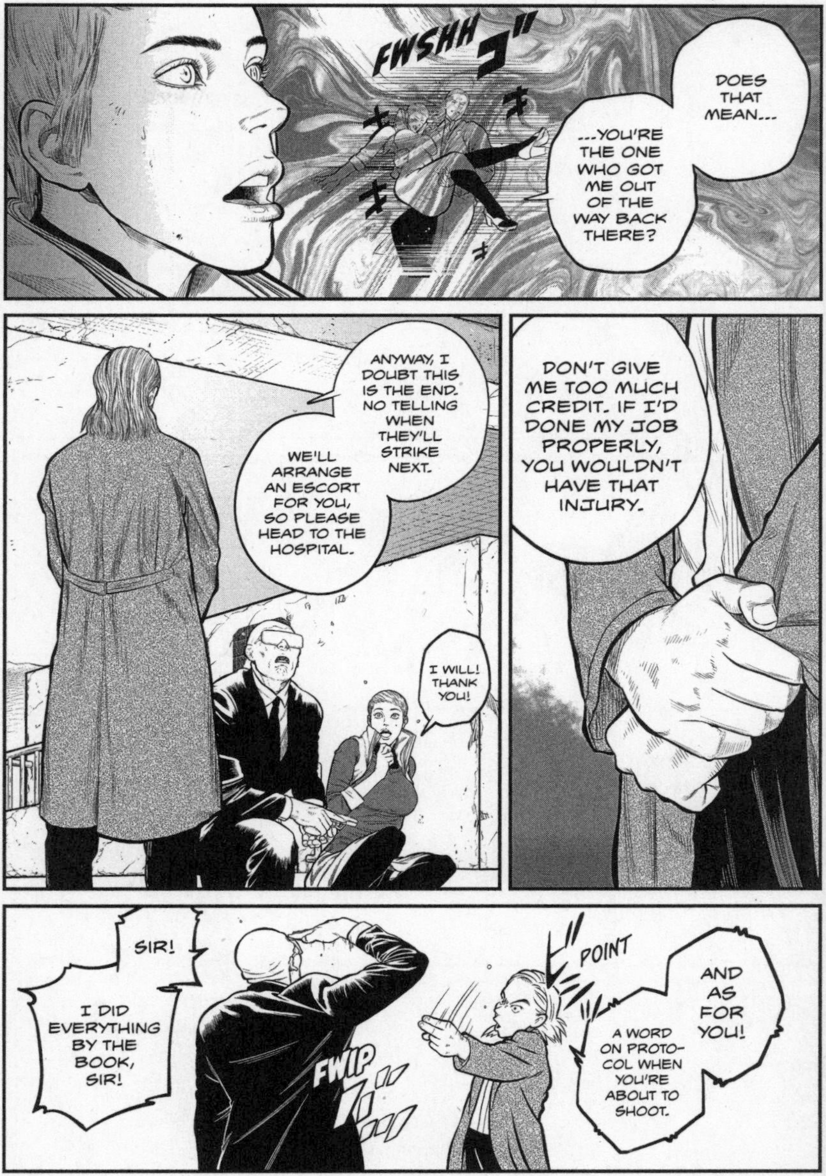
FWSHH
DOES THAT MEAN...
...YOU'RE THE ONE WHO GOT ME OUT OF THE WAY BACK THERE?
DON'T GIVE ME TOO MUCH CREDIT. IF I'D DONE MY JOB PROPERLY, YOU WOULDN'T HAVE THAT INJURY.
ANYWAY, I DOUBT THIS IS THE END. NO TELLING WHEN THEY'LL STRIKE NEXT.
WE'LL ARRANGE AN ESCORT FOR YOU, SO PLEASE HEAD TO THE HOSPITAL.
I WILL! THANK YOU!
AND AS FOR YOU!
A WORD ON PROTO-COL WHEN YOU'RE ABOUT TO SHOOT.
POINT
FWIP
SIR!
I DID EVERYTHING BY THE BOOK, SIR!

NEXT TIME, DON'T HESITATE.

慢走
SLOW

HUH?

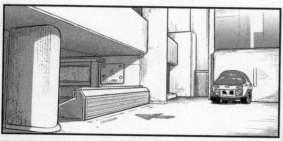

WHAT DO YOU MEAN, "HUH"?

WERE YOU LISTENING?

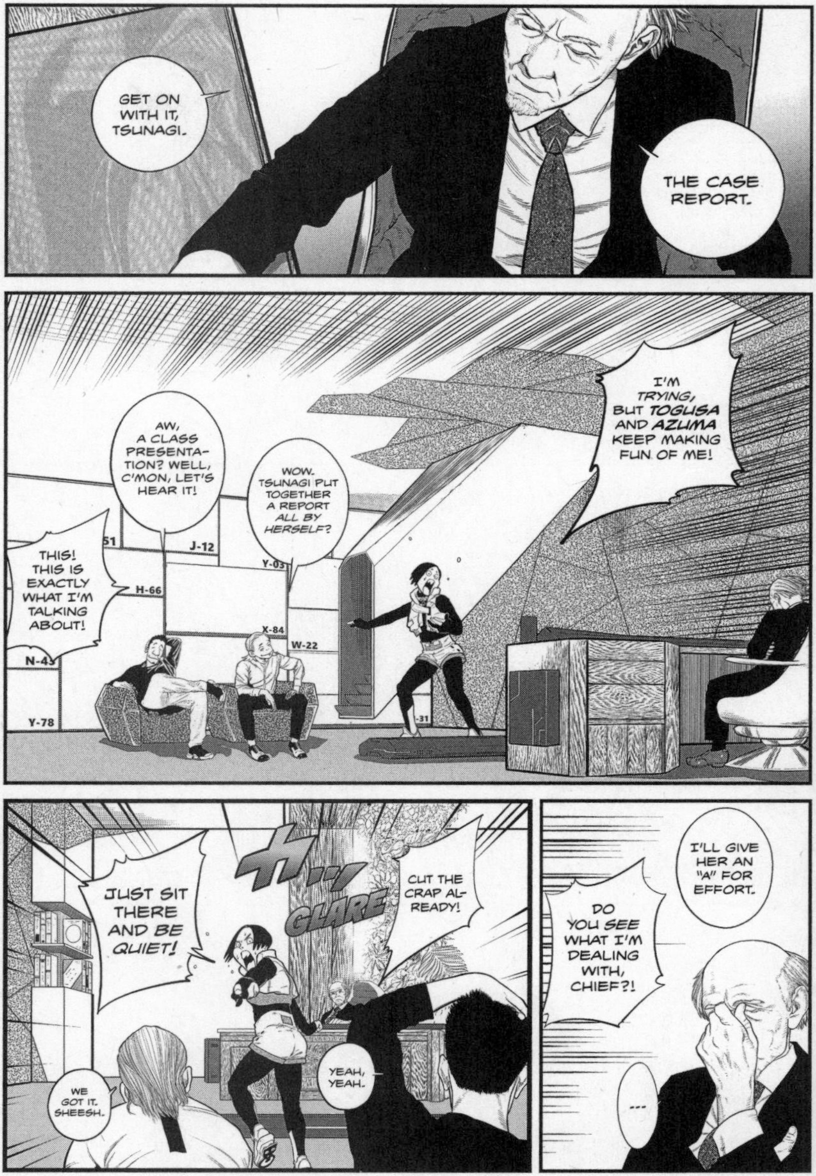
GET ON WITH IT, TSUNAGI.
THE CASE REPORT.
I'M TRYING, BUT TOGUSA AND AZUMA KEEP MAKING FUN OF ME!
WOW. TSUNAGI PUT TOGETHER A REPORT ALL BY HERSELF?
AW, A CLASS PRESENTA-TION? WELL, C'MON, LET'S HEAR IT!
THIS! THIS IS EXACTLY WHAT I'M TALKING ABOUT!
I'LL GIVE HER AN "A" FOR EFFORT.
DO YOU SEE WHAT I'M DEALING WITH, CHIEF?!

CUT THE CRAP AL-READY!
GLARE
JUST SIT THERE AND BE QUIET!
YEAH, YEAH.
WE GOT IT. SHEESH.

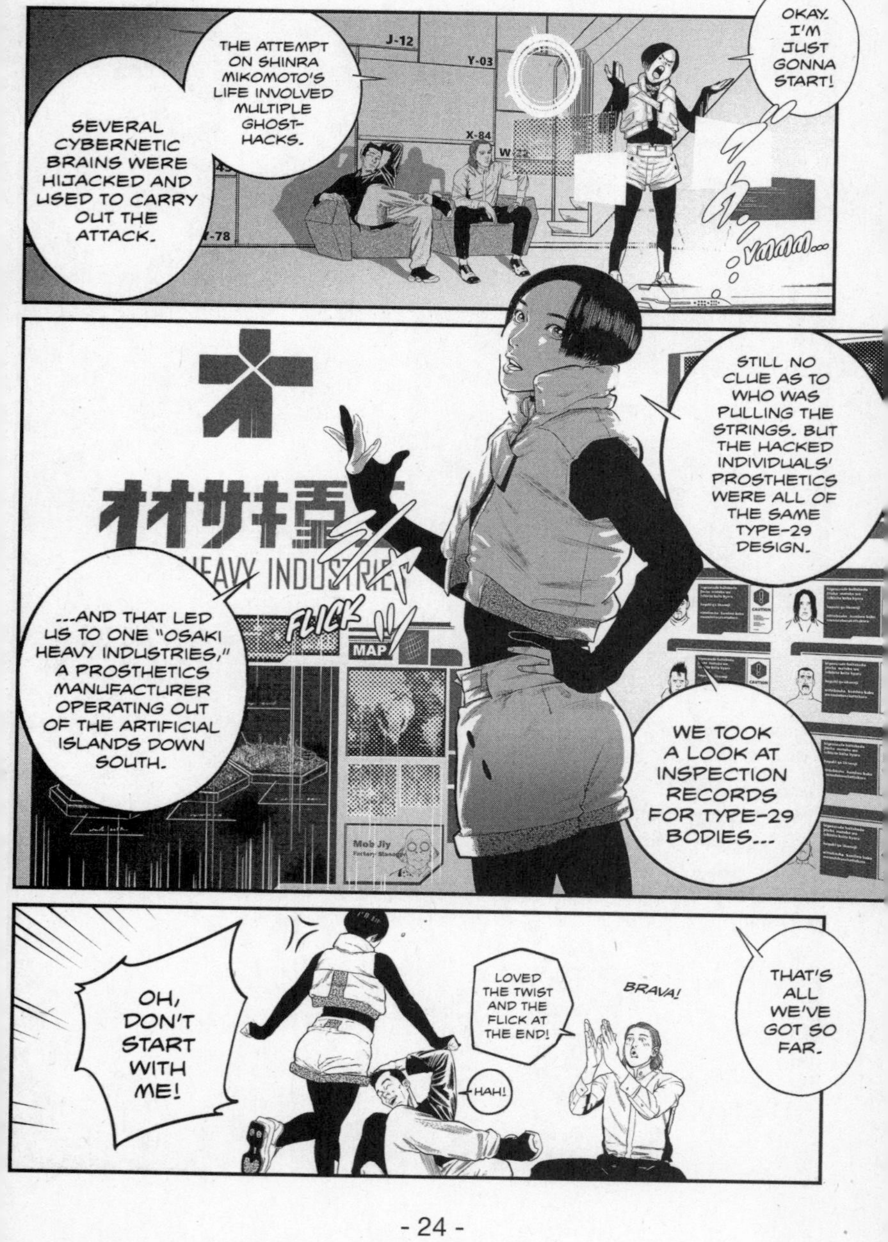
OKAY. I'M JUST GONNA START!
THE ATTEMPT ON SHINRA MIKOMOTO'S LIFE INVOLVED MULTIPLE GHOST-HACKS.
SEVERAL CYBERNETIC BRAINS WERE HIJACKED AND USED TO CARRY OUT THE ATTACK.
VMMM...
STILL NO CLUE AS TO WHO WAS PULLING THE STRINGS. BUT THE HACKED INDIVIDUALS' PROSTHETICS WERE ALL OF THE SAME TYPE-29 DESIGN.
WE TOOK A LOOK AT INSPECTION RECORDS FOR TYPE-29 BODIES...
...AND THAT LED US TO ONE "OSAKI HEAVY INDUSTRIES," A PROSTHETICS MANUFACTURER OPERATING OUT OF THE ARTIFICIAL ISLANDS DOWN SOUTH.
FLICK
MAP
Mob Jiy
THAT'S ALL WE'VE GOT SO FAR.
BRAVA!
LOVED THE TWIST AND THE FLICK AT THE END!
HAH!
OH, DON'T START WITH ME!

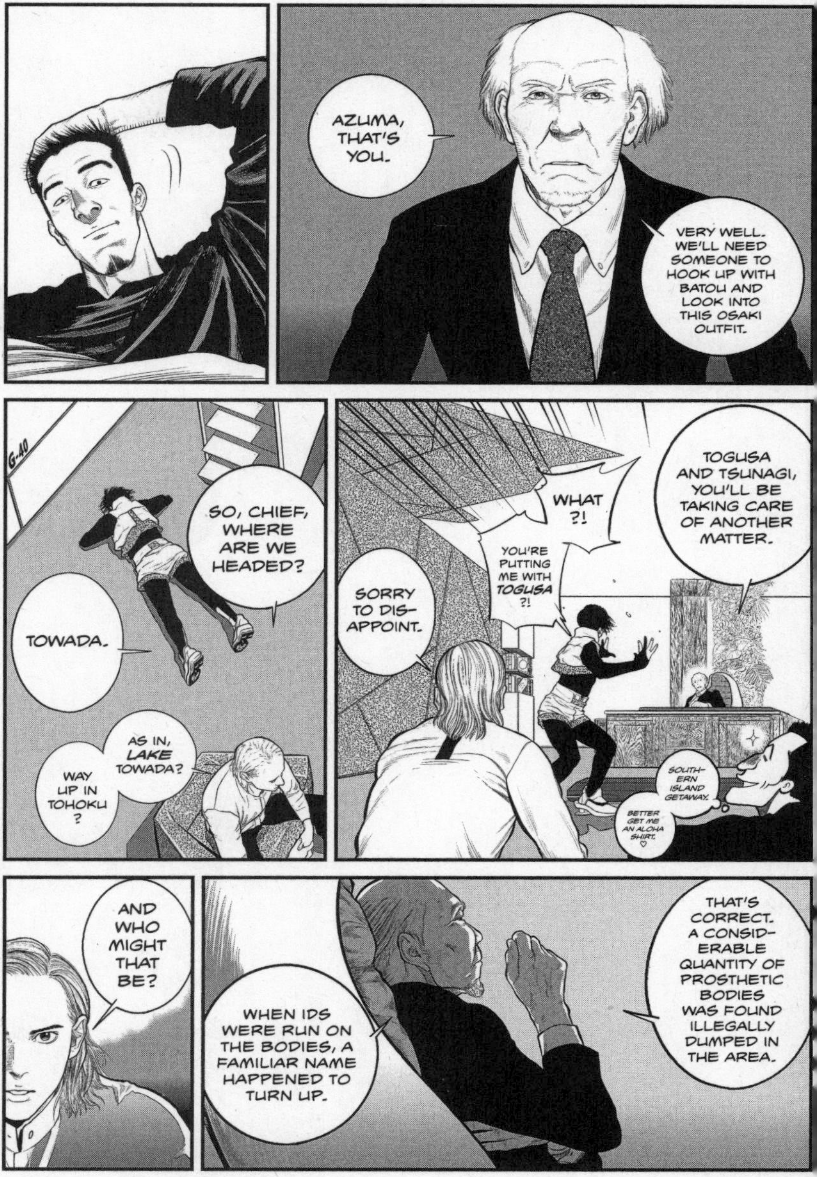
VERY WELL. WE'LL NEED SOMEONE TO HOOK UP WITH BATOU AND LOOK INTO THIS OSAKI OUTFIT.
AZUMA, THAT'S YOU.
TOGUSA AND TSUNAGI, YOU'LL BE TAKING CARE OF ANOTHER MATTER.
WHAT ?!
YOU'RE PUTTING ME WITH TOGUSA ?!
SORRY TO DIS-APPOINT.
SOUTH-ERN ISLAND GETAWAY.
BETTER GET ME AN ALOHA SHIRT. ♡
SO, CHIEF, WHERE ARE WE HEADED?
TOWADA.
AS IN, LAKE TOWADA?
WAY UP IN TOHOKU ?
THAT'S CORRECT. A CONSID-ERABLE QUANTITY OF PROSTHETIC BODIES WAS FOUND ILLEGALLY DUMPED IN THE AREA.
WHEN IDS WERE RUN ON THE BODIES, A FAMILIAR NAME HAPPENED TO TURN UP.
AND WHO MIGHT THAT BE?

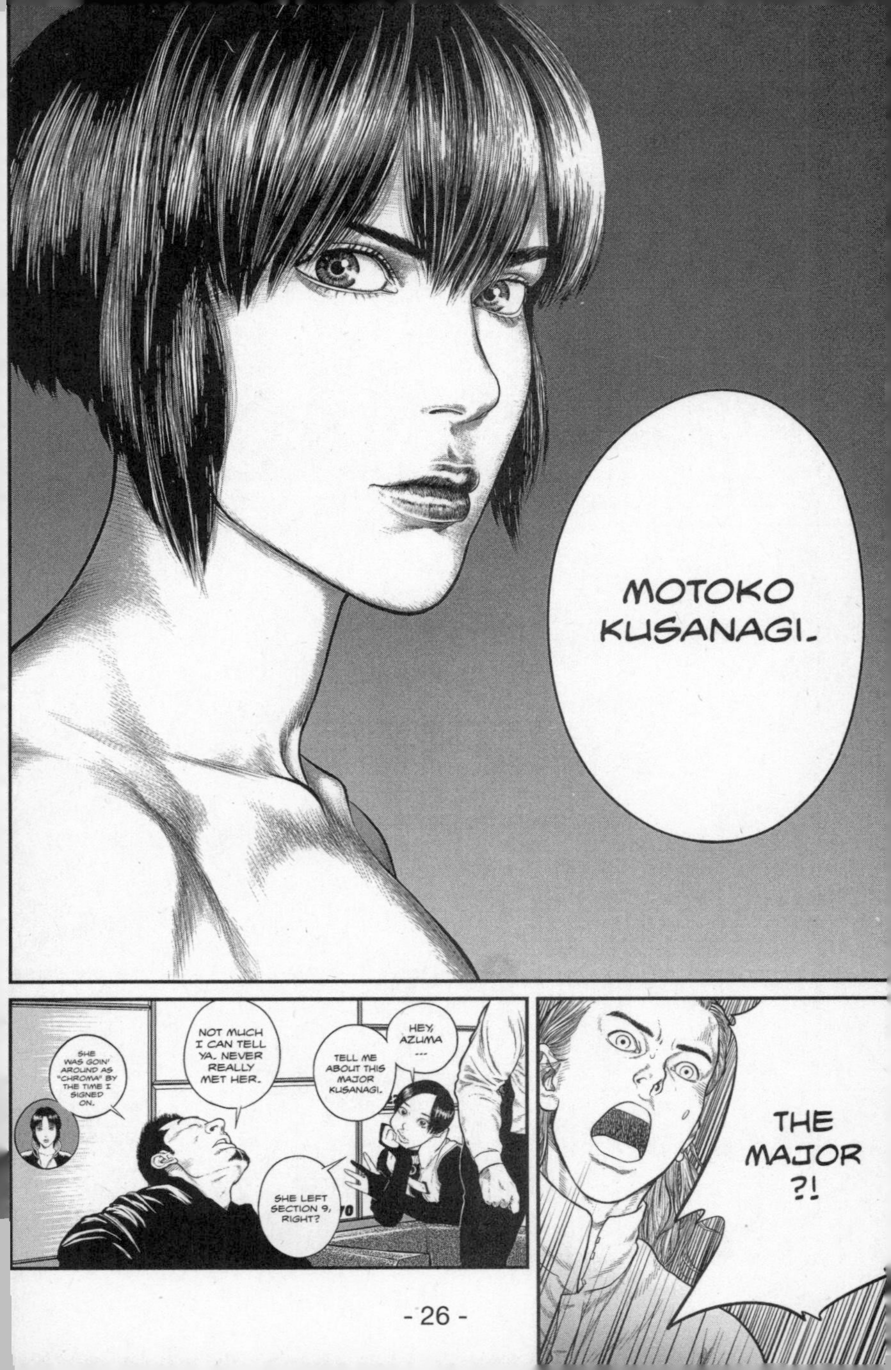
MOTOKO KUSANAGI.
THE MAJOR ?!
HEY, AZUMA ---
TELL ME ABOUT THIS MAJOR KUSANAGI.
NOT MUCH I CAN TELL YA. NEVER REALLY MET HER.
SHE WAS GOIN' AROUND AS "CHROMA" BY THE TIME I SIGNED ON.
SHE LEFT SECTION 9, RIGHT?

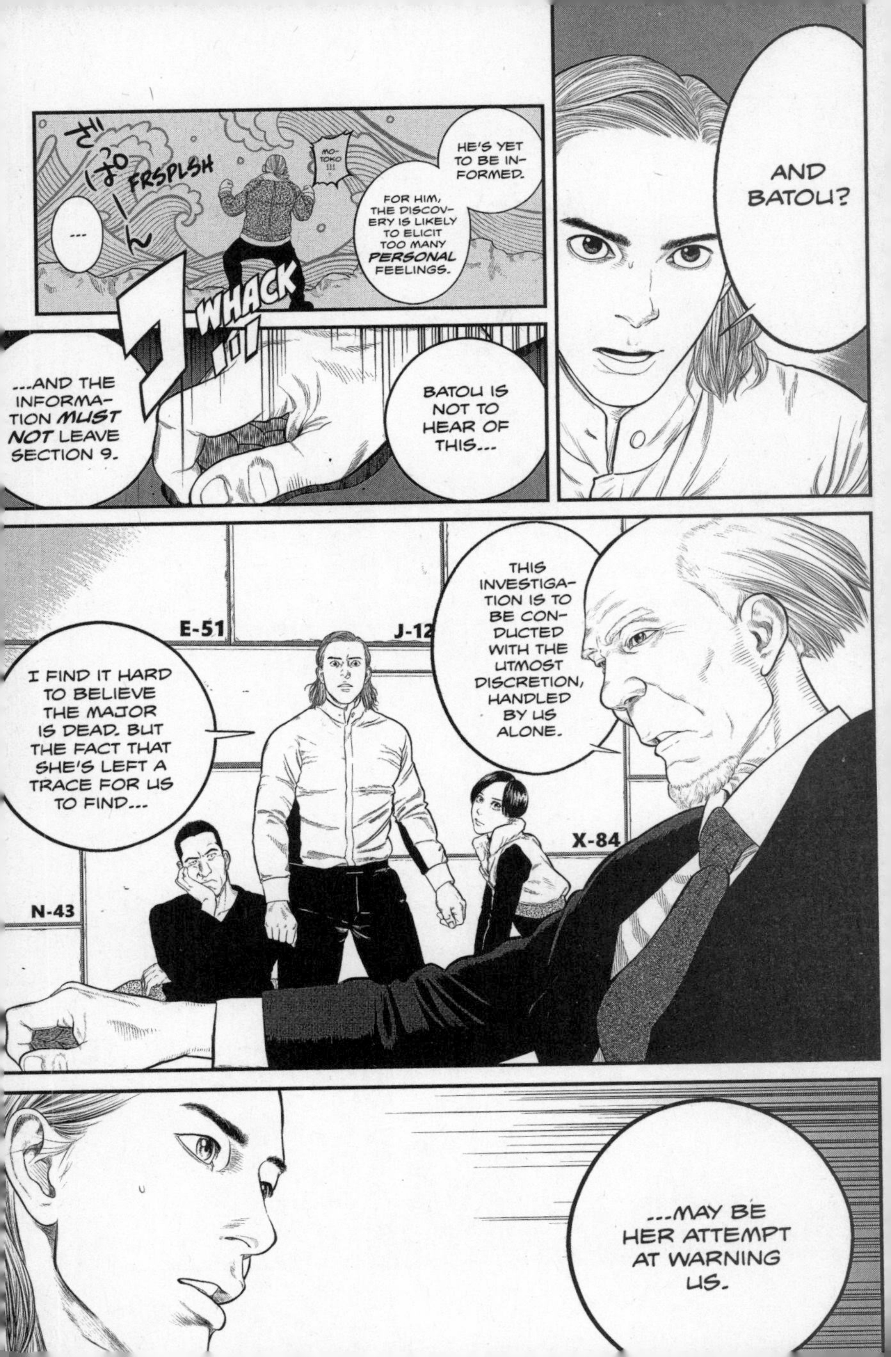
AND BATOU?
HE'S YET TO BE INFORMED.
FOR HIM, THE DISCOVERY IS LIKELY TO ELICIT TOO MANY *PERSONAL* FEELINGS.
MO-TOKO!!!
ざっぽーん
FRSPLSH
...
WHACK
BATOU IS NOT TO HEAR OF THIS...
...AND THE INFORMATION *MUST NOT* LEAVE SECTION 9.
THIS INVESTIGATION IS TO BE CONDUCTED WITH THE UTMOST DISCRETION, HANDLED BY US ALONE.
X-84
J-12
E-51
I FIND IT HARD TO BELIEVE THE MAJOR IS DEAD. BUT THE FACT THAT SHE'S LEFT A TRACE FOR US TO FIND...
N-43
...MAY BE HER ATTEMPT AT WARNING US.

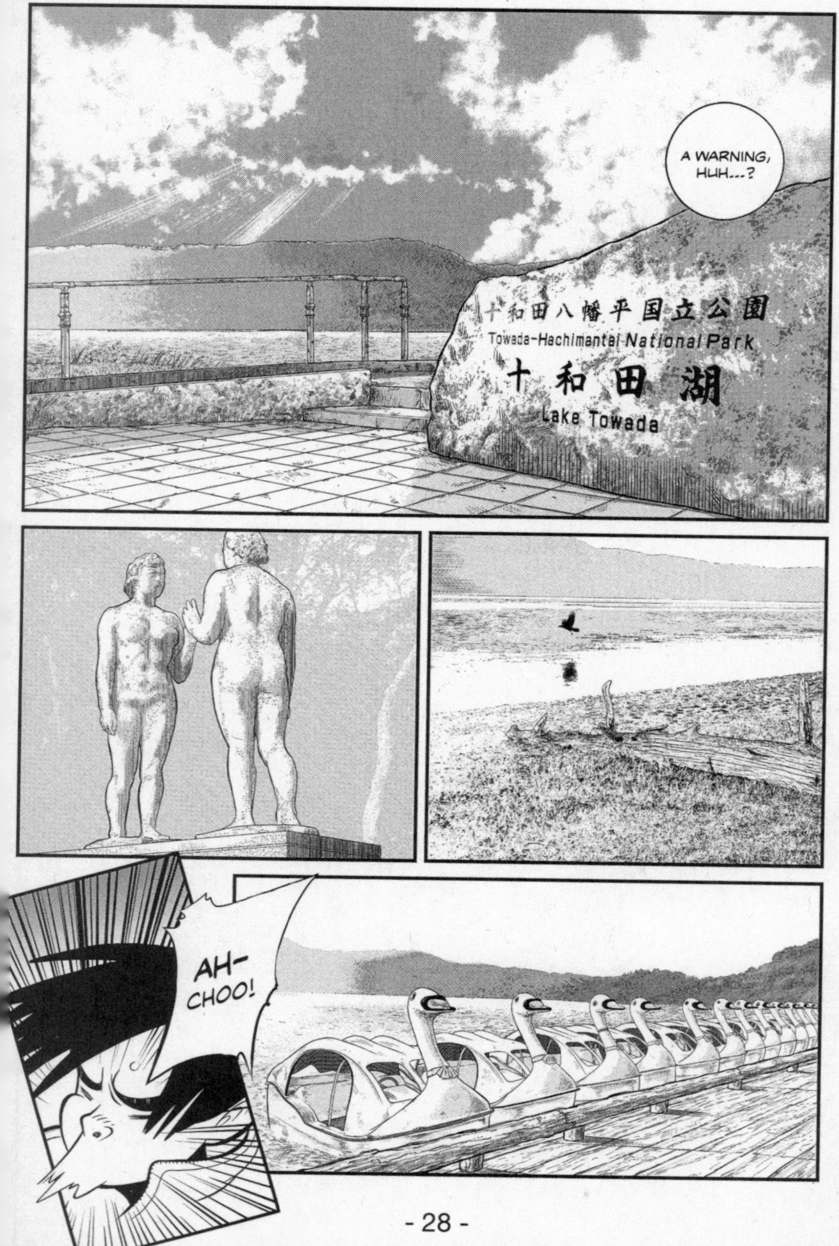
A WARNING, HUH...?
十和田八幡平国立公園
Towada-Hachimantai National Park
十和田湖
Lake Towada
AH-CHOO!

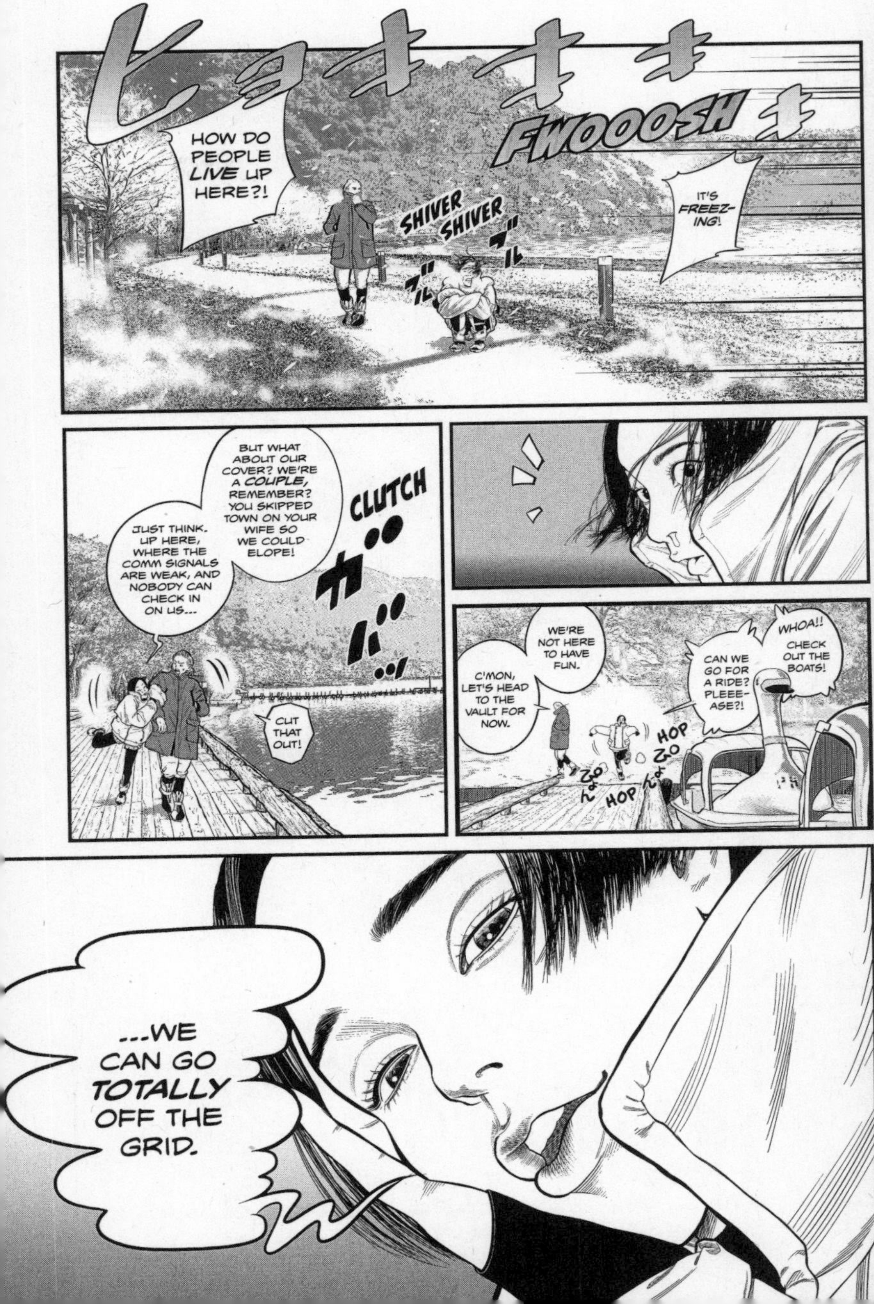
FWOOOSH
IT'S FREEZ-ING!
HOW DO PEOPLE LIVE UP HERE?!
SHIVER SHIVER
WHOA!! CHECK OUT THE BOATS!
CAN WE GO FOR A RIDE? PLEEEASE?!
WE'RE NOT HERE TO HAVE FUN.
C'MON, LET'S HEAD TO THE VAULT FOR NOW.
HOP
HOP
CLUTCH
BUT WHAT ABOUT OUR COVER? WE'RE A COUPLE, REMEMBER? YOU SKIPPED TOWN ON YOUR WIFE SO WE COULD ELOPE!
JUST THINK. UP HERE, WHERE THE COMM SIGNALS ARE WEAK, AND NOBODY CAN CHECK IN ON US...
CUT THAT OUT!
...WE CAN GO TOTALLY OFF THE GRID.

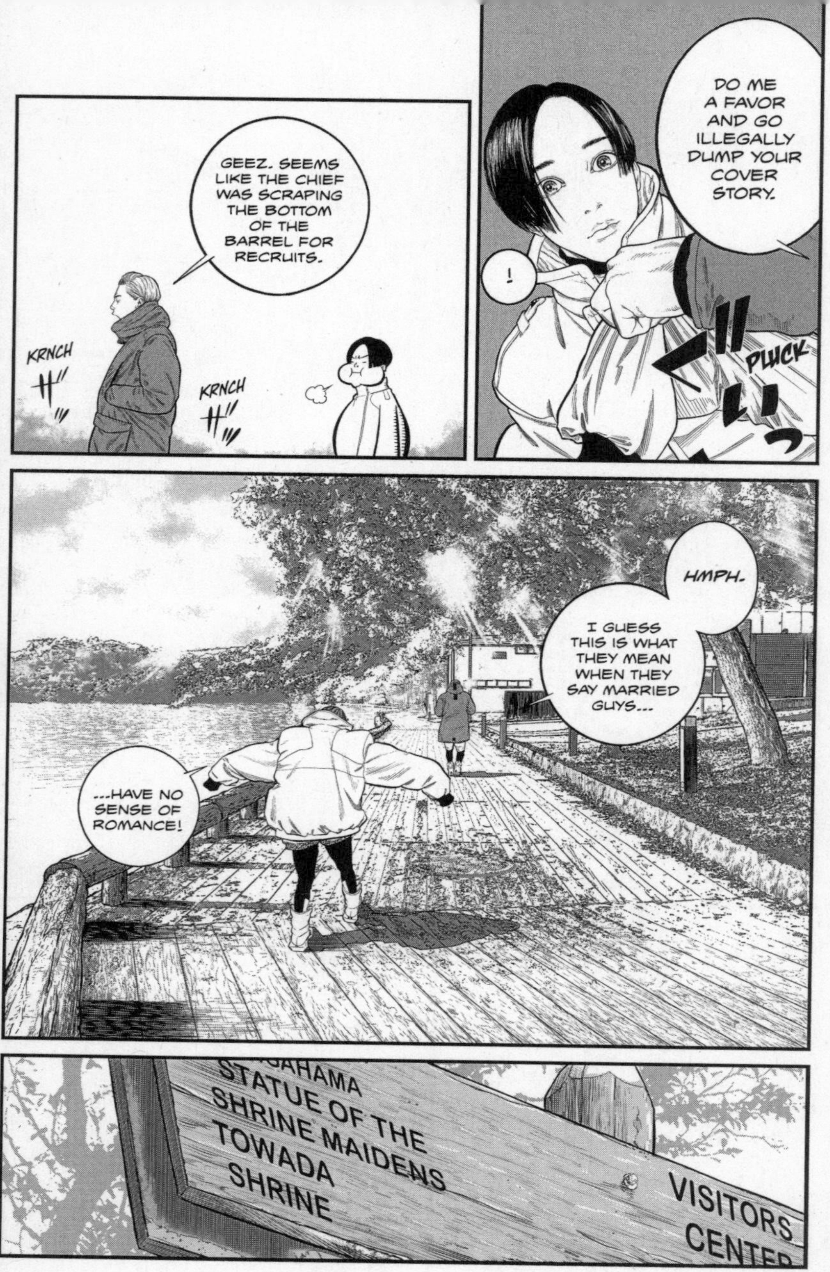

DO ME A FAVOR AND GO ILLEGALLY DUMP YOUR COVER STORY.
!
PLUCK
GEEZ. SEEMS LIKE THE CHIEF WAS SCRAPING THE BOTTOM OF THE BARREL FOR RECRUITS.
KRNCH
KRNCH
HMPH.
I GUESS THIS IS WHAT THEY MEAN WHEN THEY SAY MARRIED GUYS...
...HAVE NO SENSE OF ROMANCE!
STATUE OF THE
SHRINE OF THE MAIDENS
TOWADA SHRINE
VISITORS CENTER

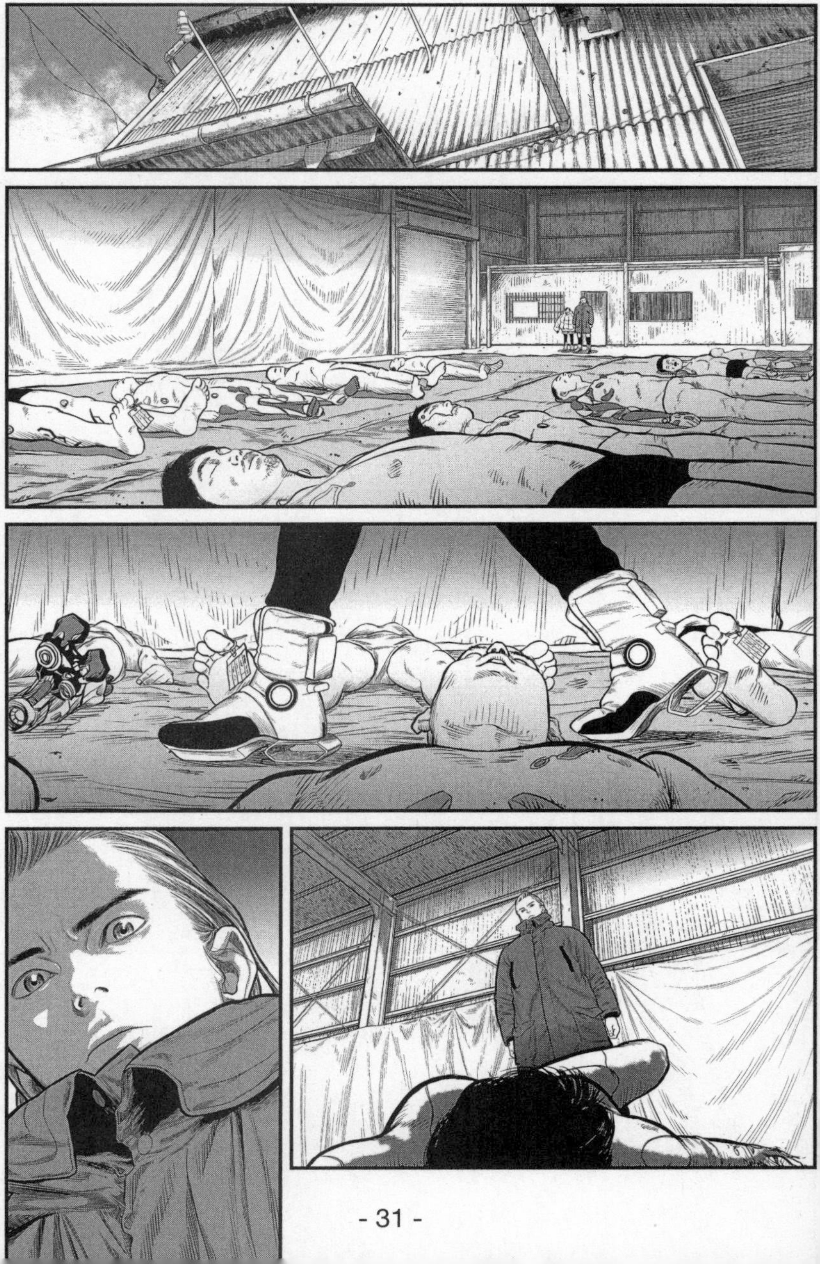

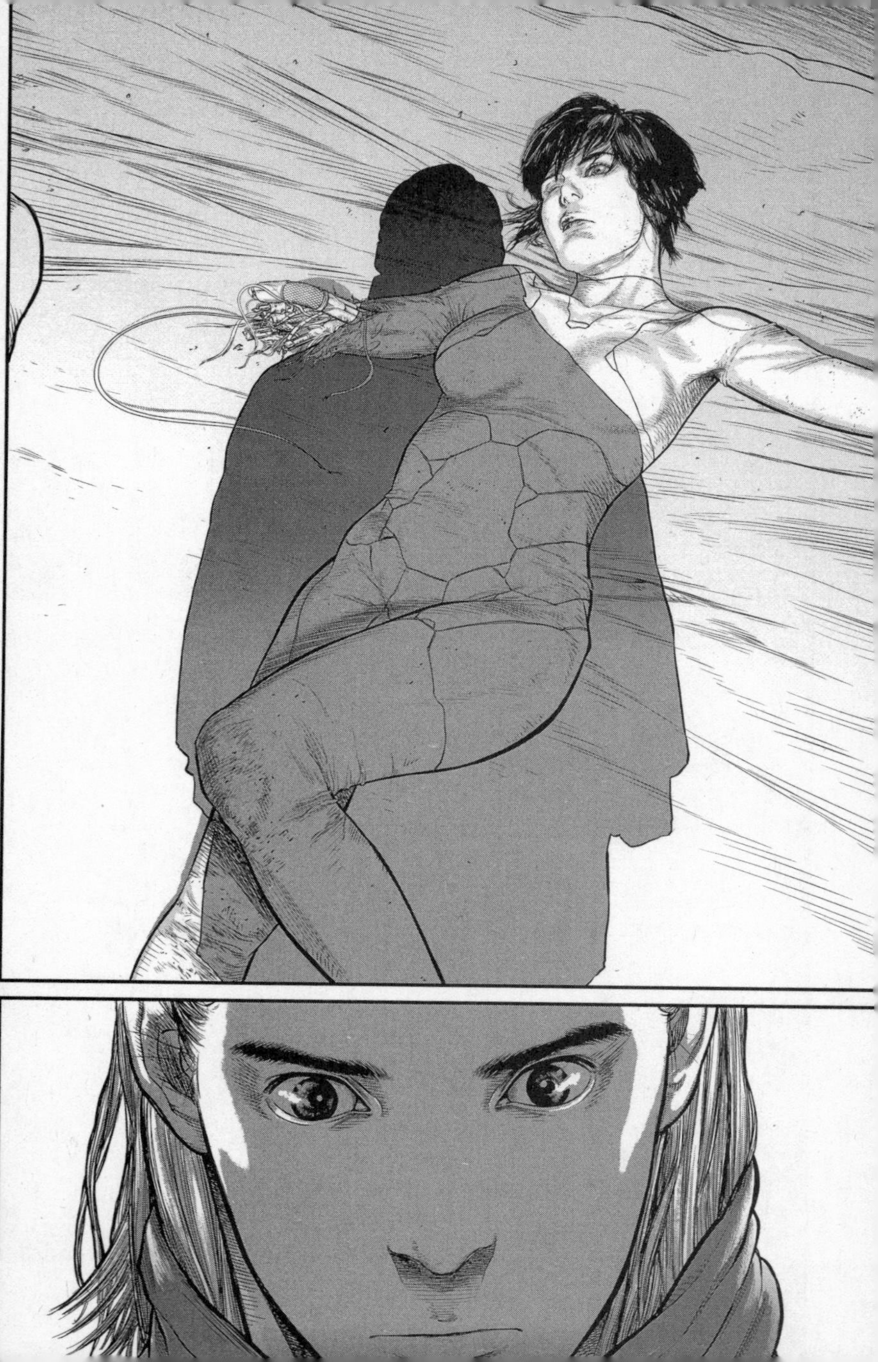

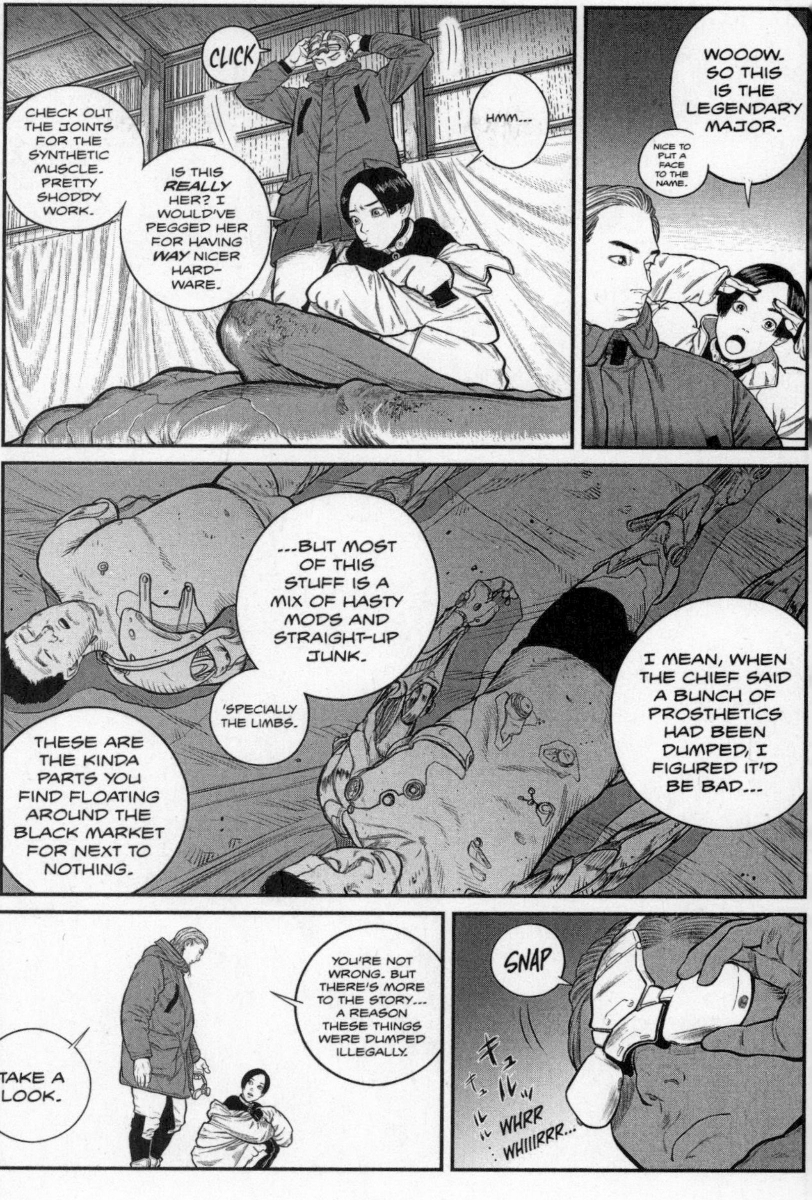
WOOOW. SO THIS IS THE LEGENDARY MAJOR.
NICE TO PUT A FACE TO THE NAME.
CLICK
HMM...
IS THIS *REALLY* HER? I WOULD'VE PEGGED HER FOR HAVING *WAY* NICER HARDWARE.
CHECK OUT THE JOINTS FOR THE SYNTHETIC MUSCLE. PRETTY SHODDY WORK.
I MEAN, WHEN THE CHIEF SAID A BUNCH OF PROSTHETICS HAD BEEN DUMPED, I FIGURED IT'D BE BAD...
...BUT MOST OF THIS STUFF IS A MIX OF HASTY MODS AND STRAIGHT-UP JUNK.
'SPECIALLY THE LIMBS.
THESE ARE THE KINDA PARTS YOU FIND FLOATING AROUND THE BLACK MARKET FOR NEXT TO NOTHING.
SNAP
キュルッ
キュルル
WHRR
WHIIIRRR...
YOU'RE NOT WRONG. BUT THERE'S MORE TO THE STORY... A REASON THESE THINGS WERE DUMPED ILLEGALLY.
TAKE A LOOK.

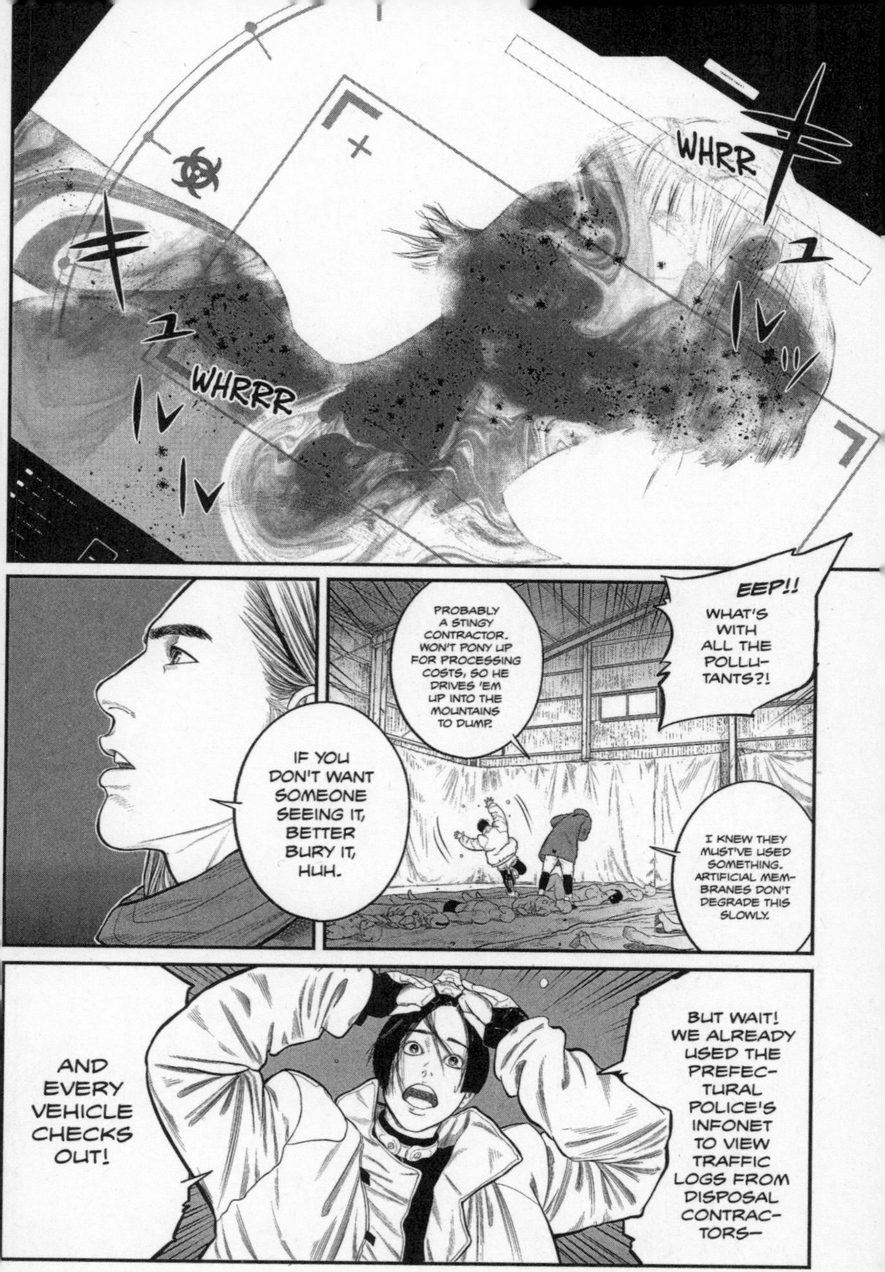
WHRR
WHRRR
EEP!! WHAT'S WITH ALL THE POLLUTANTS?!
PROBABLY A STINGY CONTRACTOR. WON'T PONY UP FOR PROCESSING COSTS, SO HE DRIVES 'EM UP INTO THE MOUNTAINS TO DUMP.
I KNEW THEY MUST'VE USED SOMETHING. ARTIFICIAL MEMBRANES DON'T DEGRADE THIS SLOWLY.
IF YOU DON'T WANT SOMEONE SEEING IT, BETTER BURY IT, HUH.
BUT WAIT! WE ALREADY USED THE PREFECTURAL POLICE'S INFONET TO VIEW TRAFFIC LOGS FROM DISPOSAL CONTRACTORS—
AND EVERY VEHICLE CHECKS OUT!

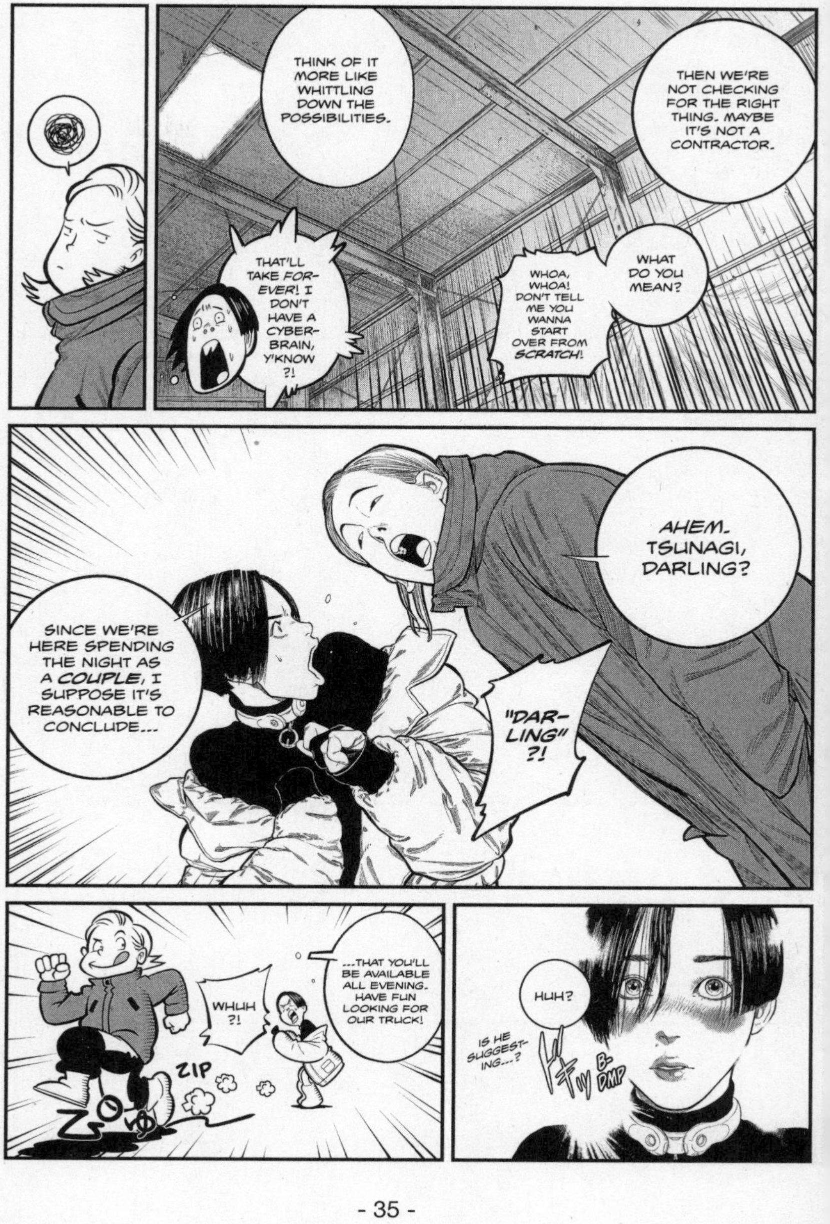
THEN WE'RE NOT CHECKING FOR THE RIGHT THING. MAYBE IT'S NOT A CONTRACTOR.
WHAT DO YOU MEAN?
WHOA, WHOA! DON'T TELL ME YOU WANNA START OVER FROM *SCRATCH*!
THINK OF IT MORE LIKE WHITTLING DOWN THE POSSIBILITIES.
THAT'LL TAKE *FOR-EVER*! I DON'T HAVE A CYBER-BRAIN, Y'KNOW ?!
AHEM. TSUNAGI, DARLING?
"DAR-LING" ?!
SINCE WE'RE HERE SPENDING THE NIGHT AS A *COUPLE*, I SUPPOSE IT'S REASONABLE TO CONCLUDE...
HUH?
IS HE SUGGEST-ING...?
B-DMP
...THAT YOU'LL BE AVAILABLE ALL EVENING. HAVE FUN LOOKING FOR OUR TRUCK!
WHUH ?!
ZIP

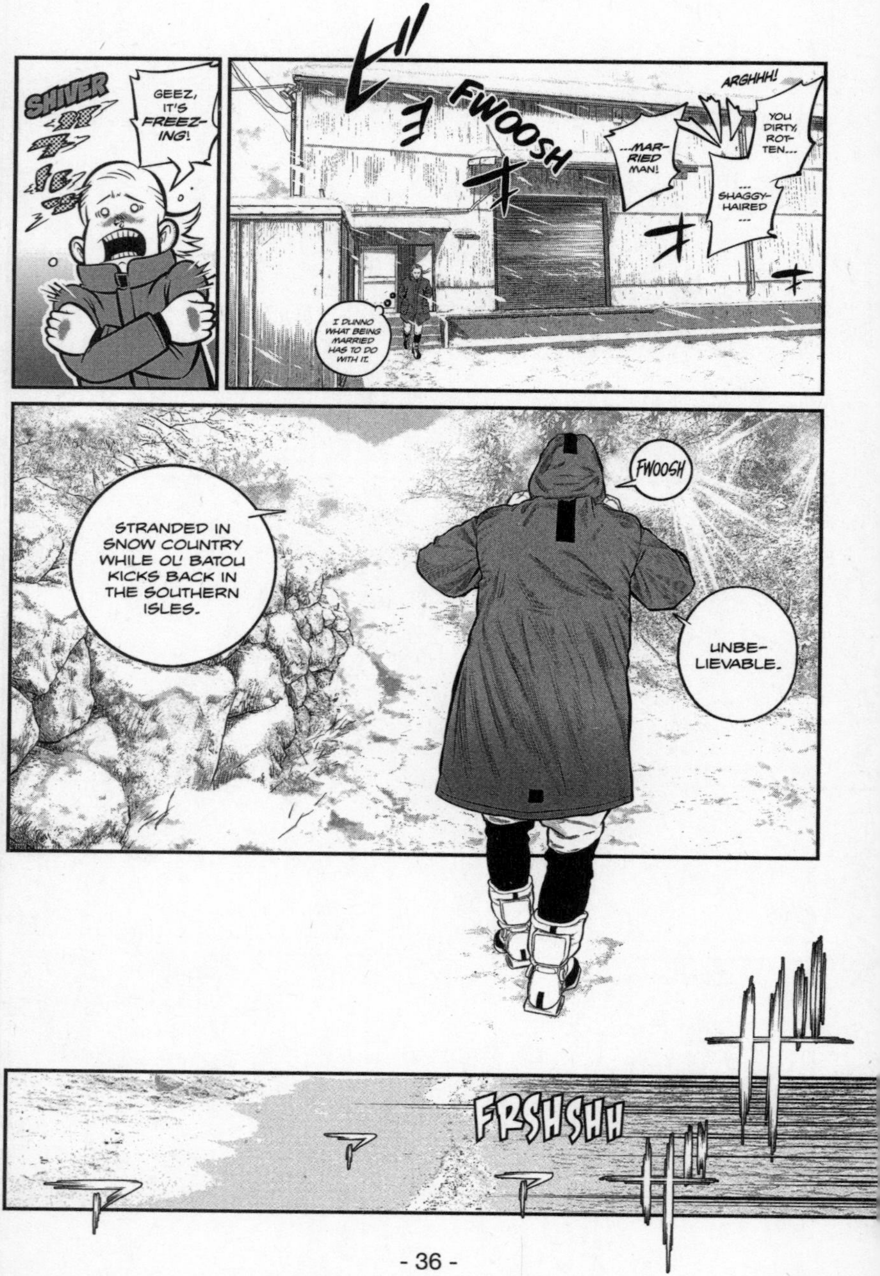
FWOOSH
ARGHHH!
YOU DIRTY, ROTTEN...
...SHAGGY-HAIRED...
...MARRIED MAN!
I DUNNO WHAT BEING MARRIED HAS TO DO WITH IT.
SHIVER
GEEZ, IT'S FREEZING!
FWOOSH
STRANDED IN SNOW COUNTRY WHILE OL' BATOU KICKS BACK IN THE SOUTHERN ISLES.
UNBELIEVABLE.
FRSHSHH

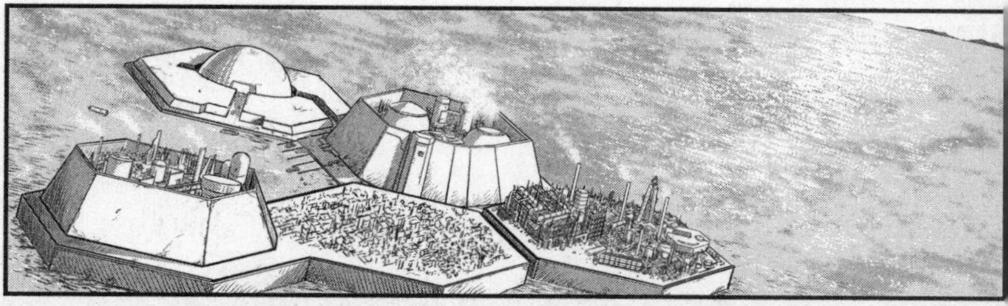

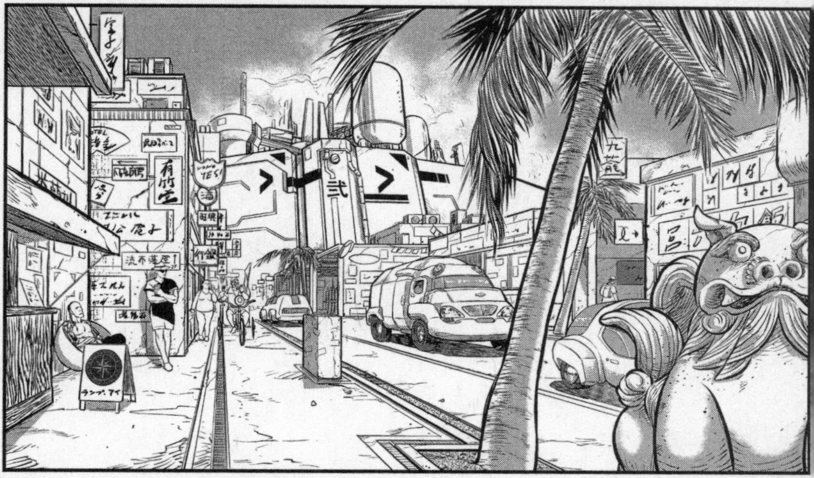
九龍
弐
YES!

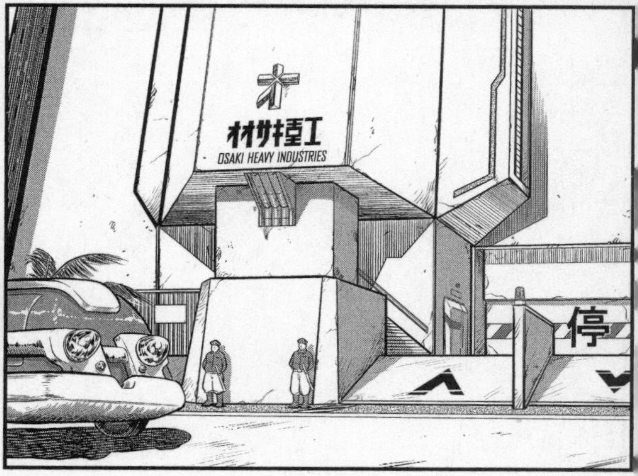
オオサキ重工
OSAKI HEAVY INDUSTRIES
停

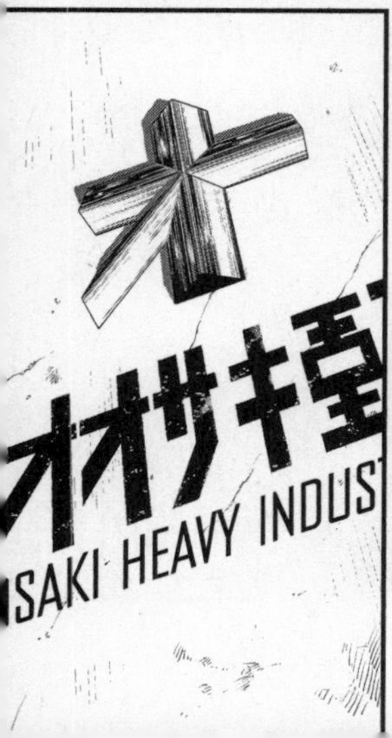
オオサキ重
SAKI HEAVY INDUST

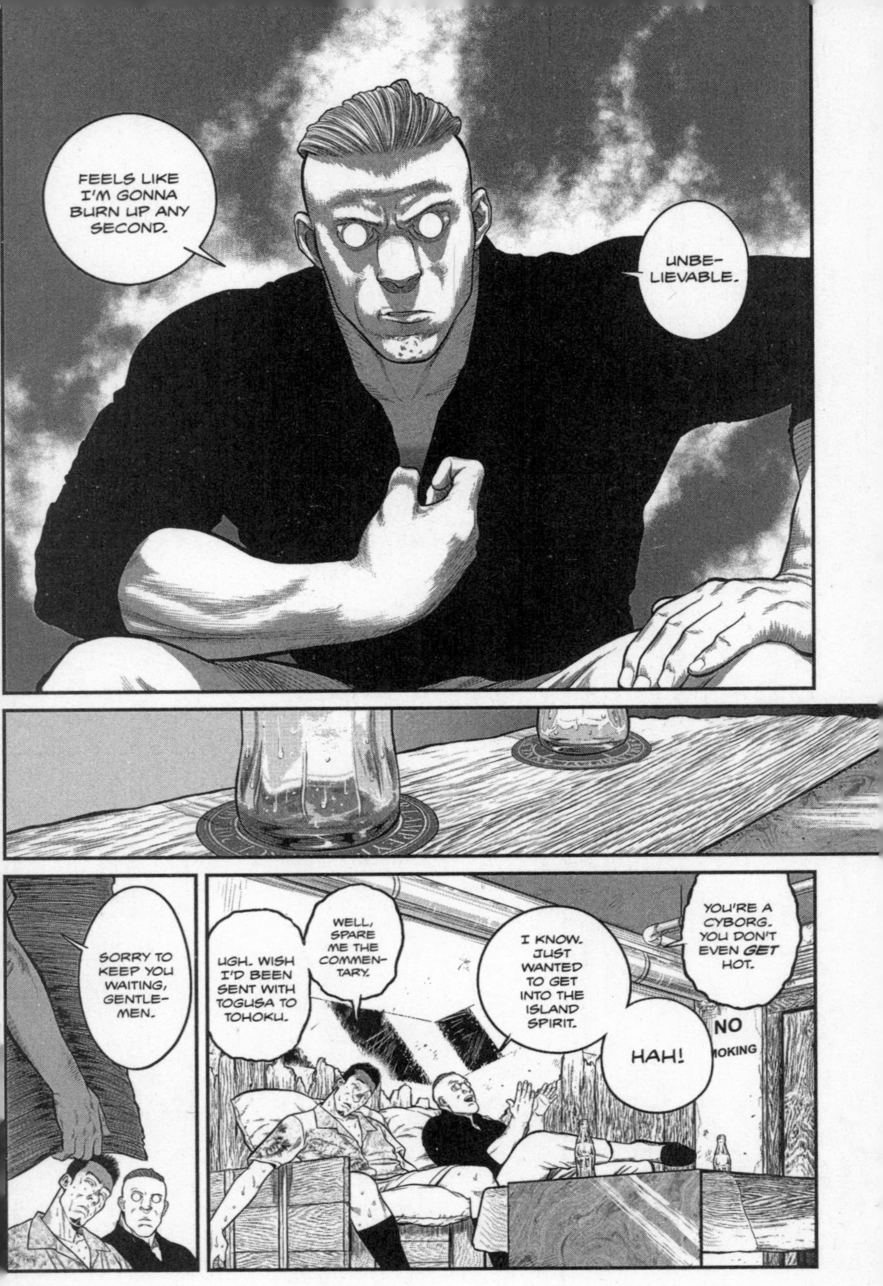

UNBE-LIEVABLE.
FEELS LIKE I'M GONNA BURN UP ANY SECOND.
YOU'RE A CYBORG. YOU DON'T EVEN *GET* HOT.
I KNOW. JUST WANTED TO GET INTO THE ISLAND SPIRIT.
HAH!
NO
MOKING
WELL, SPARE ME THE COMMENTARY.
UGH. WISH I'D BEEN SENT WITH TOGUSA TO TOHOKU.
SORRY TO KEEP YOU WAITING, GENTLEMEN.

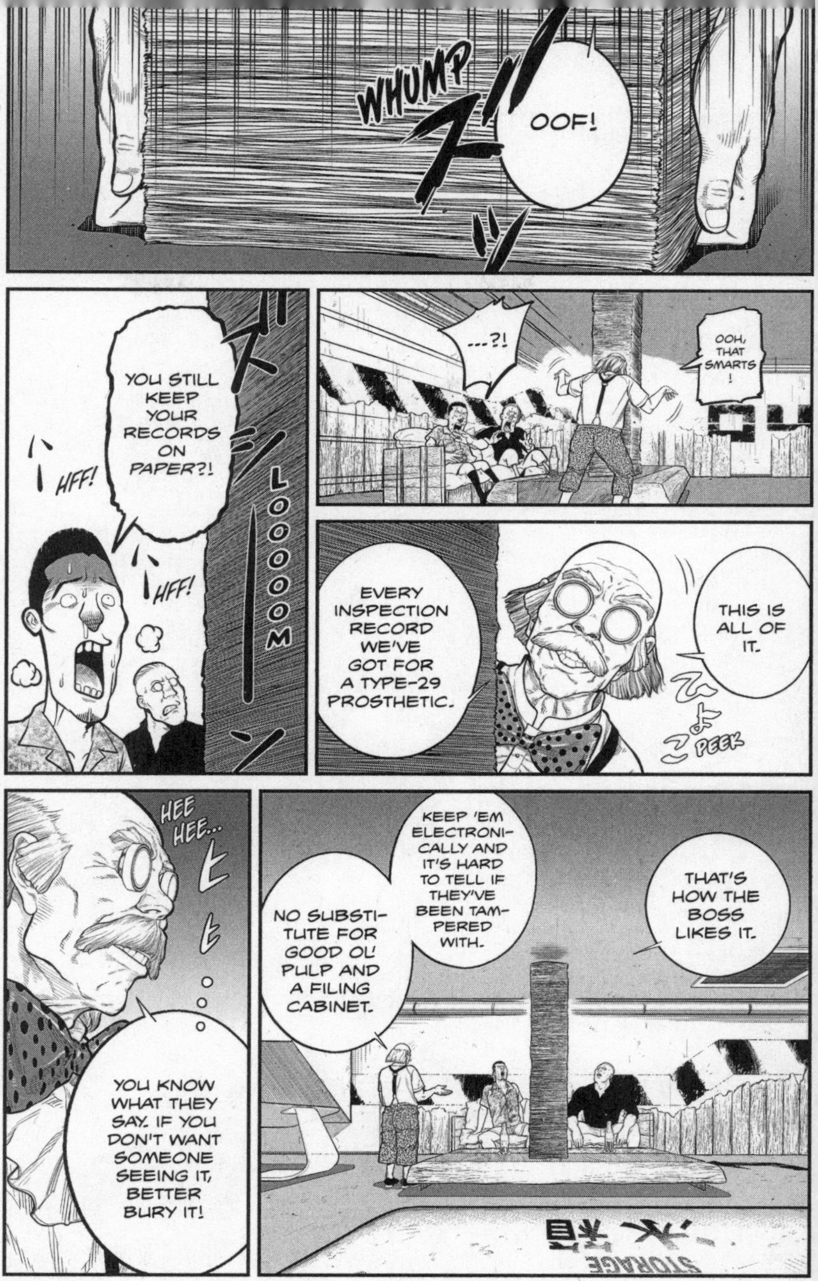
WHUMP
OOF!
OOH, THAT SMARTS!
---?!
THIS IS ALL OF IT.
PEEK
EVERY INSPECTION RECORD WE'VE GOT FOR A TYPE-29 PROSTHETIC.
LOOOOOOOM
YOU STILL KEEP YOUR RECORDS ON PAPER?!
HFF!
HFF!
THAT'S HOW THE BOSS LIKES IT.
KEEP 'EM ELECTRONICALLY AND IT'S HARD TO TELL IF THEY'VE BEEN TAMPERED WITH.
NO SUBSTITUTE FOR GOOD OL' PULP AND A FILING CABINET.
STORAGE
HEE HEE...
YOU KNOW WHAT THEY SAY. IF YOU DON'T WANT SOMEONE SEEING IT, BETTER BURY IT!

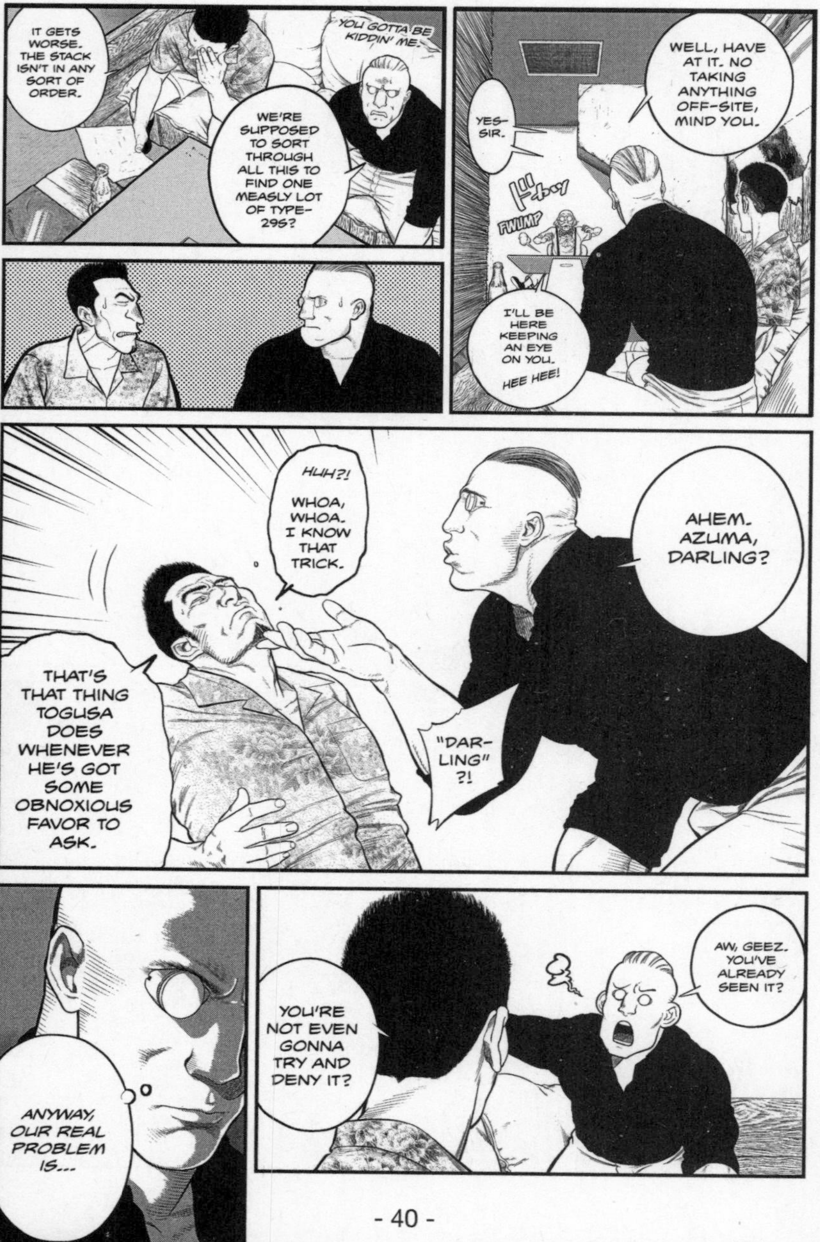
WELL, HAVE AT IT. NO TAKING ANYTHING OFF-SITE, MIND YOU.
YES-SIR.
ドカッ
FWUMP
I'LL BE HERE KEEPING AN EYE ON YOU.
HEE HEE!
YOU GOTTA BE KIDDIN' ME.
IT GETS WORSE. THE STACK ISN'T IN ANY SORT OF ORDER.
WE'RE SUPPOSED TO SORT THROUGH ALL THIS TO FIND ONE MEASLY LOT OF TYPE-29S?
AHEM. AZUMA, DARLING?
HUH?!
WHOA, WHOA. I KNOW THAT TRICK.
"DAR-LING"?!
THAT'S THAT THING TOGUSA DOES WHENEVER HE'S GOT SOME OBNOXIOUS FAVOR TO ASK.
AW, GEEZ. YOU'VE ALREADY SEEN IT?
YOU'RE NOT EVEN GONNA TRY AND DENY IT?
ANYWAY, OUR REAL PROBLEM IS...

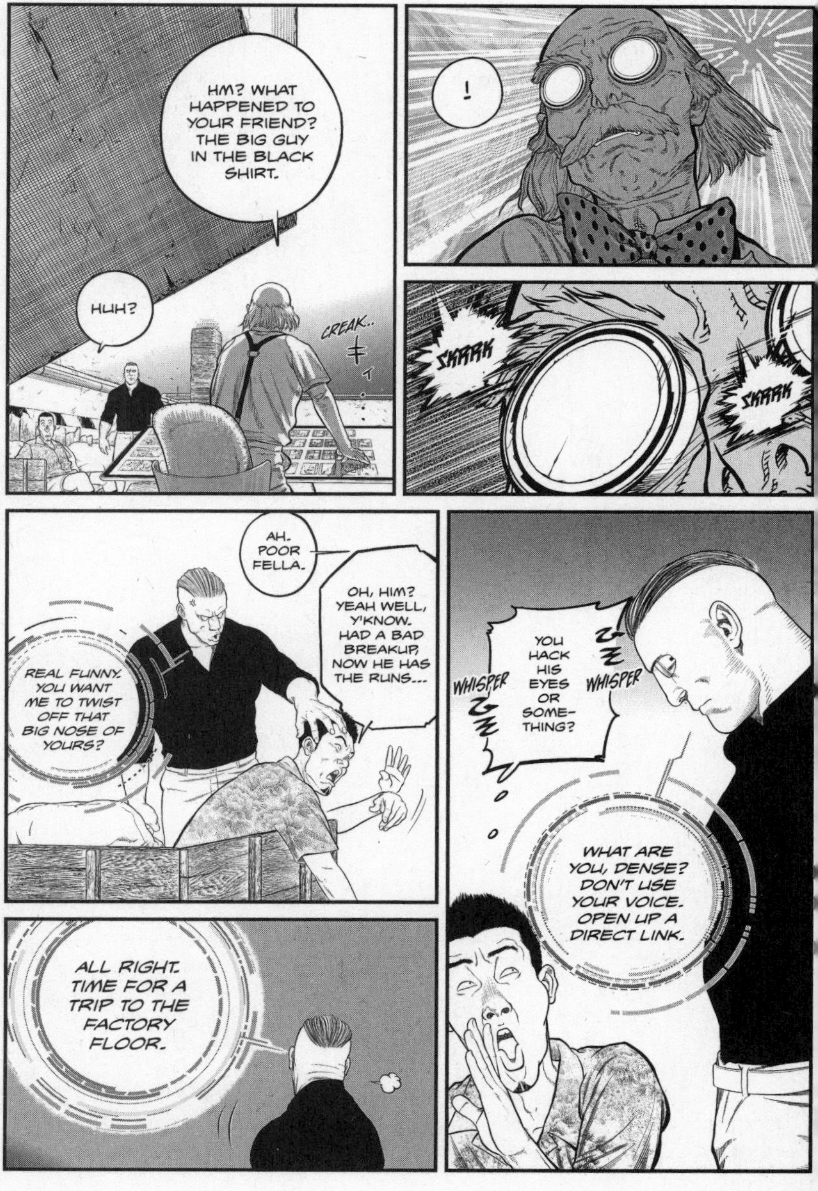
!
SKRRK
SKRRK
HM? WHAT HAPPENED TO YOUR FRIEND? THE BIG GUY IN THE BLACK SHIRT.
HUH?
CREAK..
キィ
WHISPER
WHISPER
YOU HACK HIS EYES OR SOME-THING?
WHAT ARE YOU, DENSE? DON'T USE YOUR VOICE. OPEN UP A DIRECT LINK.
AH. POOR FELLA.
OH, HIM? YEAH WELL, Y'KNOW. HAD A BAD BREAKUP, NOW HE HAS THE RUNS...
REAL FUNNY. YOU WANT ME TO TWIST OFF THAT BIG NOSE OF YOURS?
ALL RIGHT. TIME FOR A TRIP TO THE FACTORY FLOOR.

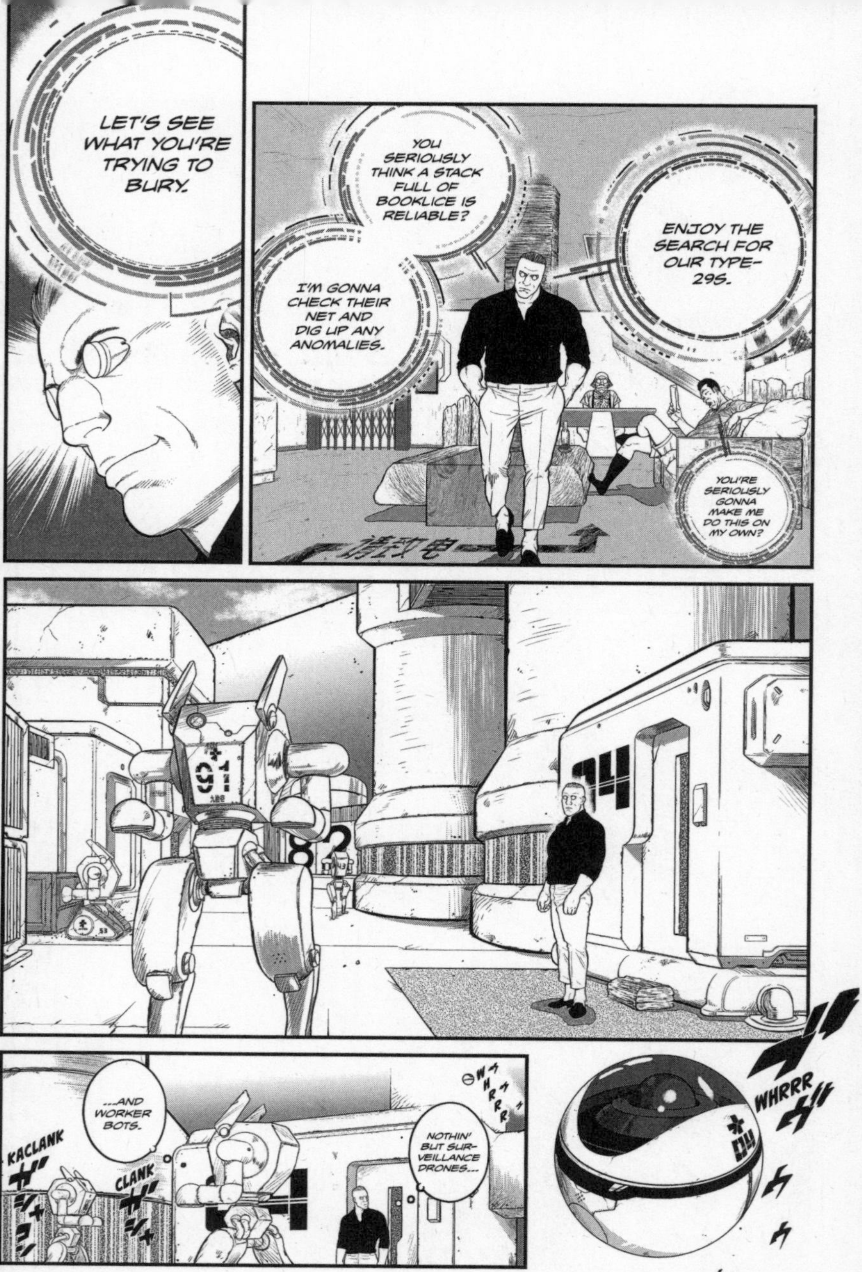
ENJOY THE SEARCH FOR OUR TYPE-29S.
YOU SERIOUSLY THINK A STACK FULL OF BOOKLICE IS RELIABLE?
I'M GONNA CHECK THEIR NET AND DIG UP ANY ANOMALIES.
YOU'RE SERIOUSLY GONNA MAKE ME DO THIS ON MY OWN?
LET'S SEE WHAT YOU'RE TRYING TO BURY.
WHRRR
WHRRR
NOTHIN' BUT SUR-VEILLANCE DRONES...
...AND WORKER BOTS.
CLANK
KACLANK

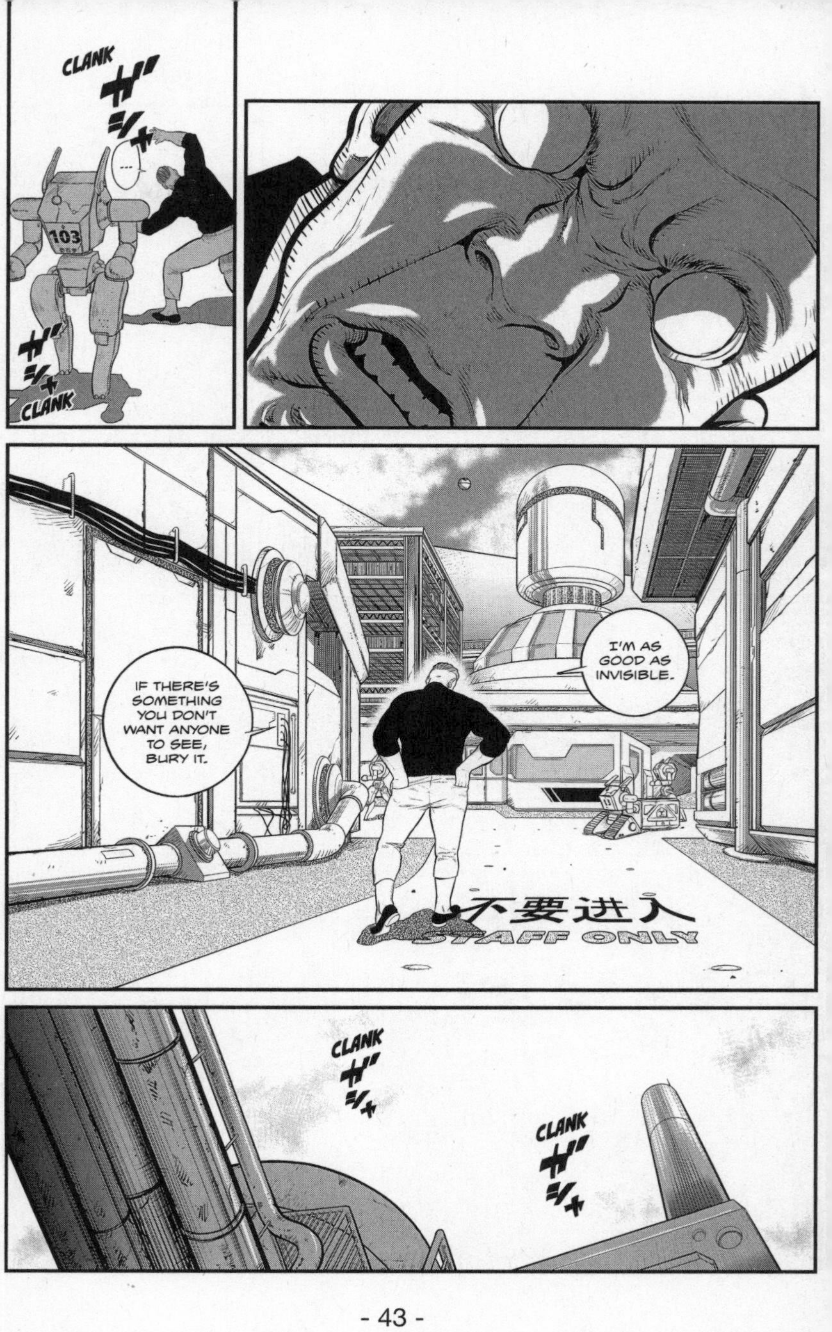
CLANK
ザシャ
...
ザシャ
CLANK
I'M AS GOOD AS INVISIBLE.
IF THERE'S SOMETHING YOU DON'T WANT ANYONE TO SEE, BURY IT.
不要进入
STAFF ONLY
CLANK
ザシャ
CLANK
ザシャ

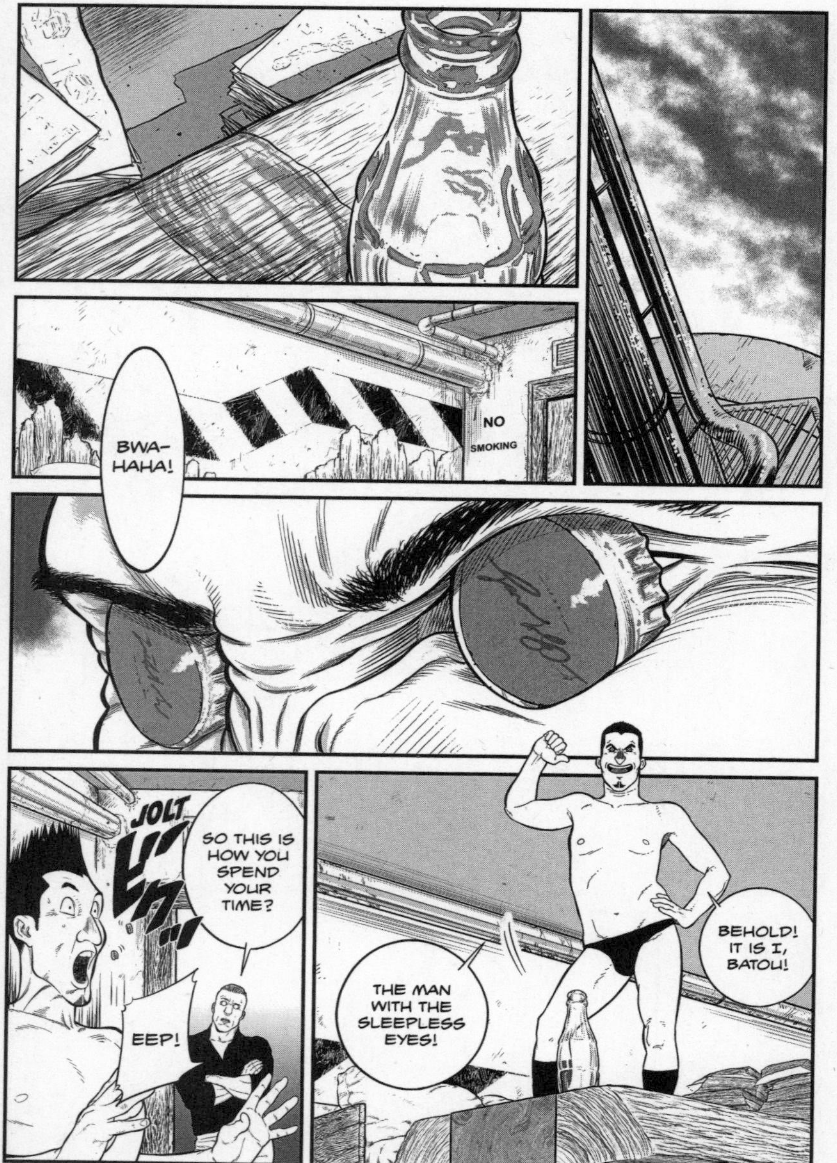
NO SMOKING
BWA-HAHA!
BEHOLD! IT IS I, BATOU!
THE MAN WITH THE SLEEPLESS EYES!
SO THIS IS HOW YOU SPEND YOUR TIME?
JOLT
EEP!

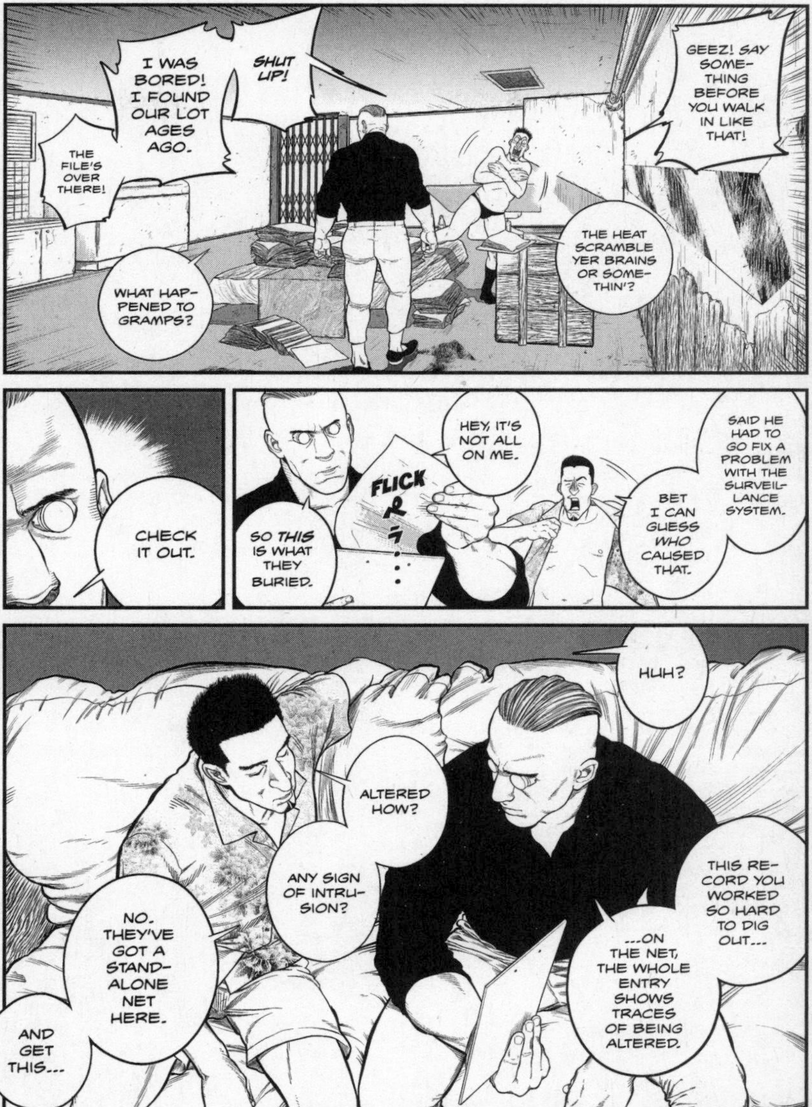
GEEZ! SAY SOMETHING BEFORE YOU WALK IN LIKE THAT!
SHUT UP!
I WAS BORED! I FOUND OUR LOT AGES AGO.
THE HEAT SCRAMBLE YER BRAINS OR SOMETHIN'?
THE FILE'S OVER THERE!
WHAT HAPPENED TO GRAMPS?
SAID HE HAD TO GO FIX A PROBLEM WITH THE SURVEILLANCE SYSTEM.
HEY, IT'S NOT ALL ON ME.
BET I CAN GUESS *WHO* CAUSED THAT.
FLICK
SO *THIS* IS WHAT THEY BURIED.
CHECK IT OUT.
HUH?
THIS RECORD YOU WORKED SO HARD TO DIG OUT...
...ON THE NET, THE WHOLE ENTRY SHOWS TRACES OF BEING ALTERED.
ALTERED HOW?
ANY SIGN OF INTRUSION?
NO. THEY'VE GOT A STANDALONE NET HERE.
AND GET THIS...

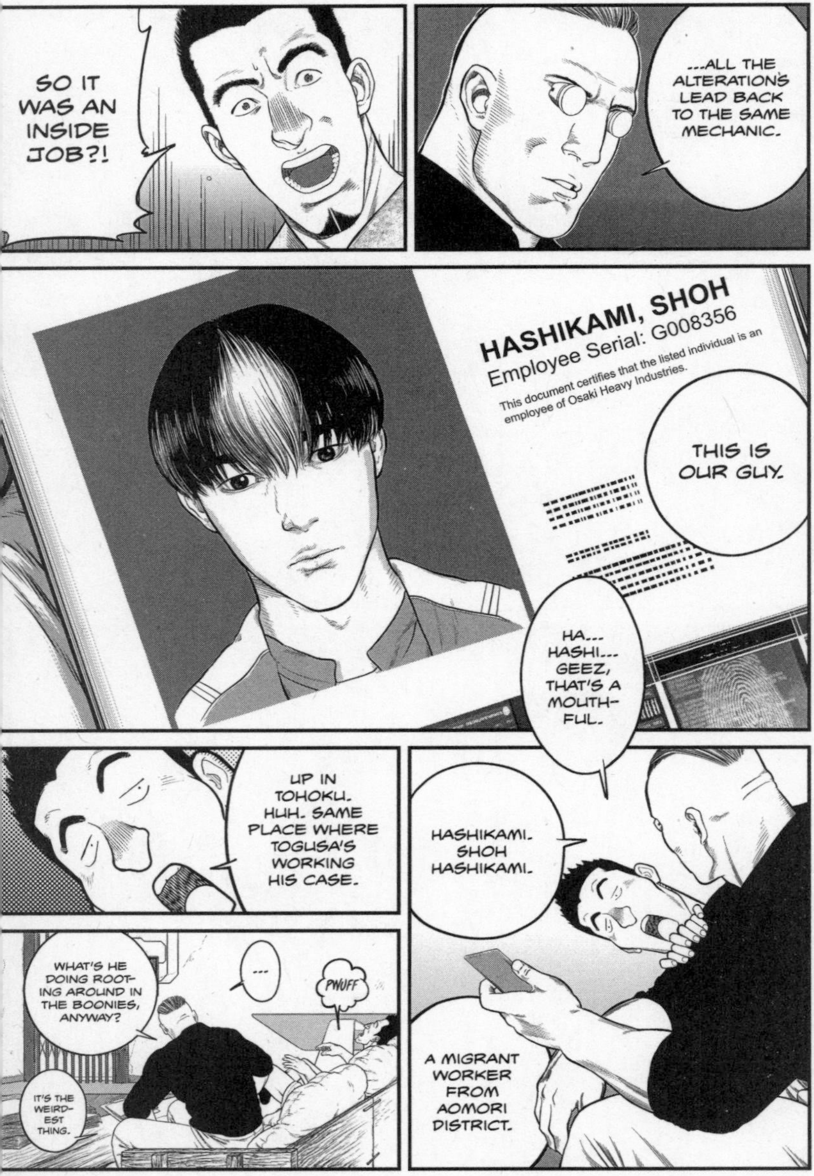
...ALL THE ALTERATIONS LEAD BACK TO THE SAME MECHANIC.
SO IT WAS AN INSIDE JOB?!
HASHIKAMI, SHOH
Employee Serial: G008356
This document certifies that the listed individual is an employee of Osaki Heavy Industries.
THIS IS OUR GUY.
HA... HASHI... GEEZ, THAT'S A MOUTHFUL.
HASHIKAMI. SHOH HASHIKAMI.
A MIGRANT WORKER FROM AOMORI DISTRICT.
UP IN TOHOKU. HUH. SAME PLACE WHERE TOGUSA'S WORKING HIS CASE.
PWUFF
...
WHAT'S HE DOING ROOTING AROUND IN THE BOONIES, ANYWAY?
IT'S THE WEIRD-EST THING.

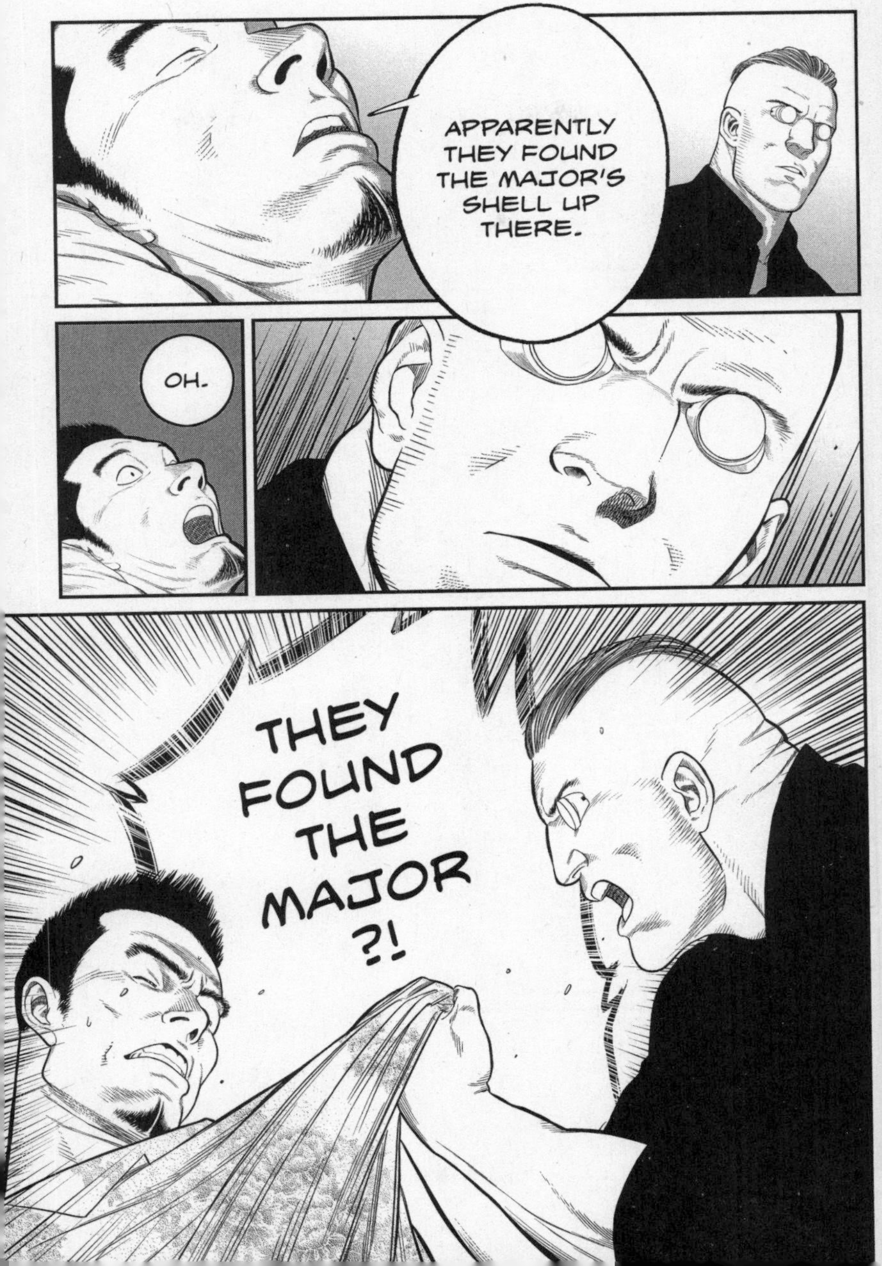
APPARENTLY THEY FOUND THE MAJOR'S SHELL UP THERE.
OH.
THEY FOUND THE MAJOR ?!

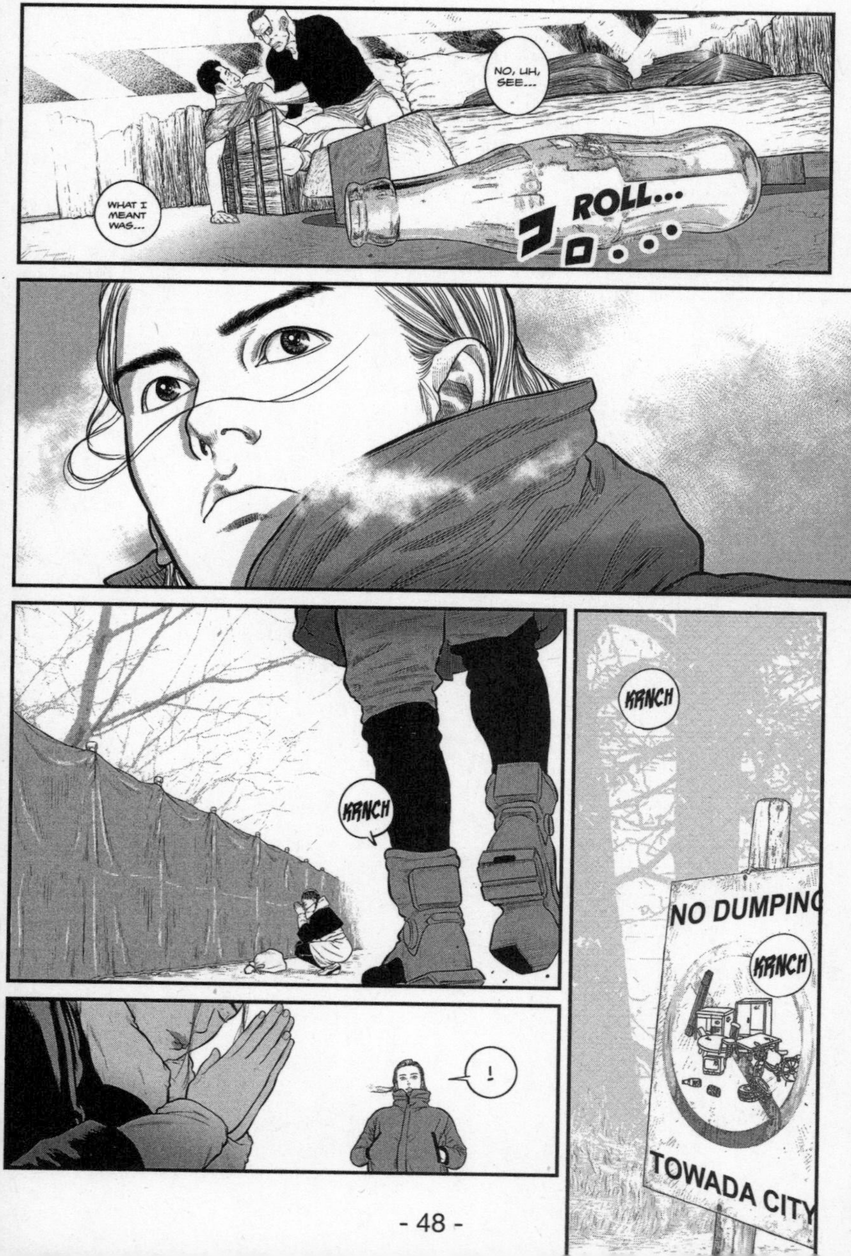
NO, UH, SEE...
ROLL...
コロ・・・
WHAT I MEANT WAS...
KRNCH
NO DUMPING
KRNCH
TOWADA CITY
KRNCH
!

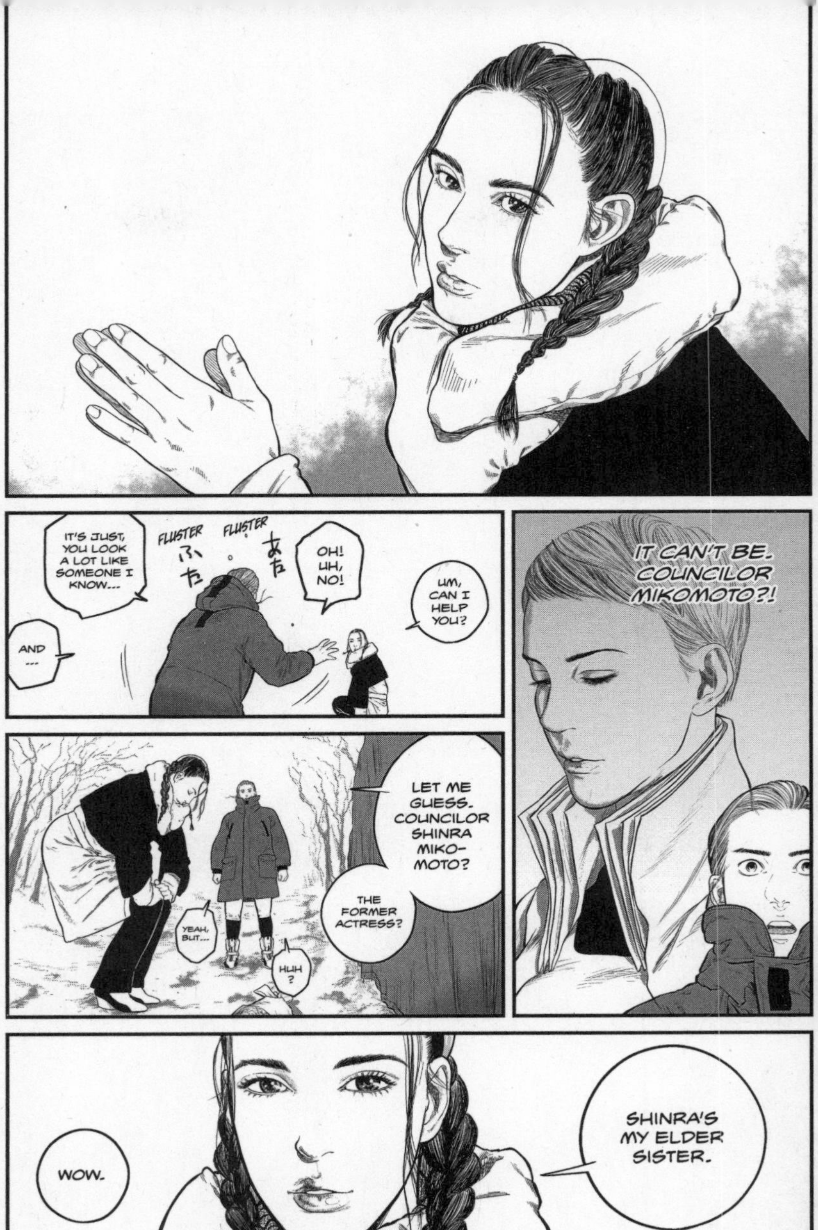
IT CAN'T BE. COUNCILOR MIKOMOTO?!
UM, CAN I HELP YOU?
OH! UH, NO!
FLUSTER あた
FLUSTER ふた
IT'S JUST, YOU LOOK A LOT LIKE SOMEONE I KNOW...
AND ...
LET ME GUESS. COUNCILOR SHINRA MIKO-MOTO?
THE FORMER ACTRESS?
HUH?
YEAH, BUT...
SHINRA'S MY ELDER SISTER.
WOW.

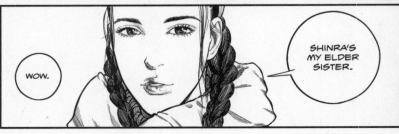

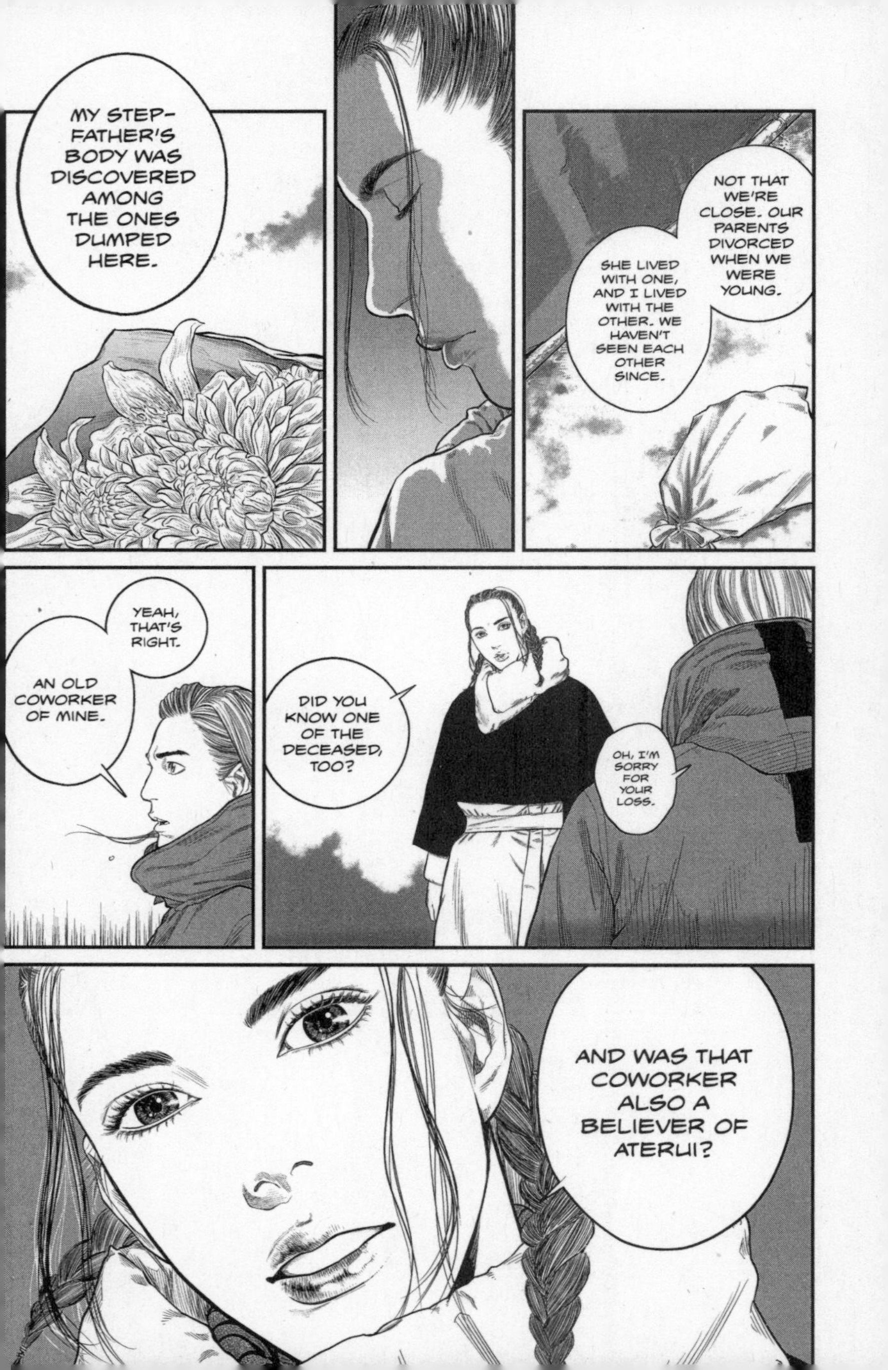
NOT THAT WE'RE CLOSE. OUR PARENTS DIVORCED WHEN WE WERE YOUNG.
SHE LIVED WITH ONE, AND I LIVED WITH THE OTHER. WE HAVEN'T SEEN EACH OTHER SINCE.
MY STEP-FATHER'S BODY WAS DISCOVERED AMONG THE ONES DUMPED HERE.
OH, I'M SORRY FOR YOUR LOSS.
DID YOU KNOW ONE OF THE DECEASED, TOO?
YEAH, THAT'S RIGHT.
AN OLD COWORKER OF MINE.
AND WAS THAT COWORKER ALSO A BELIEVER OF ATERUI?

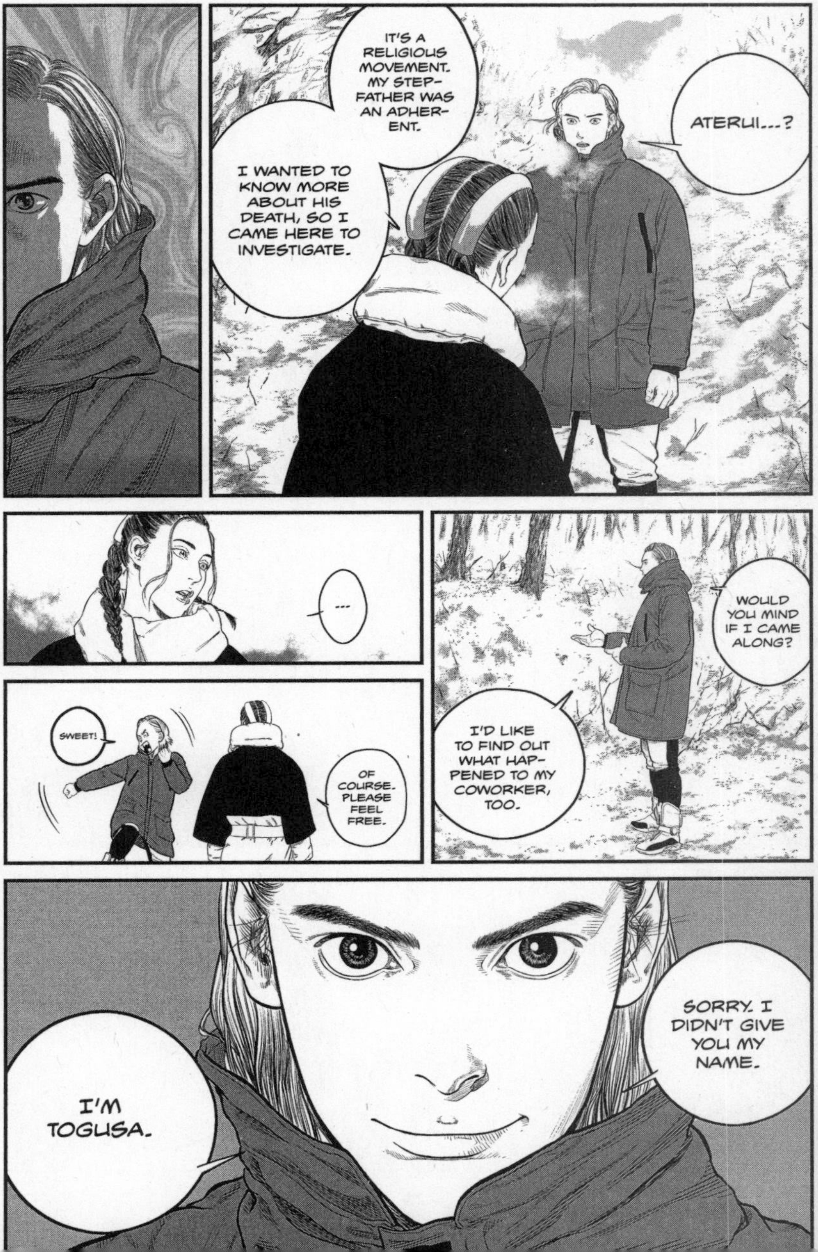
ATERUI...?
IT'S A RELIGIOUS MOVEMENT. MY STEP-FATHER WAS AN ADHER-ENT.
I WANTED TO KNOW MORE ABOUT HIS DEATH, SO I CAME HERE TO INVESTIGATE.
WOULD YOU MIND IF I CAME ALONG?
I'D LIKE TO FIND OUT WHAT HAP-PENED TO MY COWORKER, TOO.
...
OF COURSE. PLEASE FEEL FREE.
SWEET!
SORRY. I DIDN'T GIVE YOU MY NAME.
I'M TOGUSA.

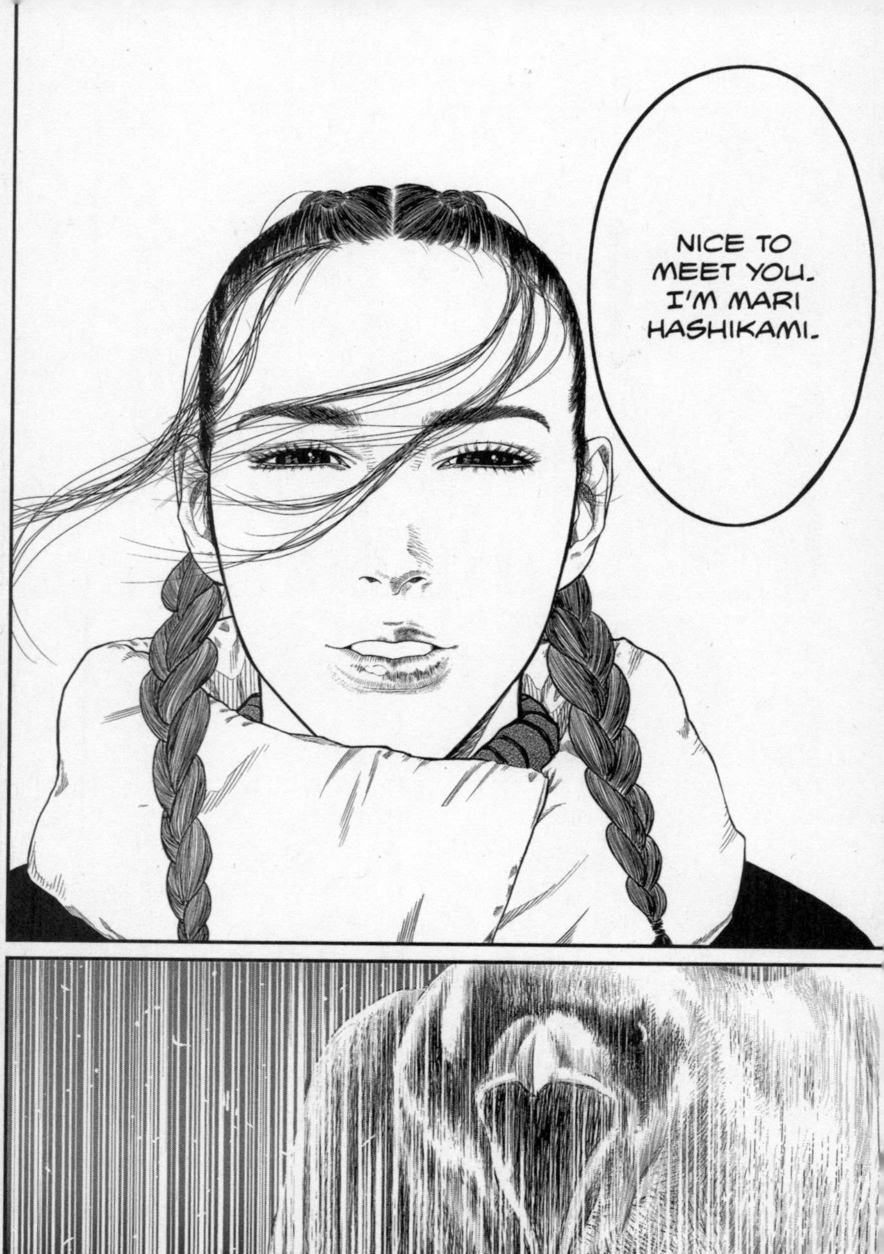
NICE TO MEET YOU. I'M MARI HASHIKAMI.

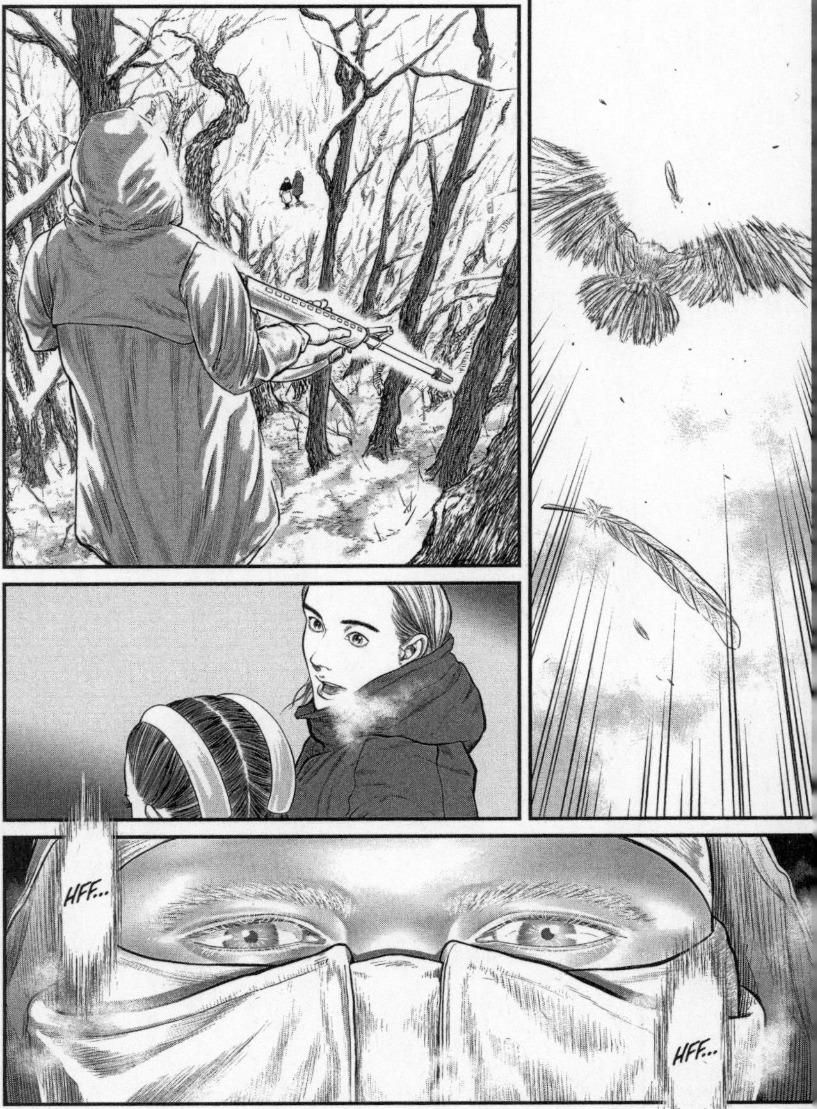
HFF...
HFF...

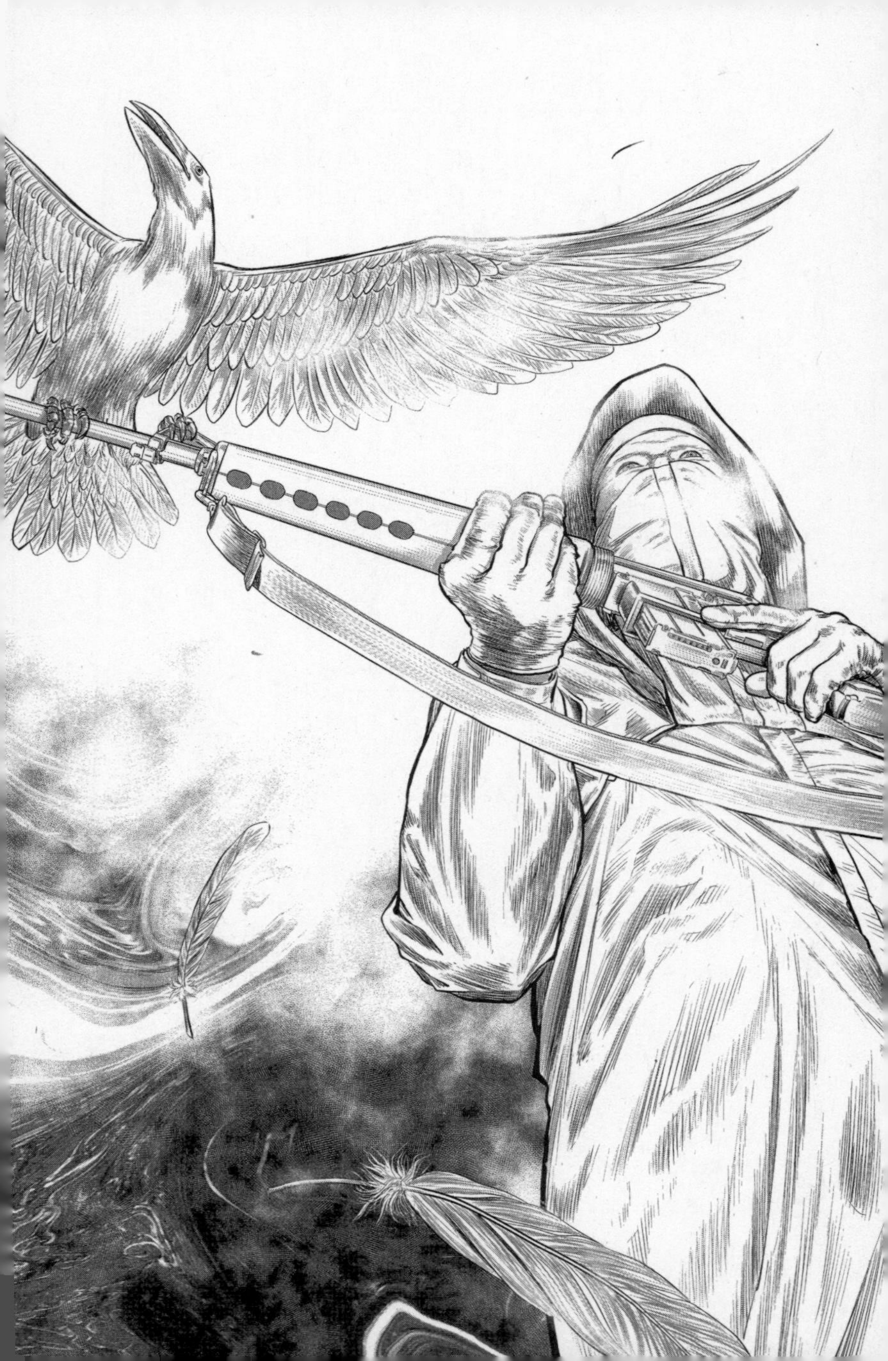

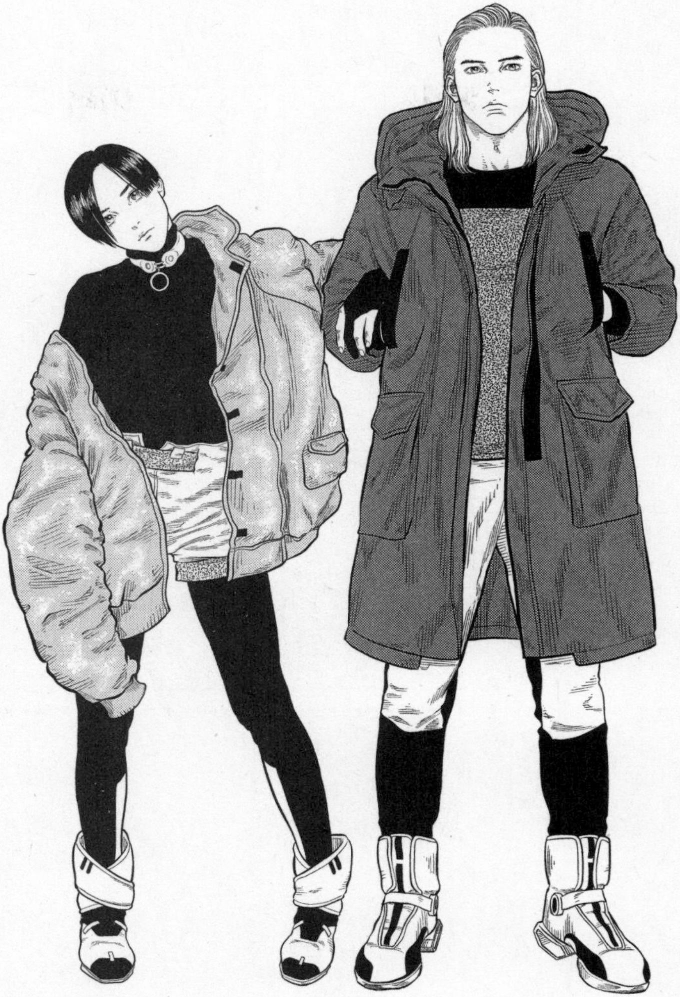

02

UNDERCOVER

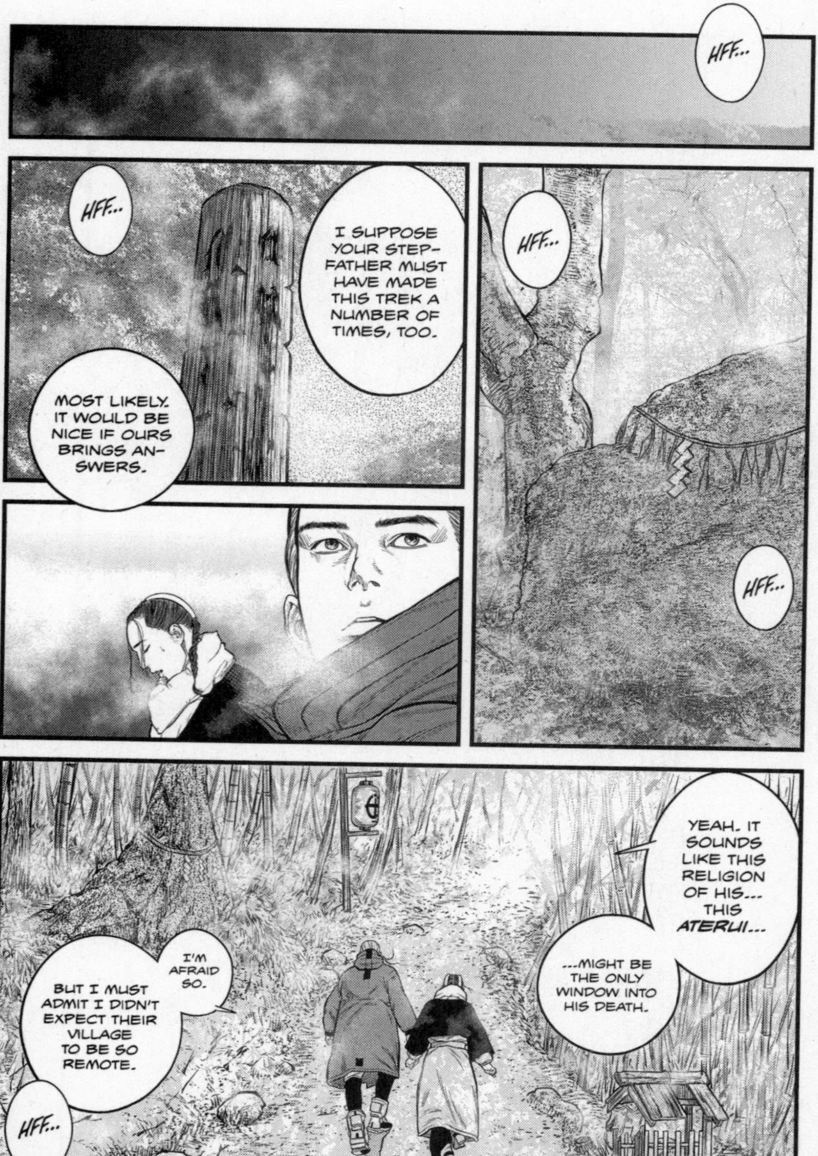
HFF...
HFF...
HFF...
HFF...
I SUPPOSE YOUR STEP-FATHER MUST HAVE MADE THIS TREK A NUMBER OF TIMES, TOO.
MOST LIKELY. IT WOULD BE NICE IF OURS BRINGS AN-SWERS.
YEAH. IT SOUNDS LIKE THIS RELIGION OF HIS... THIS ***ATERUI...***
...MIGHT BE THE ONLY WINDOW INTO HIS DEATH.
I'M AFRAID SO.
BUT I MUST ADMIT I DIDN'T EXPECT THEIR VILLAGE TO BE SO REMOTE.
HFF...

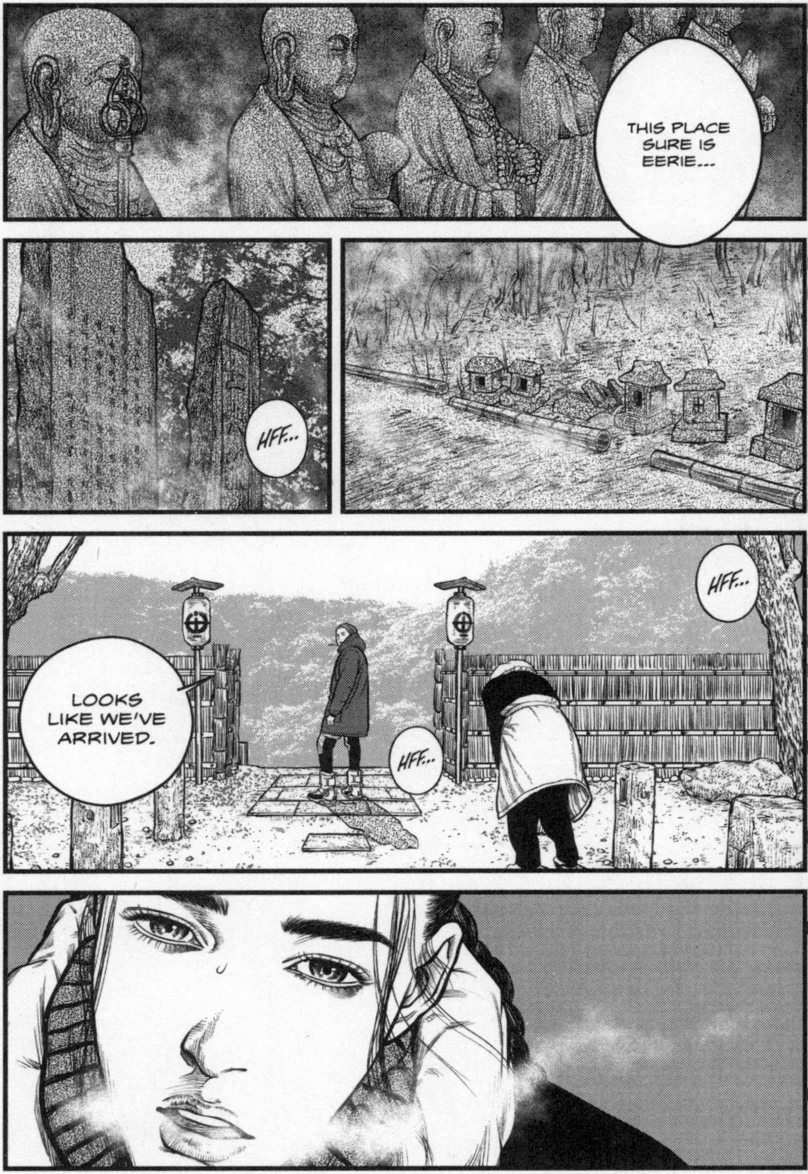
THIS PLACE SURE IS EERIE...
HFF...
HFF...
HFF...
LOOKS LIKE WE'VE ARRIVED.

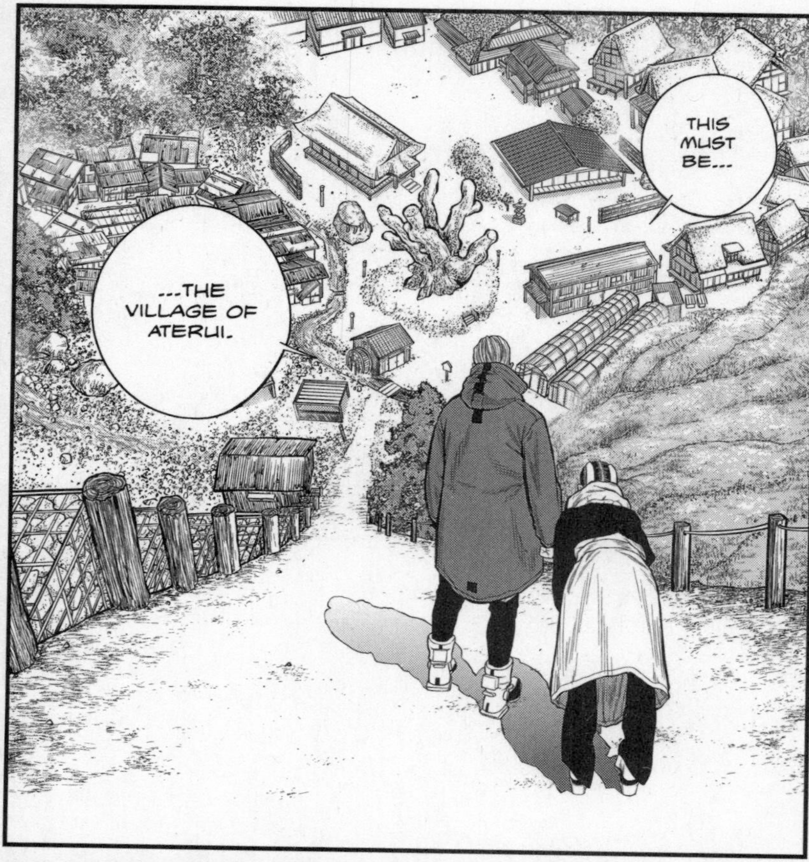
THIS MUST BE...
...THE VILLAGE OF ATERUI.

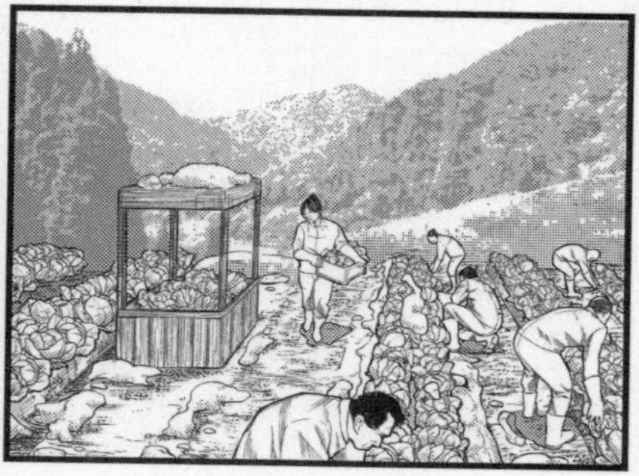

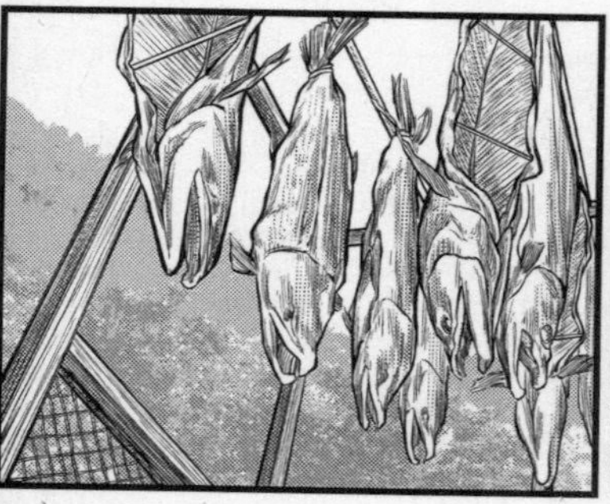

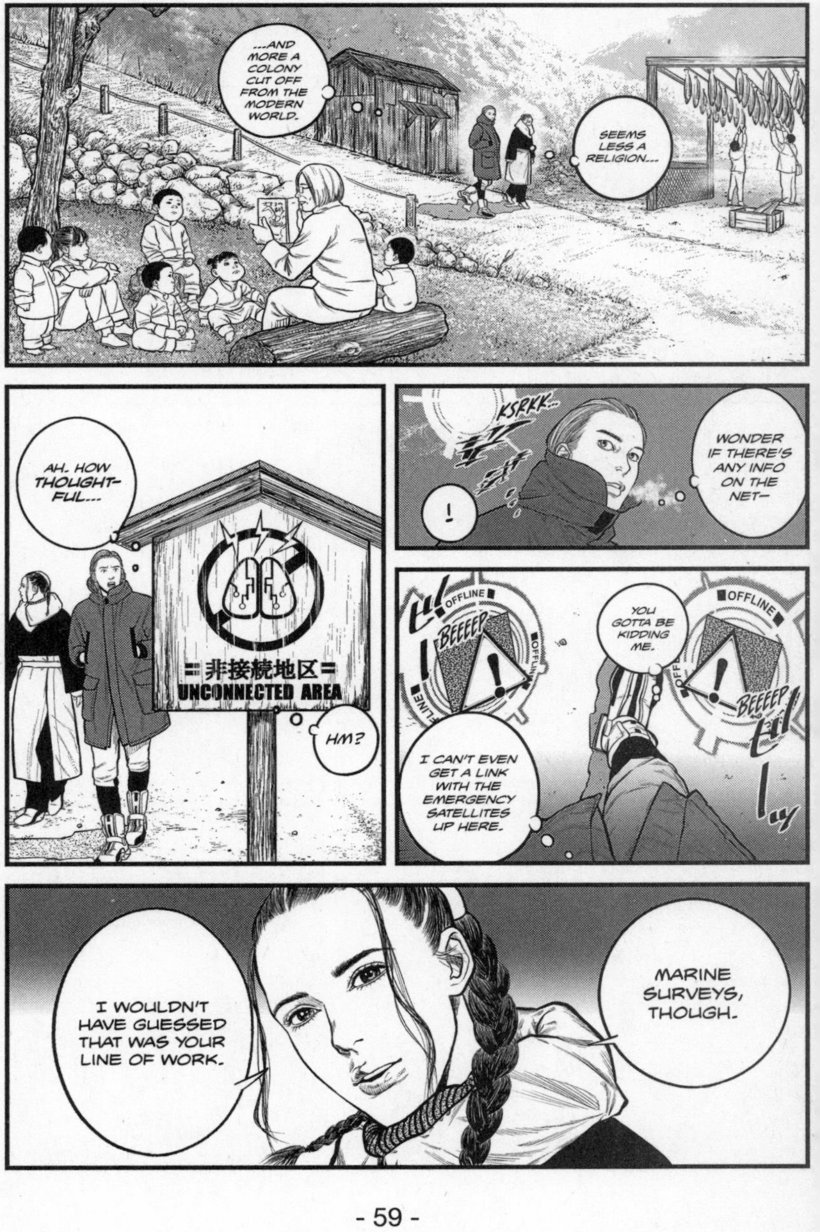
SEEMS LESS A RELIGION...
...AND MORE A COLONY CUT OFF FROM THE MODERN WORLD.
WONDER IF THERE'S ANY INFO ON THE NET—
KSRKK...
!
OFFLINE
BEEEEP
YOU GOTTA BE KIDDING ME.
I CAN'T EVEN GET A LINK WITH THE EMERGENCY SATELLITES UP HERE.
=非接続地区=
UNCONNECTED AREA
HM?
AH. HOW THOUGHT-FUL...
MARINE SURVEYS, THOUGH.
I WOULDN'T HAVE GUESSED THAT WAS YOUR LINE OF WORK.

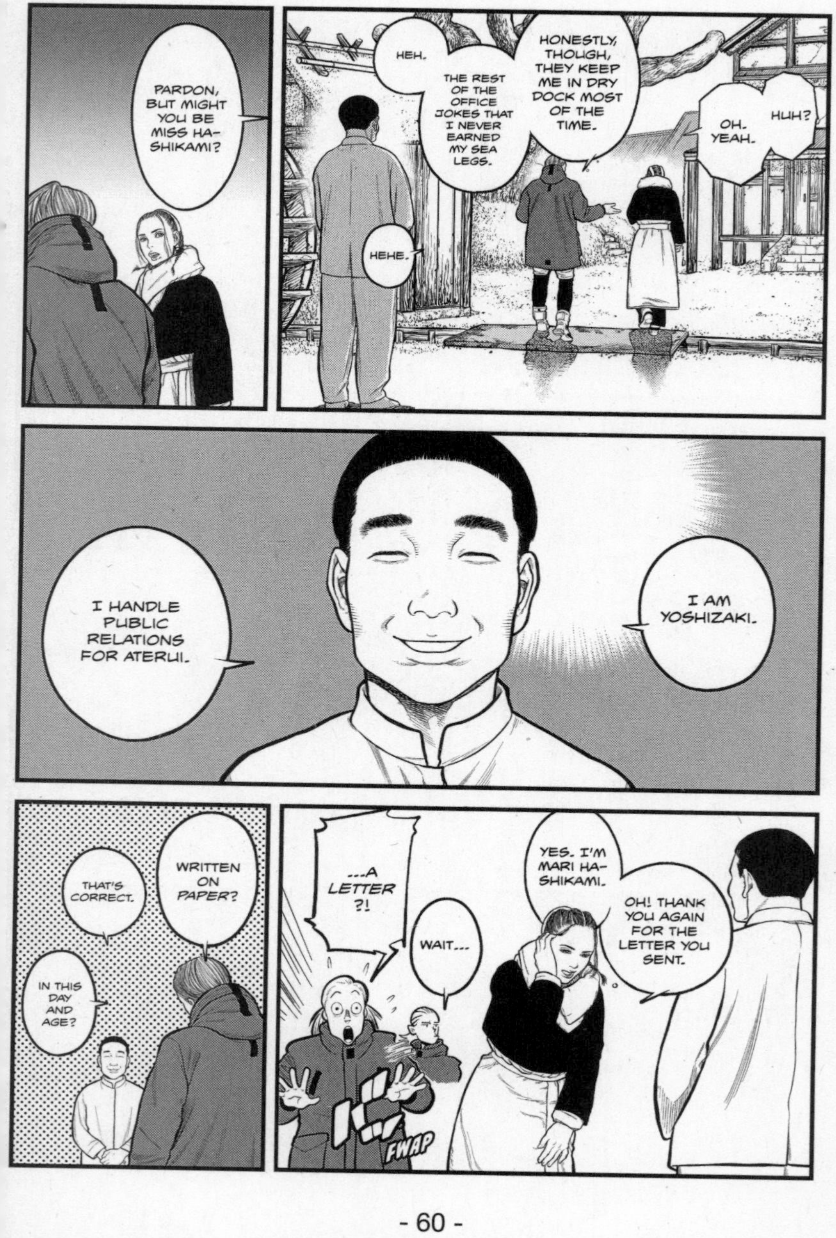
HUH?
OH. YEAH.
HONESTLY, THOUGH, THEY KEEP ME IN DRY DOCK MOST OF THE TIME.
HEH.
THE REST OF THE OFFICE JOKES THAT I NEVER EARNED MY SEA LEGS.
HEHE.
PARDON, BUT MIGHT YOU BE MISS HASHIKAMI?
I AM YOSHIZAKI.
I HANDLE PUBLIC RELATIONS FOR ATERUI.
YES. I'M MARI HASHIKAMI.
OH! THANK YOU AGAIN FOR THE LETTER YOU SENT.
WAIT...
...A LETTER ?!
FWAP
WRITTEN ON PAPER?
THAT'S CORRECT.
IN THIS DAY AND AGE?

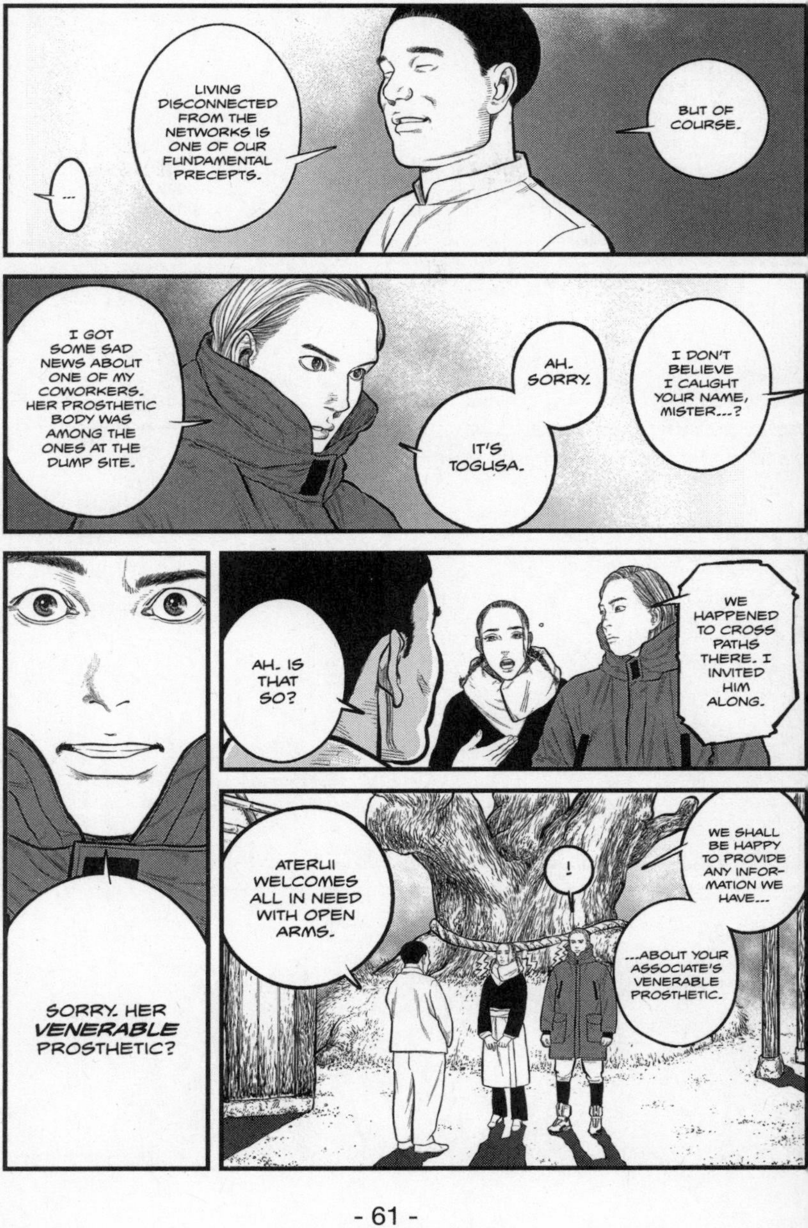
BUT OF COURSE.
LIVING DISCONNECTED FROM THE NETWORKS IS ONE OF OUR FUNDAMENTAL PRECEPTS.
...
I DON'T BELIEVE I CAUGHT YOUR NAME, MISTER...?
AH. SORRY.
IT'S TOGUSA.
I GOT SOME SAD NEWS ABOUT ONE OF MY COWORKERS. HER PROSTHETIC BODY WAS AMONG THE ONES AT THE DUMP SITE.
WE HAPPENED TO CROSS PATHS THERE. I INVITED HIM ALONG.
AH. IS THAT SO?
WE SHALL BE HAPPY TO PROVIDE ANY INFORMATION WE HAVE...
!
...ABOUT YOUR ASSOCIATE'S VENERABLE PROSTHETIC.
ATERUI WELCOMES ALL IN NEED WITH OPEN ARMS.
SORRY. HER *VENERABLE* PROSTHETIC?

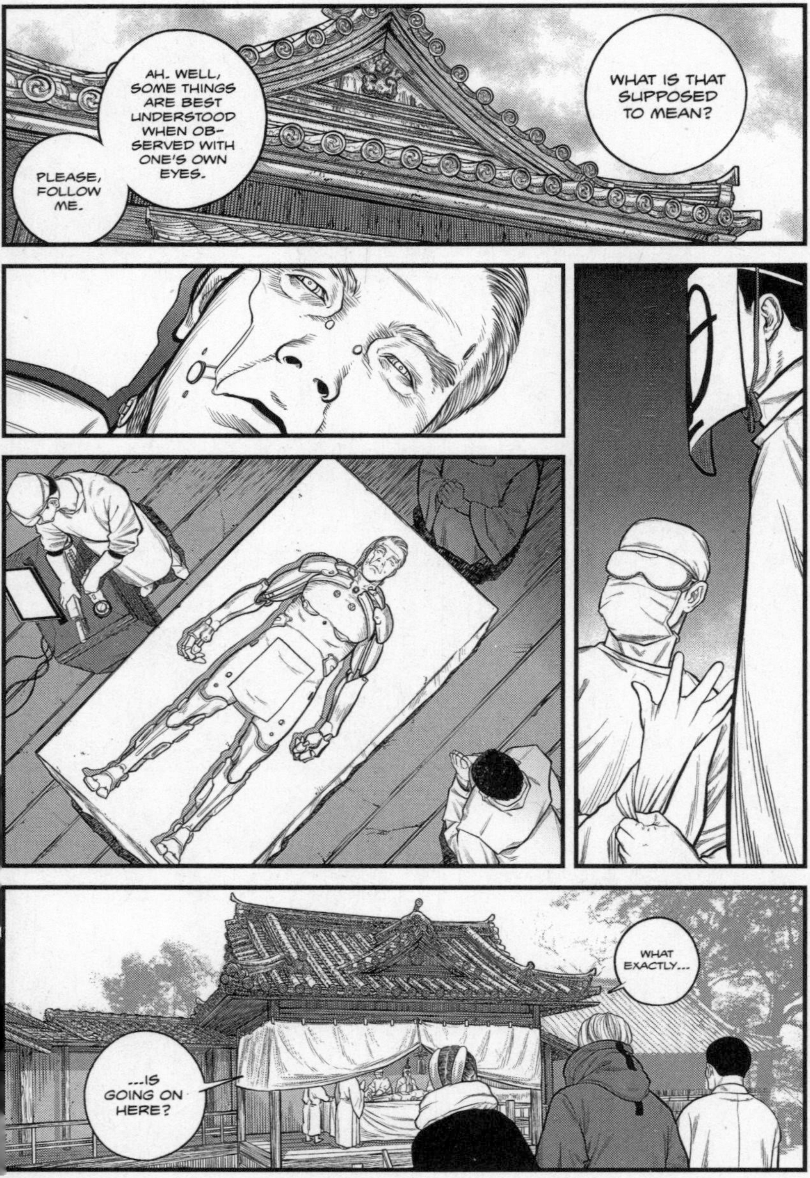
WHAT IS THAT SUPPOSED TO MEAN?
AH. WELL, SOME THINGS ARE BEST UNDERSTOOD WHEN OB-SERVED WITH ONE'S OWN EYES.
PLEASE, FOLLOW ME.
WHAT EXACTLY...
...IS GOING ON HERE?

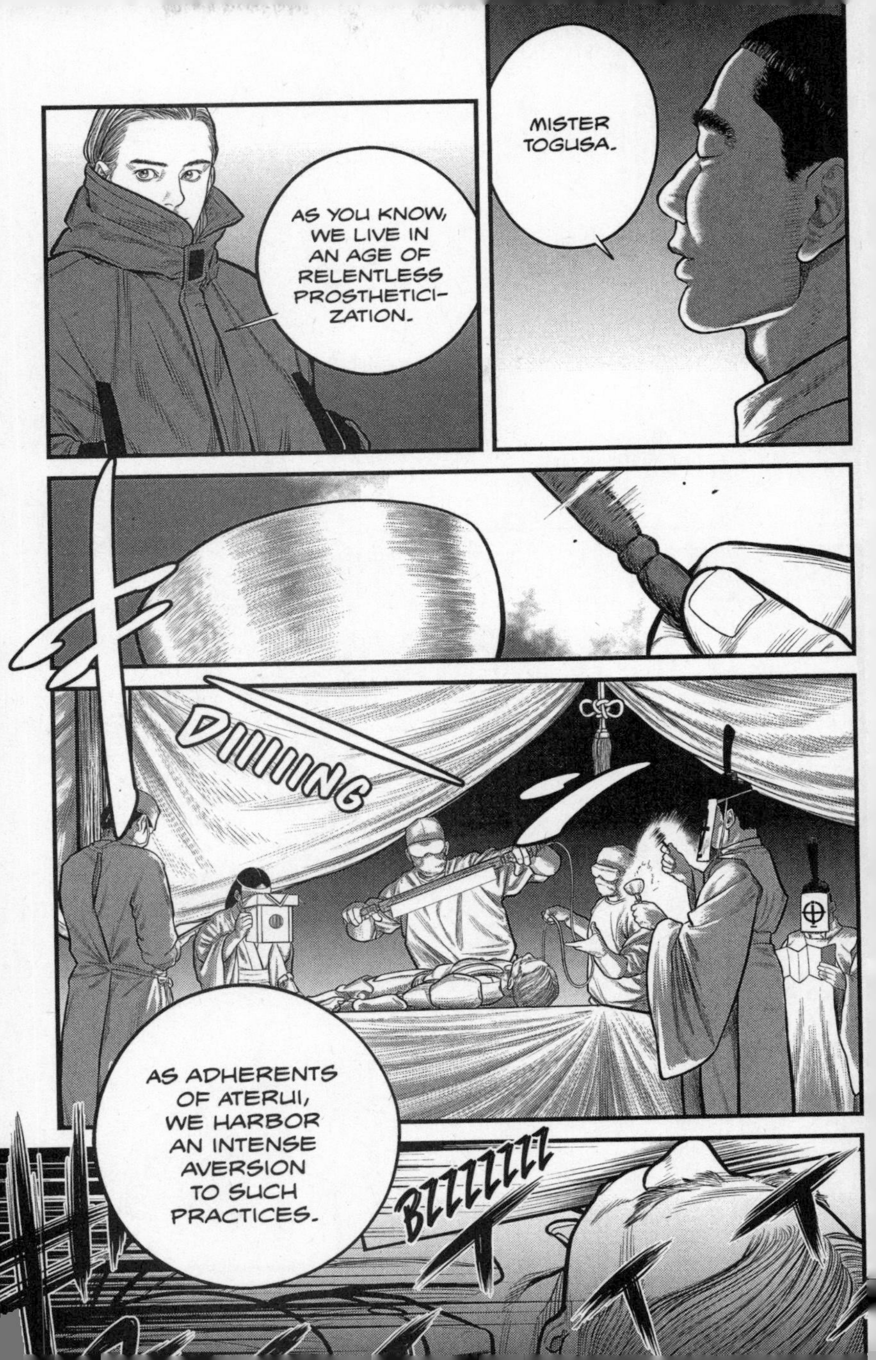
MISTER TOGUSA.
AS YOU KNOW, WE LIVE IN AN AGE OF RELENTLESS PROSTHETICI-ZATION.
DIIIIING
AS ADHERENTS OF ATERUI, WE HARBOR AN INTENSE AVERSION TO SUCH PRACTICES.
BZZZZZZZ

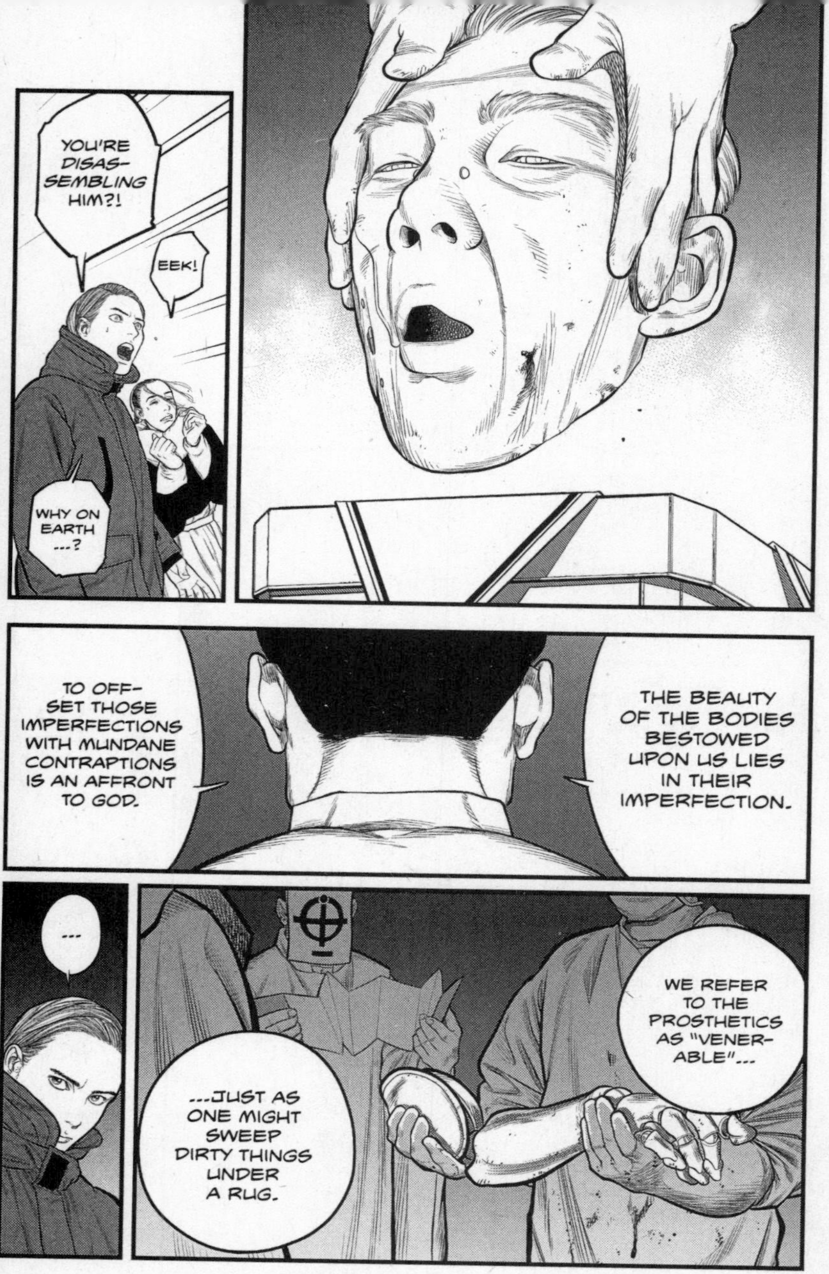
YOU'RE DISAS-SEMBLING HIM?!
EEK!
WHY ON EARTH ...?
THE BEAUTY OF THE BODIES BESTOWED UPON US LIES IN THEIR IMPERFECTION.
TO OFF-SET THOSE IMPERFECTIONS WITH MUNDANE CONTRAPTIONS IS AN AFFRONT TO GOD.
WE REFER TO THE PROSTHETICS AS "VENER-ABLE"...
...JUST AS ONE MIGHT SWEEP DIRTY THINGS UNDER A RUG.
...

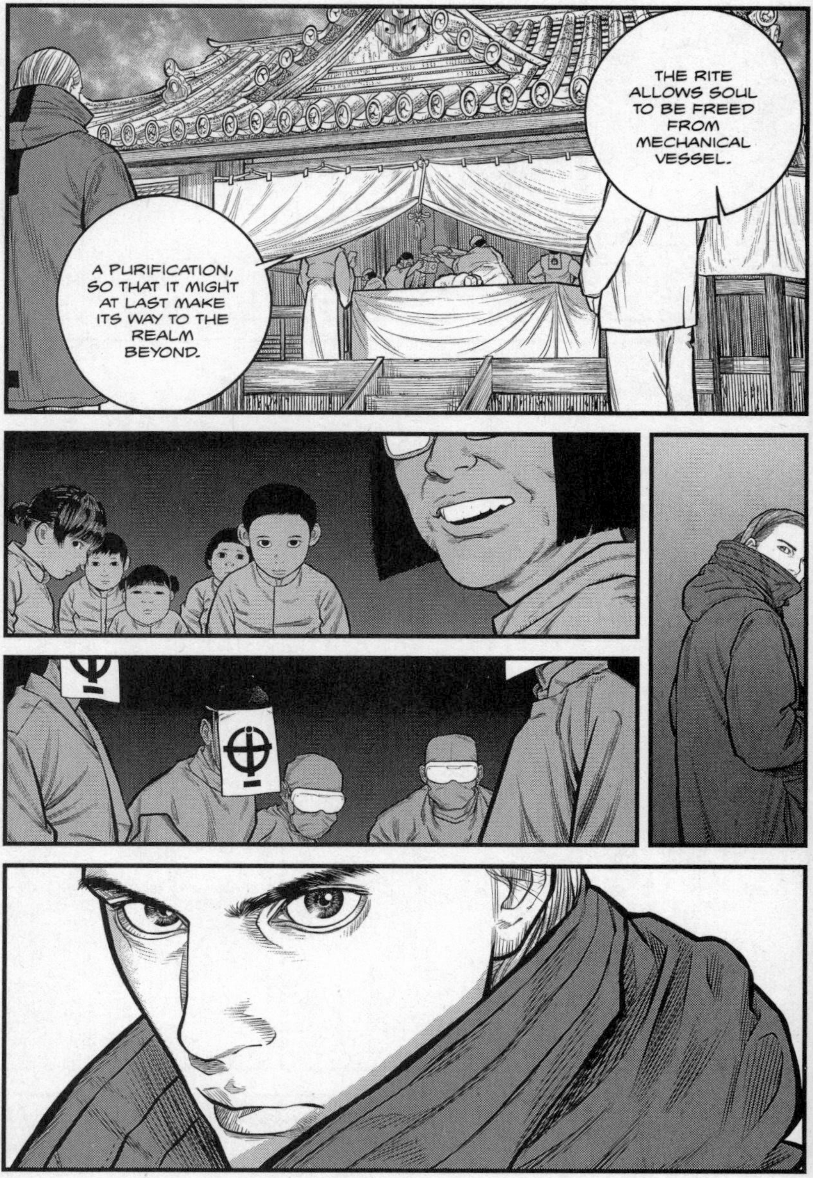
THE RITE ALLOWS SOUL TO BE FREED FROM MECHANICAL VESSEL.
A PURIFICATION, SO THAT IT MIGHT AT LAST MAKE ITS WAY TO THE REALM BEYOND.

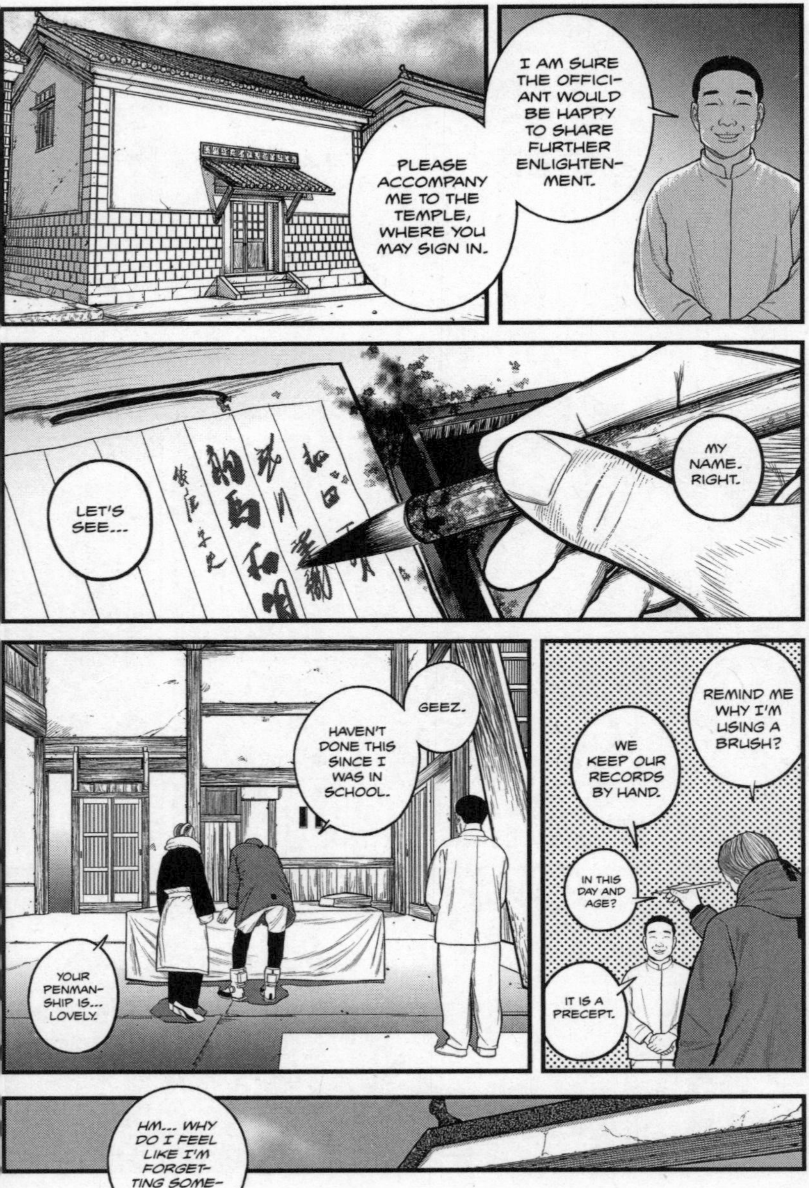
I AM SURE THE OFFICIANT WOULD BE HAPPY TO SHARE FURTHER ENLIGHTENMENT.
PLEASE ACCOMPANY ME TO THE TEMPLE, WHERE YOU MAY SIGN IN.
MY NAME. RIGHT.
LET'S SEE...
REMIND ME WHY I'M USING A BRUSH?
WE KEEP OUR RECORDS BY HAND.
IN THIS DAY AND AGE?
IT IS A PRECEPT.
GEEZ.
HAVEN'T DONE THIS SINCE I WAS IN SCHOOL.
YOUR PENMANSHIP IS... LOVELY.
HM... WHY DO I FEEL LIKE I'M FORGETTING SOMETHING...

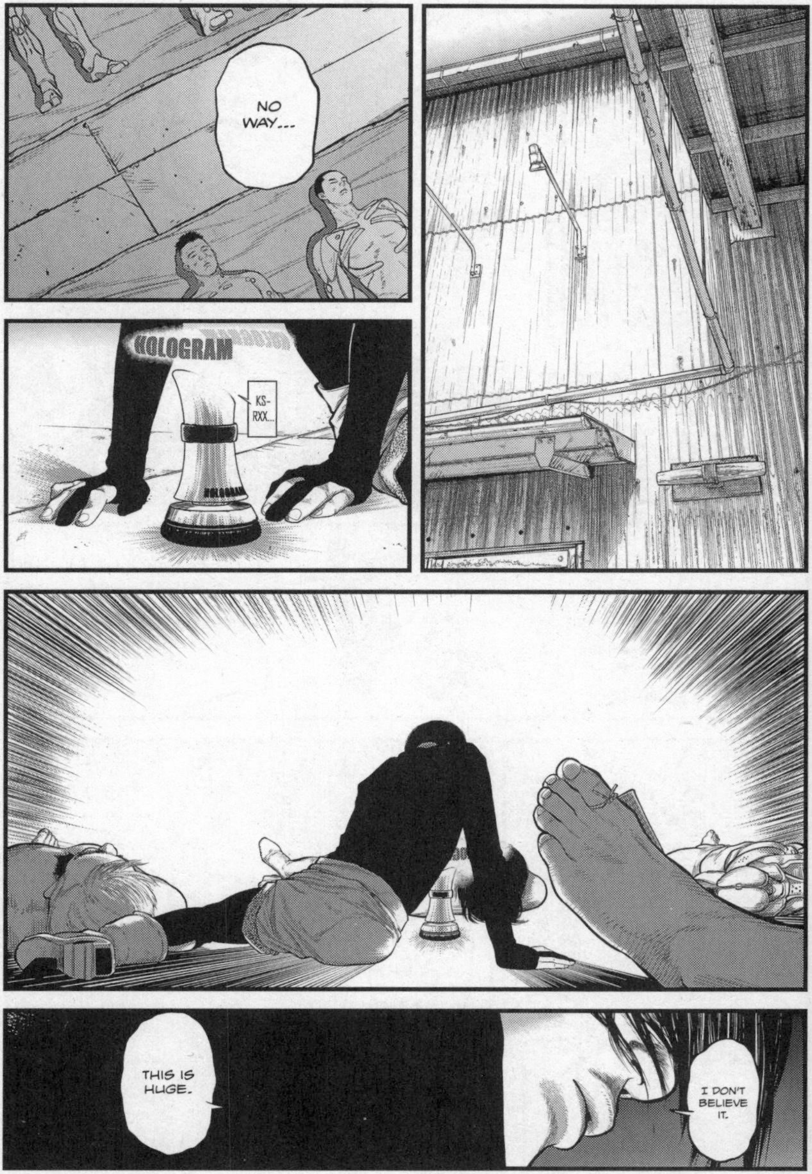
NO WAY...
HOLOGRAM
KS-RXX...
I DON'T BELIEVE IT.
THIS IS HUGE.

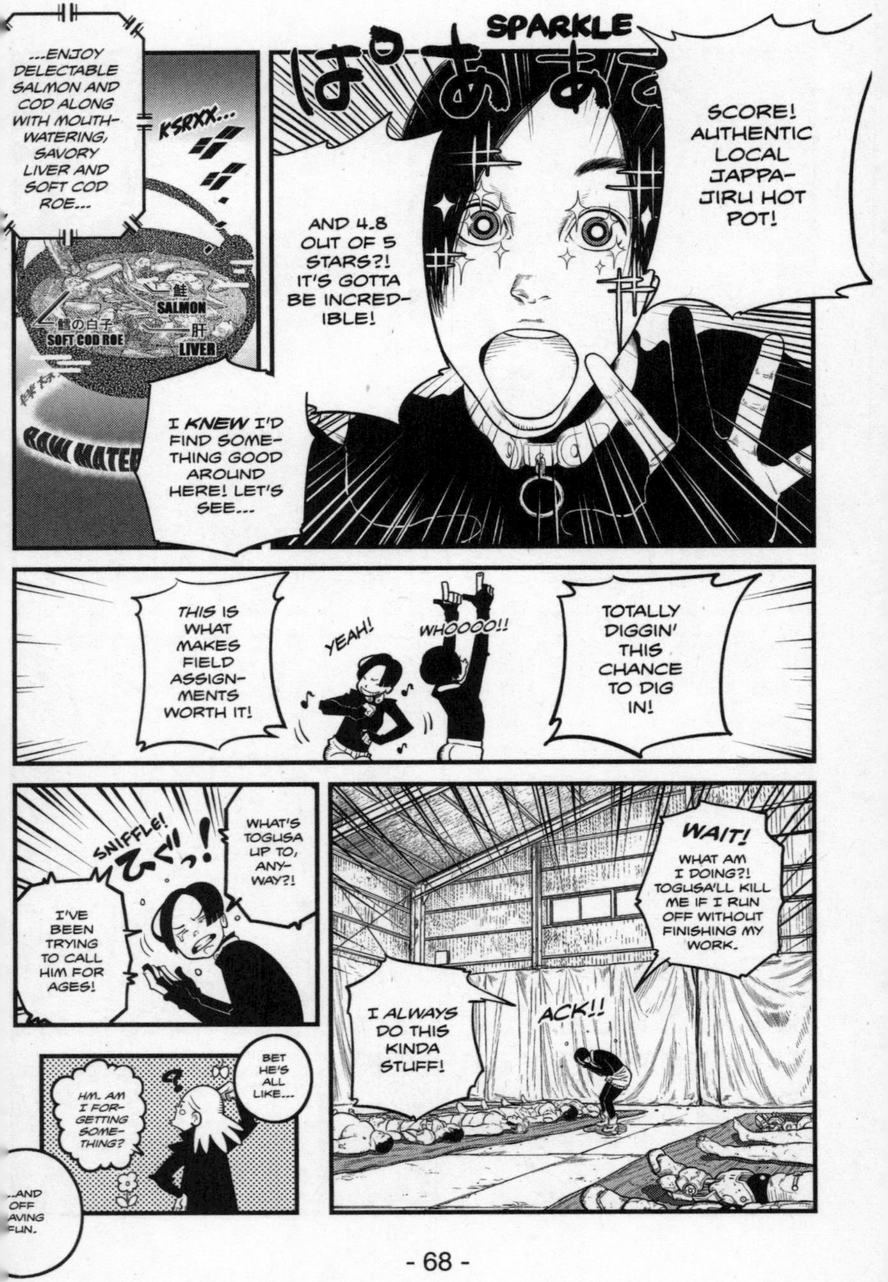
SPARKLE
SCORE! AUTHENTIC LOCAL JAPPA-JIRU HOT POT!
AND 4.8 OUT OF 5 STARS?! IT'S GOTTA BE INCREDIBLE!
...ENJOY DELECTABLE SALMON AND COD ALONG WITH MOUTH-WATERING, SAVORY LIVER AND SOFT COD ROE...
KSRXX...
鮭
SALMON
鱈の白子
SOFT COD ROE
肝
LIVER
I KNEW I'D FIND SOME-THING GOOD AROUND HERE! LET'S SEE...
TOTALLY DIGGIN' THIS CHANCE TO DIG IN!
WHOOOOO!!
YEAH!
THIS IS WHAT MAKES FIELD ASSIGN-MENTS WORTH IT!
WAIT! WHAT AM I DOING?! TOGUSA'LL KILL ME IF I RUN OFF WITHOUT FINISHING MY WORK.
ACK!!
I ALWAYS DO THIS KINDA STUFF!
WHAT'S TOGUSA UP TO, ANY-WAY?!
SNIFFLE!
I'VE BEEN TRYING TO CALL HIM FOR AGES!
BET HE'S ALL LIKE...
HM. AM I FOR-GETTING SOME-THING?
..AND OFF AVING FUN.

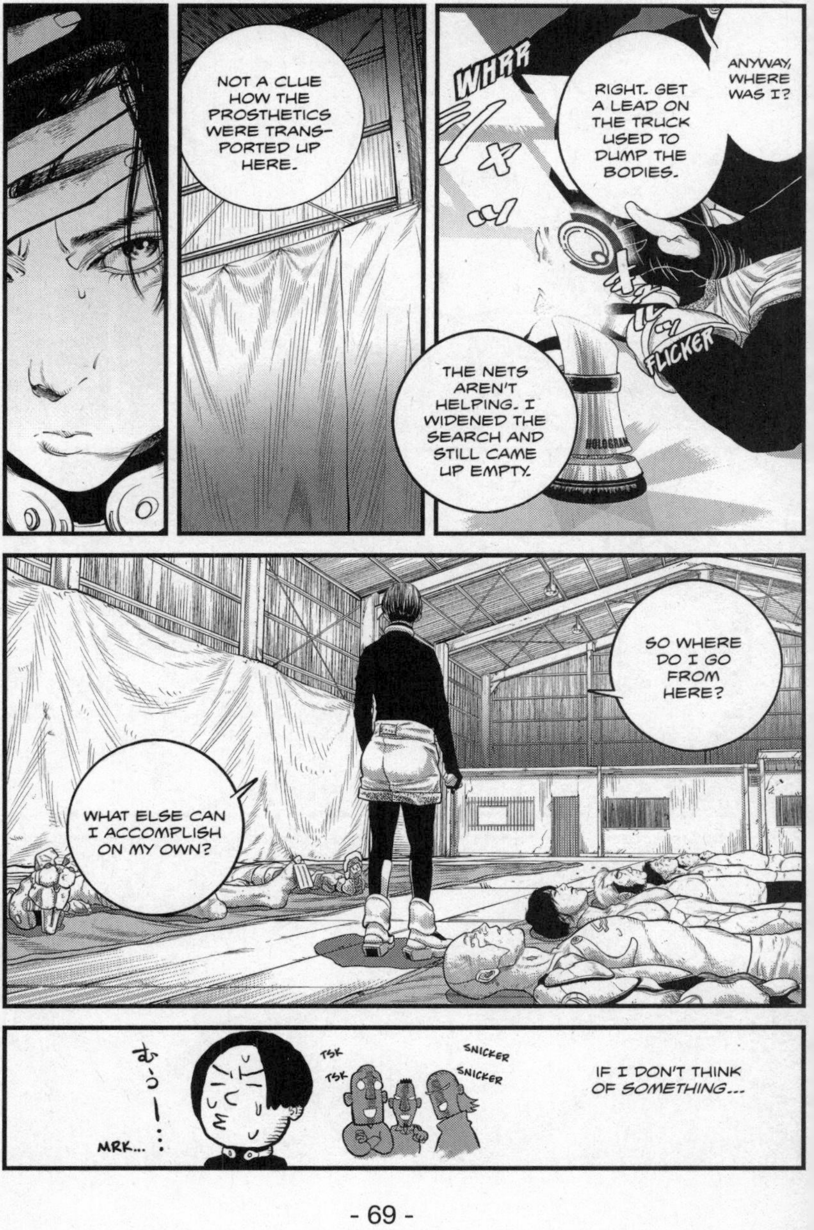
ANYWAY, WHERE WAS I?
RIGHT. GET A LEAD ON THE TRUCK USED TO DUMP THE BODIES.
WHRR
FLICKER
THE NETS AREN'T HELPING. I WIDENED THE SEARCH AND STILL CAME UP EMPTY.
NOT A CLUE HOW THE PROSTHETICS WERE TRANS-PORTED UP HERE.
SO WHERE DO I GO FROM HERE?
WHAT ELSE CAN I ACCOMPLISH ON MY OWN?
IF I DON'T THINK OF SOMETHING...
SNICKER
SNICKER
TSK
TSK
むぅー…
MRK...

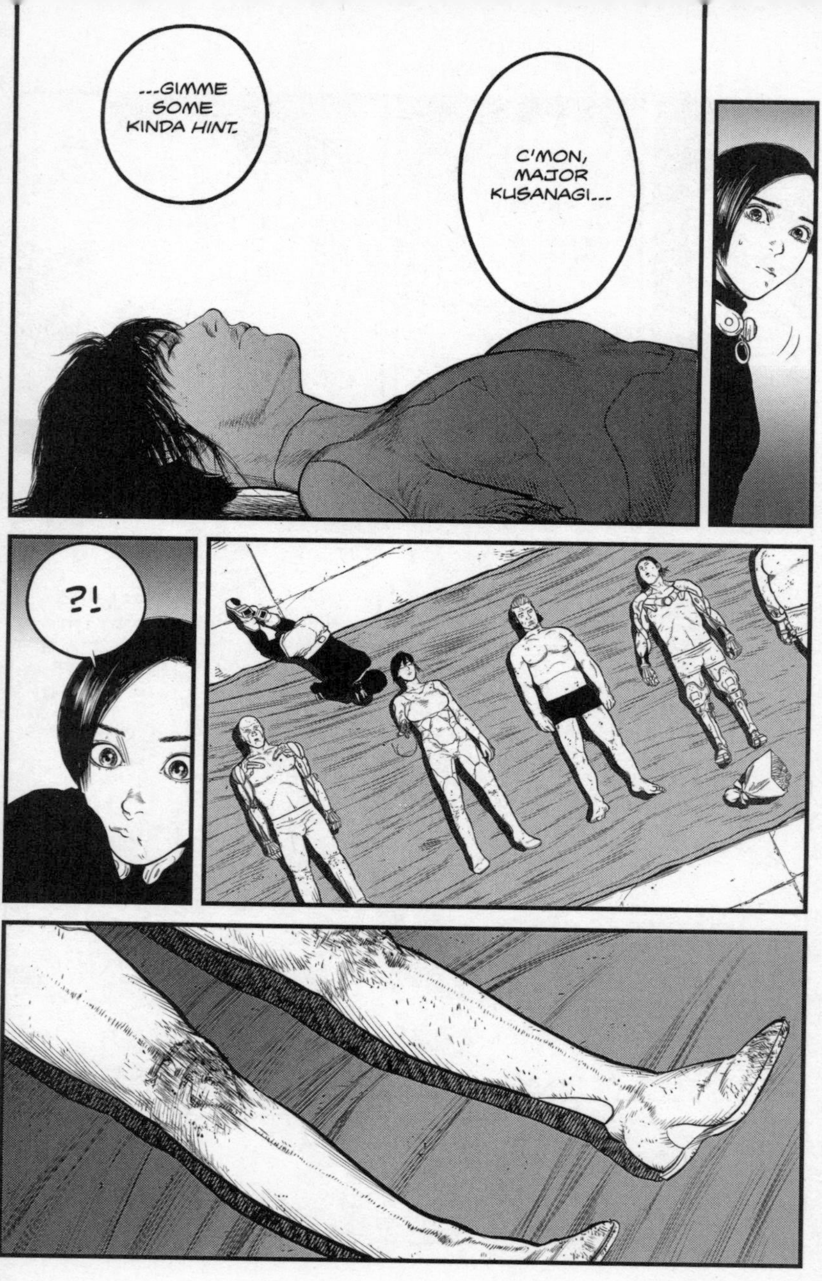
C'MON, MAJOR KUSANAGI...
...GIMME SOME KINDA HINT.
?!

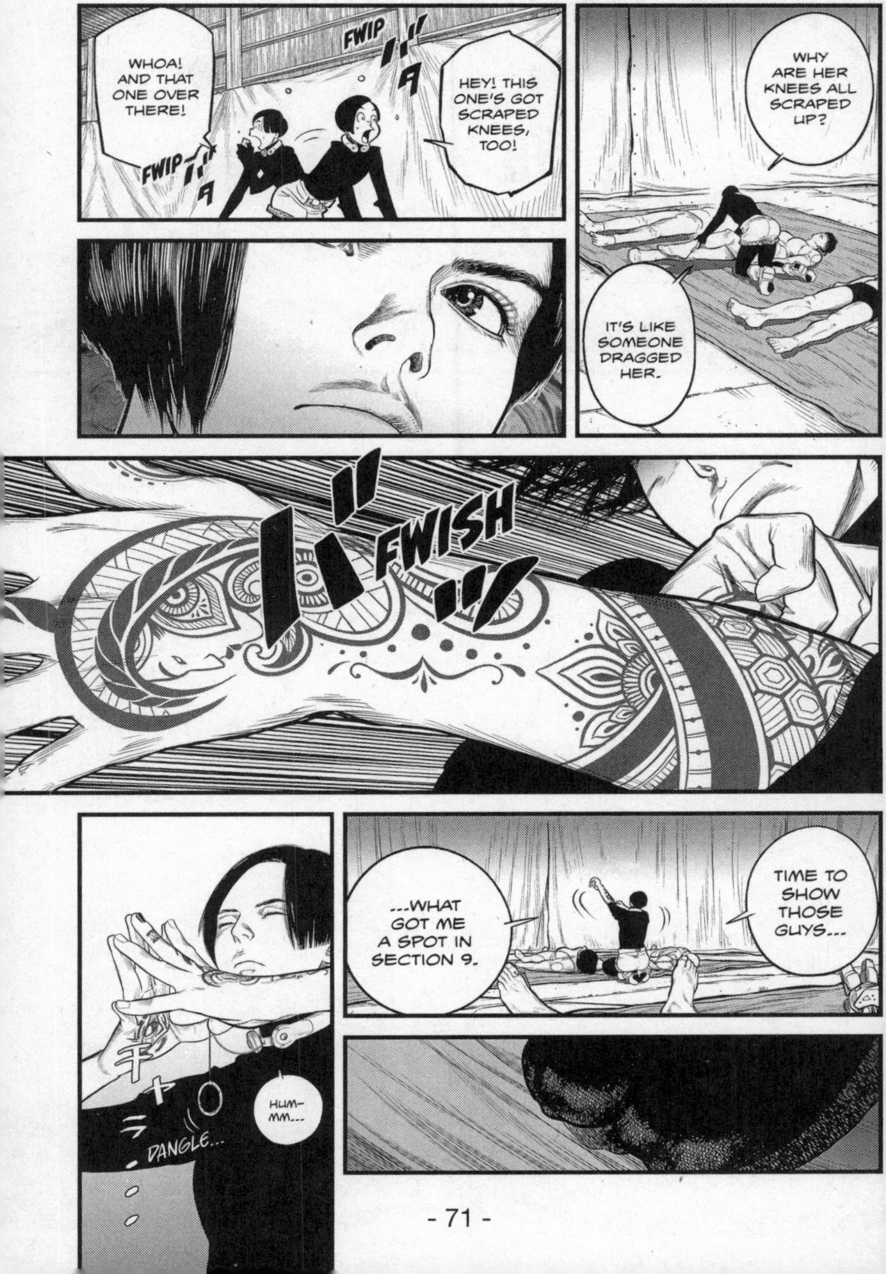
WHY ARE HER KNEES ALL SCRAPED UP?
IT'S LIKE SOMEONE DRAGGED HER.
FWIP
HEY! THIS ONE'S GOT SCRAPED KNEES, TOO!
WHOA! AND THAT ONE OVER THERE!
FWIP
FWISH
TIME TO SHOW THOSE GUYS...
...WHAT GOT ME A SPOT IN SECTION 9.
HUM-MM...
DANGLE...

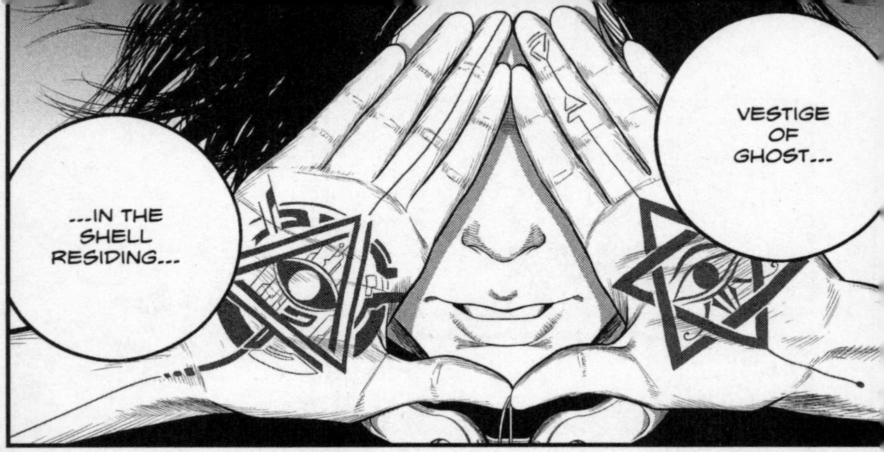
VESTIGE OF GHOST...
...IN THE SHELL RESIDING...

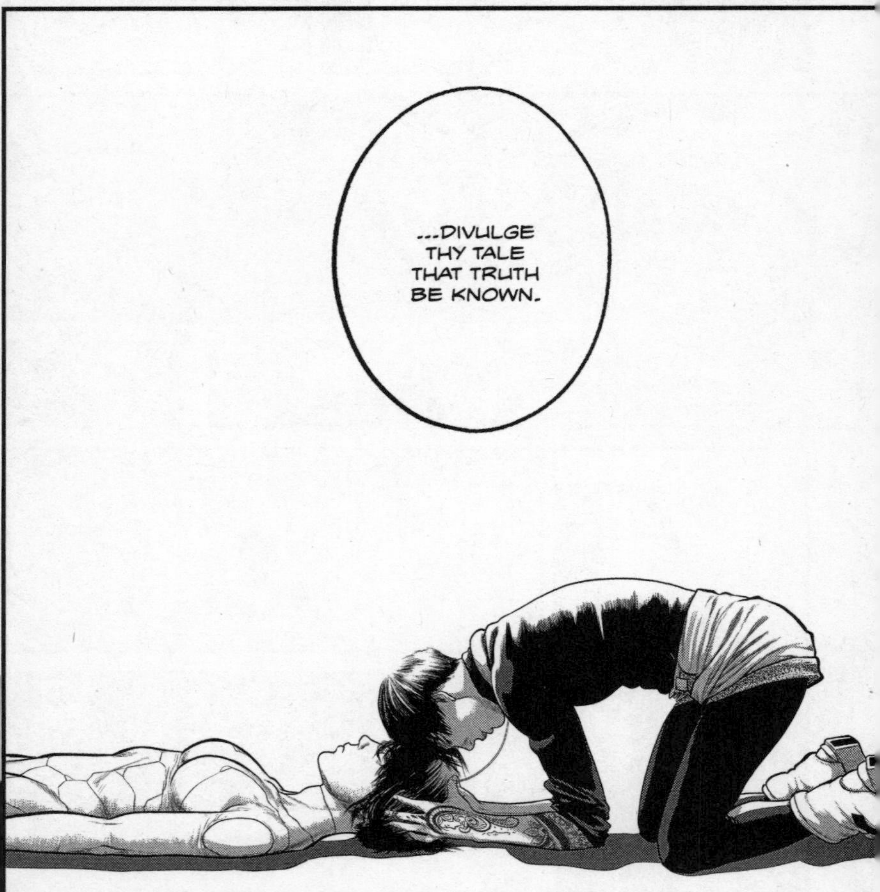
...DIVULGE THY TALE THAT TRUTH BE KNOWN.

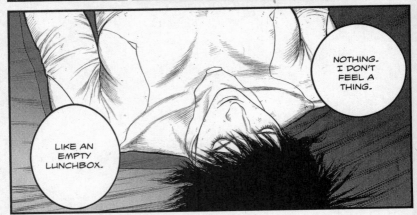

NOTHING. I DON'T FEEL A THING.

LIKE AN EMPTY LUNCHBOX.

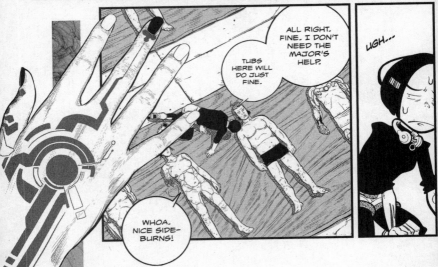

ALL RIGHT. FINE. I DON'T NEED THE MAJOR'S HELP.

TUBS HERE WILL DO JUST FINE.

UGH...

WHOA. NICE SIDE-BURNS!

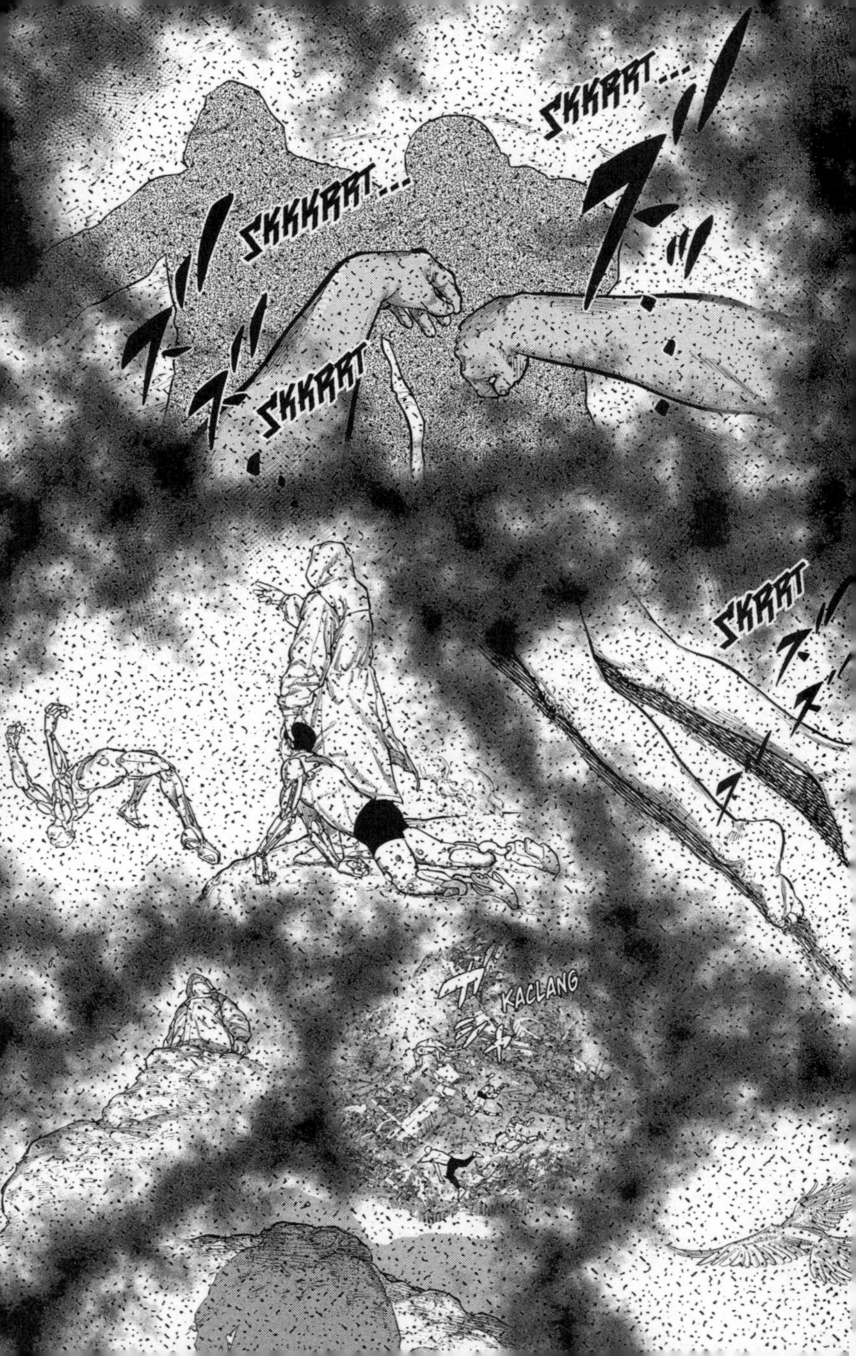
SKKRRT....
SKKKRRT...
SKKRRT
SKRRT
KACLANG

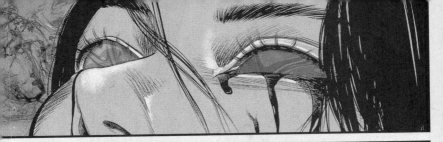

SO MUCH INTERFER-ENCE.

HFF...

HFF...

MAYBE IT'S MY PERIOD...

WHAT IN THE....

NO DUMPING

BUT AT LEAST NOW I'VE GOT SOMETHING TO WORK WITH!

FLAP

FLAP

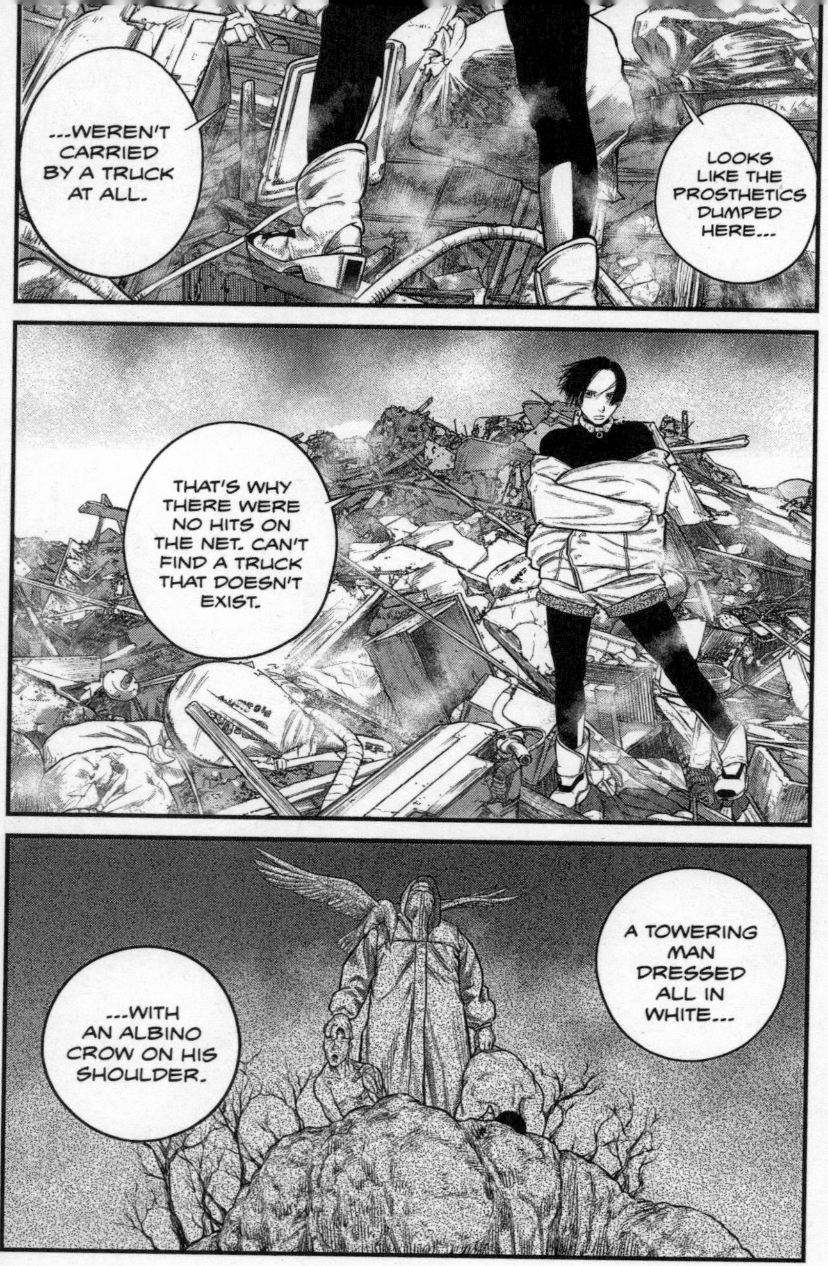
LOOKS LIKE THE PROSTHETICS DUMPED HERE...
...WEREN'T CARRIED BY A TRUCK AT ALL.
THAT'S WHY THERE WERE NO HITS ON THE NET. CAN'T FIND A TRUCK THAT DOESN'T EXIST.
A TOWERING MAN DRESSED ALL IN WHITE...
...WITH AN ALBINO CROW ON HIS SHOULDER.

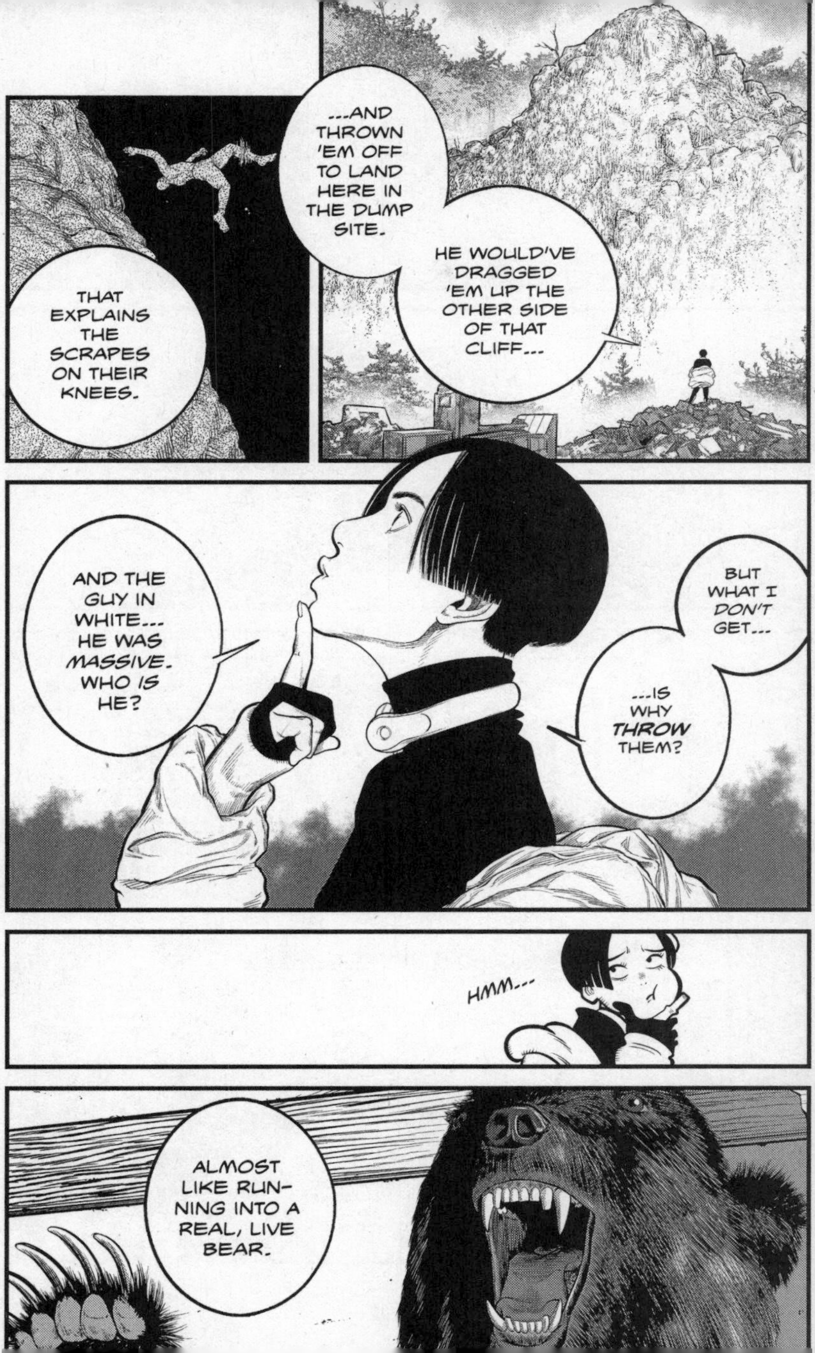
HE WOULD'VE DRAGGED 'EM UP THE OTHER SIDE OF THAT CLIFF...
...AND THROWN 'EM OFF TO LAND HERE IN THE DUMP SITE.
THAT EXPLAINS THE SCRAPES ON THEIR KNEES.
BUT WHAT I *DON'T* GET...
...IS WHY *THROW* THEM?
AND THE GUY IN WHITE... HE WAS *MASSIVE*. WHO *IS* HE?
HMM...
ALMOST LIKE RUN-NING INTO A REAL, LIVE BEAR.

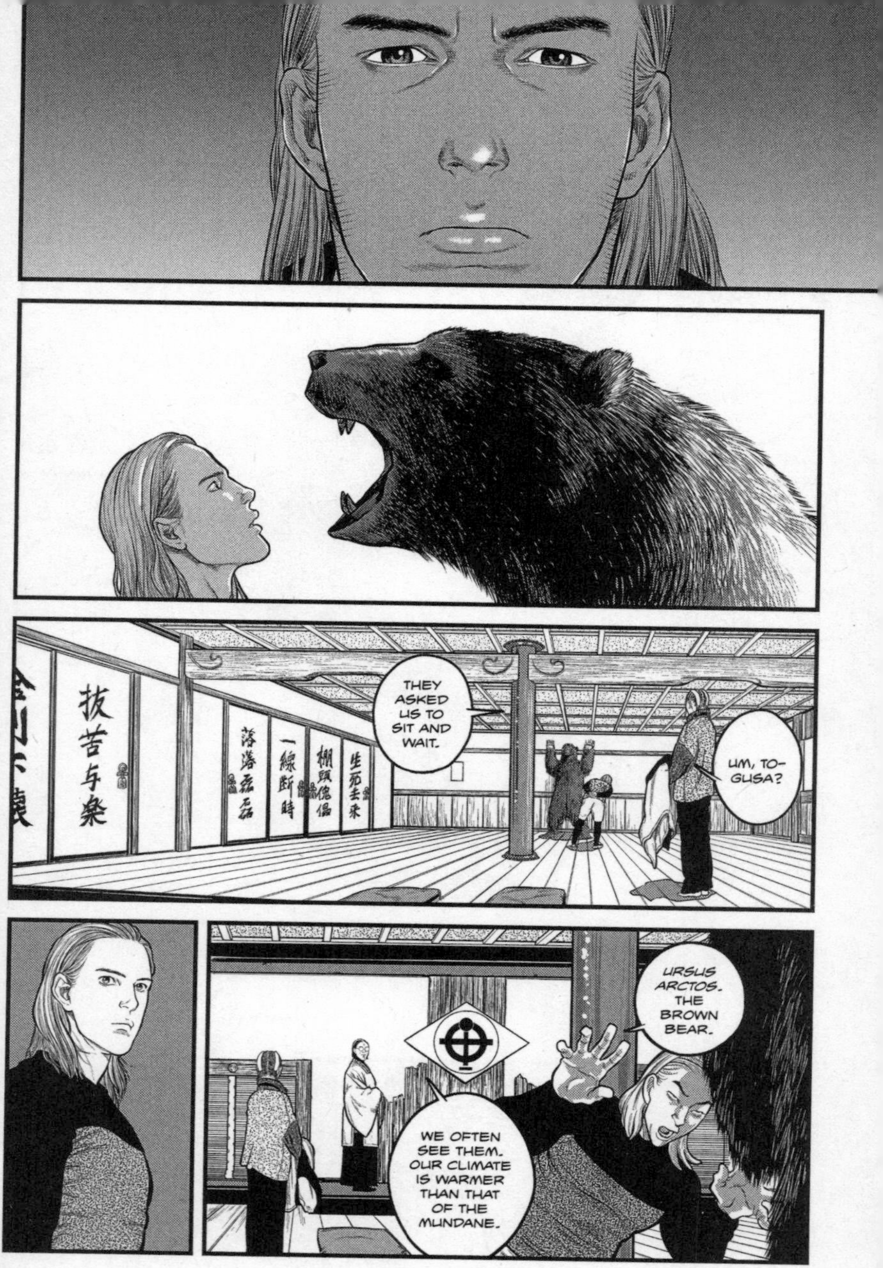
生死去来
棚頭傀儡
一線断時
落落磊磊
抜苦与楽
UM, TO-GUSA?
THEY ASKED US TO SIT AND WAIT.
URSUS ARCTOS. THE BROWN BEAR.
WE OFTEN SEE THEM. OUR CLIMATE IS WARMER THAN THAT OF THE MUNDANE.

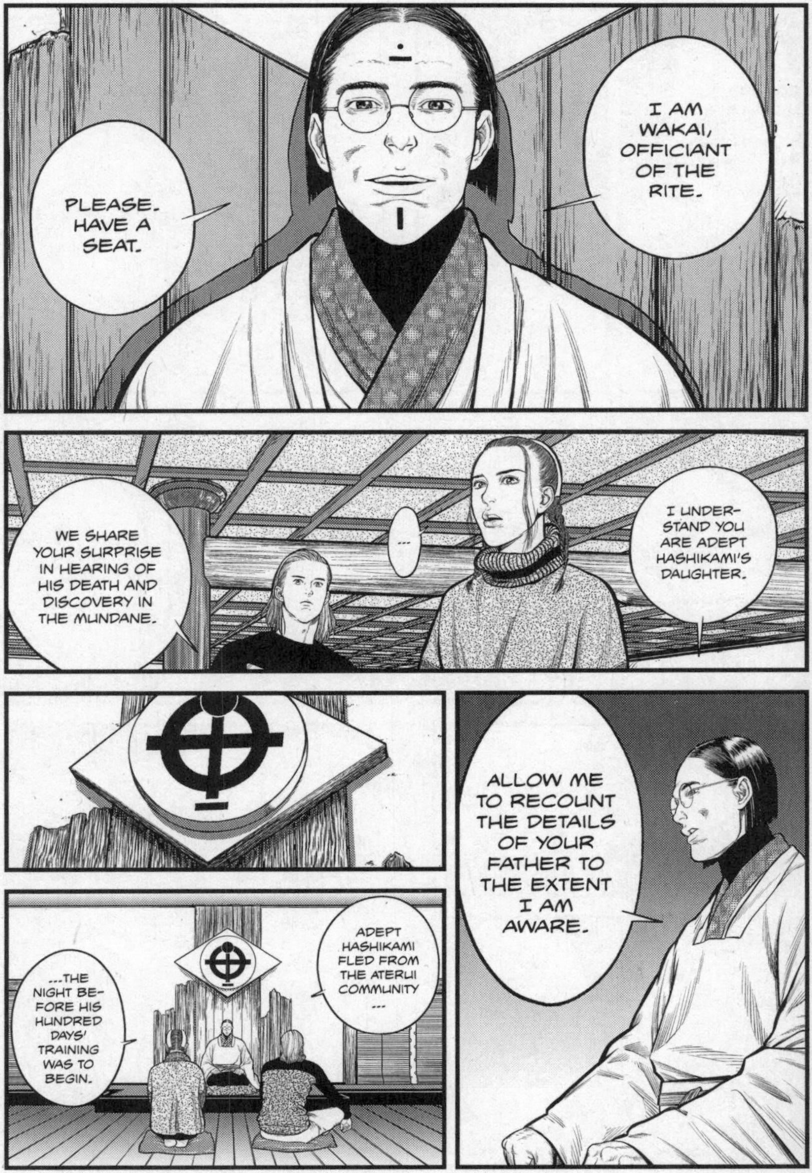
I AM WAKAI, OFFICIANT OF THE RITE.
PLEASE. HAVE A SEAT.
I UNDER-STAND YOU ARE ADEPT HASHIKAMI'S DAUGHTER.
...
WE SHARE YOUR SURPRISE IN HEARING OF HIS DEATH AND DISCOVERY IN THE MUNDANE.
ALLOW ME TO RECOUNT THE DETAILS OF YOUR FATHER TO THE EXTENT I AM AWARE.
ADEPT HASHIKAMI FLED FROM THE ATERUI COMMUNITY ...
...THE NIGHT BE-FORE HIS HUNDRED DAYS' TRAINING WAS TO BEGIN.

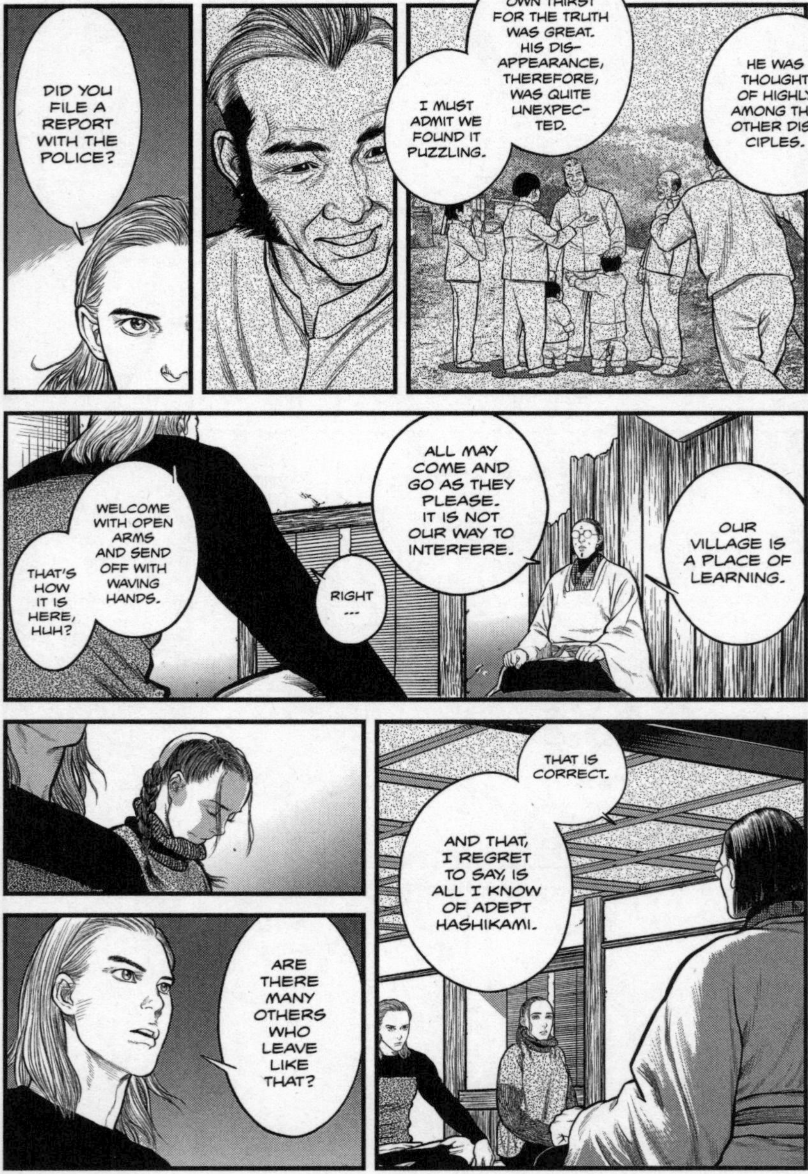
HE WAS THOUGHT OF HIGHLY AMONG THE OTHER DISCIPLES.
AND HIS OWN THIRST FOR THE TRUTH WAS GREAT. HIS DISAPPEARANCE, THEREFORE, WAS QUITE UNEXPECTED.
I MUST ADMIT WE FOUND IT PUZZLING.
DID YOU FILE A REPORT WITH THE POLICE?
OUR VILLAGE IS A PLACE OF LEARNING.
ALL MAY COME AND GO AS THEY PLEASE. IT IS NOT OUR WAY TO INTERFERE.
RIGHT ...
WELCOME WITH OPEN ARMS AND SEND OFF WITH WAVING HANDS.
THAT'S HOW IT IS HERE, HUH?
THAT IS CORRECT.
AND THAT, I REGRET TO SAY, IS ALL I KNOW OF ADEPT HASHIKAMI.
ARE THERE MANY OTHERS WHO LEAVE LIKE THAT?

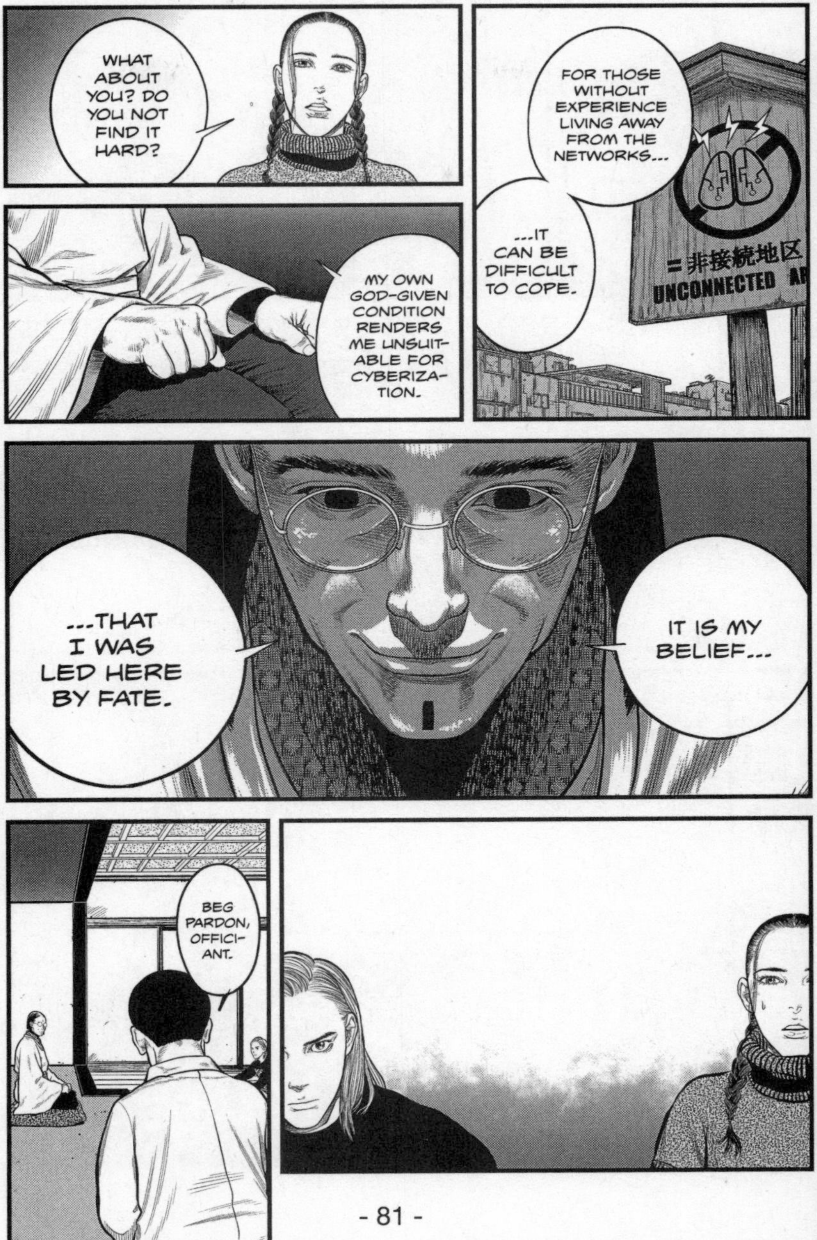
FOR THOSE WITHOUT EXPERIENCE LIVING AWAY FROM THE NETWORKS...
...IT CAN BE DIFFICULT TO COPE.
=非接続地区
UNCONNECTED AR
WHAT ABOUT YOU? DO YOU NOT FIND IT HARD?
MY OWN GOD-GIVEN CONDITION RENDERS ME UNSUITABLE FOR CYBERIZATION.
IT IS MY BELIEF...
...THAT I WAS LED HERE BY FATE.
BEG PARDON, OFFICIANT.

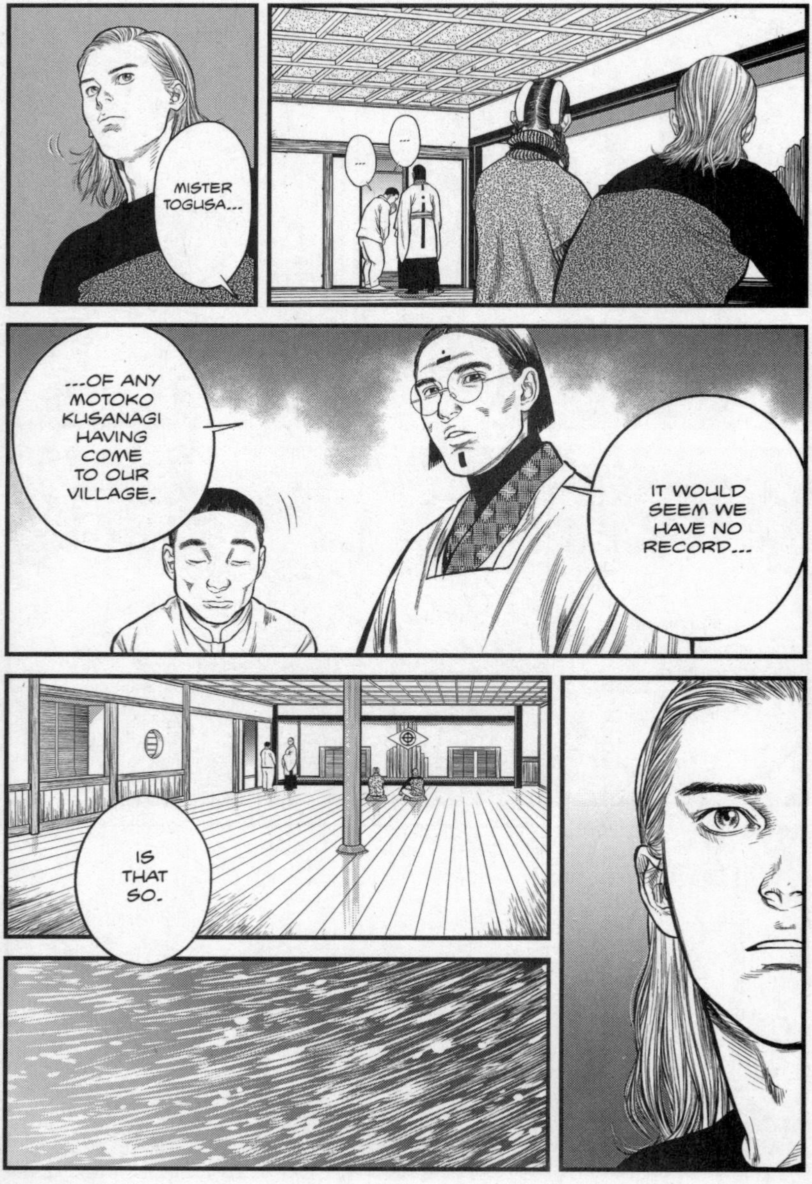
...
...
MISTER TOGUSA...
IT WOULD SEEM WE HAVE NO RECORD...
...OF ANY MOTOKO KUSANAGI HAVING COME TO OUR VILLAGE.
IS THAT SO.

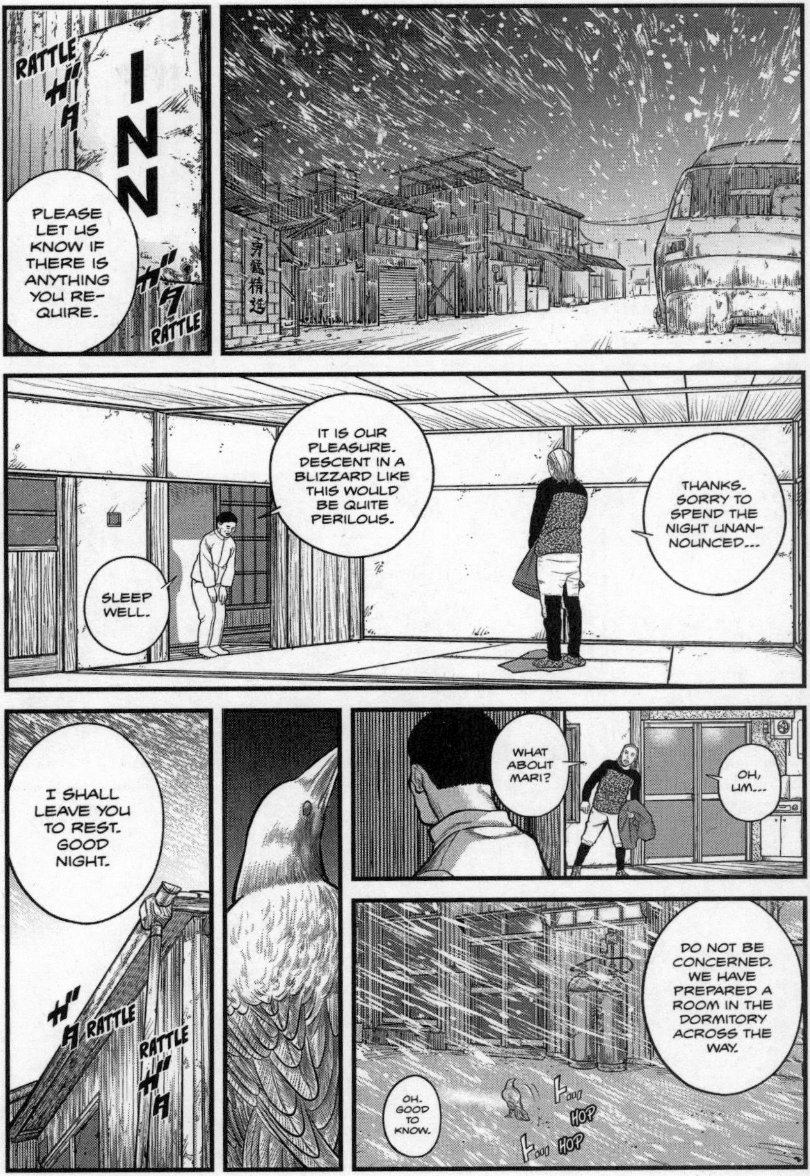
RATTLE
ガタ
INN
PLEASE LET US KNOW IF THERE IS ANYTHING YOU RE-QUIRE.
ガタ
RATTLE
THANKS. SORRY TO SPEND THE NIGHT UNAN-NOUNCED...
IT IS OUR PLEASURE. DESCENT IN A BLIZZARD LIKE THIS WOULD BE QUITE PERILOUS.
SLEEP WELL.
WHAT ABOUT MARI?
OH, UM...
DO NOT BE CONCERNED. WE HAVE PREPARED A ROOM IN THE DORMITORY ACROSS THE WAY.
ト... HOP
ト... HOP
OH. GOOD TO KNOW.
I SHALL LEAVE YOU TO REST. GOOD NIGHT.
ガタ RATTLE
RATTLE ガタ

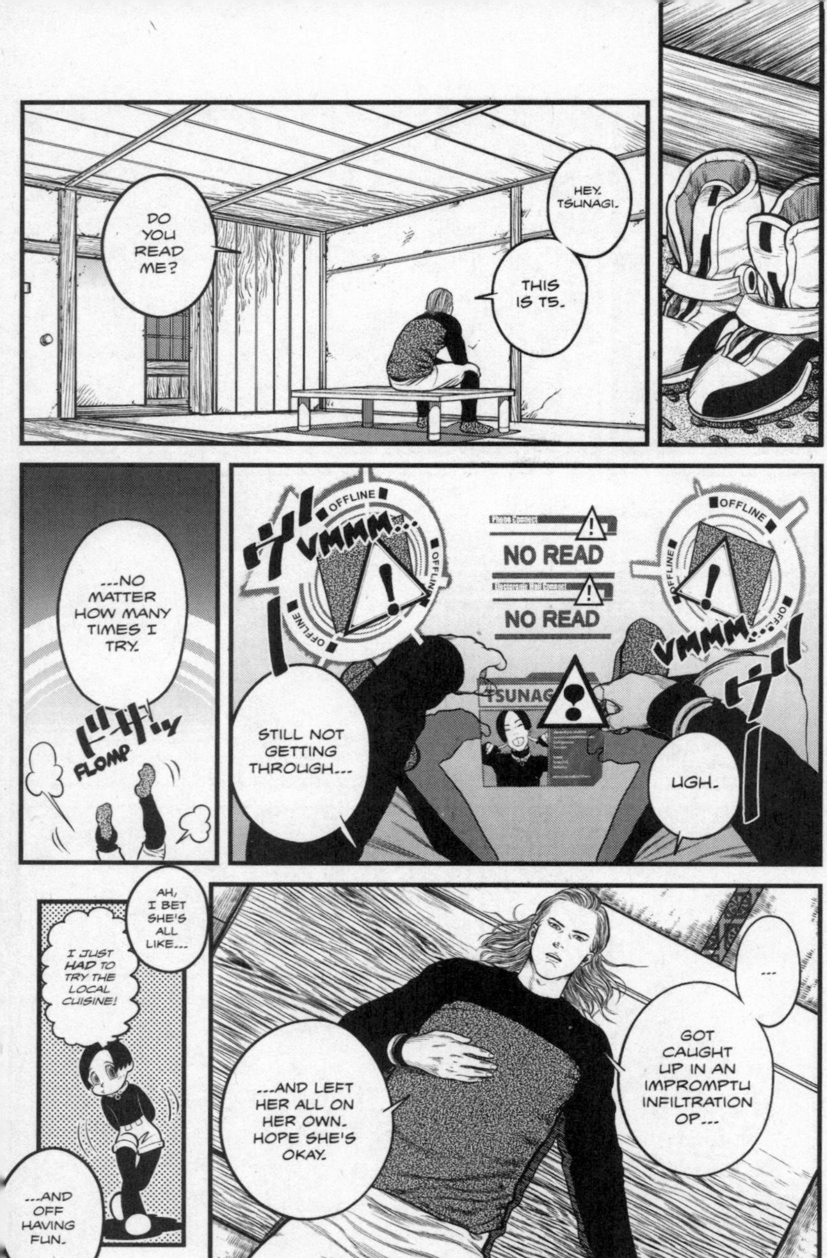
HEY. TSUNAGI.
THIS IS T5.
DO YOU READ ME?
OFFLINE
VMMM...
NO READ
NO READ
OFFLINE
VMMM...
UGH.
STILL NOT GETTING THROUGH...
...NO MATTER HOW MANY TIMES I TRY.
FLOMP
...
GOT CAUGHT UP IN AN IMPROMPTU INFILTRATION OP...
...AND LEFT HER ALL ON HER OWN. HOPE SHE'S OKAY.
AH, I BET SHE'S ALL LIKE...
I JUST *HAD* TO TRY THE LOCAL CUISINE!
...AND OFF HAVING FUN.

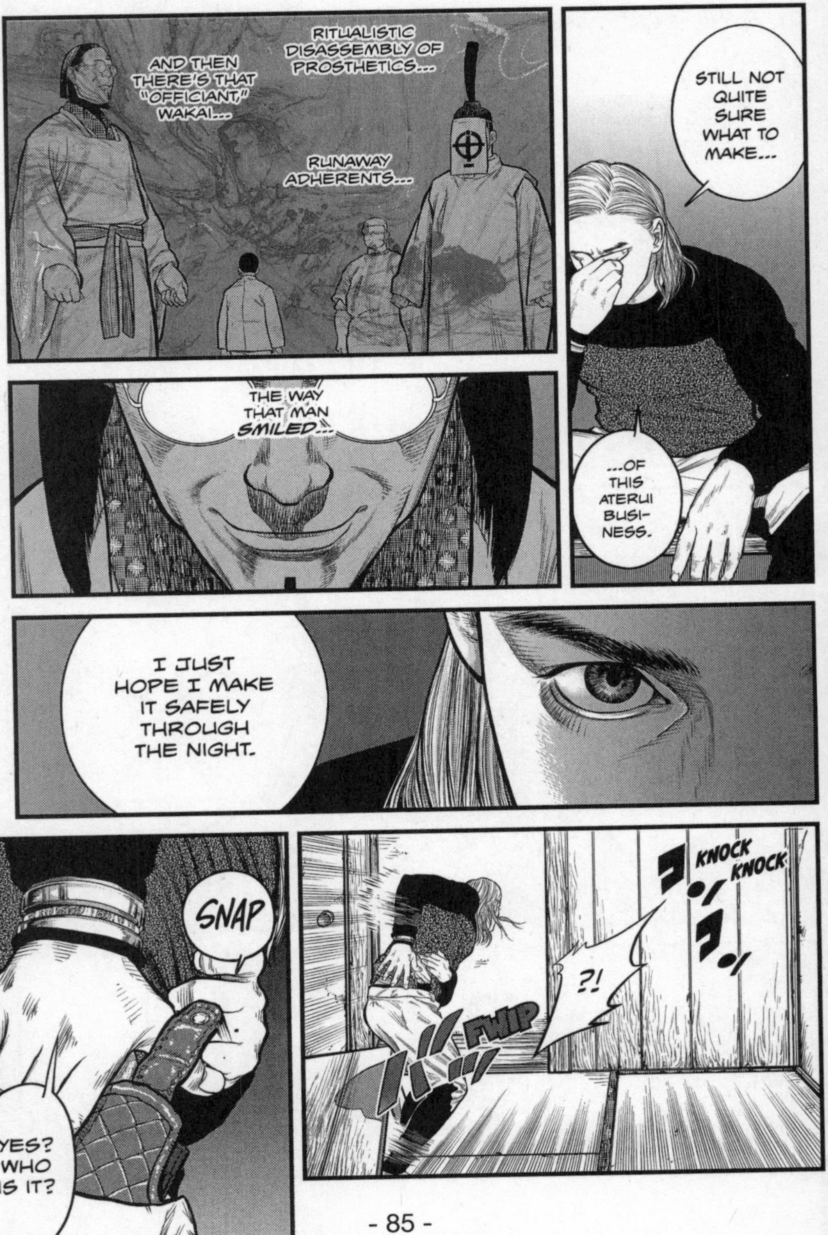
STILL NOT QUITE SURE WHAT TO MAKE...
...OF THIS ATERUI BUSINESS.
RITUALISTIC DISASSEMBLY OF PROSTHETICS...
AND THEN THERE'S THAT "OFFICIANT," WAKAI...
RUNAWAY ADHERENTS...
THE WAY THAT MAN SMILED...
I JUST HOPE I MAKE IT SAFELY THROUGH THE NIGHT.
KNOCK KNOCK
?!
FWIP
SNAP
YES? WHO IS IT?

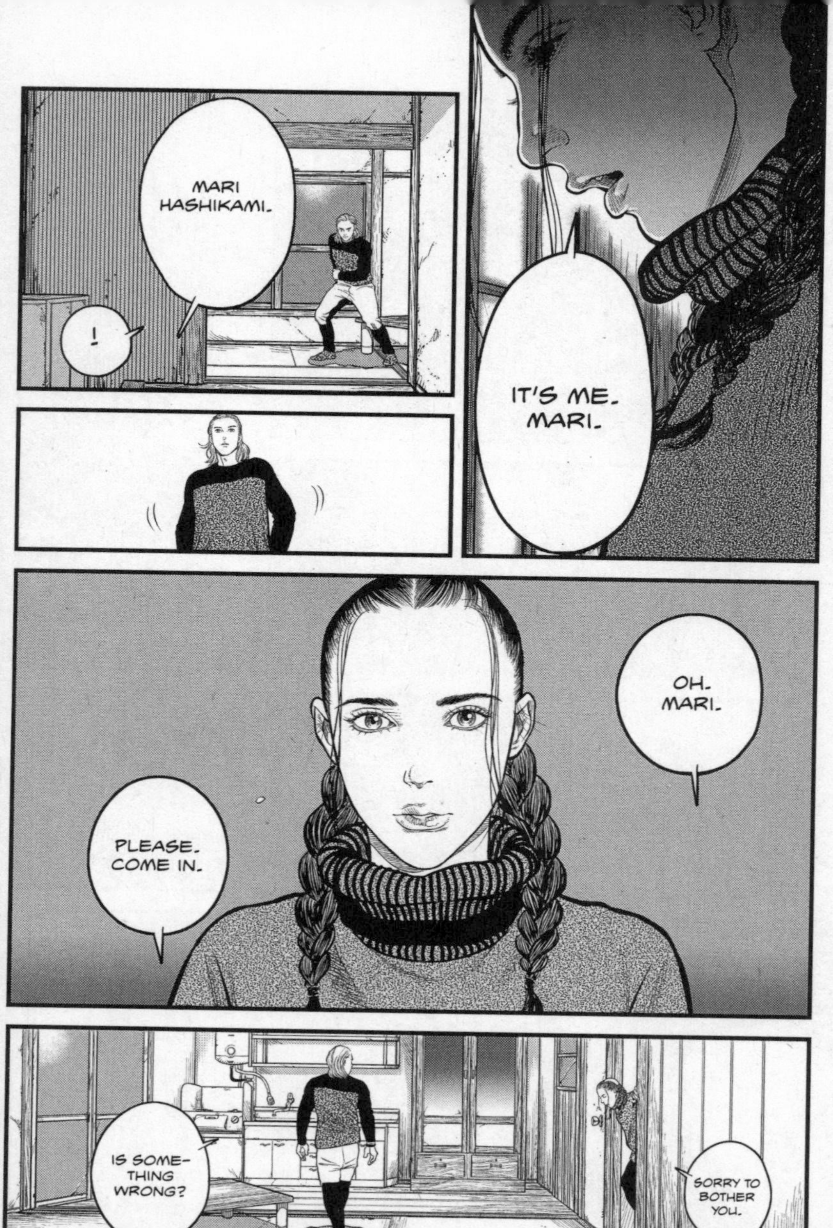
IT'S ME. MARI.
MARI HASHIKAMI.
!
OH. MARI.
PLEASE. COME IN.
SORRY TO BOTHER YOU.
IS SOME-THING WRONG?

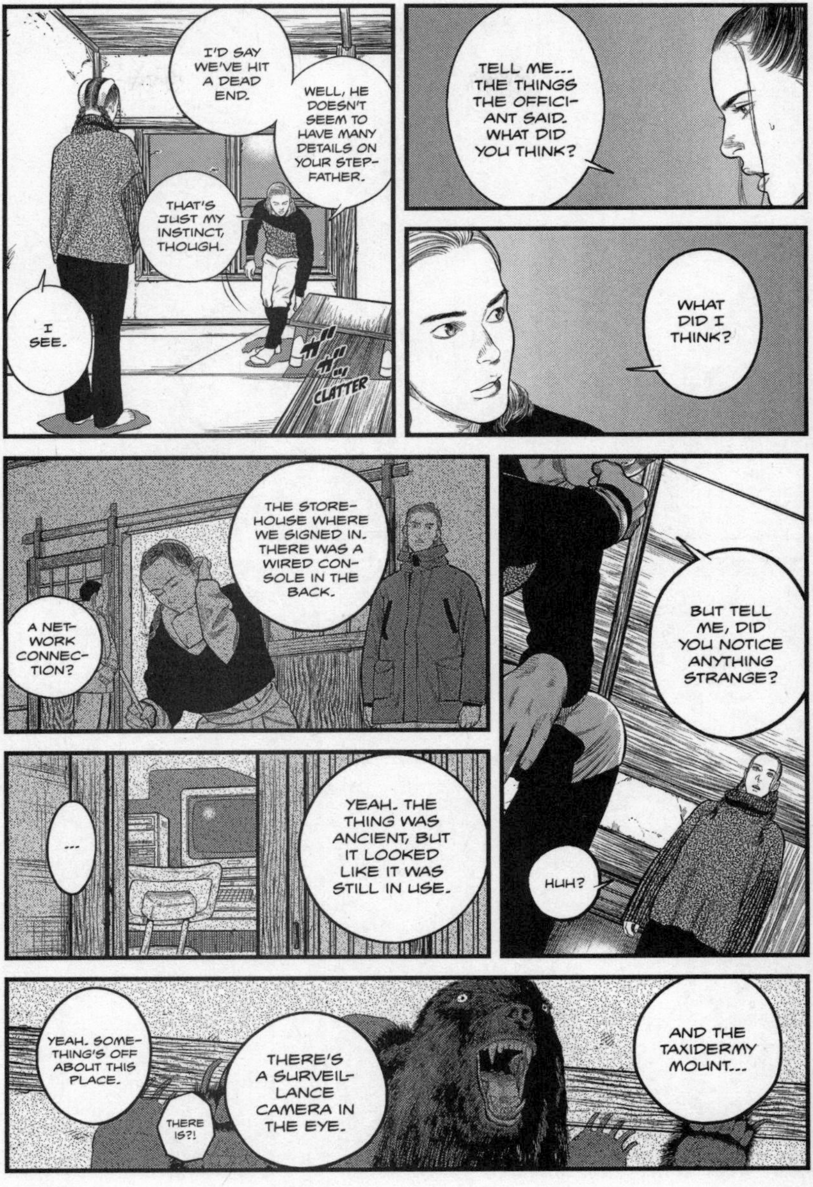
TELL ME... THE THINGS THE OFFICI-ANT SAID. WHAT DID YOU THINK?
WHAT DID I THINK?
WELL, HE DOESN'T SEEM TO HAVE MANY DETAILS ON YOUR STEP-FATHER.
I'D SAY WE'VE HIT A DEAD END.
THAT'S JUST MY INSTINCT, THOUGH.
CLATTER
I SEE.
BUT TELL ME, DID YOU NOTICE ANYTHING STRANGE?
HUH?
THE STORE-HOUSE WHERE WE SIGNED IN. THERE WAS A WIRED CON-SOLE IN THE BACK.
A NET-WORK CONNEC-TION?
YEAH. THE THING WAS ANCIENT, BUT IT LOOKED LIKE IT WAS STILL IN USE.
...
AND THE TAXIDERMY MOUNT...
THERE'S A SURVEIL-LANCE CAMERA IN THE EYE.
THERE IS?!
YEAH. SOME-THING'S OFF ABOUT THIS PLACE.

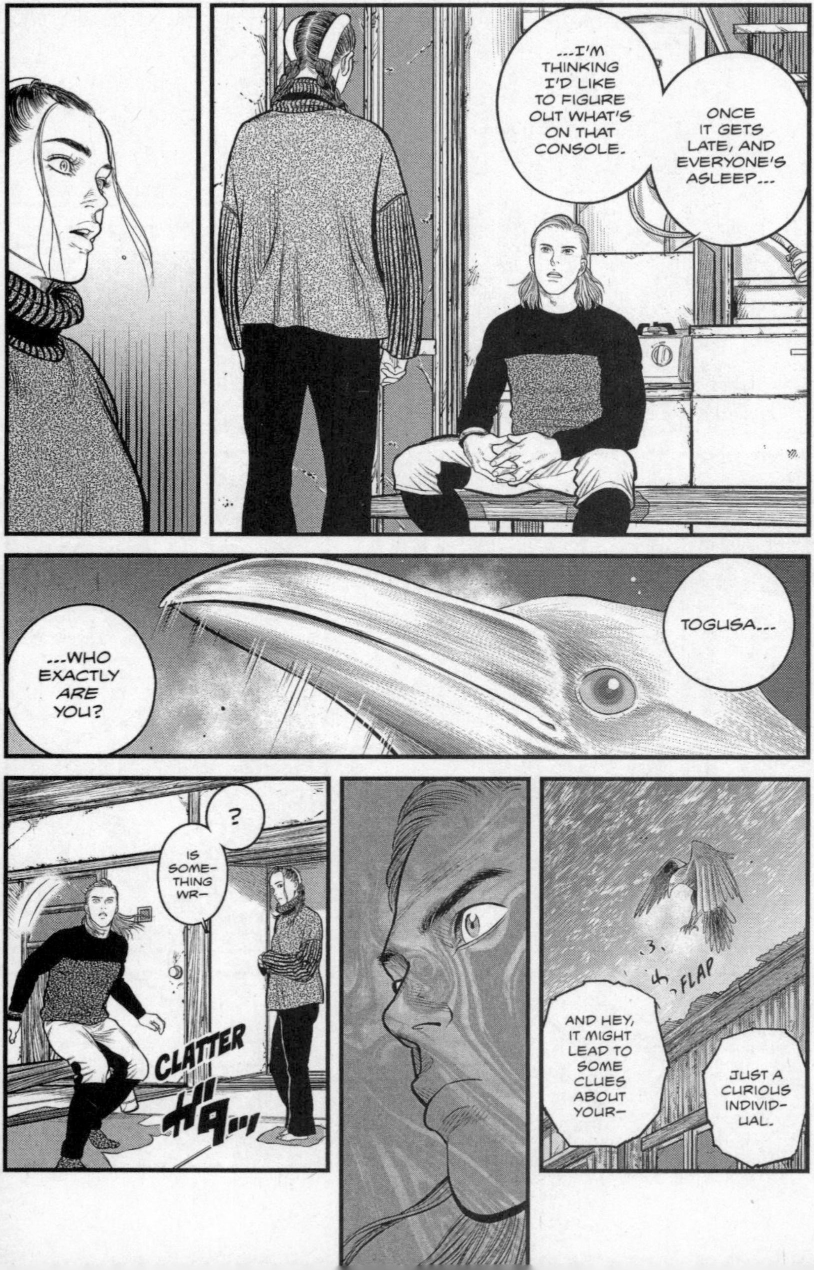
ONCE IT GETS LATE, AND EVERYONE'S ASLEEP...
...I'M THINKING I'D LIKE TO FIGURE OUT WHAT'S ON THAT CONSOLE.
TOGUSA...
...WHO EXACTLY ARE YOU?
FLAP
JUST A CURIOUS INDIVIDUAL.
AND HEY, IT MIGHT LEAD TO SOME CLUES ABOUT YOUR—
?
IS SOME-THING WR—
CLATTER
ガタッ

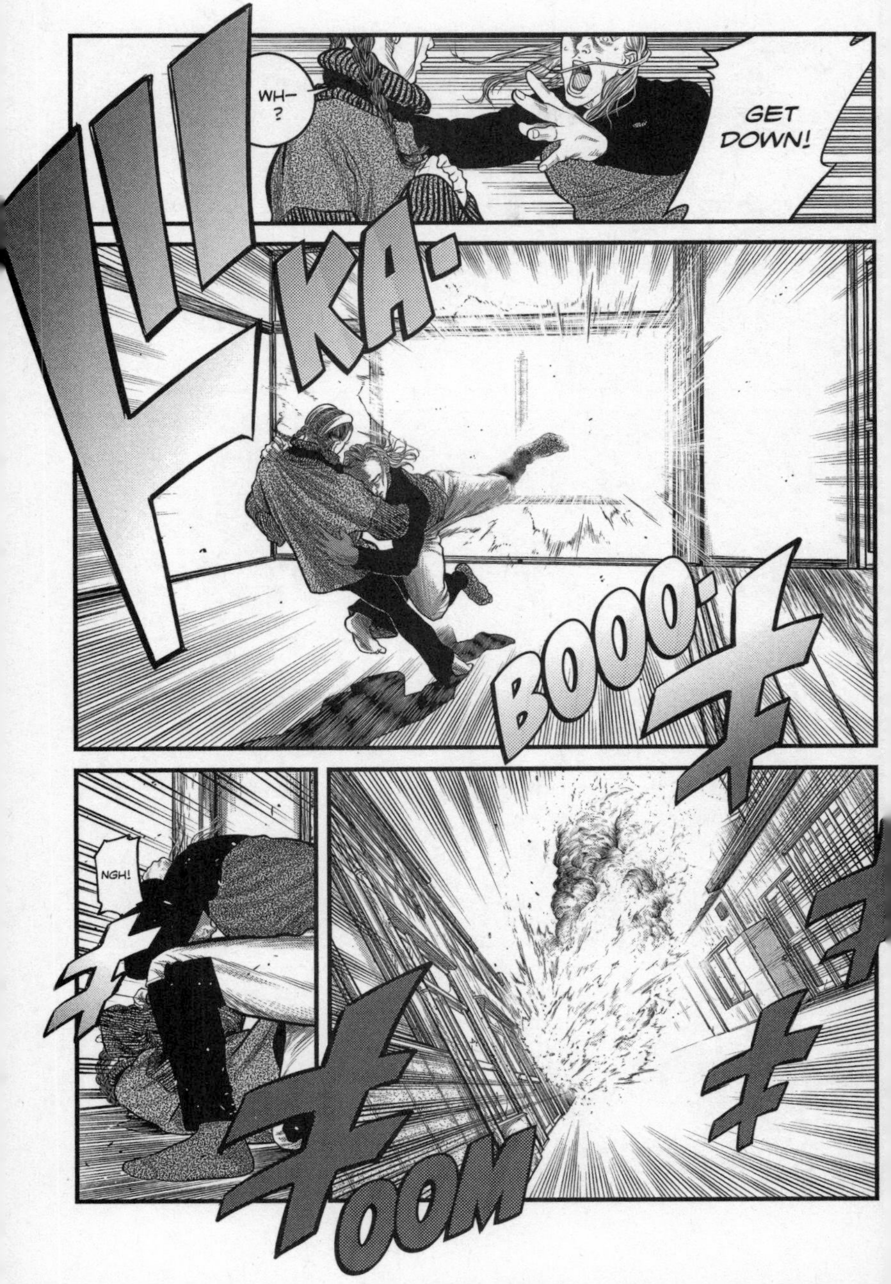
GET DOWN!
WH- ?
KA-
BOOO-
OOM
NGH!

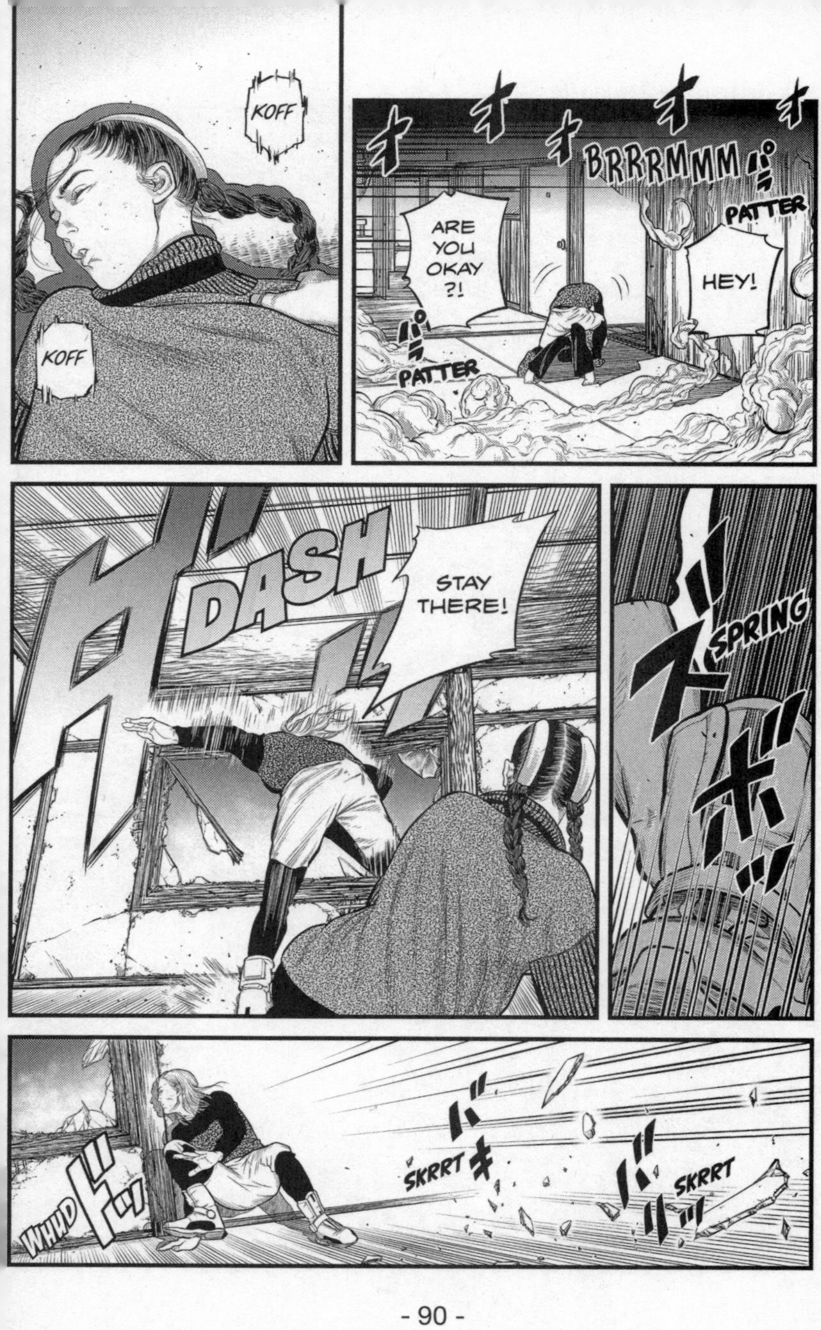
BRRRMMM
PATTER
HEY!
ARE YOU OKAY ?!
PATTER
KOFF
KOFF
SPRING
STAY THERE!
DASH
SKRRT
SKRRT
WHUD

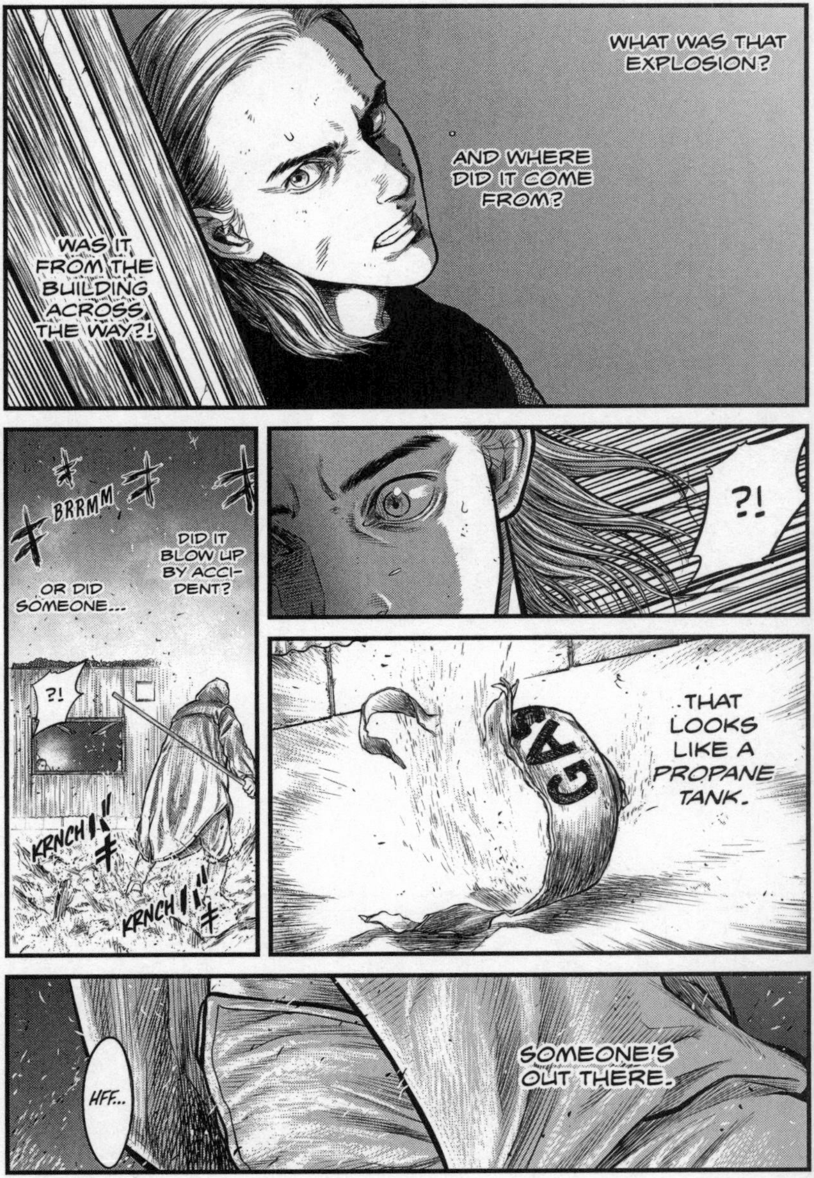
WHAT WAS THAT EXPLOSION?
AND WHERE DID IT COME FROM?
WAS IT FROM THE BUILDING ACROSS THE WAY?!
?!
..THAT LOOKS LIKE A PROPANE TANK.
GAS
BRRMM
DID IT BLOW UP BY ACCI-DENT?
OR DID SOMEONE...
?!
KRNCH
KRNCH
SOMEONE'S OUT THERE.
HFF...

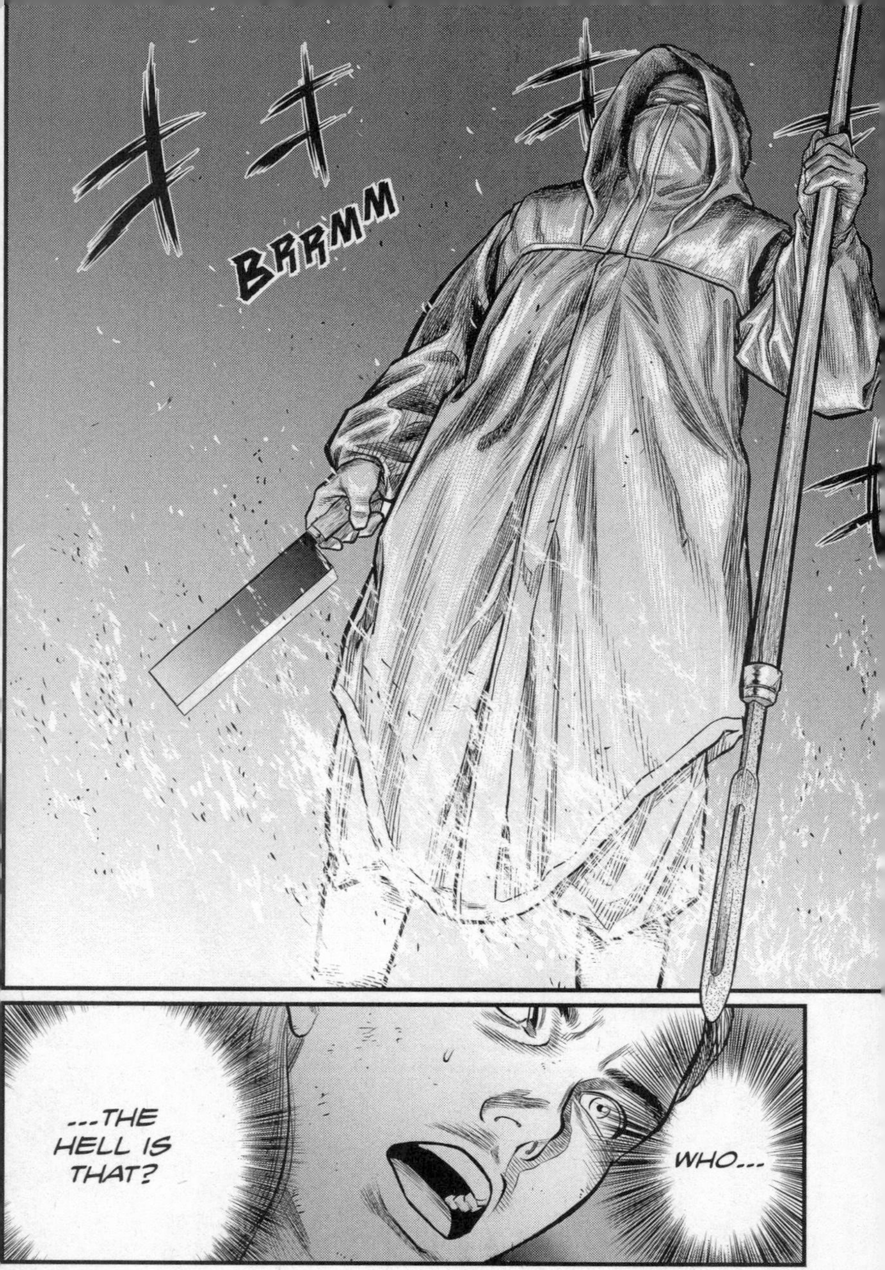
BRRMM
WHO...
...THE HELL IS THAT?

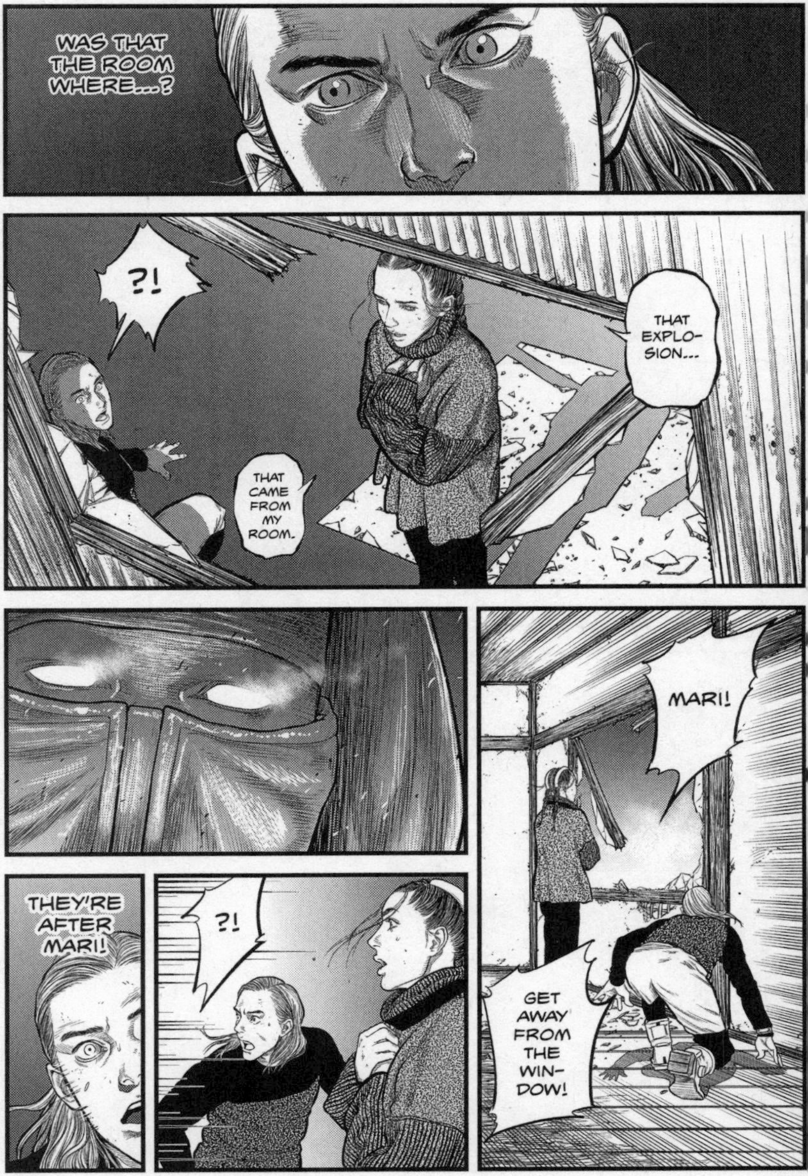
WAS THAT THE ROOM WHERE...?
THAT EXPLO-SION...
?!
THAT CAME FROM MY ROOM.
MARI!
GET AWAY FROM THE WIN-DOW!
?!
THEY'RE AFTER MARI!

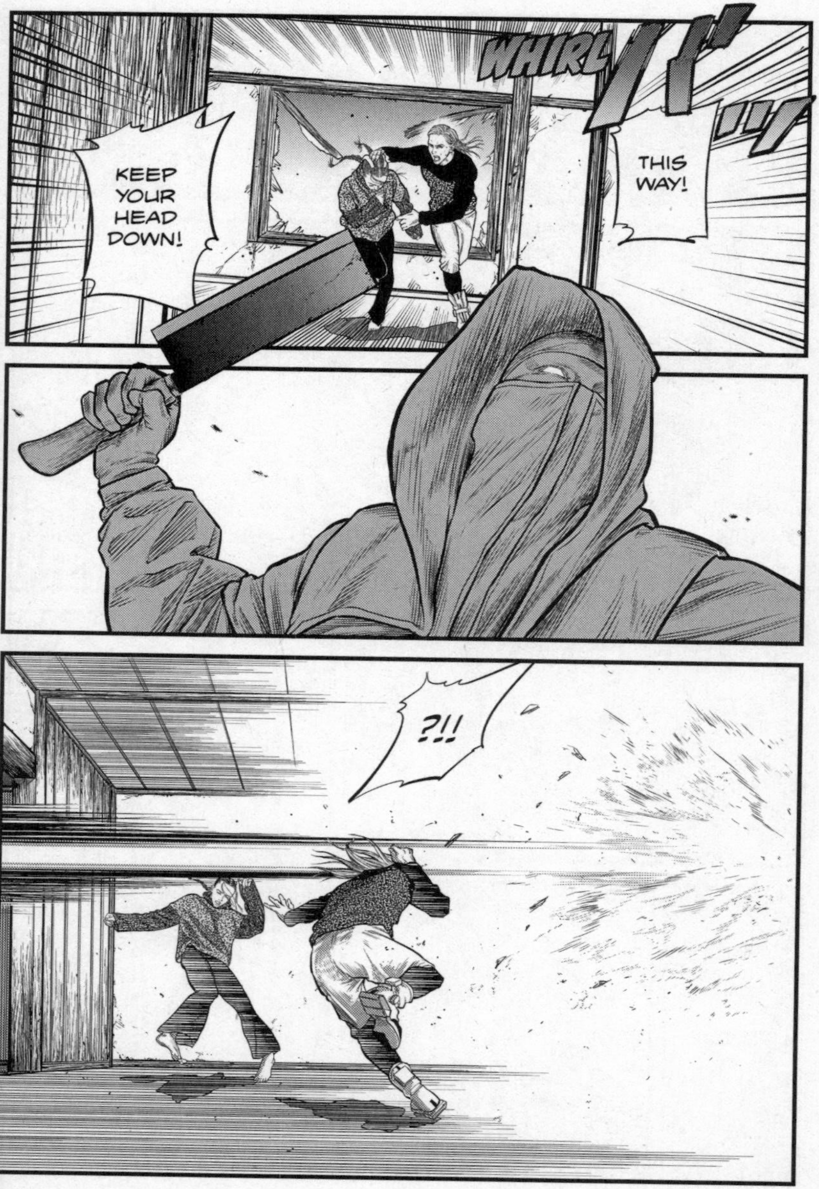
WHIRL
THIS WAY!
KEEP YOUR HEAD DOWN!
?!!

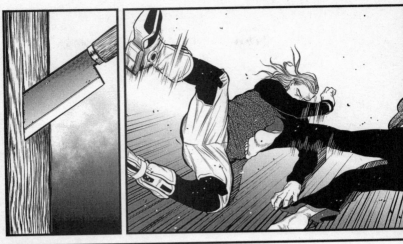

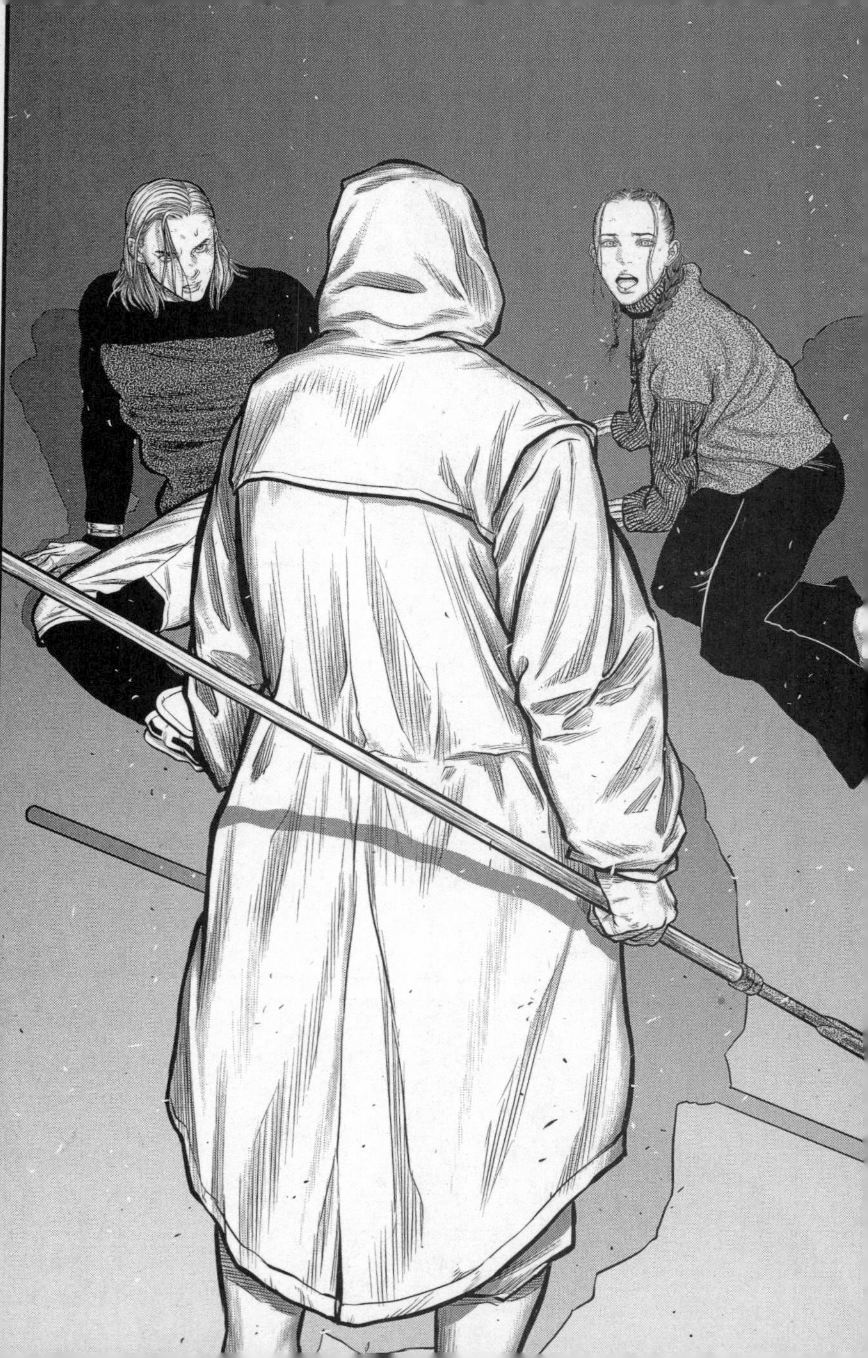

03
WHITE BEAR

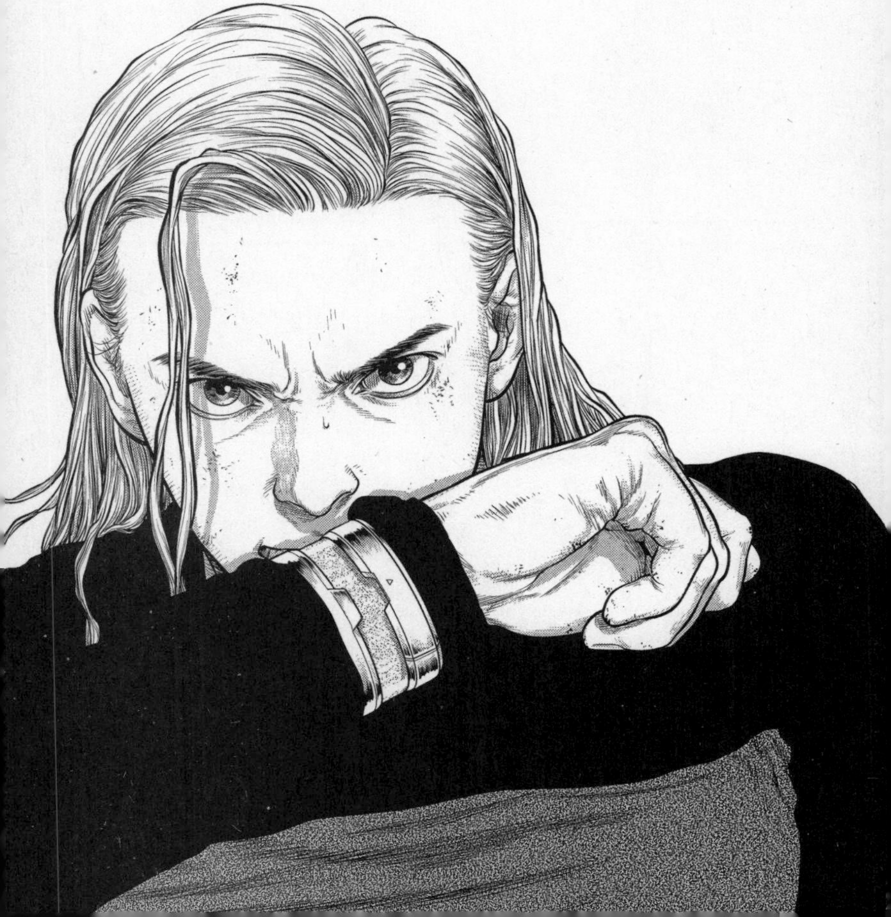

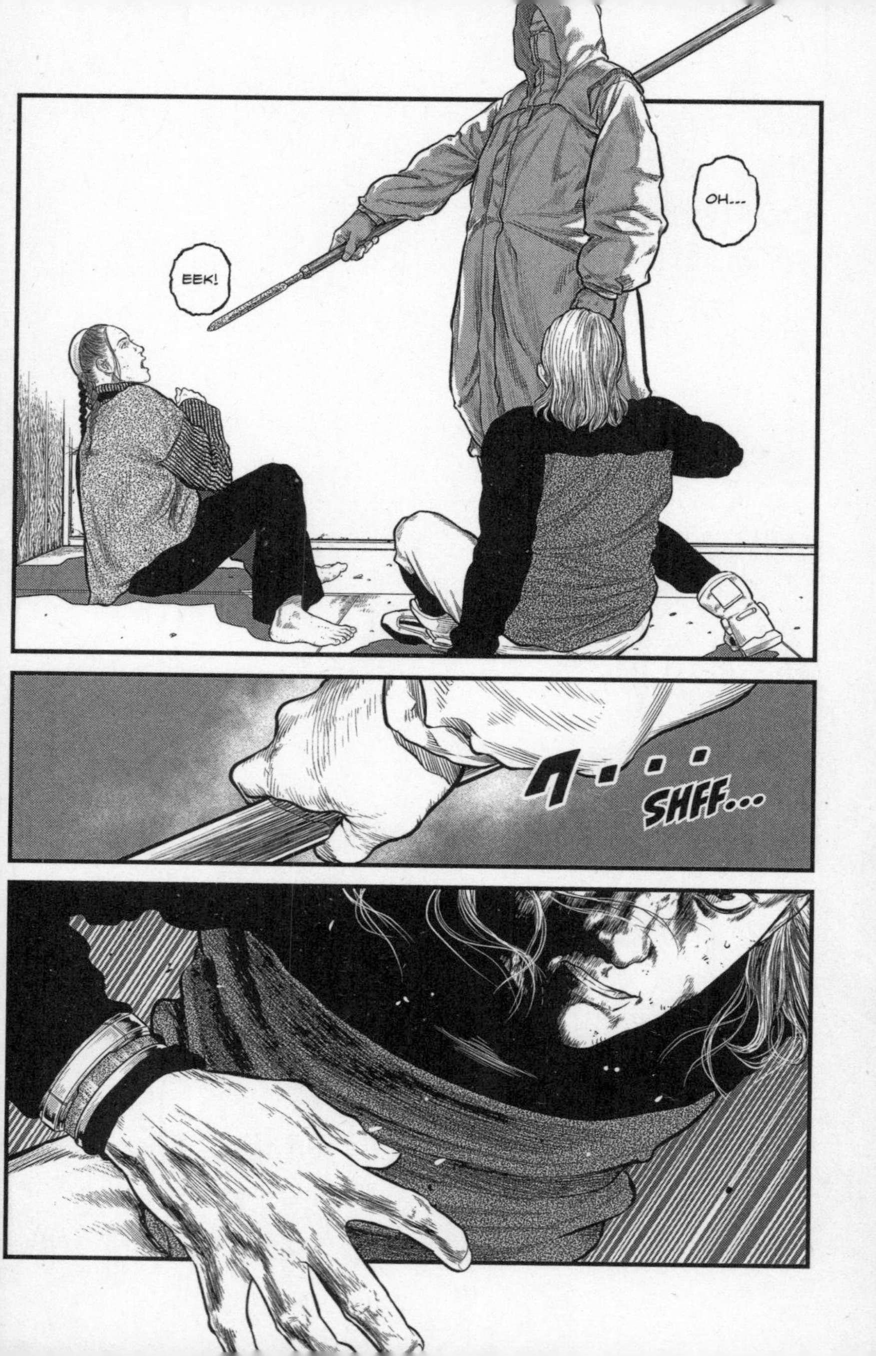
OH...
EEK!
ク...
SHFF...

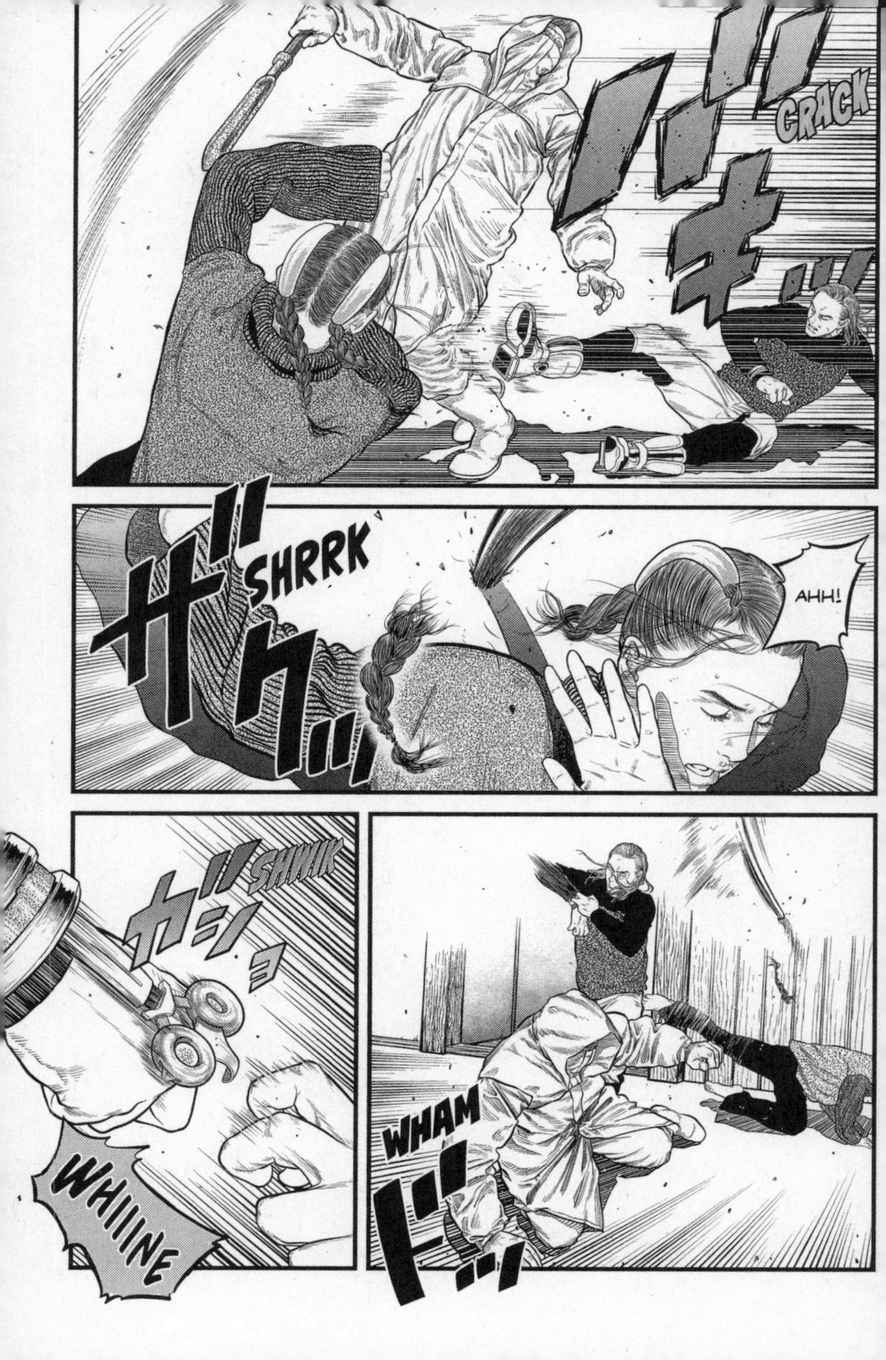
CRACK
AHH!
SHRRK
WHAM
SHWIK
WHIIINE

BZZRRT

HHACK

WE HAVE TO RUN!

MARI! GET UP!

OW!!

WHUMP

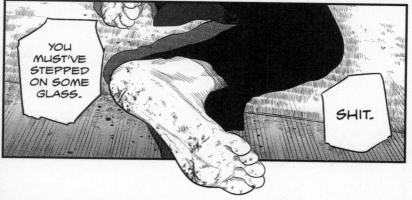

YOU MUST'VE STEPPED ON SOME GLASS.

SHIT.

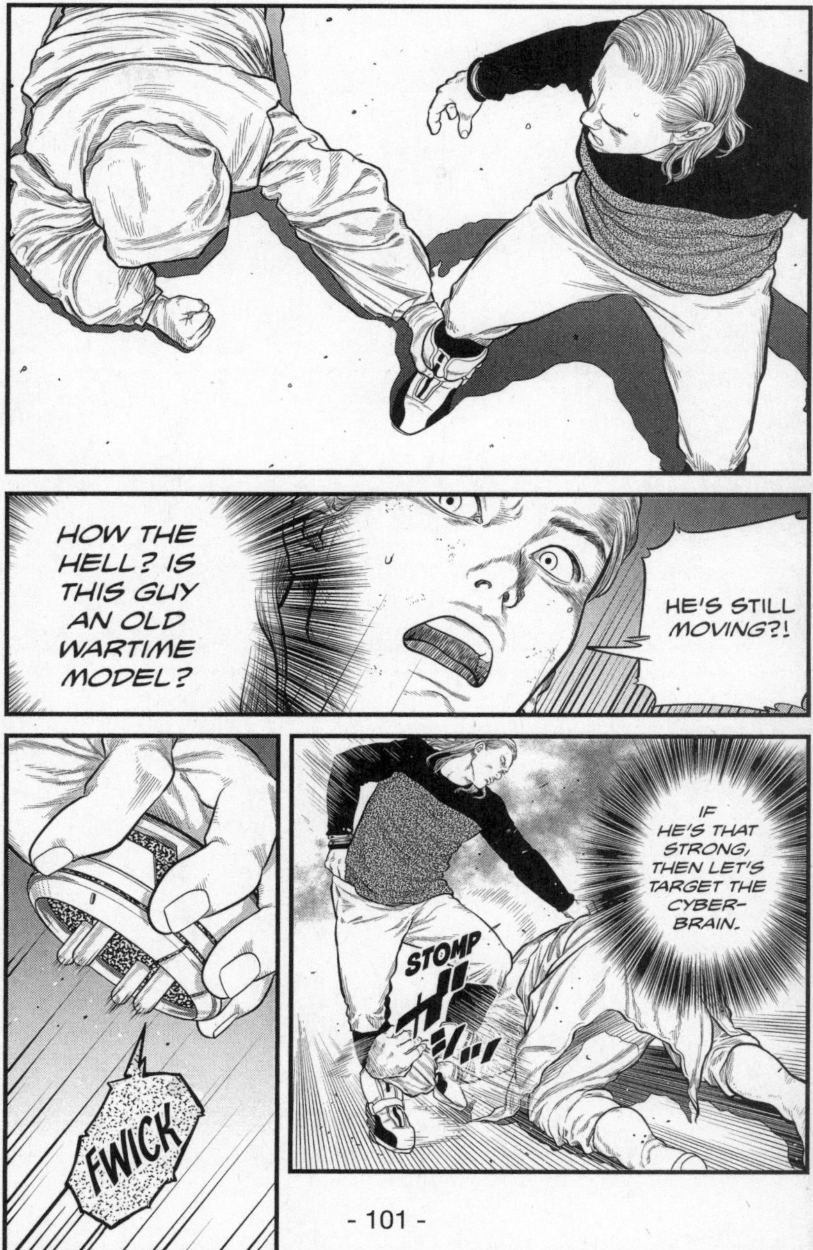
HE'S STILL MOVING?!
HOW THE HELL? IS THIS GUY AN OLD WARTIME MODEL?
IF HE'S THAT STRONG, THEN LET'S TARGET THE CYBER-BRAIN.
STOMP
FWICK

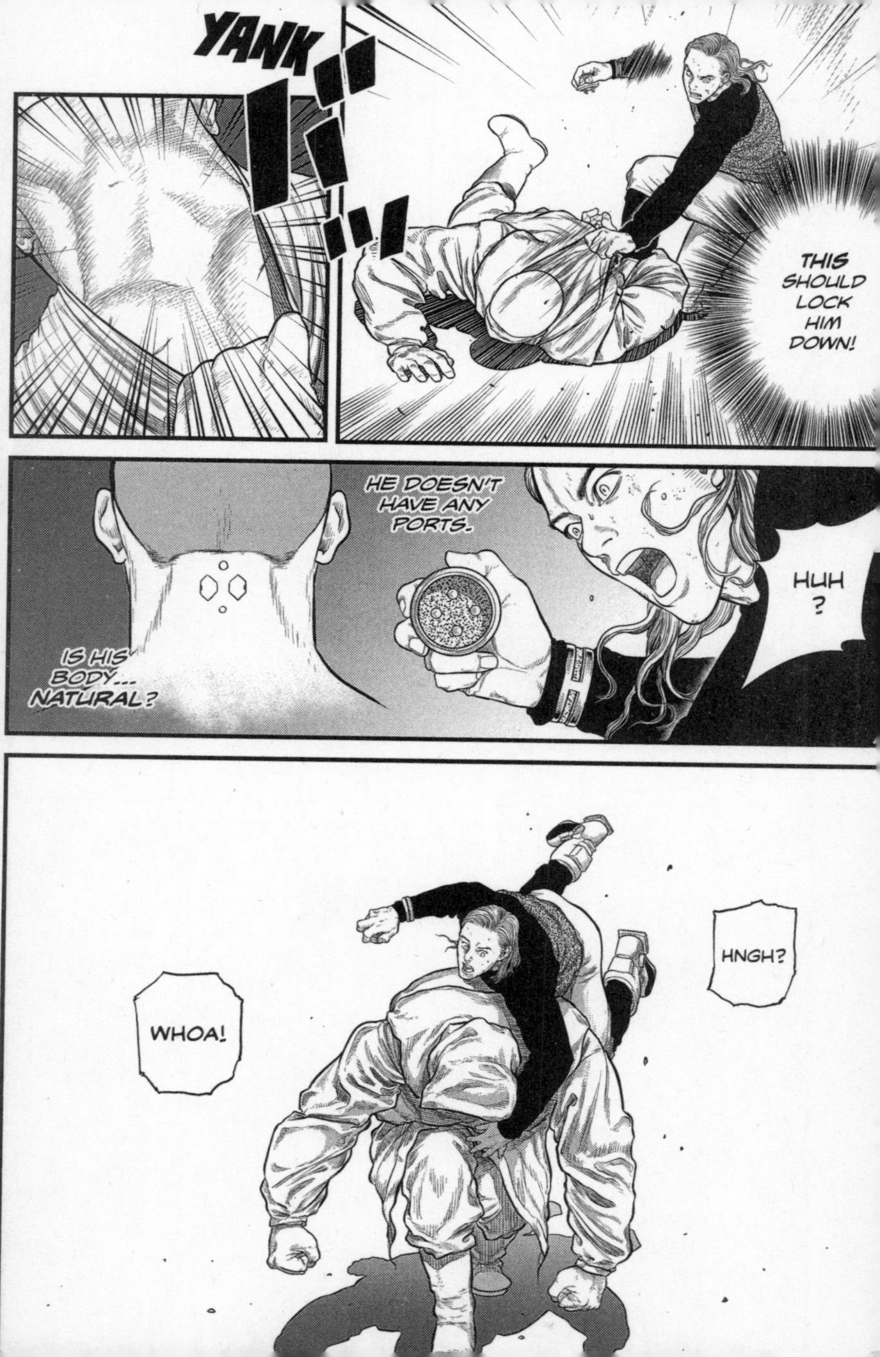
THIS SHOULD LOCK HIM DOWN!
YANK
HUH?
HE DOESN'T HAVE ANY PORTS.
IS HIS BODY... NATURAL?
HNGH?
WHOA!

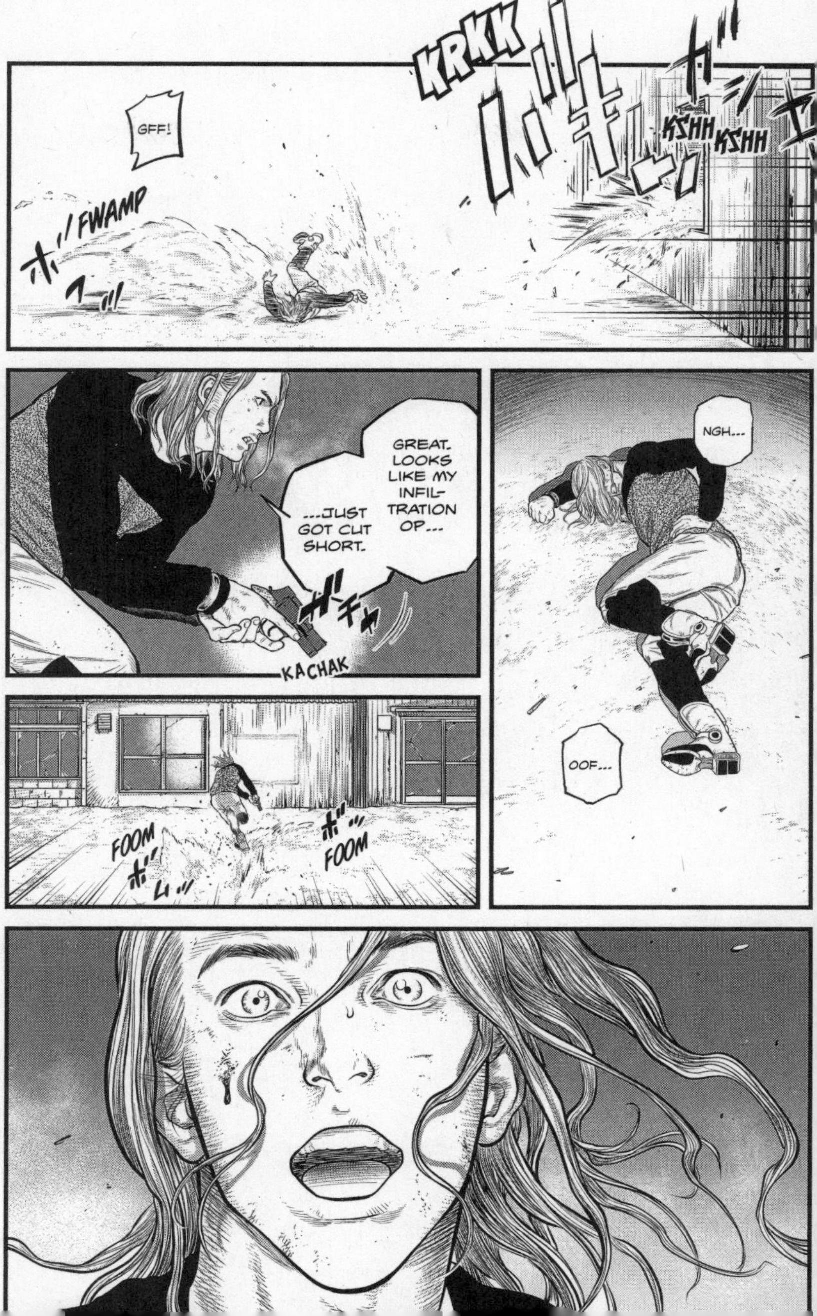
KRKK
KSHH KSHH
GFF!
FWAMP
NGH...
OOF...
GREAT. LOOKS LIKE MY INFIL-TRATION OP...
...JUST GOT CUT SHORT.
KACHAK
FOOM
FOOM

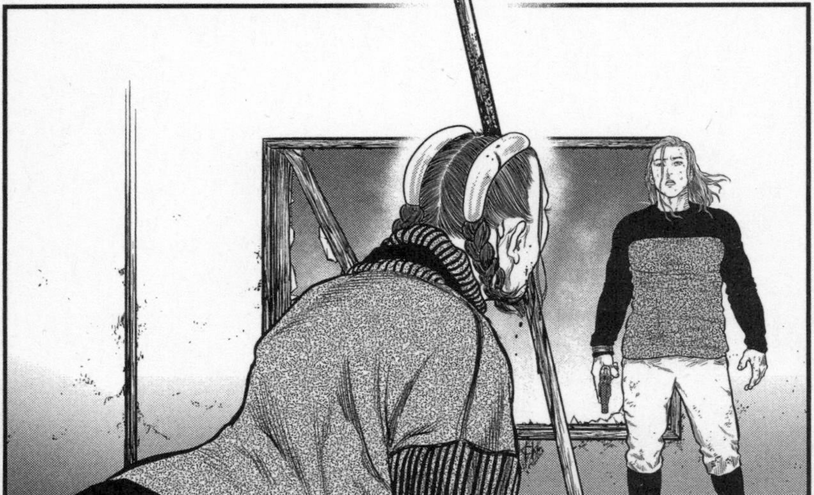
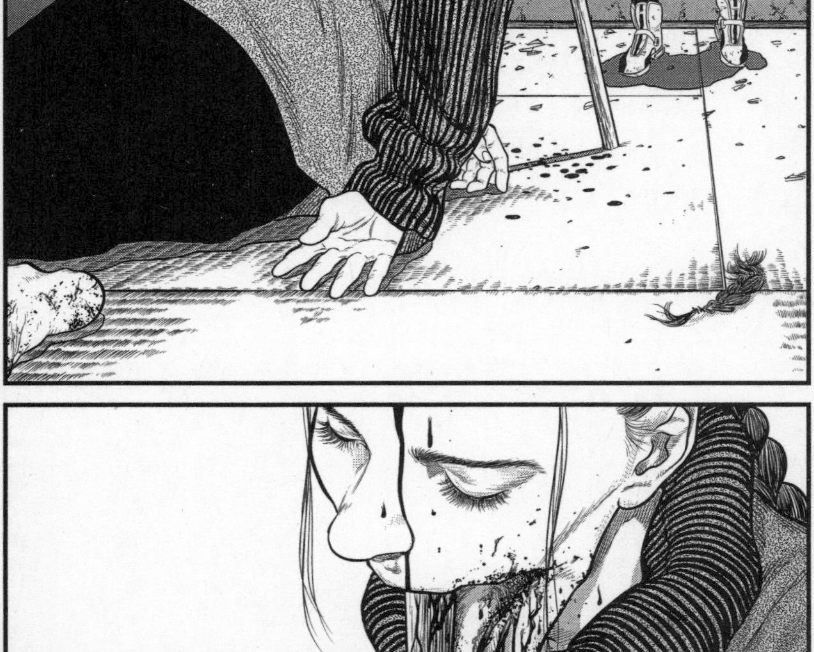

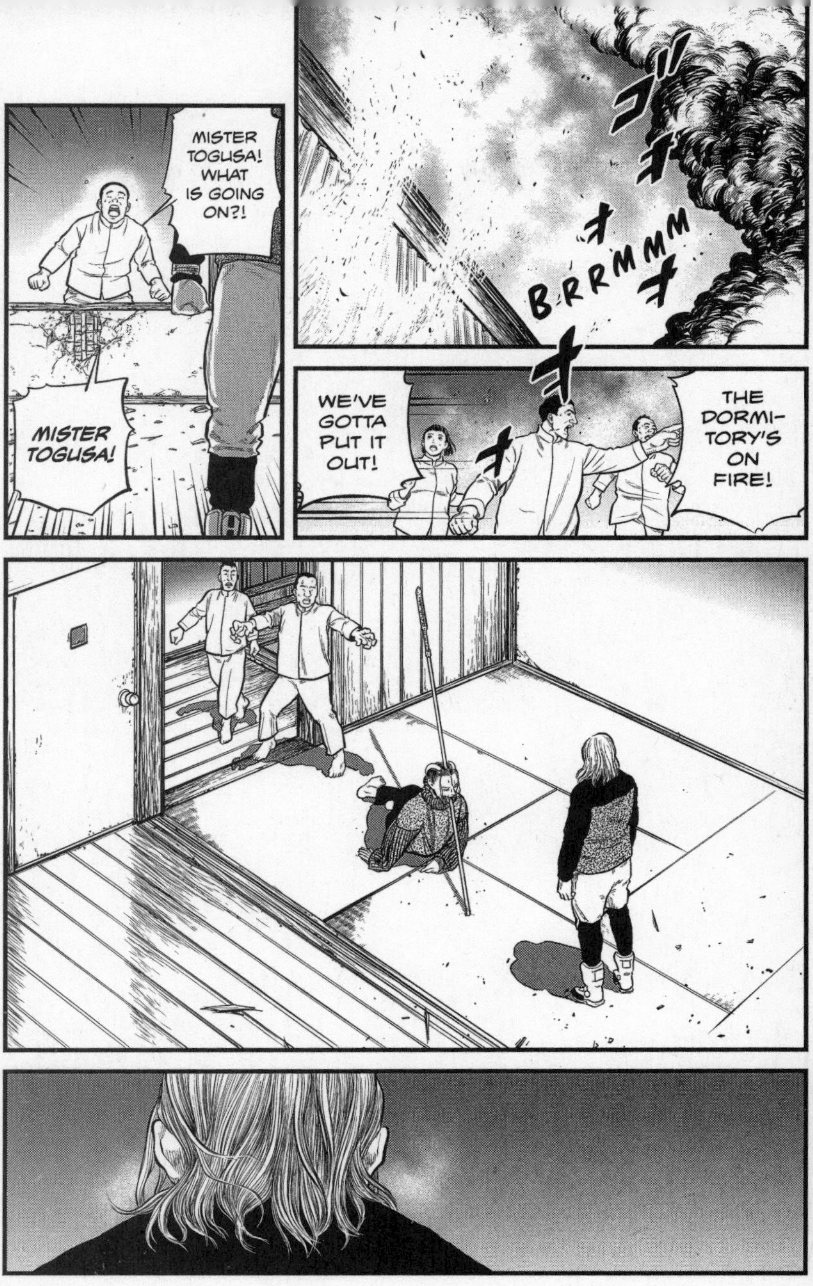
BRRMMM
THE DORMITORY'S ON FIRE!
WE'VE GOTTA PUT IT OUT!
MISTER TOGUSA! WHAT IS GOING ON?!
MISTER TOGUSA!

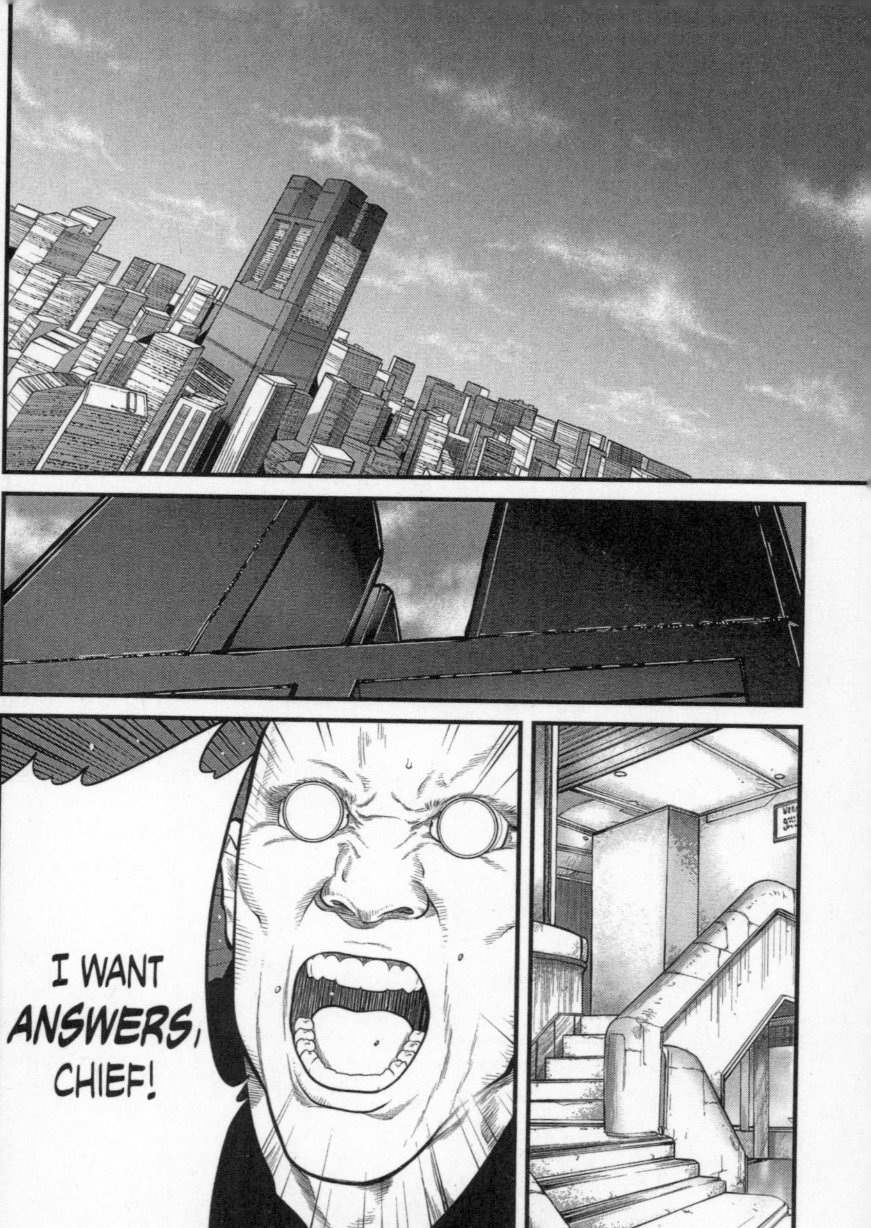
I WANT ANSWERS, CHIEF!

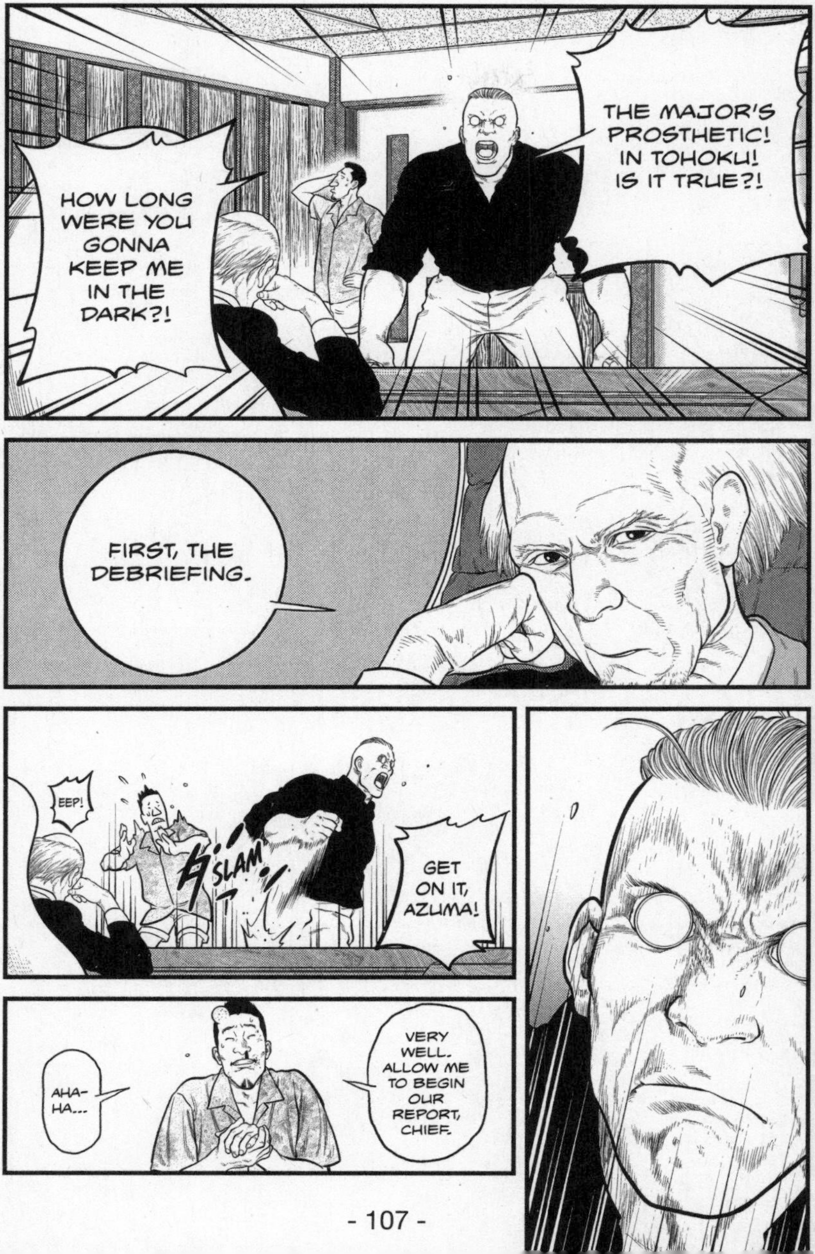
THE MAJOR'S PROSTHETIC! IN TOHOKU! IS IT TRUE?!
HOW LONG WERE YOU GONNA KEEP ME IN THE DARK?!
FIRST, THE DEBRIEFING.
GET ON IT, AZUMA!
SLAM
EEP!
VERY WELL. ALLOW ME TO BEGIN OUR REPORT, CHIEF.
AHA-HA...

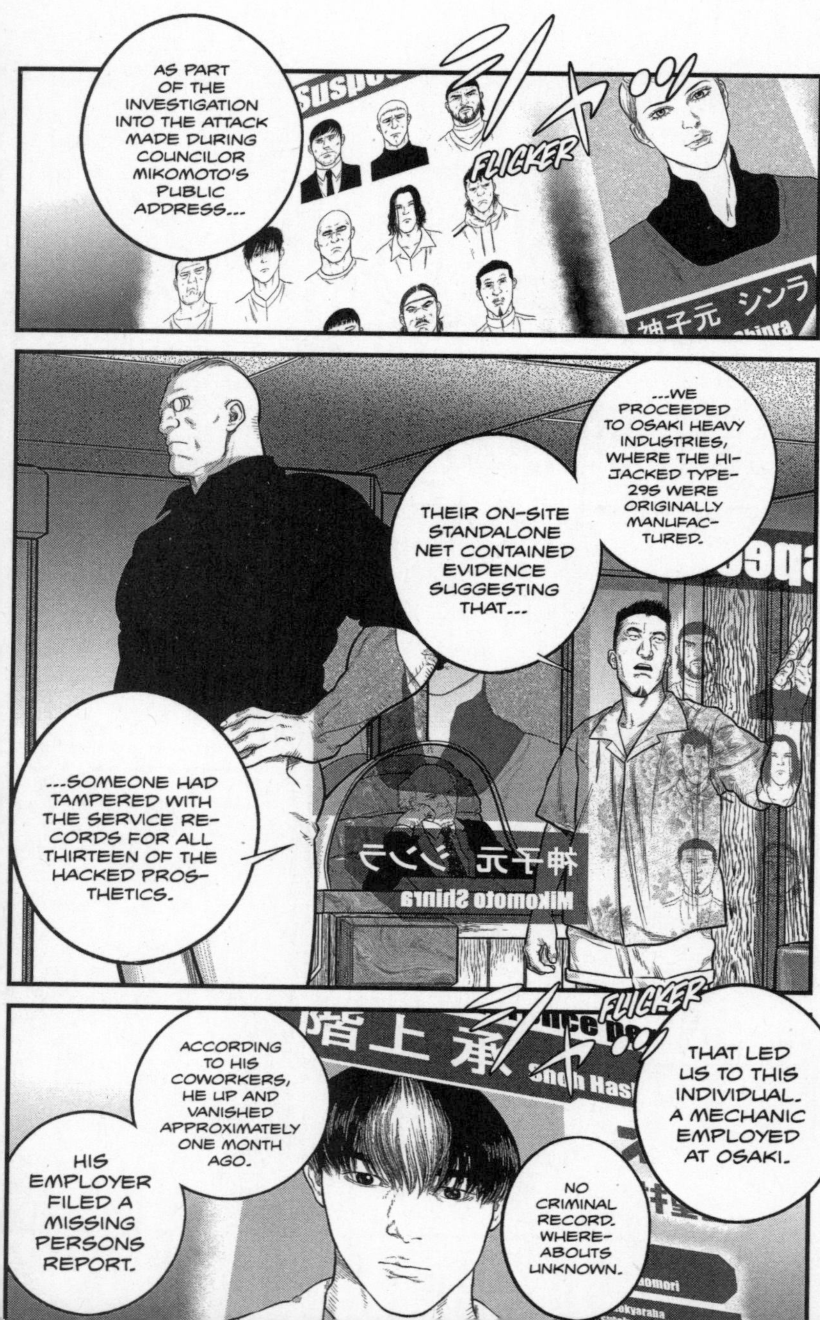
AS PART OF THE INVESTIGATION INTO THE ATTACK MADE DURING COUNCILOR MIKOMOTO'S PUBLIC ADDRESS...
FLICKER
神子元 シンラ
...WE PROCEEDED TO OSAKI HEAVY INDUSTRIES, WHERE THE HI-JACKED TYPE-29S WERE ORIGINALLY MANUFAC-TURED.
THEIR ON-SITE STANDALONE NET CONTAINED EVIDENCE SUGGESTING THAT...
...SOMEONE HAD TAMPERED WITH THE SERVICE RE-CORDS FOR ALL THIRTEEN OF THE HACKED PROS-THETICS.
神子元 シンラ
Mikomoto Shinra
FLICKER
階上 承
THAT LED US TO THIS INDIVIDUAL. A MECHANIC EMPLOYED AT OSAKI.
NO CRIMINAL RECORD. WHERE-ABOUTS UNKNOWN.
ACCORDING TO HIS COWORKERS, HE UP AND VANISHED APPROXIMATELY ONE MONTH AGO.
HIS EMPLOYER FILED A MISSING PERSONS REPORT.

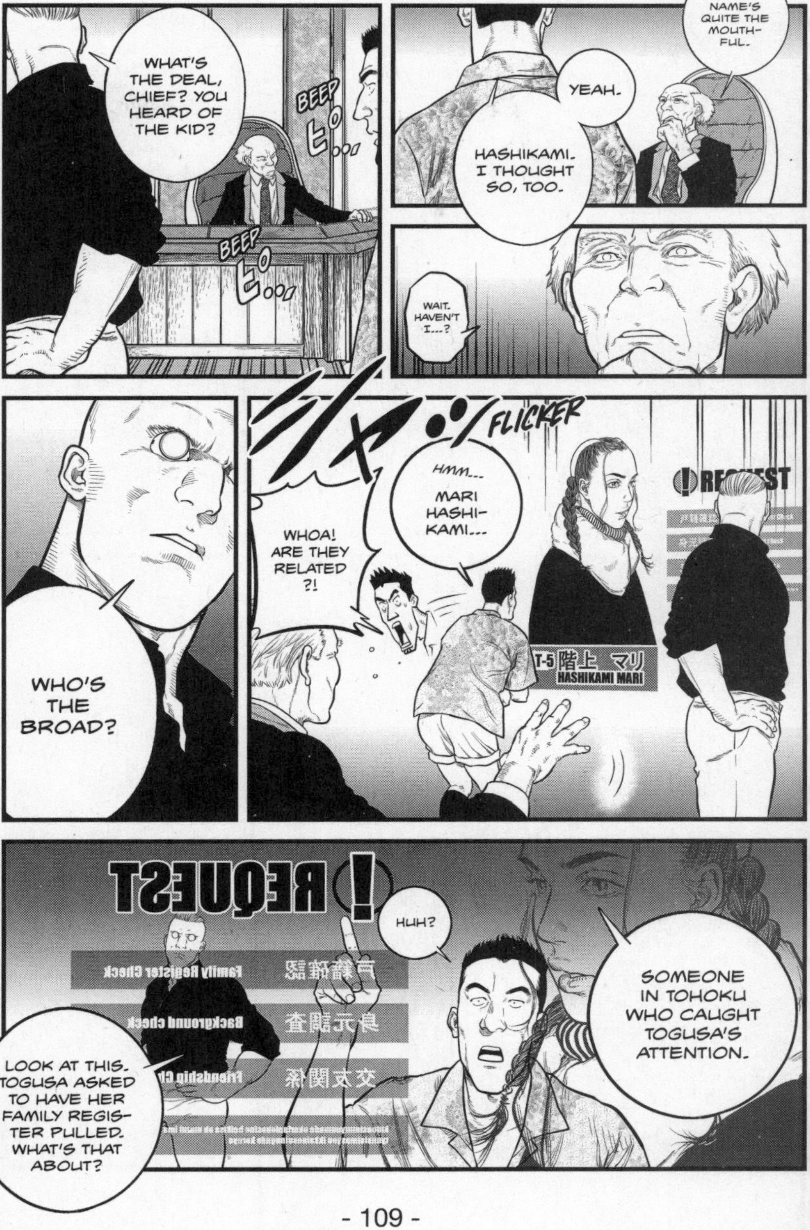
HIS SURNAME'S QUITE THE MOUTHFUL.
YEAH.
HASHIKAMI. I THOUGHT SO, TOO.
WAIT. HAVEN'T I...?
WHAT'S THE DEAL, CHIEF? YOU HEARD OF THE KID?
BEEP
BEEP
FLICKER
REQUEST
HMM... MARI HASHIKAMI...
WHOA! ARE THEY RELATED ?!
T-5 階上 マリ HASHIKAMI MARI
WHO'S THE BROAD?
SOMEONE IN TOHOKU WHO CAUGHT TOGUSA'S ATTENTION.
HUH?
REQUEST
LOOK AT THIS. TOGUSA ASKED TO HAVE HER FAMILY REGISTER PULLED. WHAT'S THAT ABOUT?

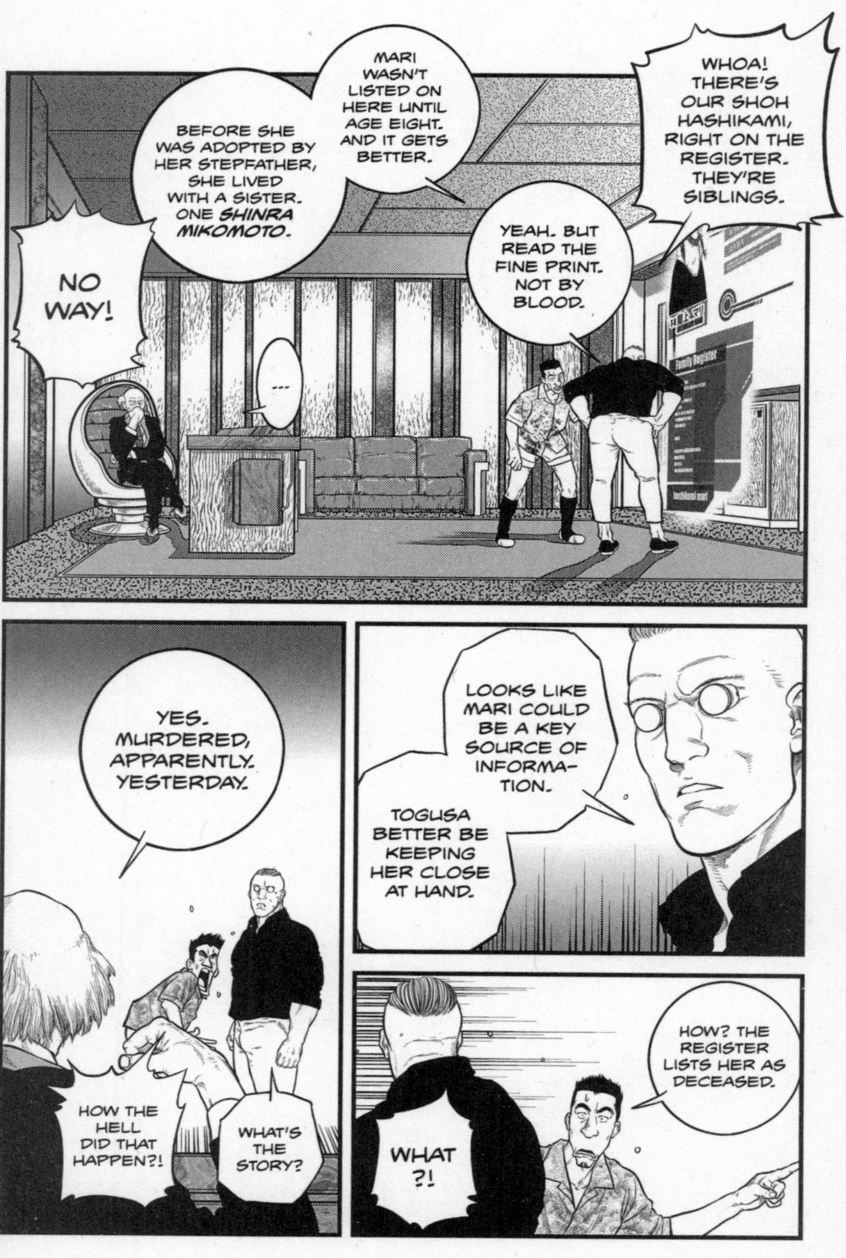

WHOA! THERE'S OUR SHOH HASHIKAMI, RIGHT ON THE REGISTER. THEY'RE SIBLINGS.
YEAH. BUT READ THE FINE PRINT. NOT BY BLOOD.
MARI WASN'T LISTED ON HERE UNTIL AGE EIGHT. AND IT GETS BETTER.
BEFORE SHE WAS ADOPTED BY HER STEPFATHER, SHE LIVED WITH A SISTER. ONE *SHINRA MIKOMOTO*.
NO WAY!
...
Family Register
LOOKS LIKE MARI COULD BE A KEY SOURCE OF INFORMATION.
TOGUSA BETTER BE KEEPING HER CLOSE AT HAND.
HOW? THE REGISTER LISTS HER AS DECEASED.
WHAT?!
YES. MURDERED, APPARENTLY. YESTERDAY.
WHAT'S THE STORY?
HOW THE HELL DID THAT HAPPEN?!

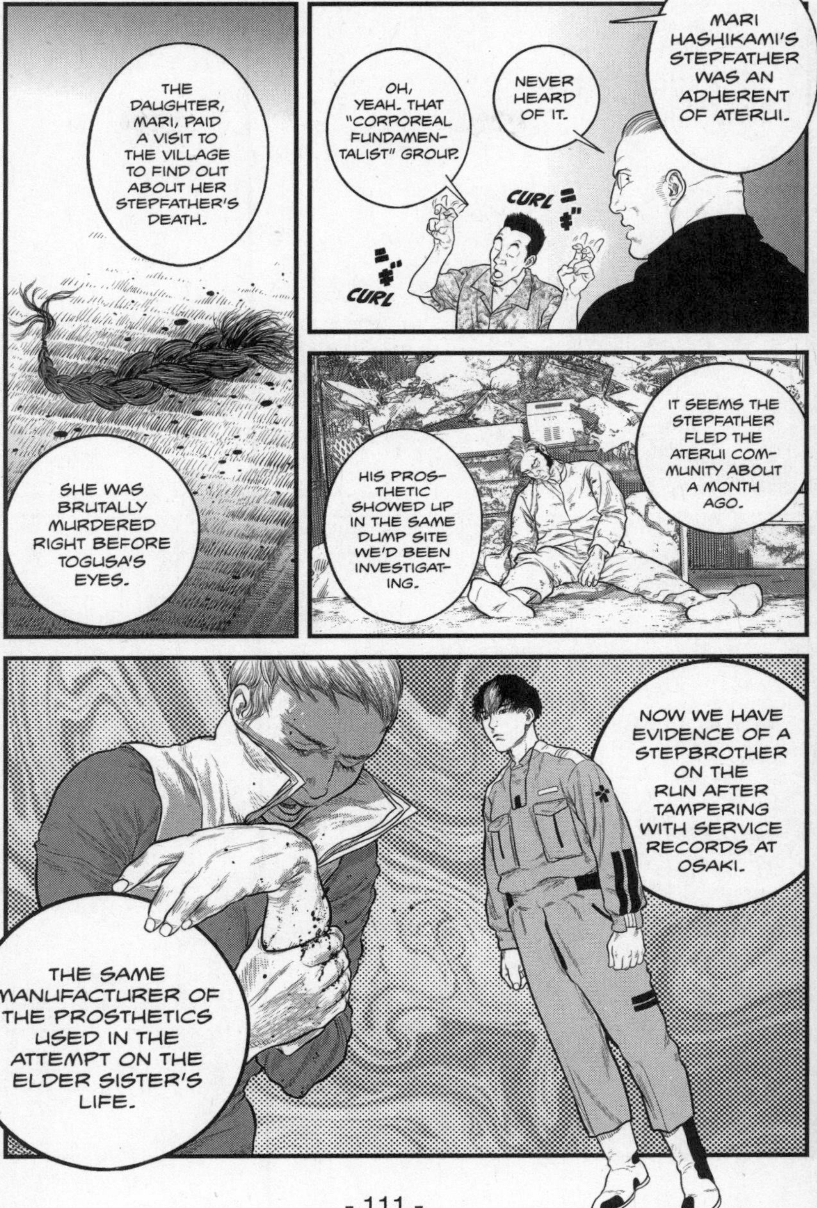
MARI HASHIKAMI'S STEPFATHER WAS AN ADHERENT OF ATERUI.
NEVER HEARD OF IT.
OH, YEAH. THAT "CORPOREAL FUNDAMENTALIST" GROUP.
CURL
CURL
IT SEEMS THE STEPFATHER FLED THE ATERUI COMMUNITY ABOUT A MONTH AGO.
HIS PROSTHETIC SHOWED UP IN THE SAME DUMP SITE WE'D BEEN INVESTIGATING.
THE DAUGHTER, MARI, PAID A VISIT TO THE VILLAGE TO FIND OUT ABOUT HER STEPFATHER'S DEATH.
SHE WAS BRUTALLY MURDERED RIGHT BEFORE TOGUSA'S EYES.
NOW WE HAVE EVIDENCE OF A STEPBROTHER ON THE RUN AFTER TAMPERING WITH SERVICE RECORDS AT OSAKI.
THE SAME MANUFACTURER OF THE PROSTHETICS USED IN THE ATTEMPT ON THE ELDER SISTER'S LIFE.

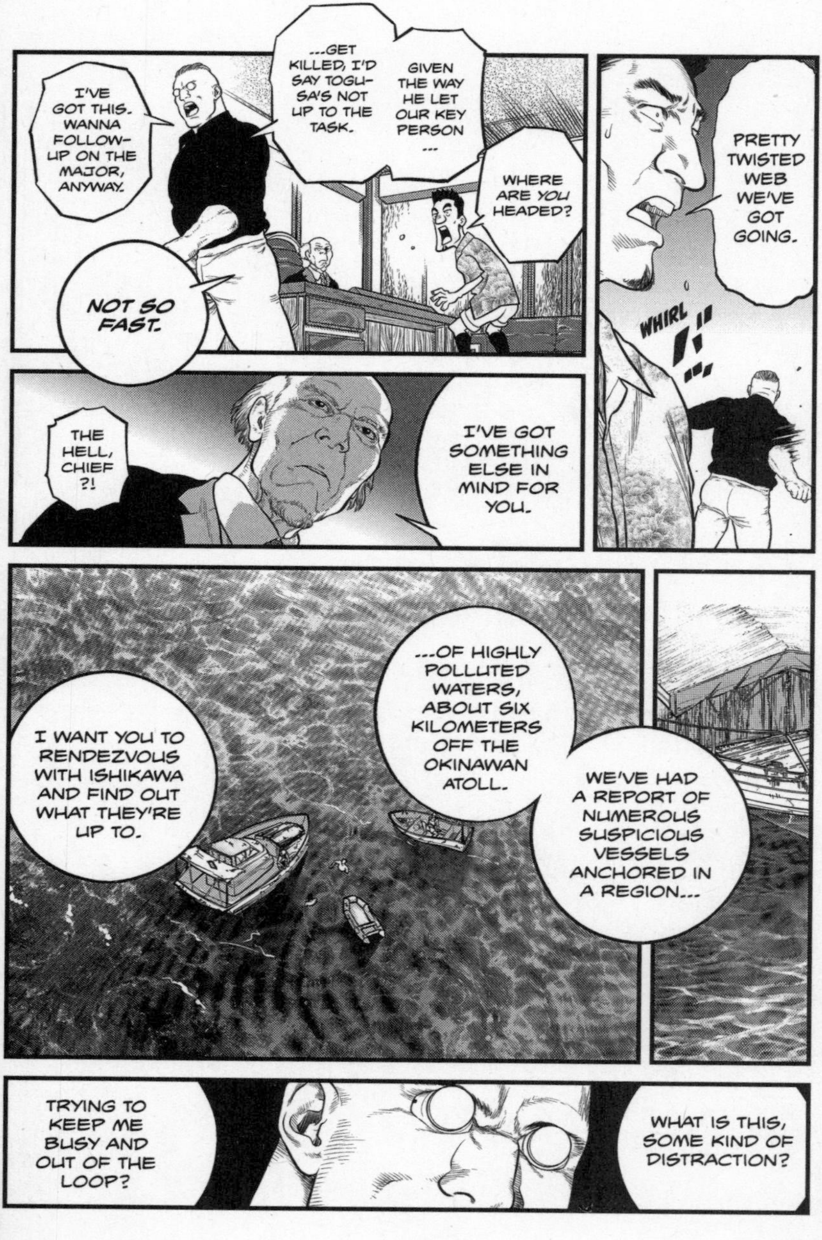
PRETTY TWISTED WEB WE'VE GOT GOING.
WHIRL
GIVEN THE WAY HE LET OUR KEY PERSON ...
...GET KILLED, I'D SAY TOGUSA'S NOT UP TO THE TASK.
WHERE ARE YOU HEADED?
I'VE GOT THIS. WANNA FOLLOW-UP ON THE MAJOR, ANYWAY.
NOT SO FAST.
I'VE GOT SOMETHING ELSE IN MIND FOR YOU.
THE HELL, CHIEF?!
WE'VE HAD A REPORT OF NUMEROUS SUSPICIOUS VESSELS ANCHORED IN A REGION...
...OF HIGHLY POLLUTED WATERS, ABOUT SIX KILOMETERS OFF THE OKINAWAN ATOLL.
I WANT YOU TO RENDEZVOUS WITH ISHIKAWA AND FIND OUT WHAT THEY'RE UP TO.
WHAT IS THIS, SOME KIND OF DISTRACTION?
TRYING TO KEEP ME BUSY AND OUT OF THE LOOP?

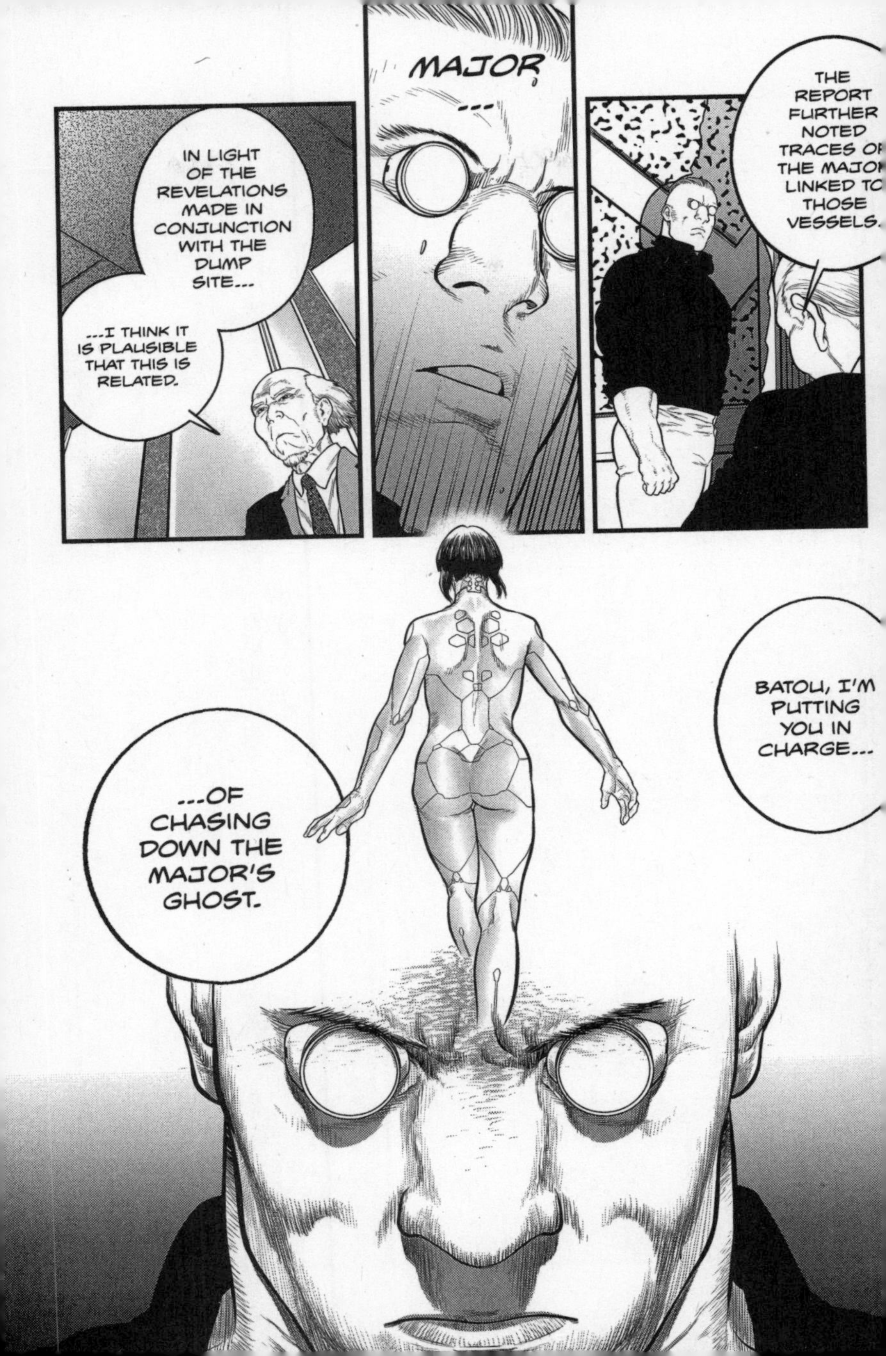
THE REPORT FURTHER NOTED TRACES OF THE MAJOR LINKED TO THOSE VESSELS.
MAJOR ...
IN LIGHT OF THE REVELATIONS MADE IN CONJUNCTION WITH THE DUMP SITE...
...I THINK IT IS PLAUSIBLE THAT THIS IS RELATED.
BATOU, I'M PUTTING YOU IN CHARGE...
...OF CHASING DOWN THE MAJOR'S GHOST.

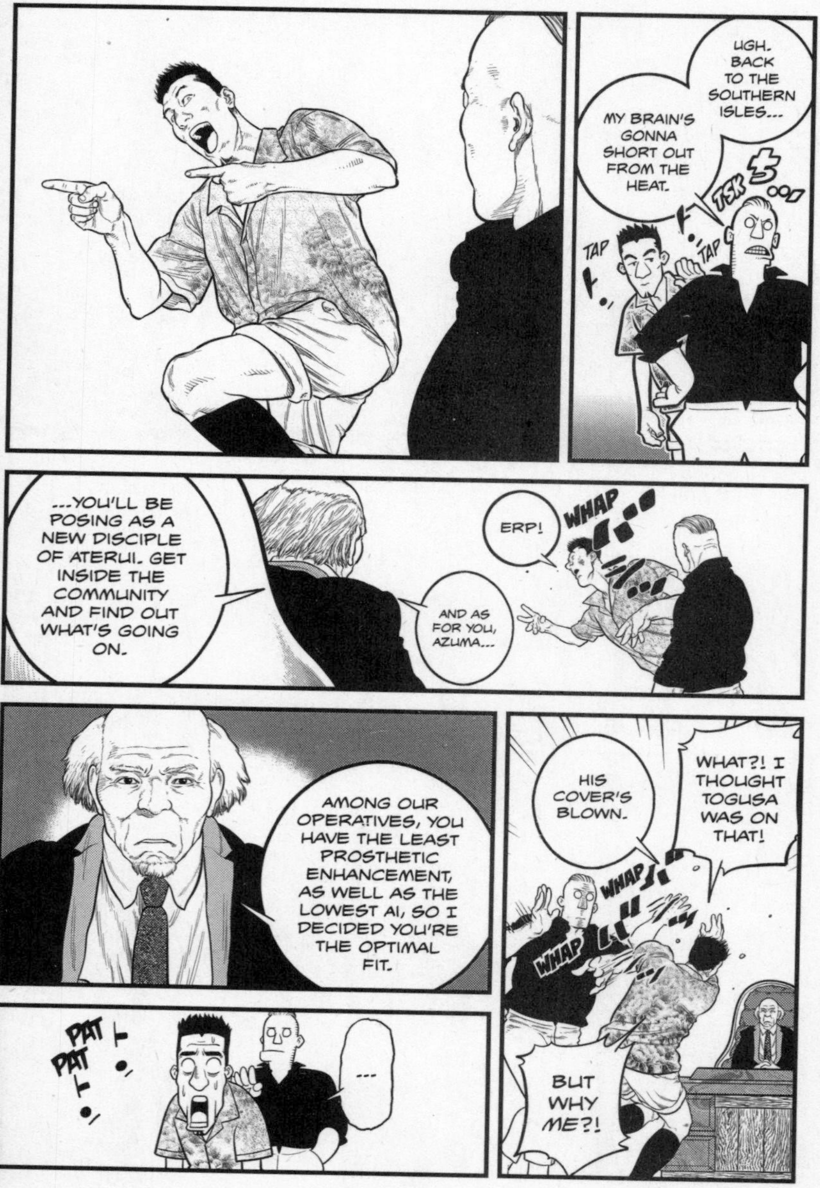
UGH. BACK TO THE SOUTHERN ISLES...
MY BRAIN'S GONNA SHORT OUT FROM THE HEAT.
TSK
TAP
TAP
WHAP
ERP!
AND AS FOR YOU, AZUMA...
...YOU'LL BE POSING AS A NEW DISCIPLE OF ATERUI. GET INSIDE THE COMMUNITY AND FIND OUT WHAT'S GOING ON.
WHAT?! I THOUGHT TOGUSA WAS ON THAT!
HIS COVER'S BLOWN.
WHAP
WHAP
WHAP
BUT WHY ME?!
AMONG OUR OPERATIVES, YOU HAVE THE LEAST PROSTHETIC ENHANCEMENT, AS WELL AS THE LOWEST AI, SO I DECIDED YOU'RE THE OPTIMAL FIT.
...
PAT
PAT

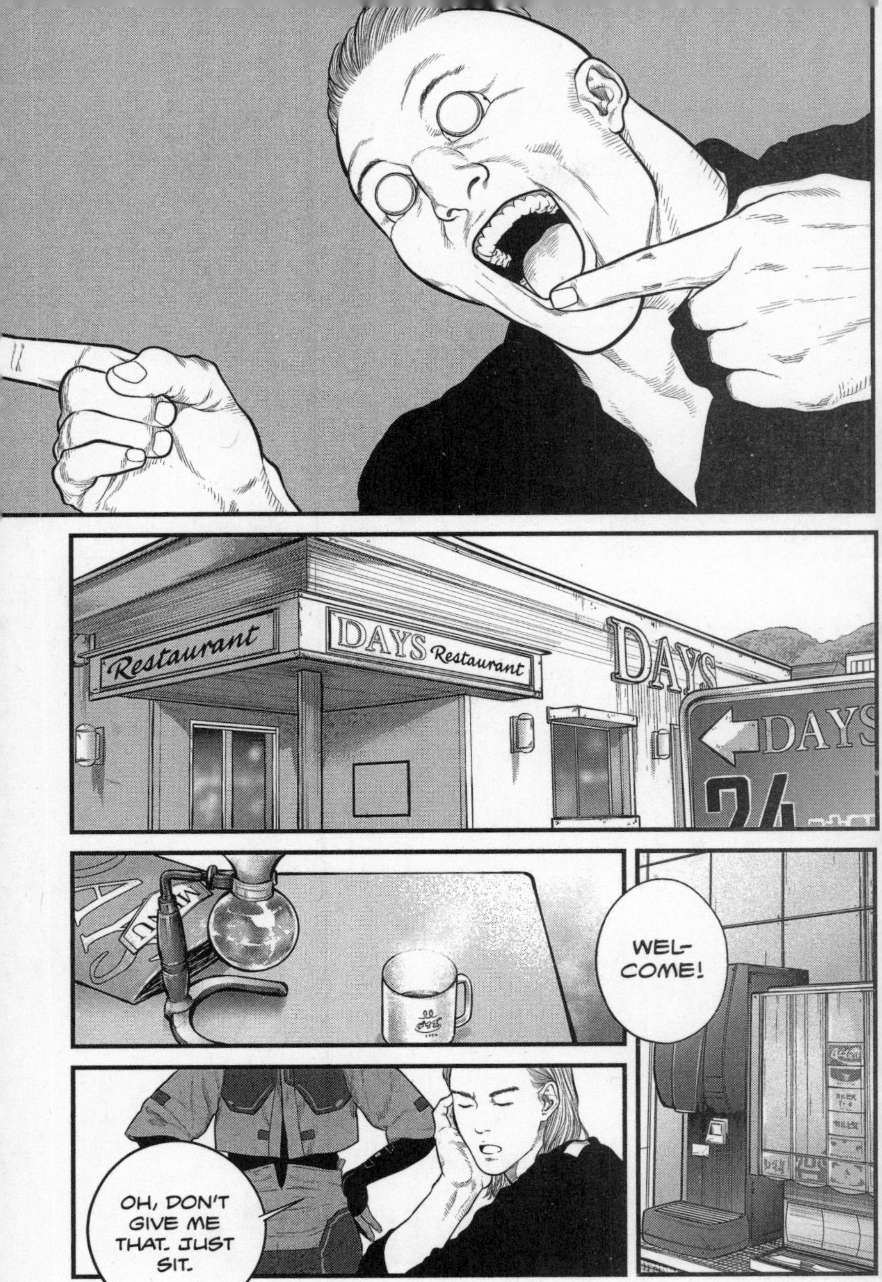
DAYS Restaurant
Restaurant
DAYS
DAYS
WEL-
COME!
MENU
OH, DON'T
GIVE ME
THAT. JUST
SIT.

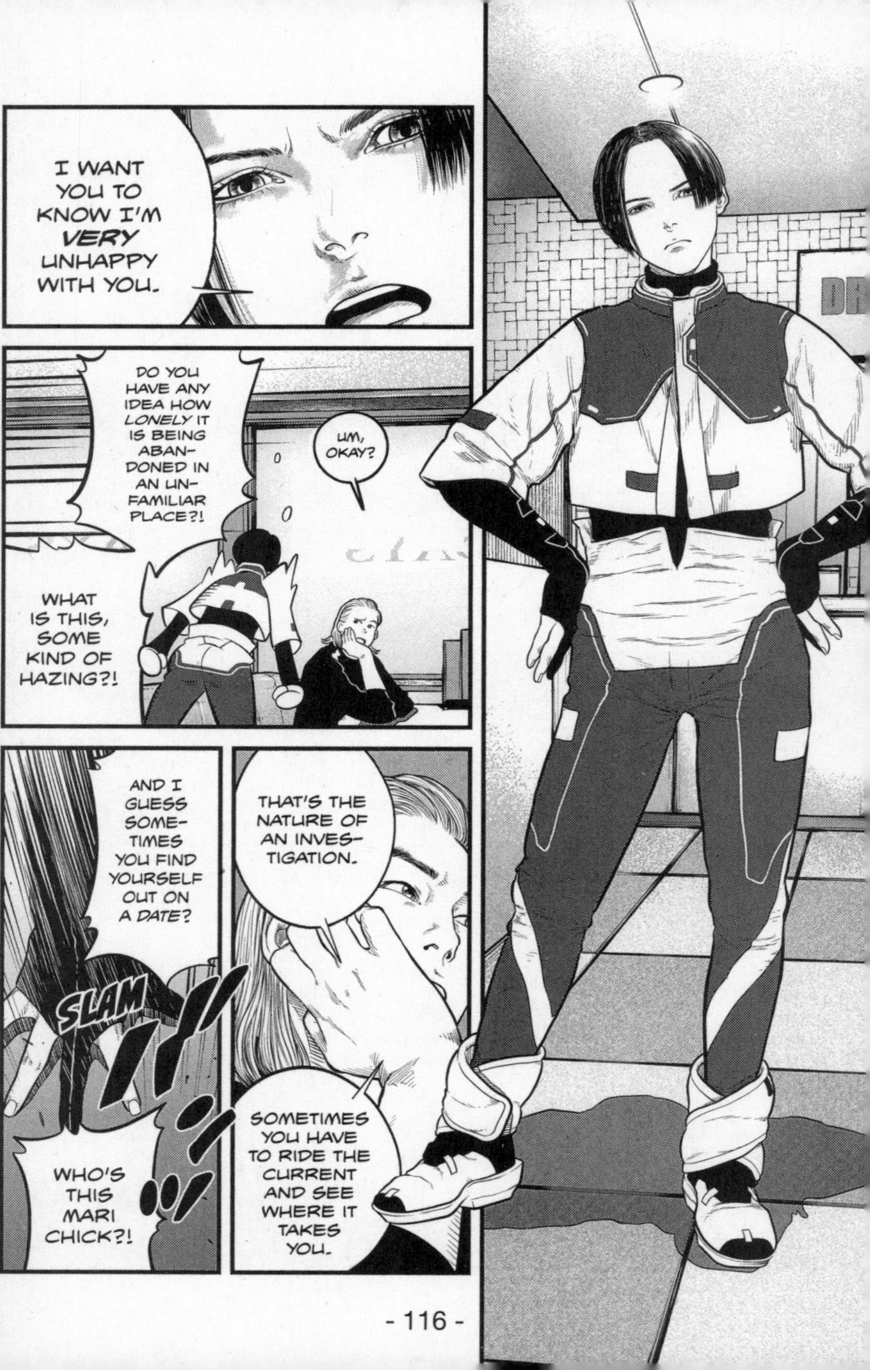
I WANT YOU TO KNOW I'M *VERY* UNHAPPY WITH YOU.
DO YOU HAVE ANY IDEA HOW *LONELY* IT IS BEING ABAN-DONED IN AN UN-FAMILIAR PLACE?!
UM, OKAY?
WHAT IS THIS, SOME KIND OF HAZING?!
THAT'S THE NATURE OF AN INVES-TIGATION.
SOMETIMES YOU HAVE TO RIDE THE CURRENT AND SEE WHERE IT TAKES YOU.
AND I GUESS SOME-TIMES YOU FIND YOURSELF OUT ON A *DATE*?
SLAM
WHO'S THIS MARI CHICK?!

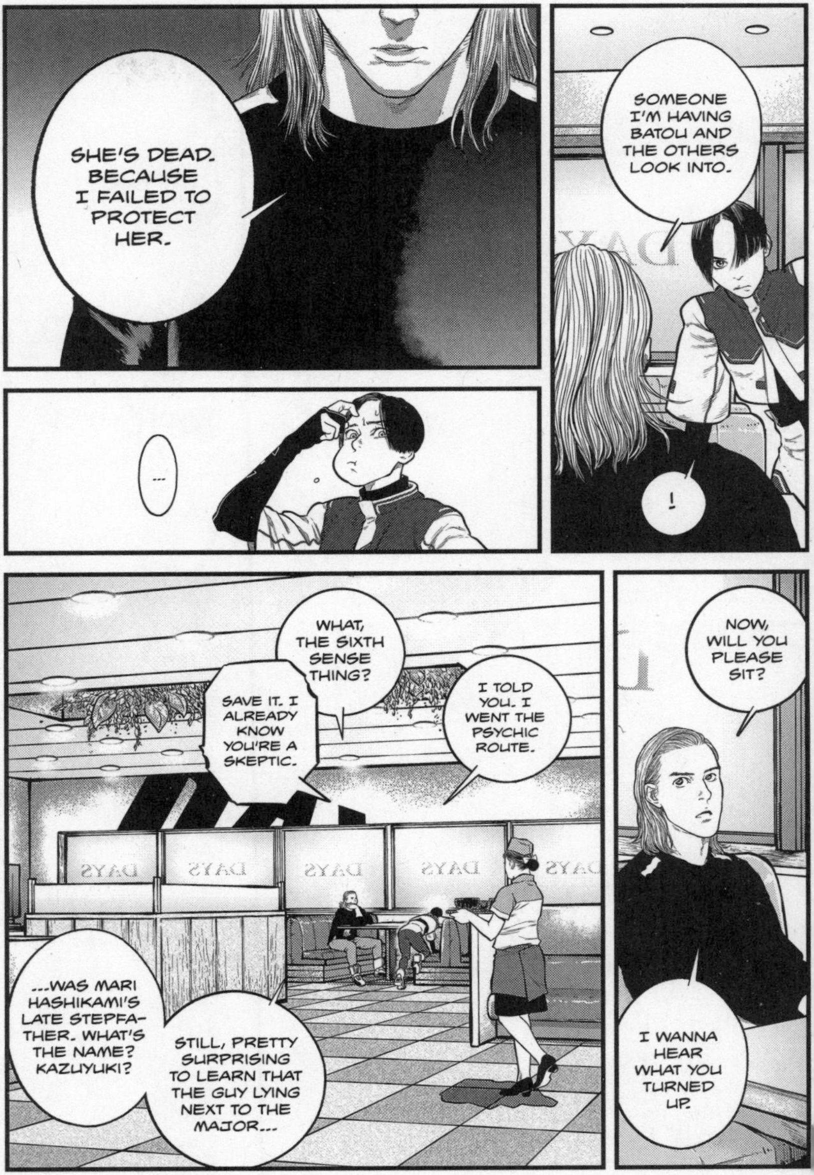
SOMEONE I'M HAVING BATOU AND THE OTHERS LOOK INTO.
!
SHE'S DEAD. BECAUSE I FAILED TO PROTECT HER.
...
NOW, WILL YOU PLEASE SIT?
I WANNA HEAR WHAT YOU TURNED UP.
I TOLD YOU. I WENT THE PSYCHIC ROUTE.
WHAT, THE SIXTH SENSE THING?
SAVE IT. I ALREADY KNOW YOU'RE A SKEPTIC.
STILL, PRETTY SURPRISING TO LEARN THAT THE GUY LYING NEXT TO THE MAJOR...
...WAS MARI HASHIKAMI'S LATE STEPFA-THER. WHAT'S THE NAME? KAZUYUKI?

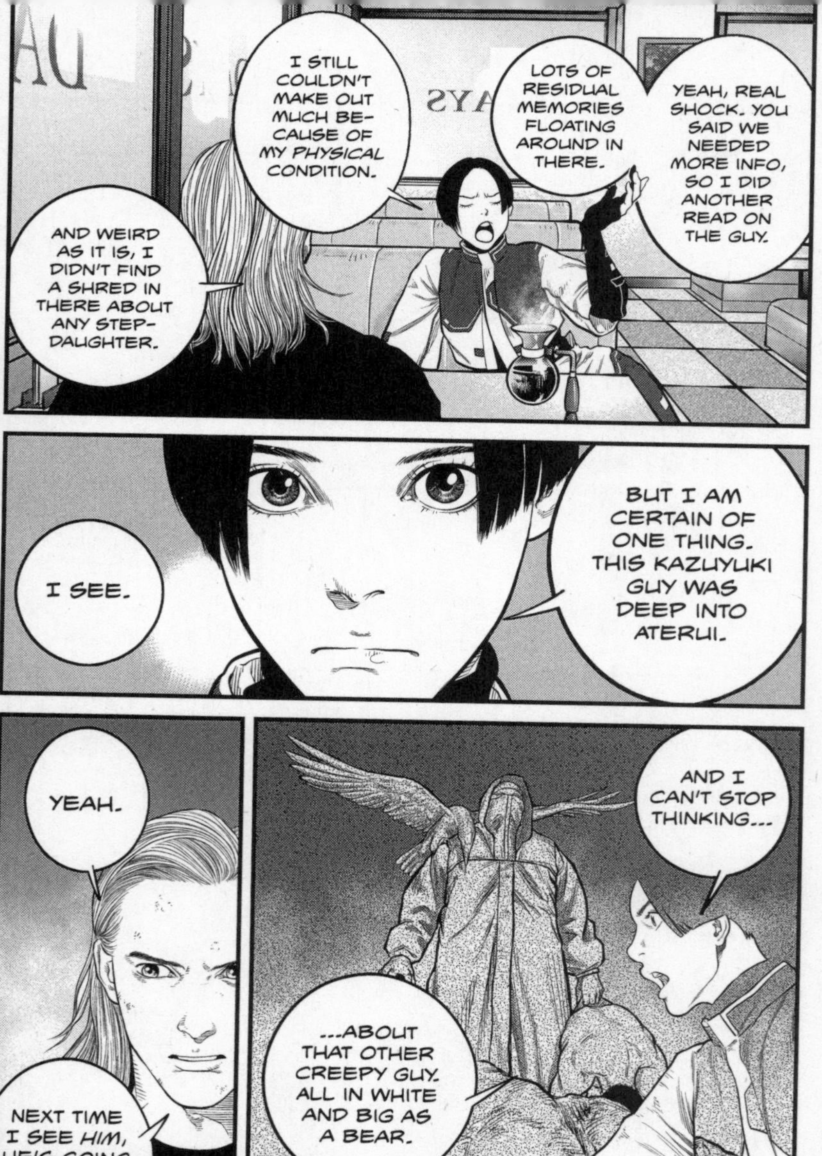
YEAH, REAL SHOCK. YOU SAID WE NEEDED MORE INFO, SO I DID ANOTHER READ ON THE GUY.
LOTS OF RESIDUAL MEMORIES FLOATING AROUND IN THERE.
I STILL COULDN'T MAKE OUT MUCH BE-CAUSE OF MY *PHYSICAL* CONDITION.
AND WEIRD AS IT IS, I DIDN'T FIND A SHRED IN THERE ABOUT ANY STEP-DAUGHTER.
BUT I AM CERTAIN OF ONE THING. THIS KAZUYUKI GUY WAS DEEP INTO ATERUI.
I SEE.
AND I CAN'T STOP THINKING...
...ABOUT THAT OTHER CREEPY GUY. ALL IN WHITE AND BIG AS A BEAR.
YEAH.
NEXT TIME I SEE *HIM*, HE'S GOING STRAIGHT INTO A PEN.

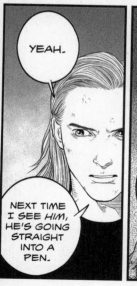

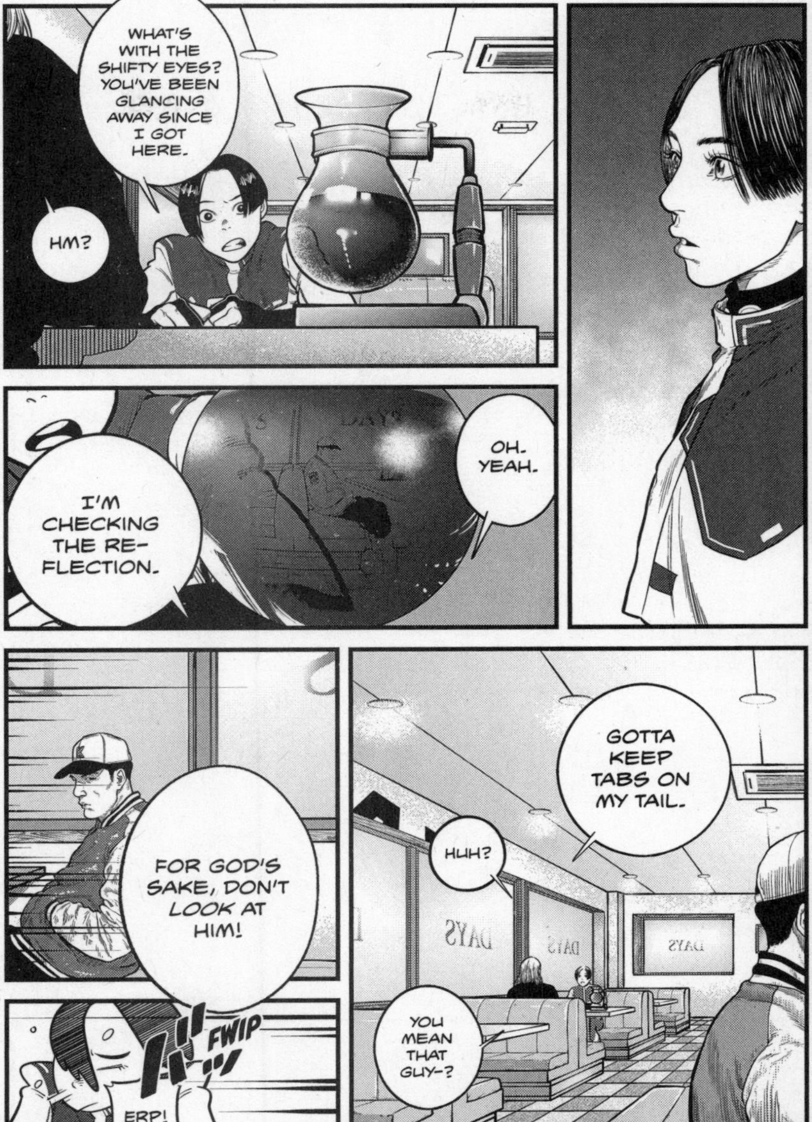

WHAT'S WITH THE SHIFTY EYES? YOU'VE BEEN GLANCING AWAY SINCE I GOT HERE.
HM?
OH. YEAH.
I'M CHECKING THE RE-FLECTION.
GOTTA KEEP TABS ON MY TAIL.
HUH?
YOU MEAN THAT GUY-?
FOR GOD'S SAKE, DON'T LOOK AT HIM!
FWIP
ERP!

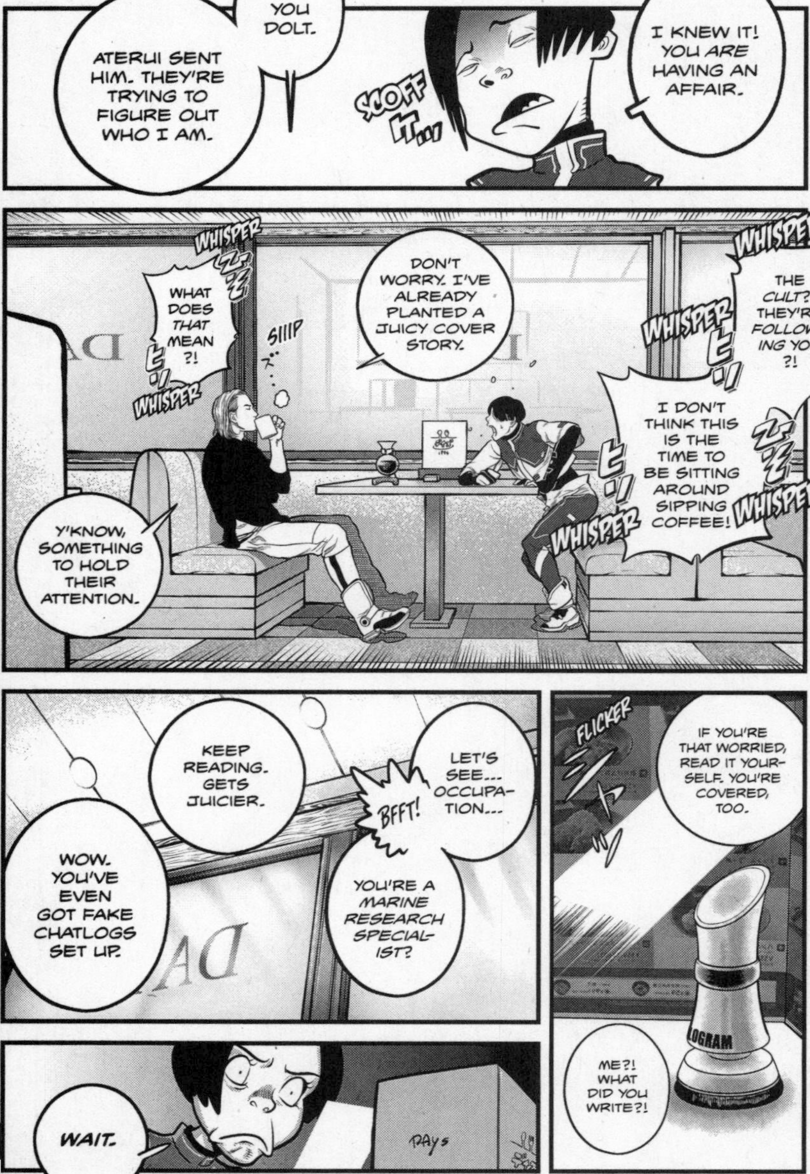
I KNEW IT! YOU *ARE* HAVING AN AFFAIR.
SCOFF
NO, YOU DOLT.
ATERUI SENT HIM. THEY'RE TRYING TO FIGURE OUT WHO I AM.
WHISPER
THE *CULT*?! THEY'RE *FOLLOWING* YOU?!
WHISPER
I DON'T THINK THIS IS THE TIME TO BE SITTING AROUND SIPPING COFFEE!
WHISPER
WHISPER
DON'T WORRY. I'VE ALREADY PLANTED A JUICY COVER STORY.
SIIIP
WHISPER
WHAT DOES *THAT* MEAN?!
WHISPER
Y'KNOW, SOMETHING TO HOLD THEIR ATTENTION.
FLICKER
IF YOU'RE THAT WORRIED, READ IT YOURSELF. YOU'RE COVERED, TOO.
LOGRAM
ME?! WHAT DID YOU WRITE?!
LET'S SEE... OCCUPATION...
BFFT!
KEEP READING. GETS JUICIER.
YOU'RE A *MARINE RESEARCH SPECIALIST*?
WOW. YOU'VE EVEN GOT FAKE CHATLOGS SET UP.
WAIT.
DAYS

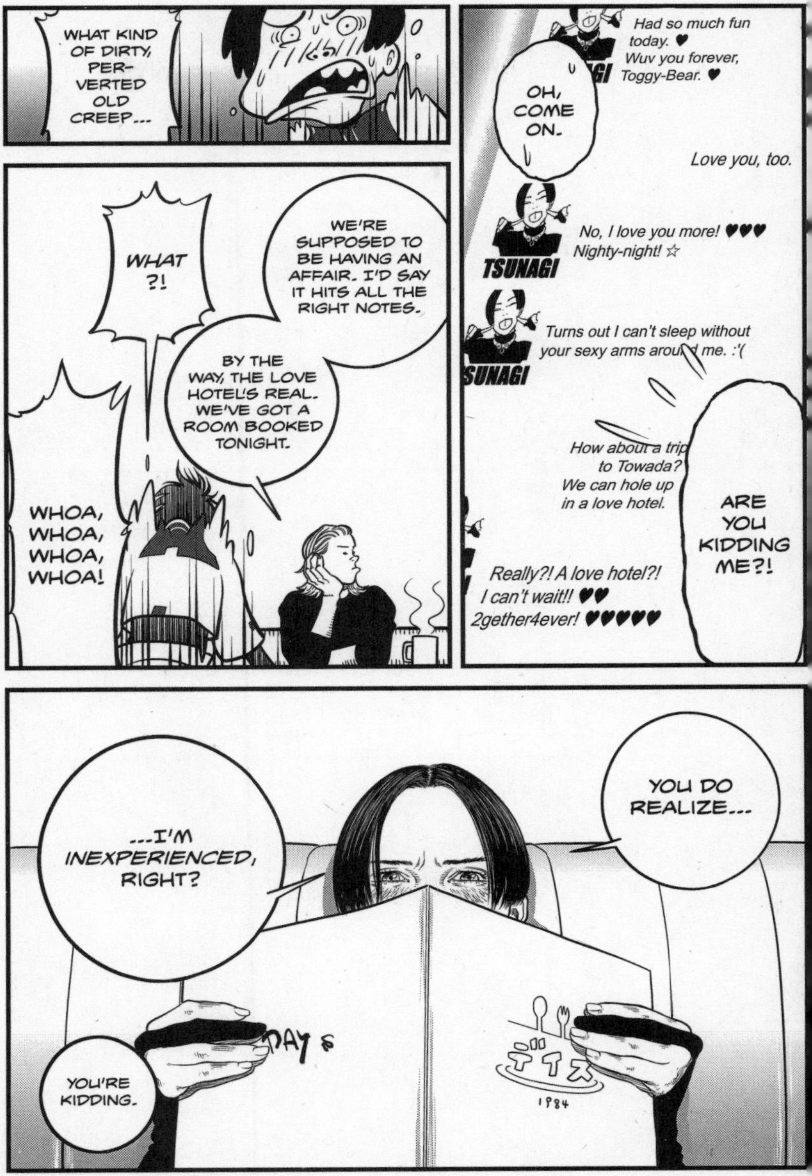
Had so much fun today. ♥
Wuv you forever, Toggy-Bear. ♥
OH, COME ON.
Love you, too.
TSUNAGI
No, I love you more! ♥♥♥
Nighty-night! ☆
TSUNAGI
Turns out I can't sleep without your sexy arms arou d me. :'(
How about a trip to Towada?
We can hole up in a love hotel.
Really?! A love hotel?!
I can't wait!! ♥♥
2gether4ever! ♥♥♥♥♥
ARE YOU KIDDING ME?!
WHAT KIND OF DIRTY, PER-VERTED OLD CREEP...
WHAT?!
WE'RE SUPPOSED TO BE HAVING AN AFFAIR. I'D SAY IT HITS ALL THE RIGHT NOTES.
BY THE WAY, THE LOVE HOTEL'S REAL. WE'VE GOT A ROOM BOOKED TONIGHT.
WHOA, WHOA, WHOA, WHOA!
YOU DO REALIZE...
...I'M INEXPERIENCED, RIGHT?
YOU'RE KIDDING.
DAYS
デイズ
1984

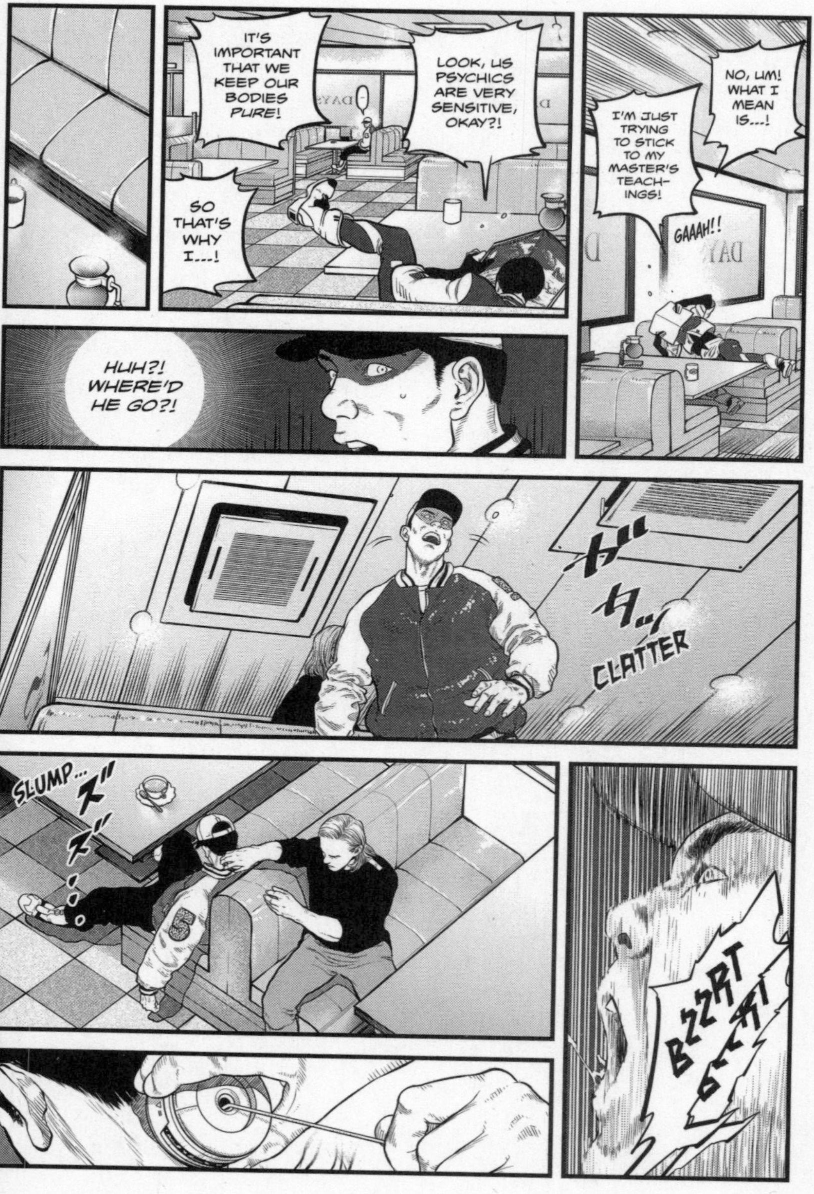
NO, UM! WHAT I MEAN IS...!
I'M JUST TRYING TO STICK TO MY MASTER'S TEACH-INGS!
GAAAH!!
LOOK, US PSYCHICS ARE VERY SENSITIVE, OKAY?!
IT'S IMPORTANT THAT WE KEEP OUR BODIES PURE!
SO THAT'S WHY I...!
HUH?! WHERE'D HE GO?!
CLATTER
BZZRT
SLUMP...

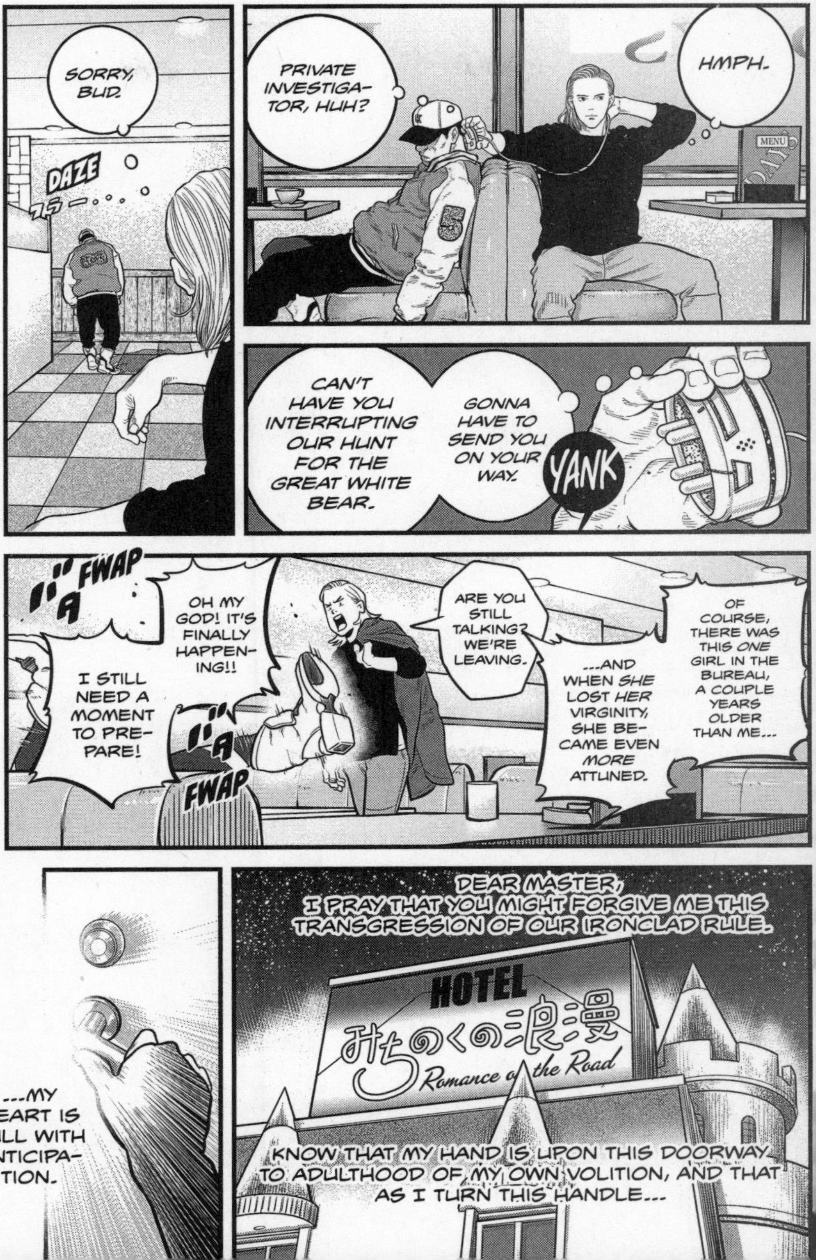
HMPH.
PRIVATE INVESTIGATOR, HUH?
GONNA HAVE TO SEND YOU ON YOUR WAY.
YANK
CAN'T HAVE YOU INTERRUPTING OUR HUNT FOR THE GREAT WHITE BEAR.
SORRY, BUD.
DAZE
OF COURSE, THERE WAS THIS *ONE* GIRL IN THE BUREAU, A COUPLE YEARS OLDER THAN ME...
...AND WHEN *SHE* LOST HER VIRGINITY, SHE BECAME EVEN *MORE* ATTUNED.
ARE YOU STILL TALKING? WE'RE LEAVING.
OH MY GOD! IT'S FINALLY HAPPENING!!
FWAP
I STILL NEED A MOMENT TO PREPARE!
FWAP
DEAR MASTER, I PRAY THAT YOU MIGHT FORGIVE ME THIS TRANSGRESSION OF OUR IRONCLAD RULE.
HOTEL
みちのくの浪漫
Romance on the Road
KNOW THAT MY HAND IS UPON THIS DOORWAY TO ADULTHOOD OF MY OWN VOLITION, AND THAT AS I TURN THIS HANDLE...
...MY HEART IS FULL WITH ANTICIPATION.

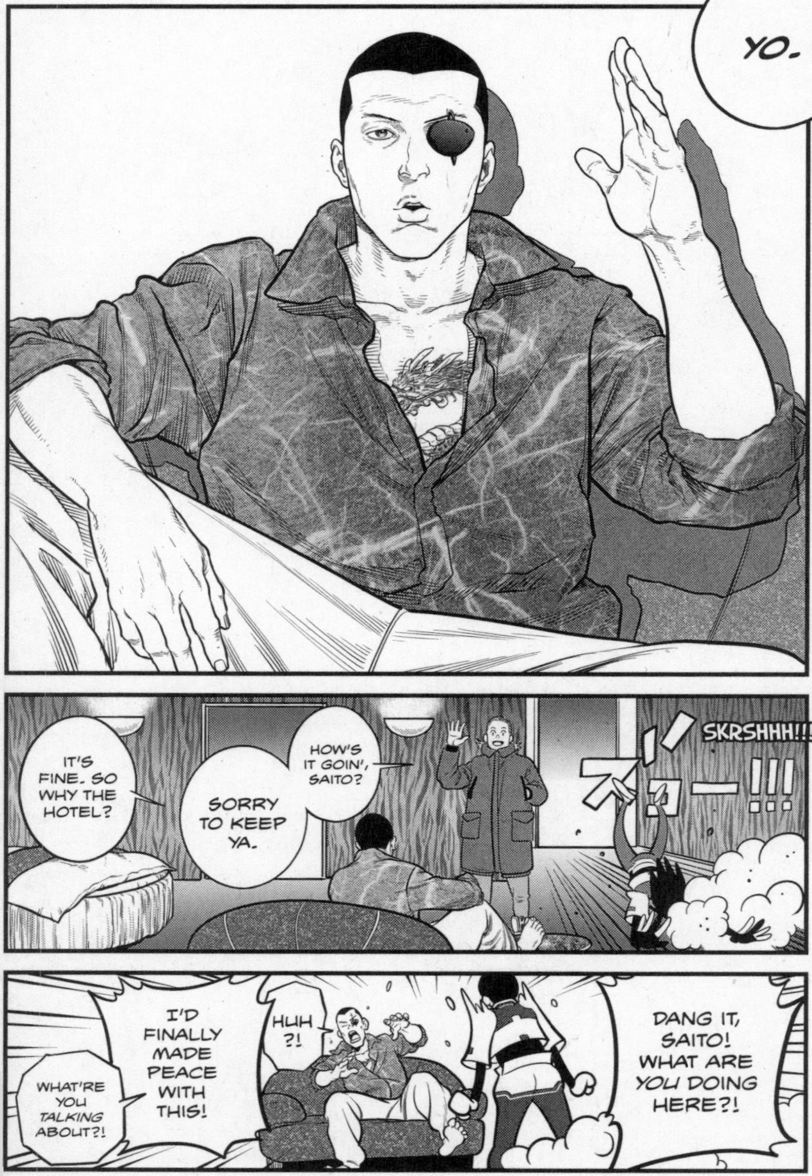
YO.
SKRSHHH!!!
HOW'S IT GOIN', SAITO?
SORRY TO KEEP YA.
IT'S FINE. SO WHY THE HOTEL?
DANG IT, SAITO! WHAT ARE *YOU* DOING HERE?!
HUH?!
I'D FINALLY MADE PEACE WITH THIS!
WHAT'RE YOU *TALKING* ABOUT?!

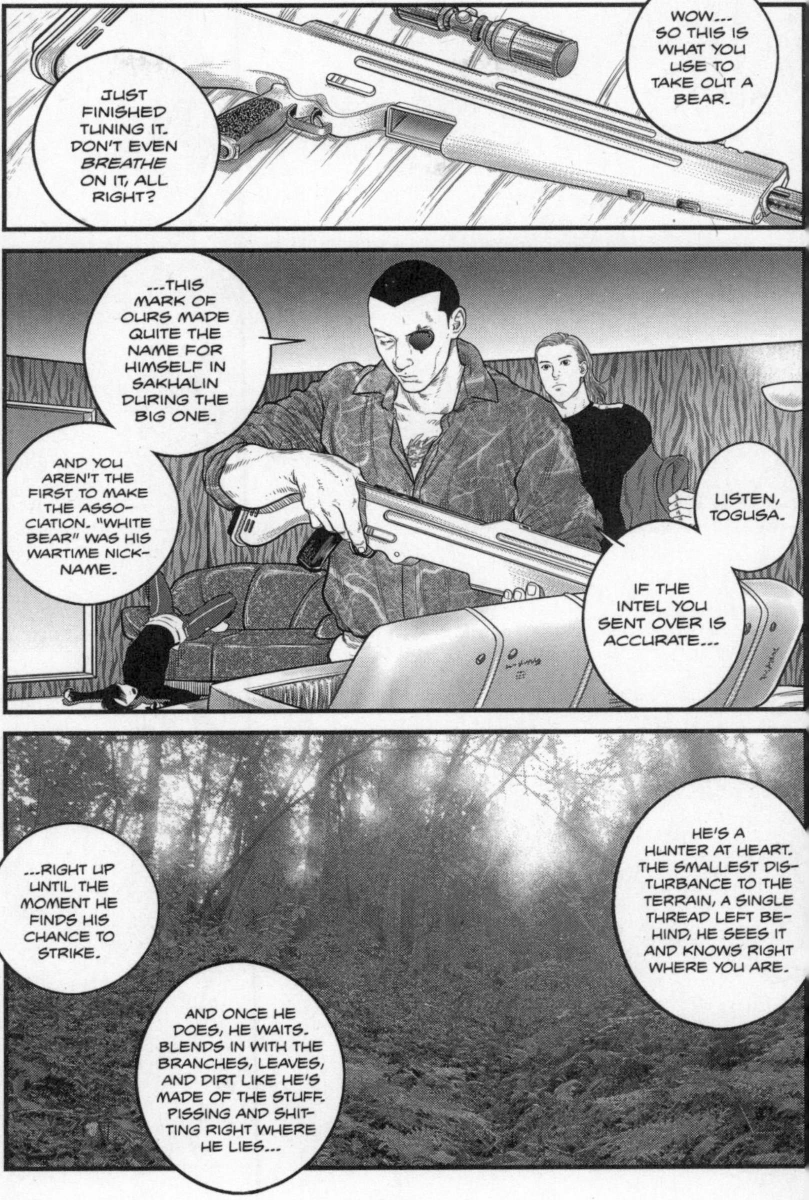
WOW... SO THIS IS WHAT YOU USE TO TAKE OUT A BEAR.
JUST FINISHED TUNING IT. DON'T EVEN *BREATHE* ON IT, ALL RIGHT?
...THIS MARK OF OURS MADE QUITE THE NAME FOR HIMSELF IN SAKHALIN DURING THE BIG ONE.
AND YOU AREN'T THE FIRST TO MAKE THE ASSO-CIATION. "WHITE BEAR" WAS HIS WARTIME NICK-NAME.
LISTEN, TOGUSA.
IF THE INTEL YOU SENT OVER IS ACCURATE...
HE'S A HUNTER AT HEART. THE SMALLEST DIS-TURBANCE TO THE TERRAIN, A SINGLE THREAD LEFT BE-HIND, HE SEES IT AND KNOWS RIGHT WHERE YOU ARE.
AND ONCE HE DOES, HE WAITS. BLENDS IN WITH THE BRANCHES, LEAVES, AND DIRT LIKE HE'S MADE OF THE STUFF. PISSING AND SHIT-TING RIGHT WHERE HE LIES...
...RIGHT UP UNTIL THE MOMENT HE FINDS HIS CHANCE TO STRIKE.

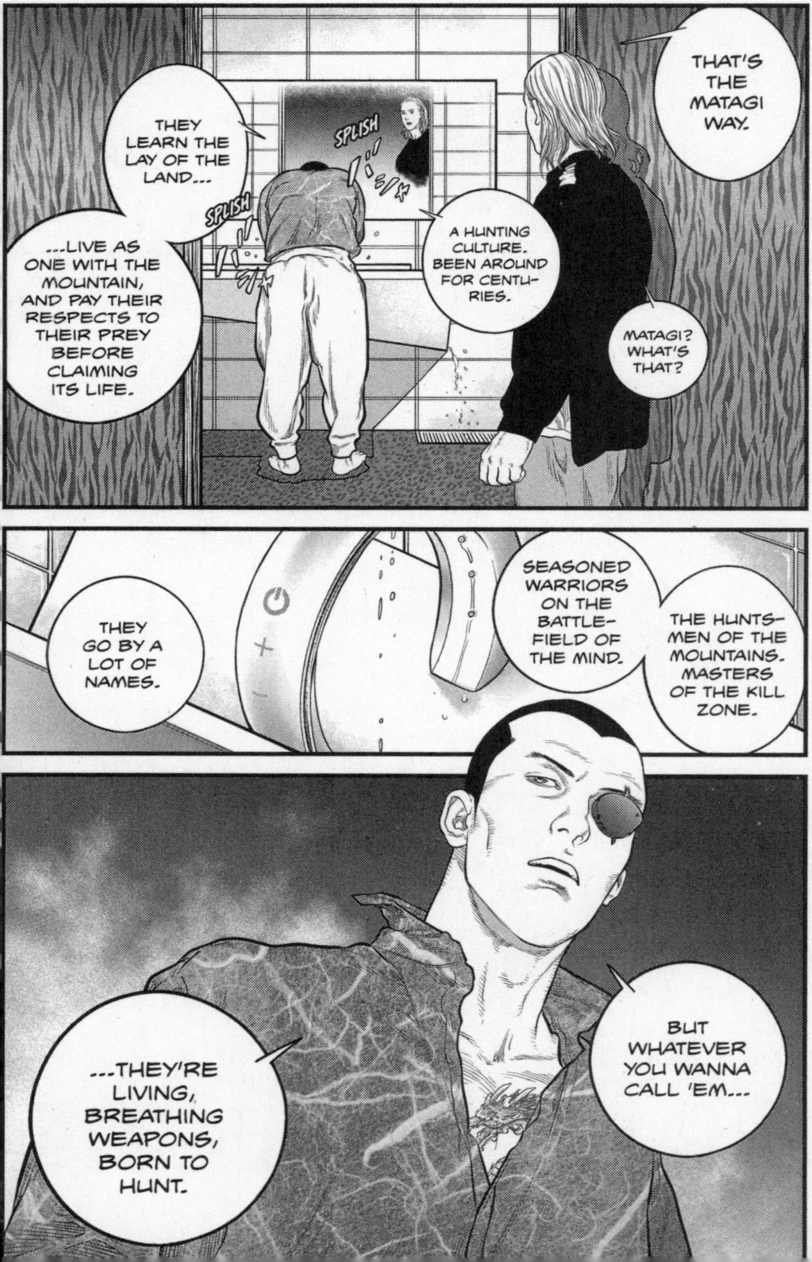
THAT'S THE MATAGI WAY.
MATAGI? WHAT'S THAT?
A HUNTING CULTURE. BEEN AROUND FOR CENTU-RIES.
SPLISH
THEY LEARN THE LAY OF THE LAND...
SPLISH
...LIVE AS ONE WITH THE MOUNTAIN, AND PAY THEIR RESPECTS TO THEIR PREY BEFORE CLAIMING ITS LIFE.
THE HUNTS-MEN OF THE MOUNTAINS. MASTERS OF THE KILL ZONE.
SEASONED WARRIORS ON THE BATTLE-FIELD OF THE MIND.
THEY GO BY A LOT OF NAMES.
BUT WHATEVER YOU WANNA CALL 'EM...
...THEY'RE LIVING, BREATHING WEAPONS, BORN TO HUNT.

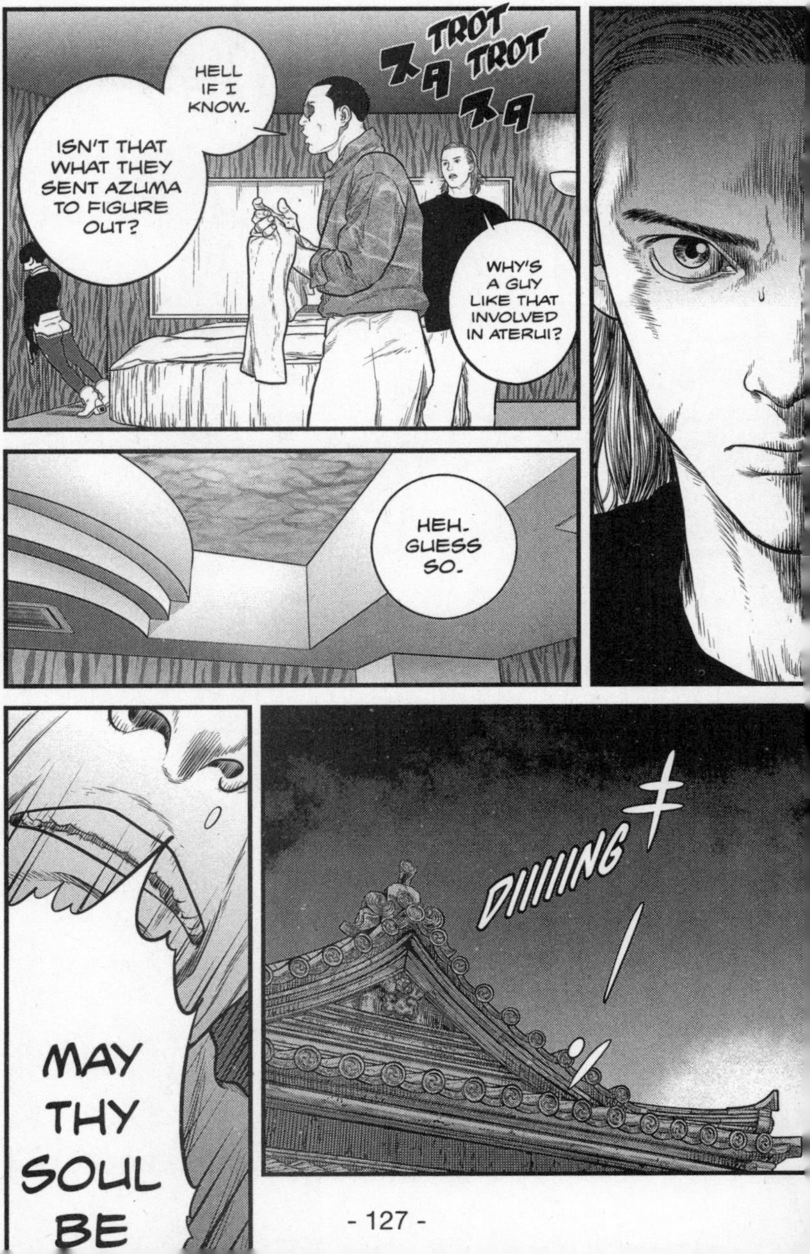
TROT TROT
スタ スタ
WHY'S A GUY LIKE THAT INVOLVED IN ATERUI?
HELL IF I KNOW.
ISN'T THAT WHAT THEY SENT AZUMA TO FIGURE OUT?
HEH. GUESS SO.
DIIIIING
MAY THY SOUL BE

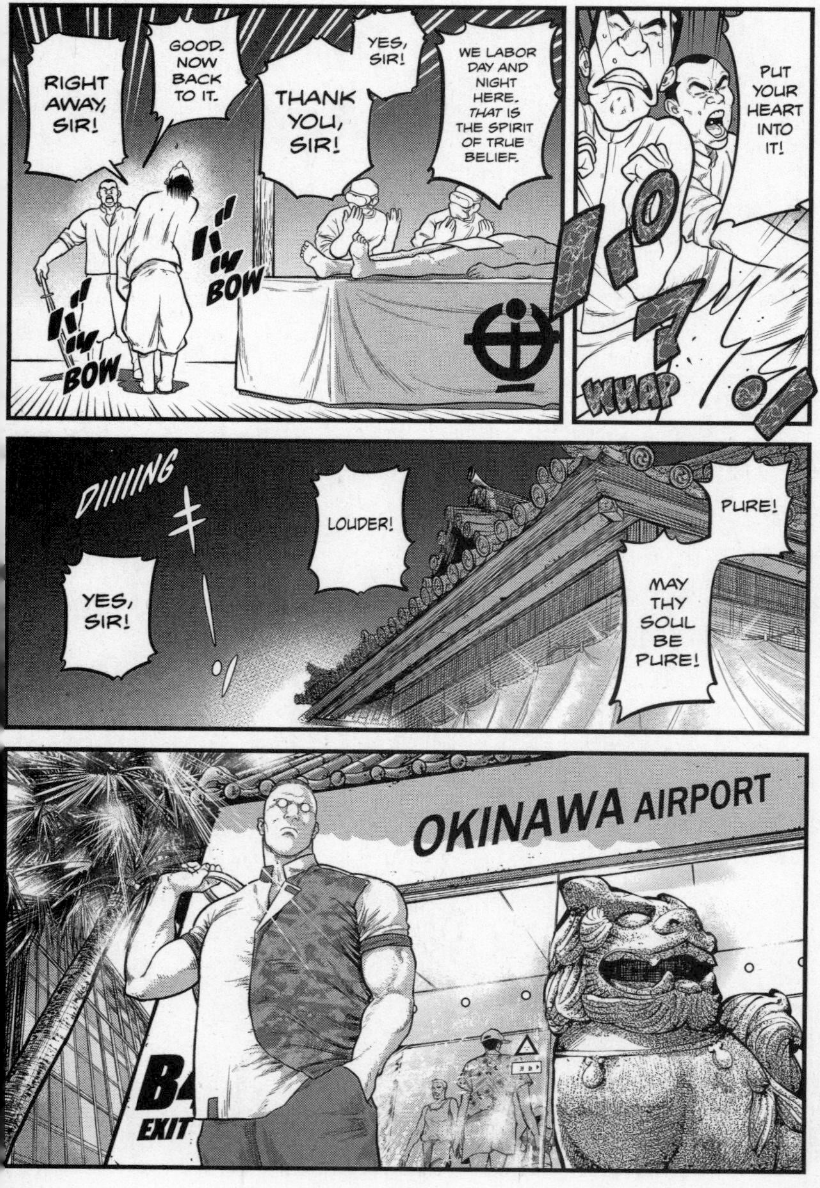
PUT YOUR HEART INTO IT!
WHAP
WE LABOR DAY AND NIGHT HERE. THAT IS THE SPIRIT OF TRUE BELIEF.
YES, SIR!
THANK YOU, SIR!
GOOD. NOW BACK TO IT.
RIGHT AWAY, SIR!
BOW
BOW
PURE!
MAY THY SOUL BE PURE!
LOUDER!
YES, SIR!
DIIIIING
OKINAWA AIRPORT
EXIT

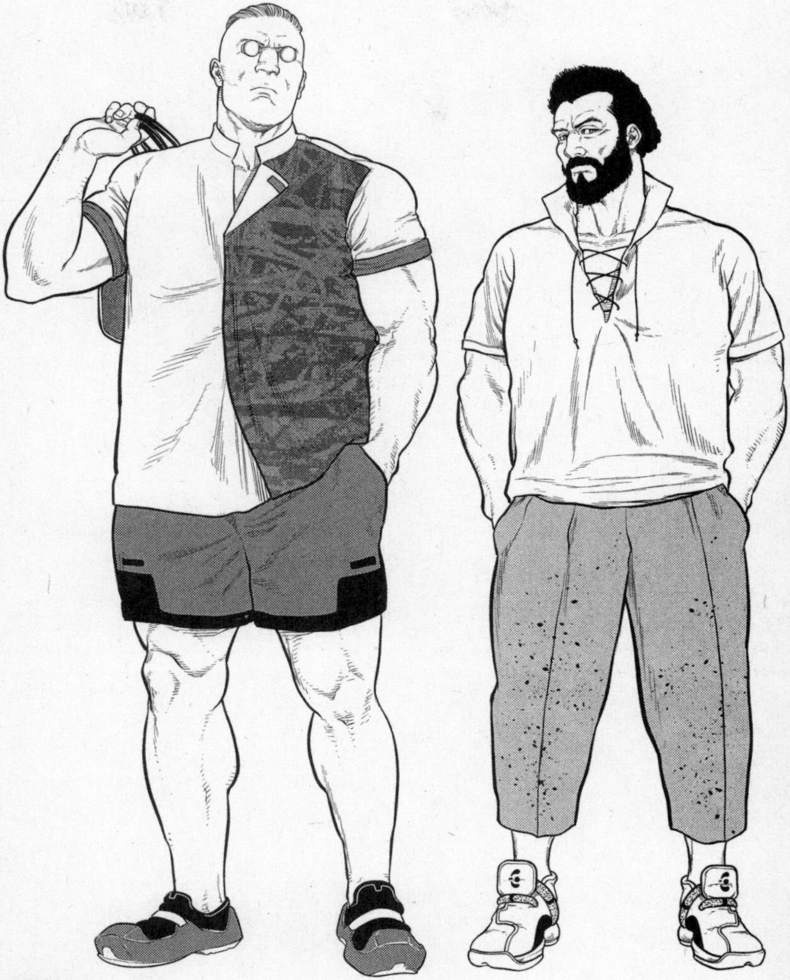

04

STORMING

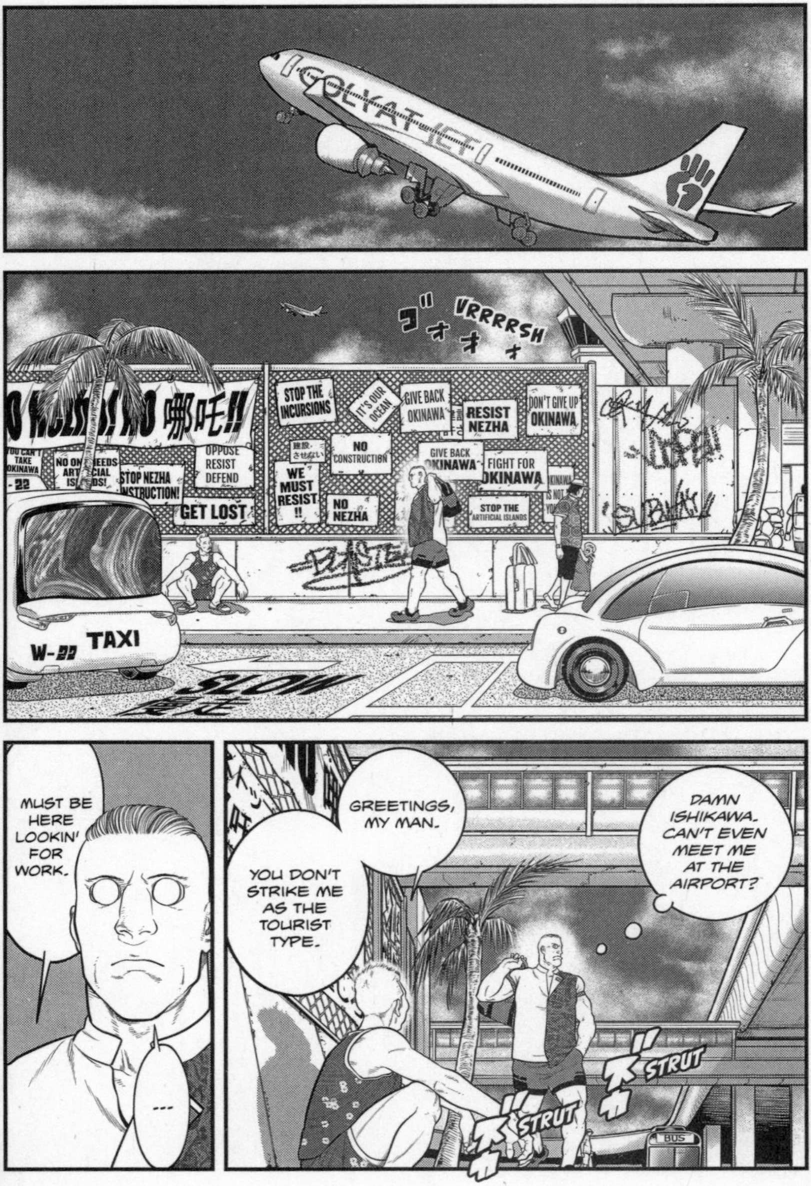
GOLYAT JET
ゴオオオ
VRRRRSH
STOP THE INCURSIONS
IT'S OUR OCEAN
GIVE BACK OKINAWA
RESIST NEZHA
DON'T GIVE UP OKINAWA
OPPOSE RESIST DEFEND
建設させない
WE MUST RESIST !!
NO CONSTRUCTION
GIVE BACK OKINAWA
FIGHT FOR OKINAWA
STOP NEZHA
GET LOST
NO NEZHA
STOP THE ARTIFICIAL ISLANDS
TAXI
W-22
SLOW
DAMN ISHIKAWA. CAN'T EVEN MEET ME AT THE AIRPORT?
GREETINGS, MY MAN.
YOU DON'T STRIKE ME AS THE TOURIST TYPE.
ズカ STRUT
ズカ STRUT
BUS
MUST BE HERE LOOKIN' FOR WORK.
...

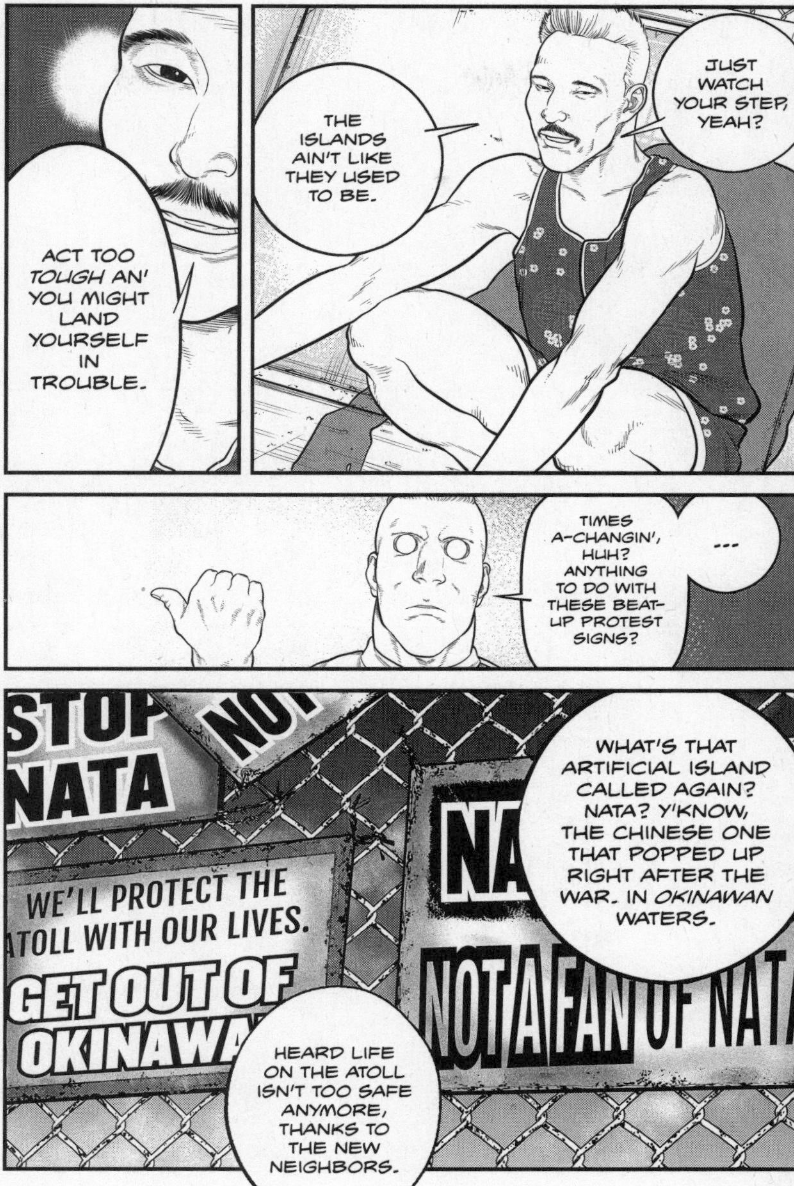
JUST WATCH YOUR STEP, YEAH?
THE ISLANDS AIN'T LIKE THEY USED TO BE.
ACT TOO *TOUGH* AN' YOU MIGHT LAND YOURSELF IN TROUBLE.
...
TIMES A-CHANGIN', HUH? ANYTHING TO DO WITH THESE BEAT-UP PROTEST SIGNS?
NOT A FAN OF NATA
WHAT'S THAT ARTIFICIAL ISLAND CALLED AGAIN? NATA? Y'KNOW, THE CHINESE ONE THAT POPPED UP RIGHT AFTER THE WAR. IN *OKINAWAN* WATERS.
STOP NATA
WE'LL PROTECT THE ATOLL WITH OUR LIVES.
GET OUT OF OKINAWA
HEARD LIFE ON THE ATOLL ISN'T TOO SAFE ANYMORE, THANKS TO THE NEW NEIGHBORS.

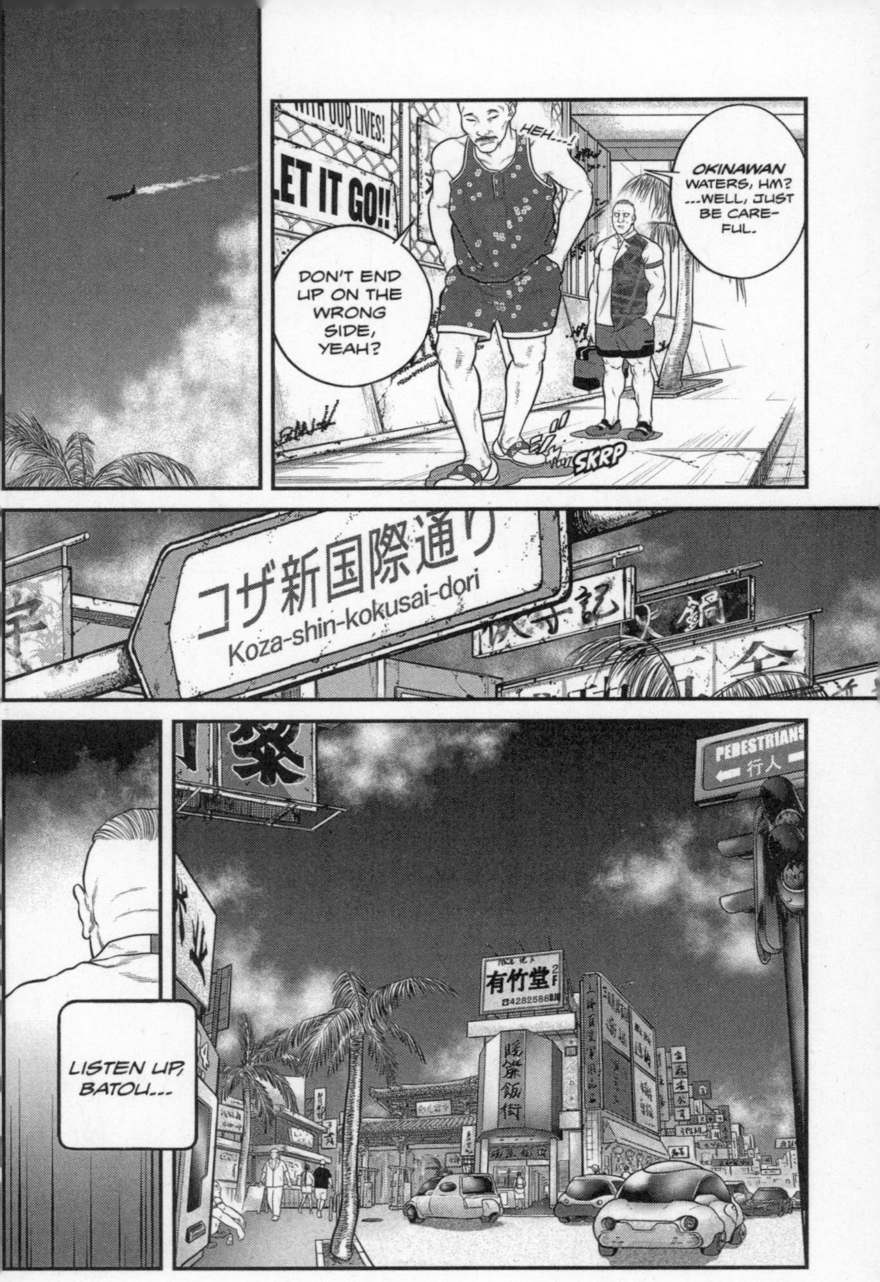
OKINAWAN WATERS, HM? ...WELL, JUST BE CAREFUL.
HEH...!
WITH OUR LIVES!
LET IT GO!!
DON'T END UP ON THE WRONG SIDE, YEAH?
SKRP
コザ新国際通り
Koza-shin-kokusai-dori
PEDESTRIANS
行人
有竹堂
LISTEN UP, BATOU...

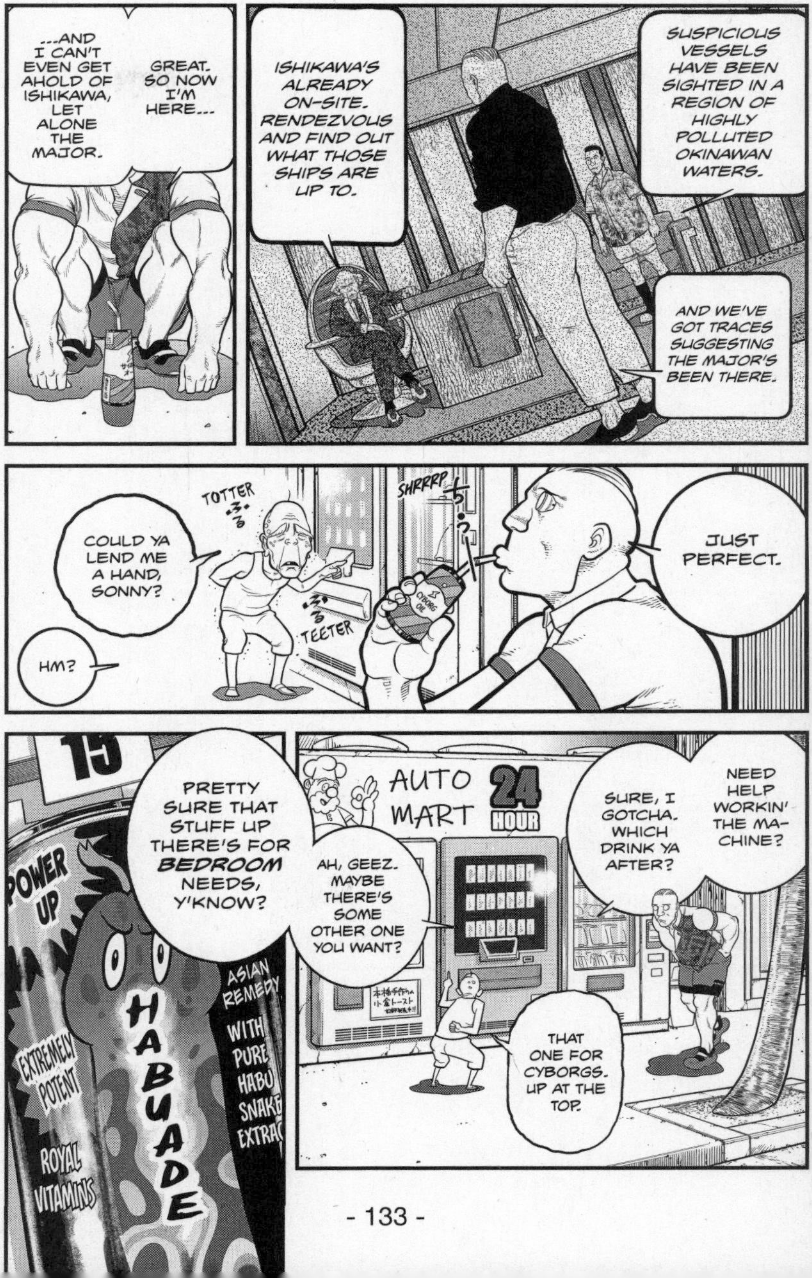
SUSPICIOUS VESSELS HAVE BEEN SIGHTED IN A REGION OF HIGHLY POLLUTED OKINAWAN WATERS.
AND WE'VE GOT TRACES SUGGESTING THE MAJOR'S BEEN THERE.
ISHIKAWA'S ALREADY ON-SITE. RENDEZVOUS AND FIND OUT WHAT THOSE SHIPS ARE UP TO.
GREAT. SO NOW I'M HERE...
...AND I CAN'T EVEN GET AHOLD OF ISHIKAWA, LET ALONE THE MAJOR.
SHRRRP
JUST PERFECT.
CYBORG OIL
TOTTER
COULD YA LEND ME A HAND, SONNY?
TEETER
HM?
NEED HELP WORKIN' THE MA-CHINE?
SURE, I GOTCHA. WHICH DRINK YA AFTER?
AUTO MART
24 HOUR
THAT ONE FOR CYBORGS. UP AT THE TOP.
AH, GEEZ. MAYBE THERE'S SOME OTHER ONE YOU WANT?
PRETTY SURE THAT STUFF UP THERE'S FOR ***BEDROOM*** NEEDS, Y'KNOW?
15
POWER UP
HABUADE
ASIAN REMEDY
WITH PURE HABU SNAKE EXTRAC
EXTREMELY POTENT
ROYAL VITAMINS

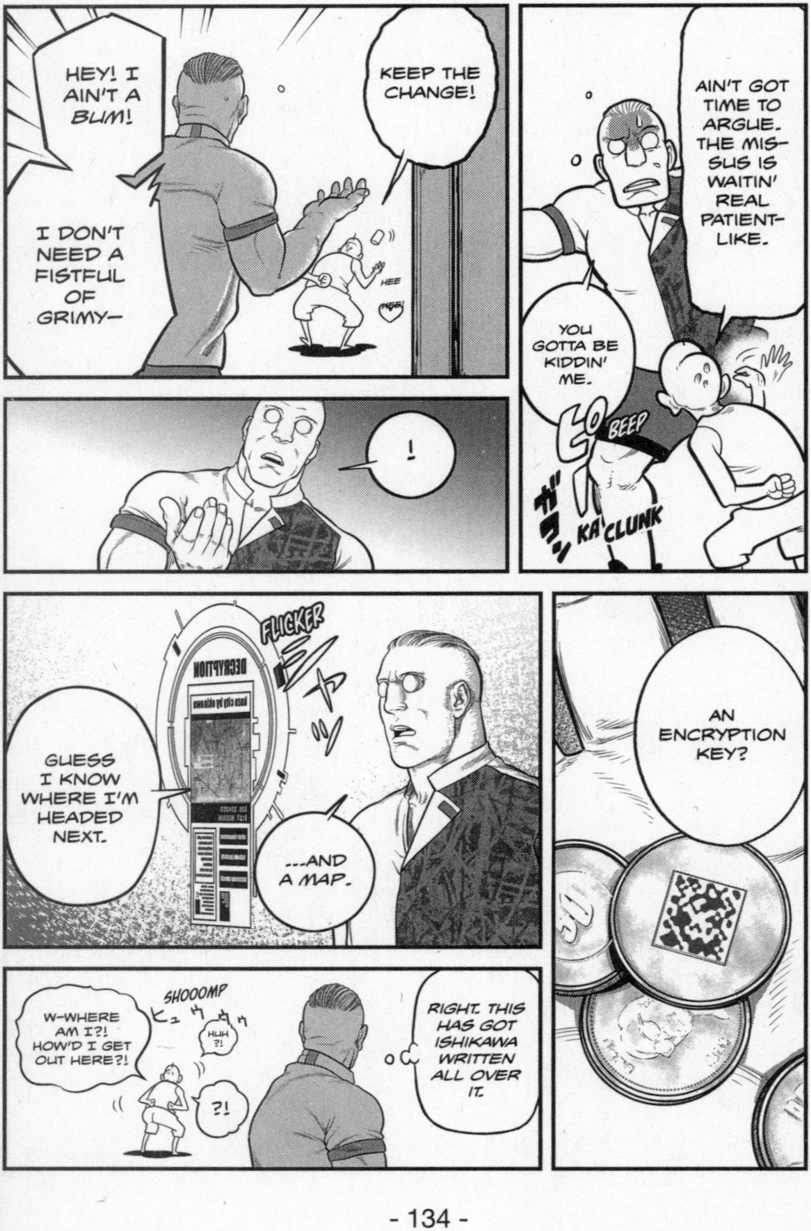
AIN'T GOT TIME TO ARGUE. THE MIS-SUS IS WAITIN' REAL PATIENT-LIKE.
YOU GOTTA BE KIDDIN' ME.
BEEP
KA CLUNK
KEEP THE CHANGE!
HEY! I AIN'T A BUM!
I DON'T NEED A FISTFUL OF GRIMY—
HEE HEE!
!
AN ENCRYPTION KEY?
FLICKER
DECRYPTION
...AND A MAP.
GUESS I KNOW WHERE I'M HEADED NEXT.
RIGHT. THIS HAS GOT ISHIKAWA WRITTEN ALL OVER IT.
SHOOOMP
HUH ?!
?!
W-WHERE AM I?! HOW'D I GET OUT HERE?!

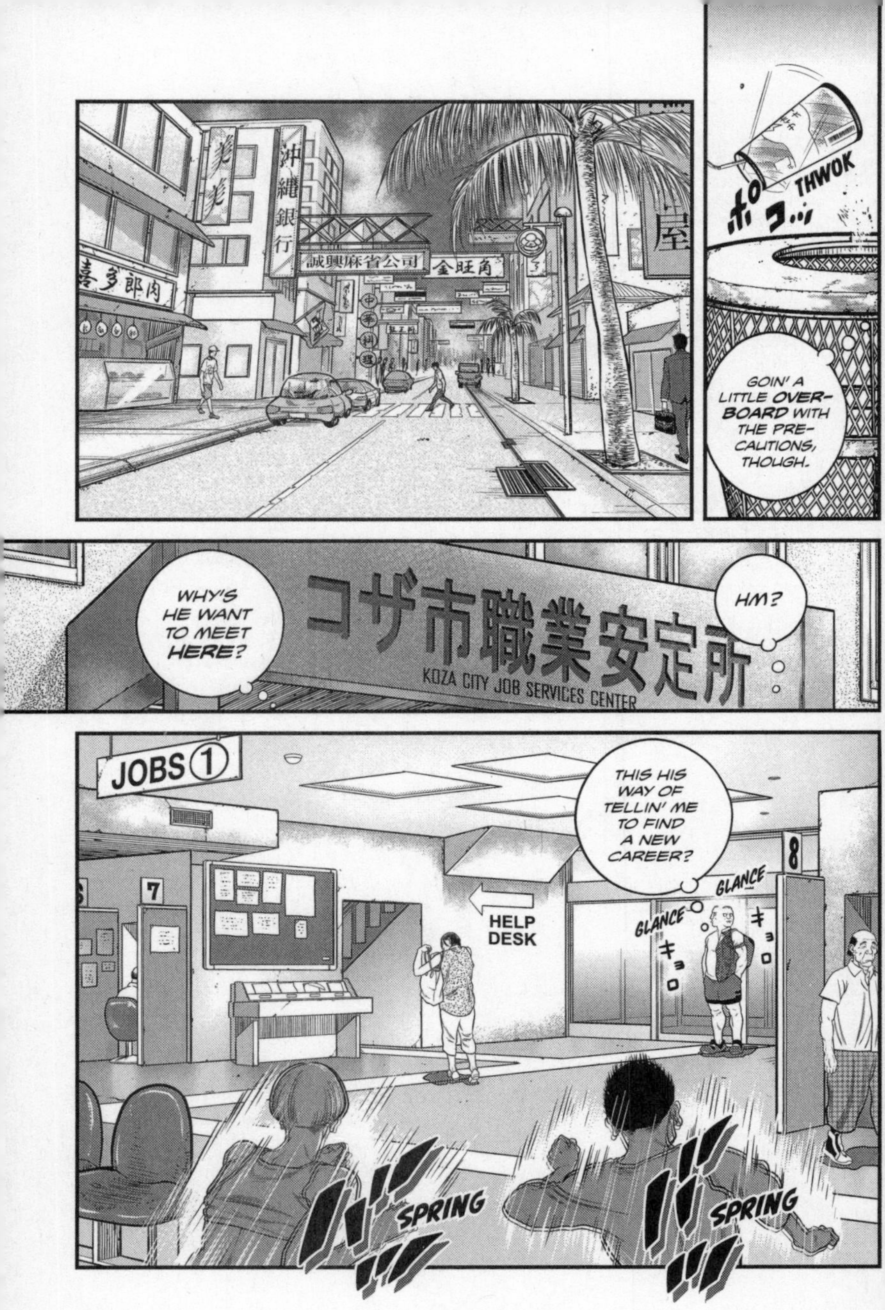

ホコッ
THWOK
GOIN' A LITTLE OVER-BOARD WITH THE PRE-CAUTIONS, THOUGH.
HM?
コザ市職業安定所
KOZA CITY JOB SERVICES CENTER
WHY'S HE WANT TO MEET HERE?
8
THIS HIS WAY OF TELLIN' ME TO FIND A NEW CAREER?
GLANCE
キョロ
GLANCE
キョロ
HELP DESK
JOBS ①
7
SPRING
SPRING

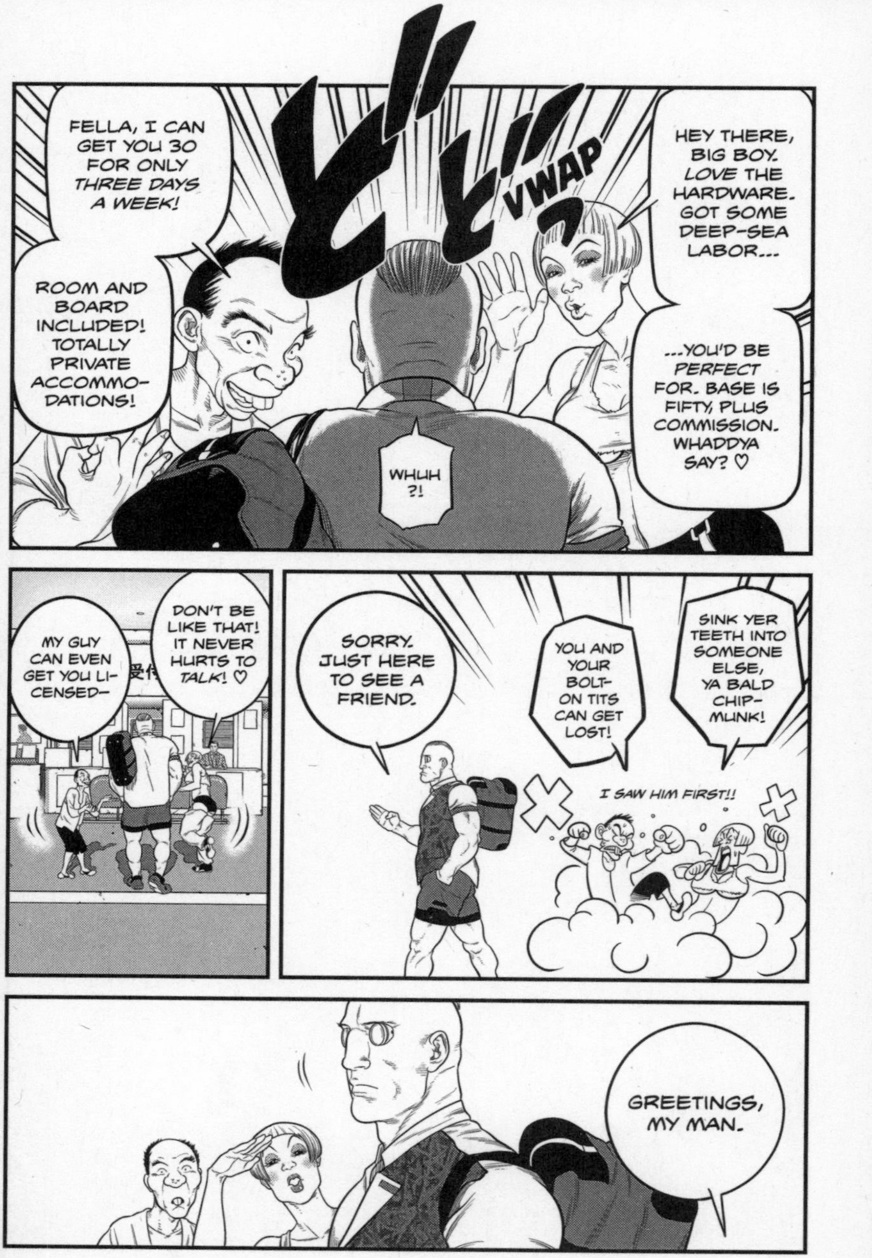
HEY THERE, BIG BOY. LOVE THE HARDWARE. GOT SOME DEEP-SEA LABOR...
...YOU'D BE PERFECT FOR. BASE IS FIFTY, PLUS COMMISSION. WHADDYA SAY? ♡
VWAP
FELLA, I CAN GET YOU 30 FOR ONLY THREE DAYS A WEEK!
ROOM AND BOARD INCLUDED! TOTALLY PRIVATE ACCOMMO-DATIONS!
WHUH ?!
SINK YER TEETH INTO SOMEONE ELSE, YA BALD CHIP-MUNK!
YOU AND YOUR BOLT-ON TITS CAN GET LOST!
SORRY. JUST HERE TO SEE A FRIEND.
I SAW HIM FIRST!!
DON'T BE LIKE THAT! IT NEVER HURTS TO TALK! ♡
MY GUY CAN EVEN GET YOU LI-CENSED-
GREETINGS, MY MAN.

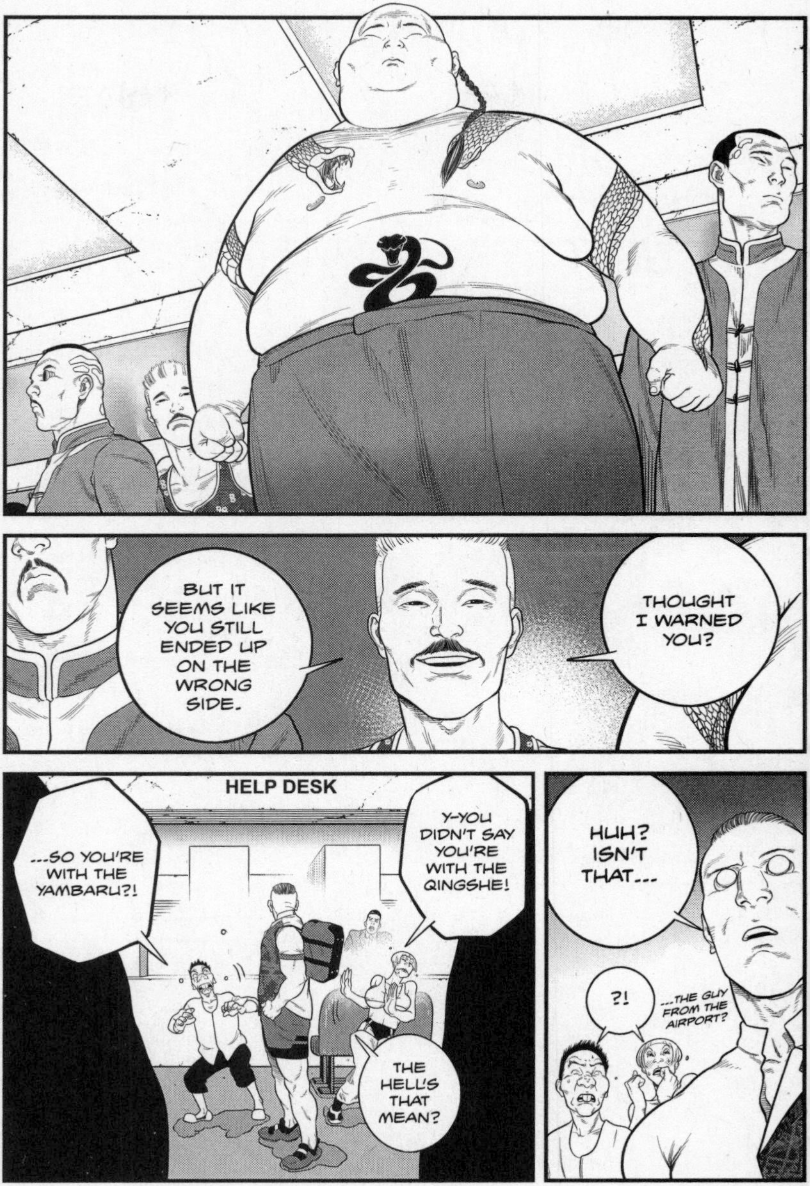
THOUGHT I WARNED YOU?
BUT IT SEEMS LIKE YOU STILL ENDED UP ON THE WRONG SIDE.
HUH? ISN'T THAT...
...THE GUY FROM THE AIRPORT?
?!
HELP DESK
Y-YOU DIDN'T SAY YOU'RE WITH THE QINGSHE!
...SO YOU'RE WITH THE YAMBARU?!
THE HELL'S THAT MEAN?

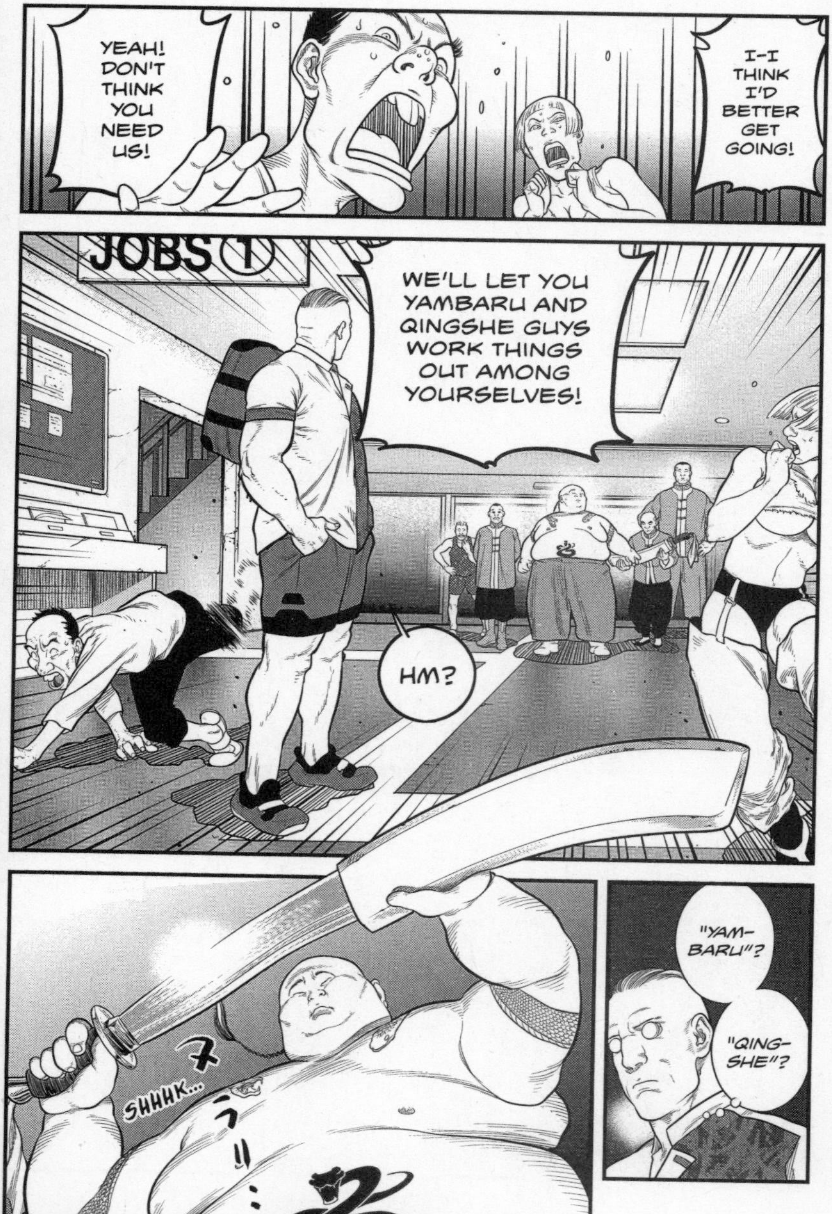
I-I THINK I'D BETTER GET GOING!
YEAH! DON'T THINK YOU NEED US!
JOBS ①
WE'LL LET YOU YAMBARU AND QINGSHE GUYS WORK THINGS OUT AMONG YOURSELVES!
HM?
"YAM-BARU"?
"QING-SHE"?
SHHHK...

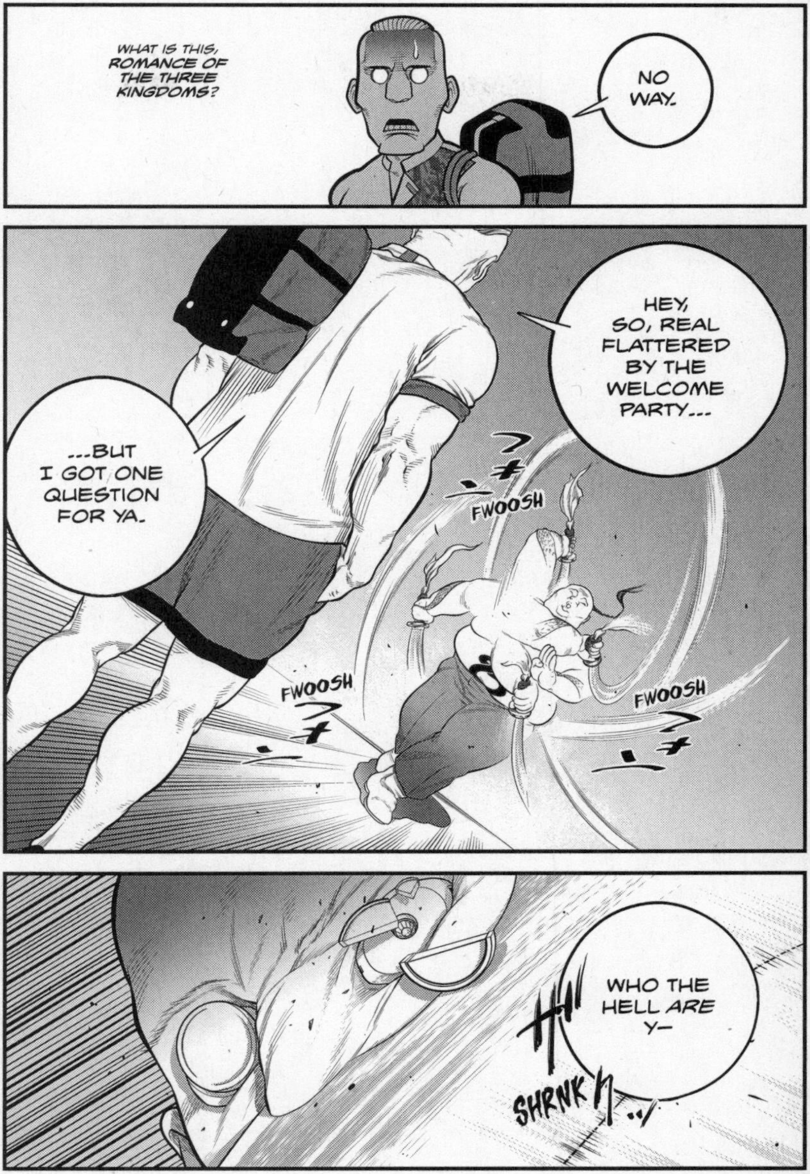
NO WAY.
WHAT IS THIS, ROMANCE OF THE THREE KINGDOMS?
HEY, SO, REAL FLATTERED BY THE WELCOME PARTY...
...BUT I GOT ONE QUESTION FOR YA.
FWOOSH
FWOOSH
FWOOSH
WHO THE HELL ARE Y—
SHRNK

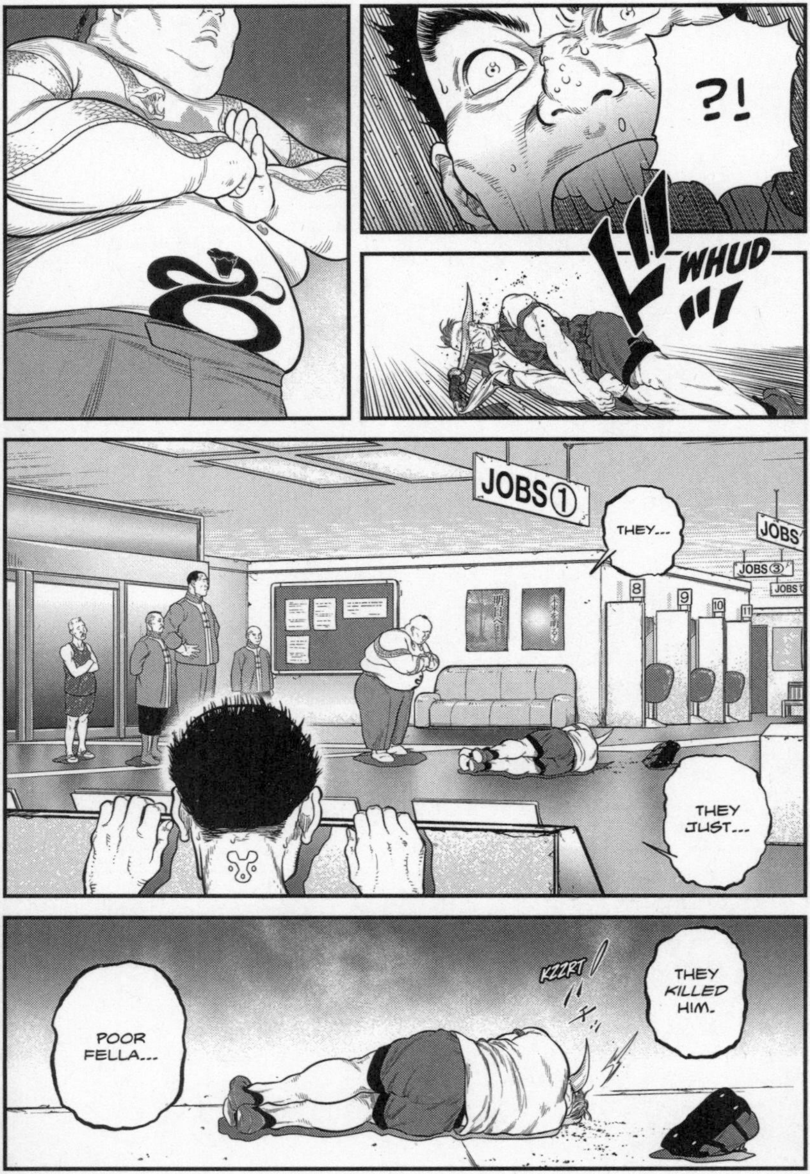
?!
WHUD
JOBS ①
THEY...
JOBS
JOBS ③
THEY JUST...
THEY KILLED HIM.
KZZRT
POOR FELLA...

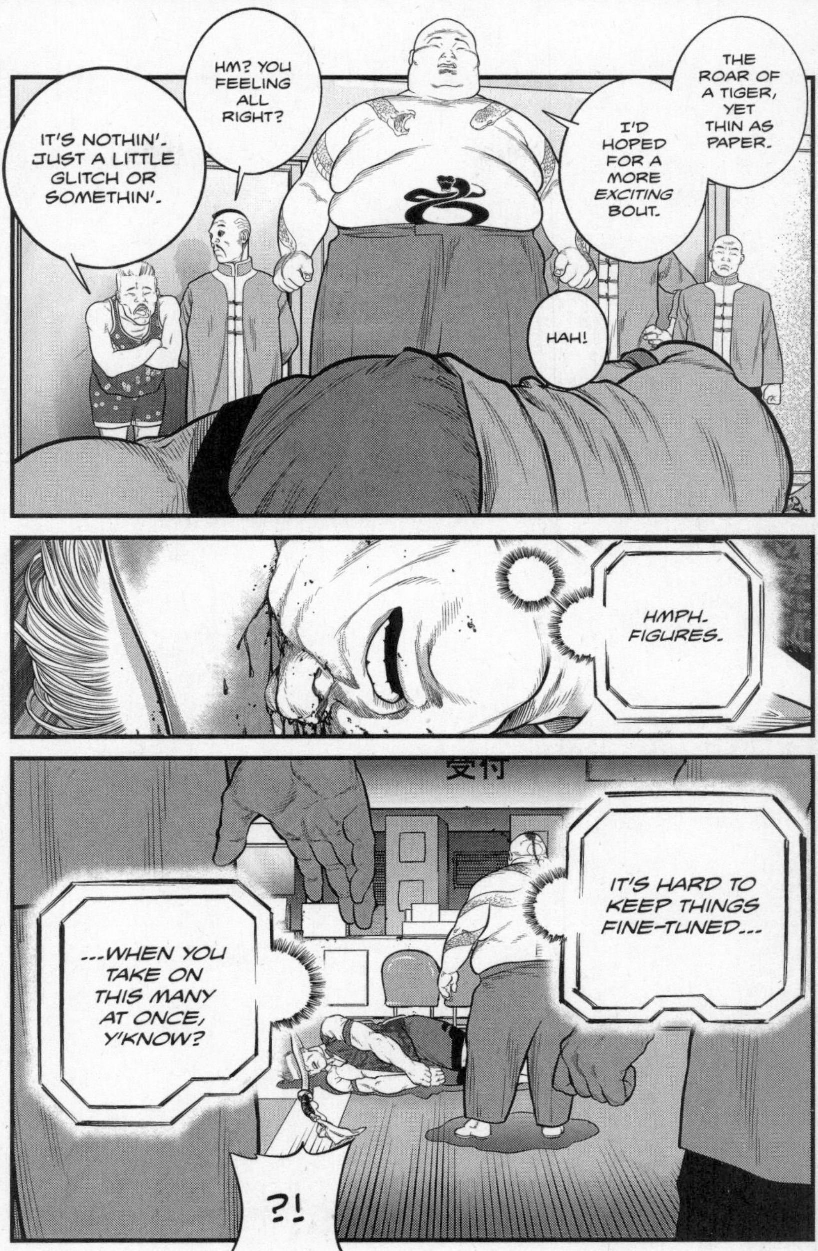
THE ROAR OF A TIGER, YET THIN AS PAPER.
I'D HOPED FOR A MORE EXCITING BOUT.
HAH!
HM? YOU FEELING ALL RIGHT?
IT'S NOTHIN'. JUST A LITTLE GLITCH OR SOMETHIN'.
HMPH. FIGURES.
受付
IT'S HARD TO KEEP THINGS FINE-TUNED...
...WHEN YOU TAKE ON THIS MANY AT ONCE, Y'KNOW?
?!

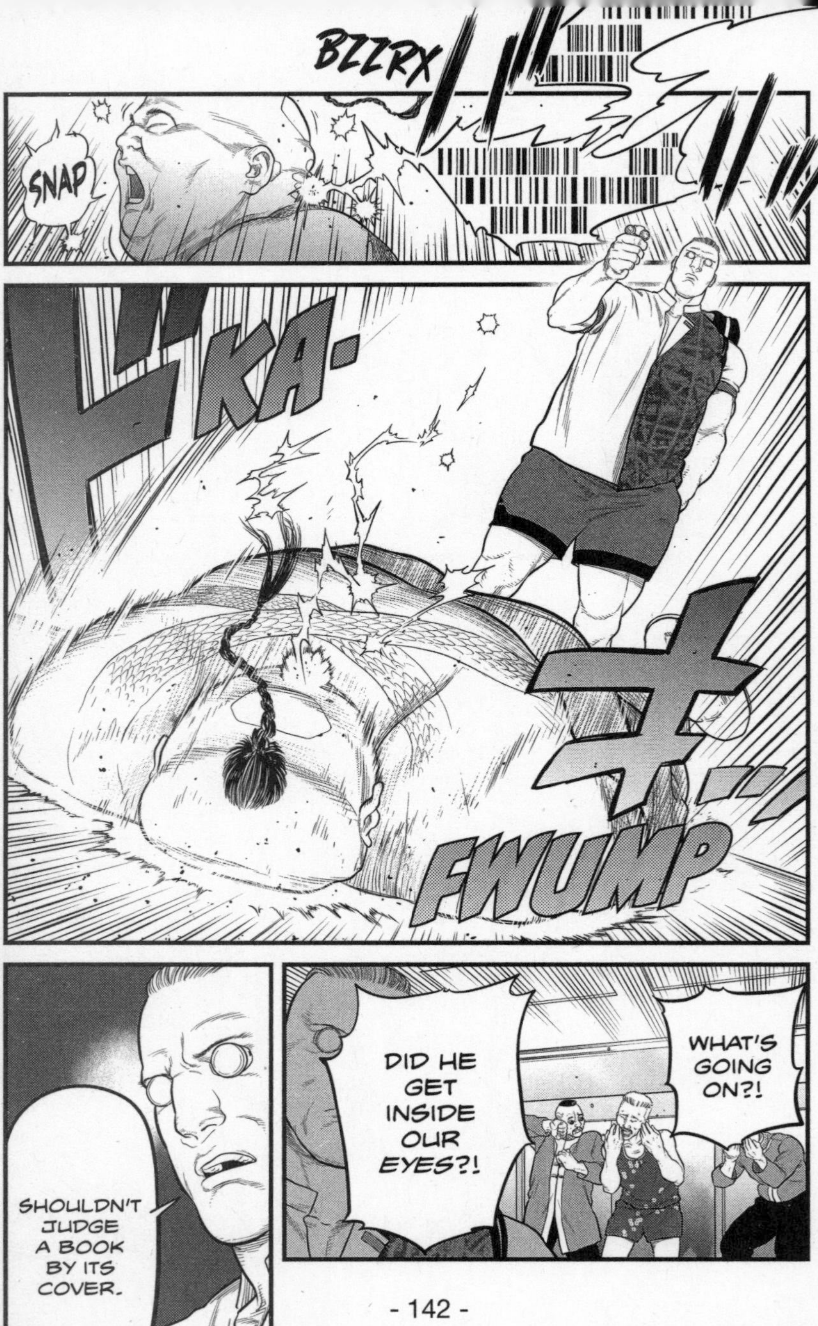
BZZRX
SNAP
KA-
FWUMP
WHAT'S GOING ON?!
DID HE GET INSIDE OUR EYES?!
SHOULDN'T JUDGE A BOOK BY ITS COVER.

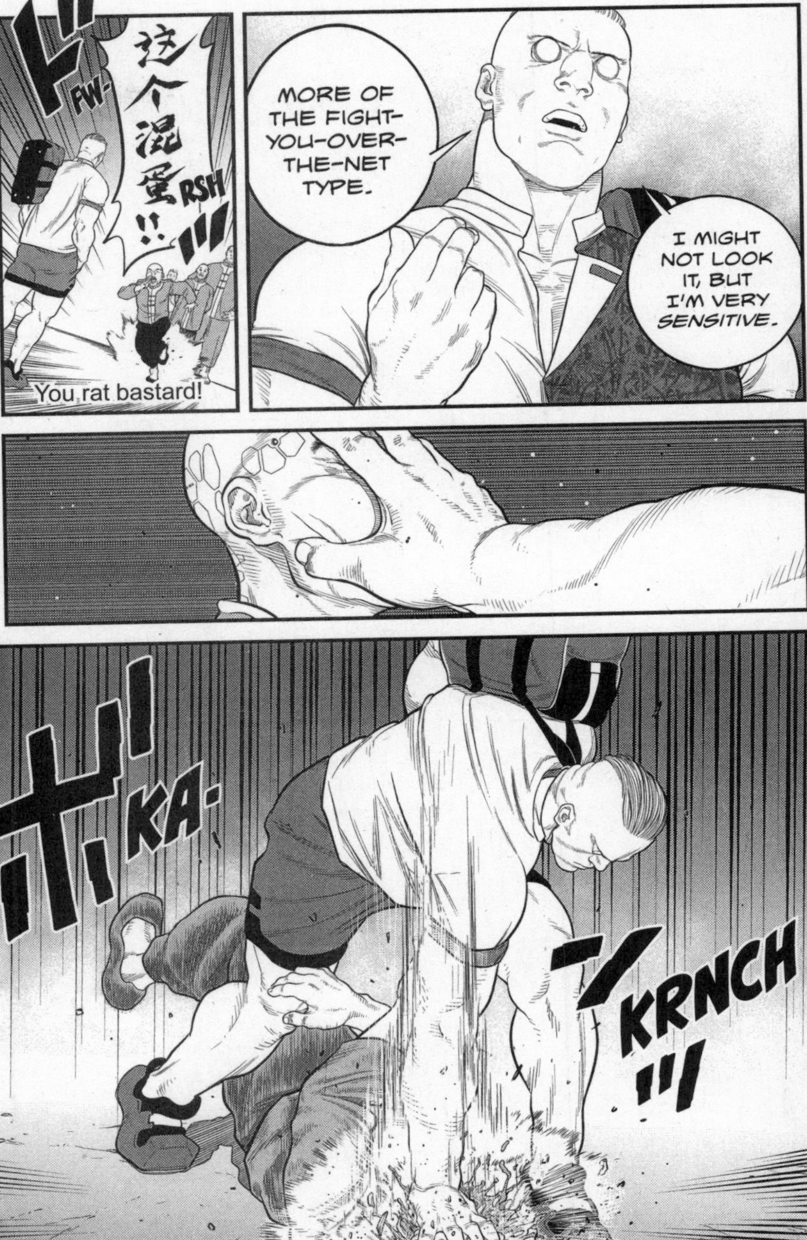

MORE OF THE FIGHT-YOU-OVER-THE-NET TYPE.
I MIGHT NOT LOOK IT, BUT I'M VERY SENSITIVE.
FW-
RSH!!!
这个混蛋!!
You rat bastard!
KA-
KRNCH!!!

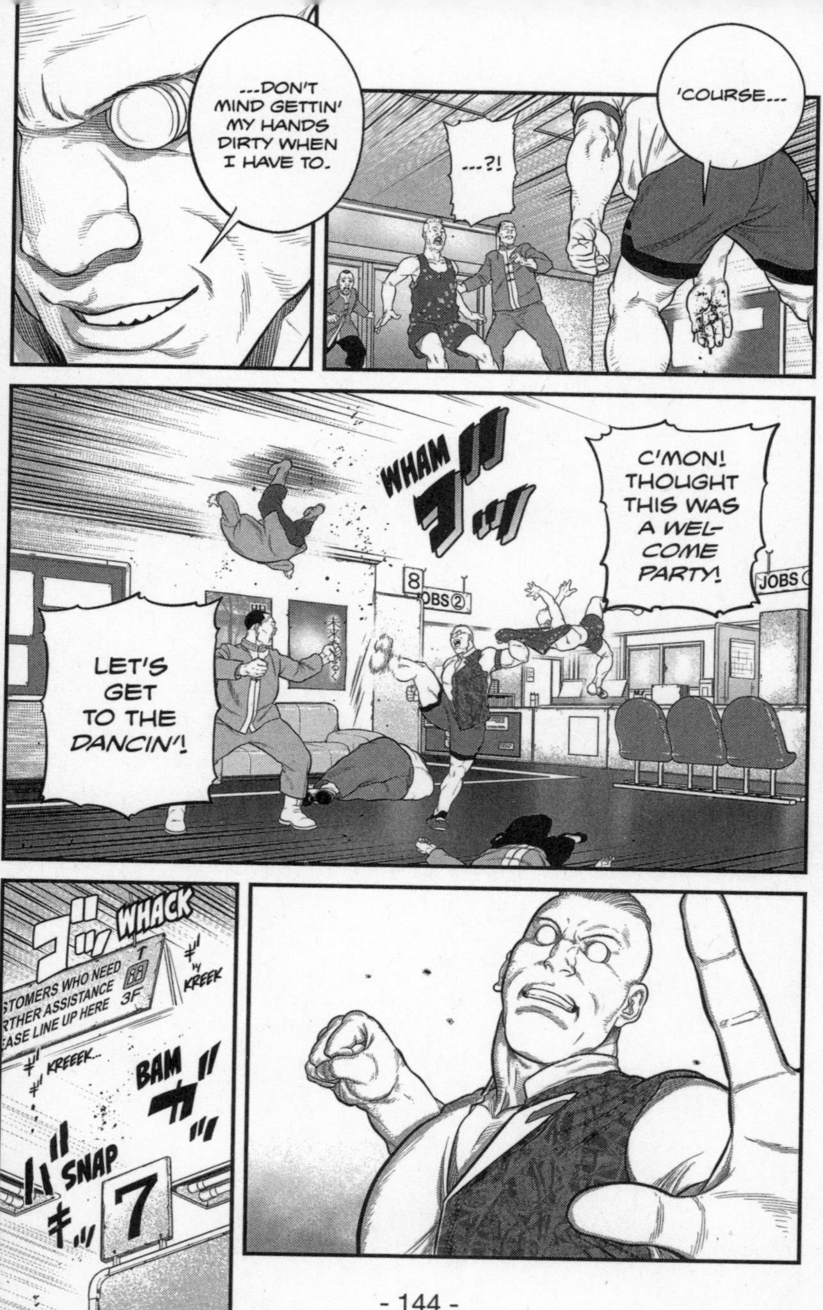
'COURSE...
...?!
...DON'T MIND GETTIN' MY HANDS DIRTY WHEN I HAVE TO.
WHAM
C'MON! THOUGHT THIS WAS A WEL-COME PARTY!
8
JOBS ②
JOBS
LET'S GET TO THE DANCIN'!
WHACK
STOMERS WHO NEED
RTHER ASSISTANCE
EASE LINE UP HERE
3F
KREEK
KREEEK...
BAM
SNAP
7

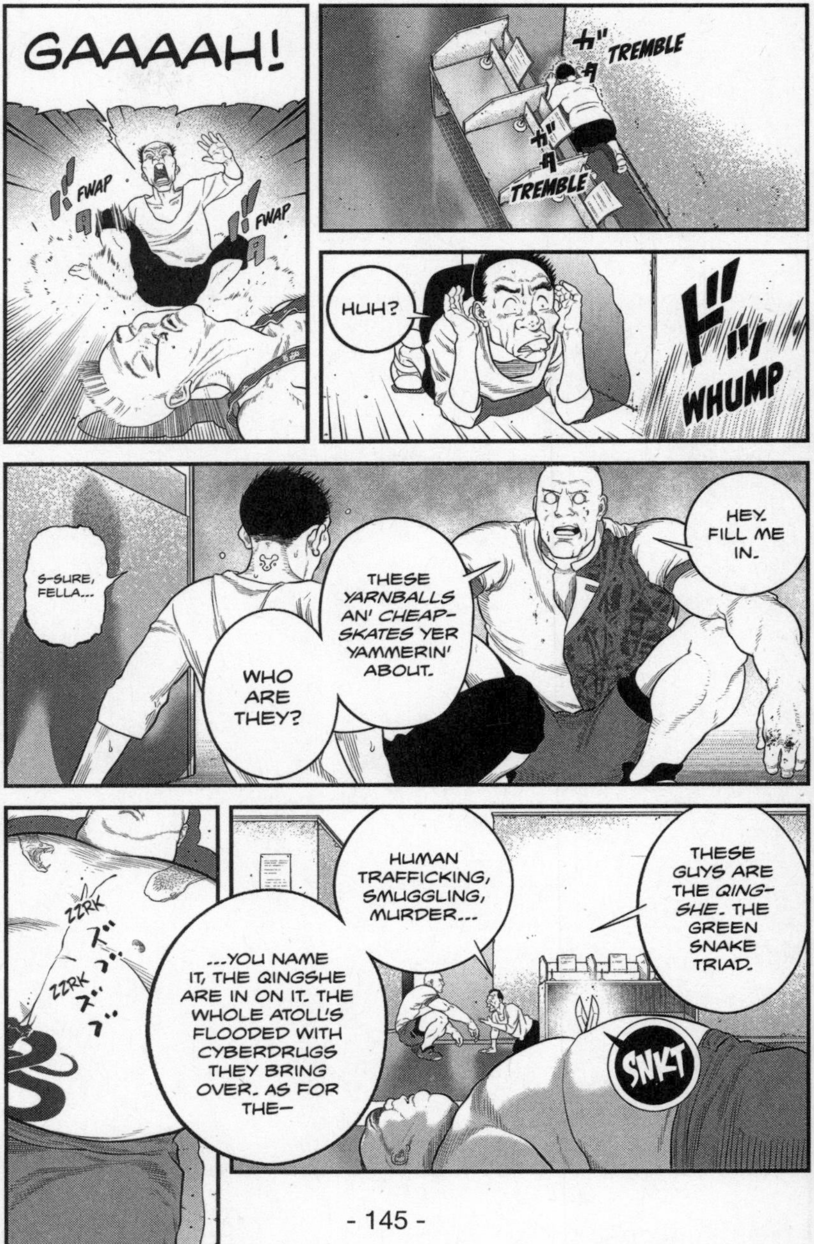
ガタ TREMBLE
ガタ TREMBLE
HUH?
ドッ WHUMP
GAAAAH!
FWAP
FWAP
HEY. FILL ME IN.
THESE YARNBALLS AN' CHEAP-SKATES YER YAMMERIN' ABOUT.
WHO ARE THEY?
S-SURE, FELLA...
THESE GUYS ARE THE QING-SHE. THE GREEN SNAKE TRIAD.
HUMAN TRAFFICKING, SMUGGLING, MURDER...
...YOU NAME IT, THE QINGSHE ARE IN ON IT. THE WHOLE ATOLL'S FLOODED WITH CYBERDRUGS THEY BRING OVER. AS FOR THE—
SNKT
ZZRK
ZZRK

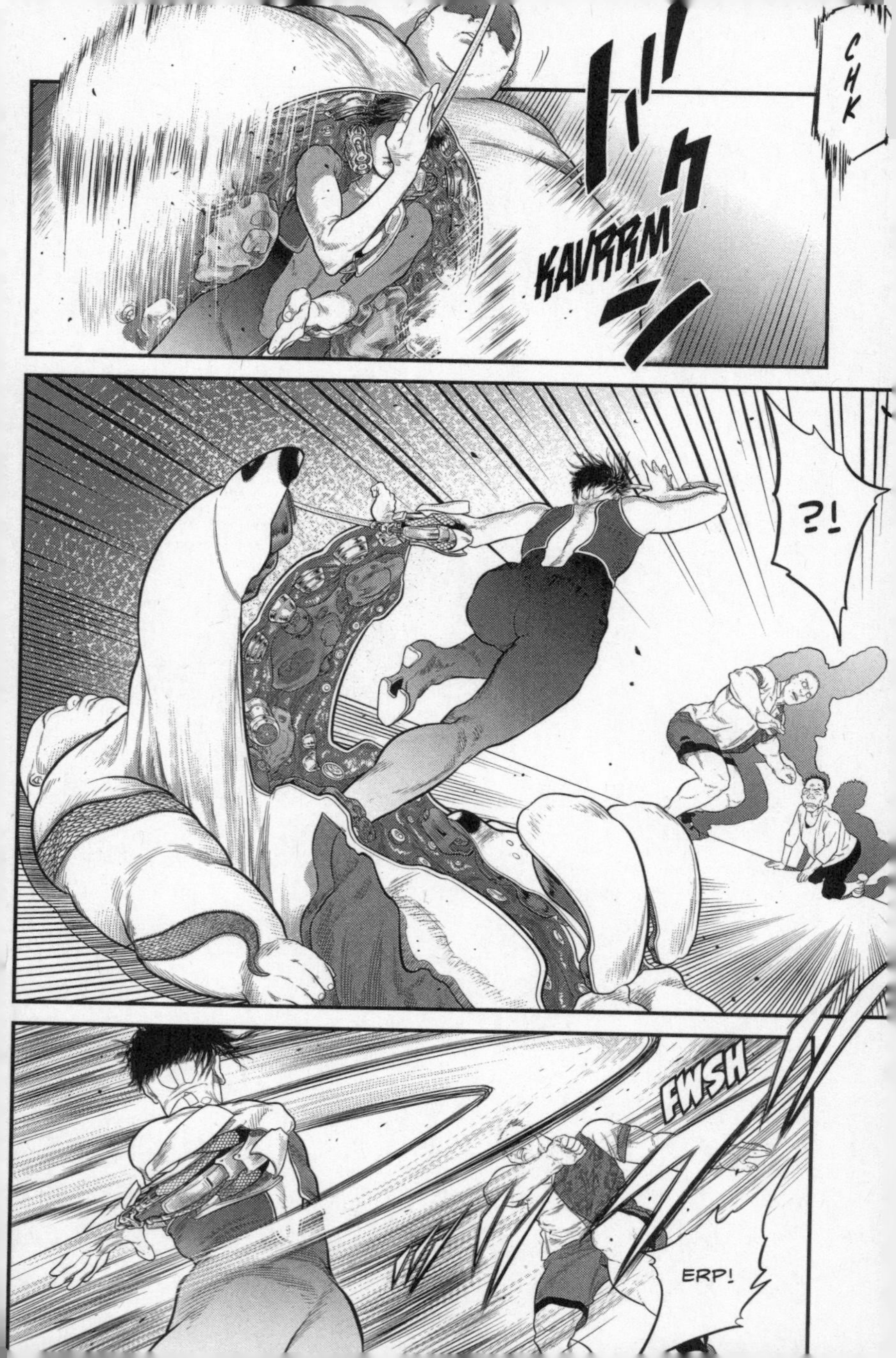
CHK
KAVRRM
?!
FWSH
ERP!

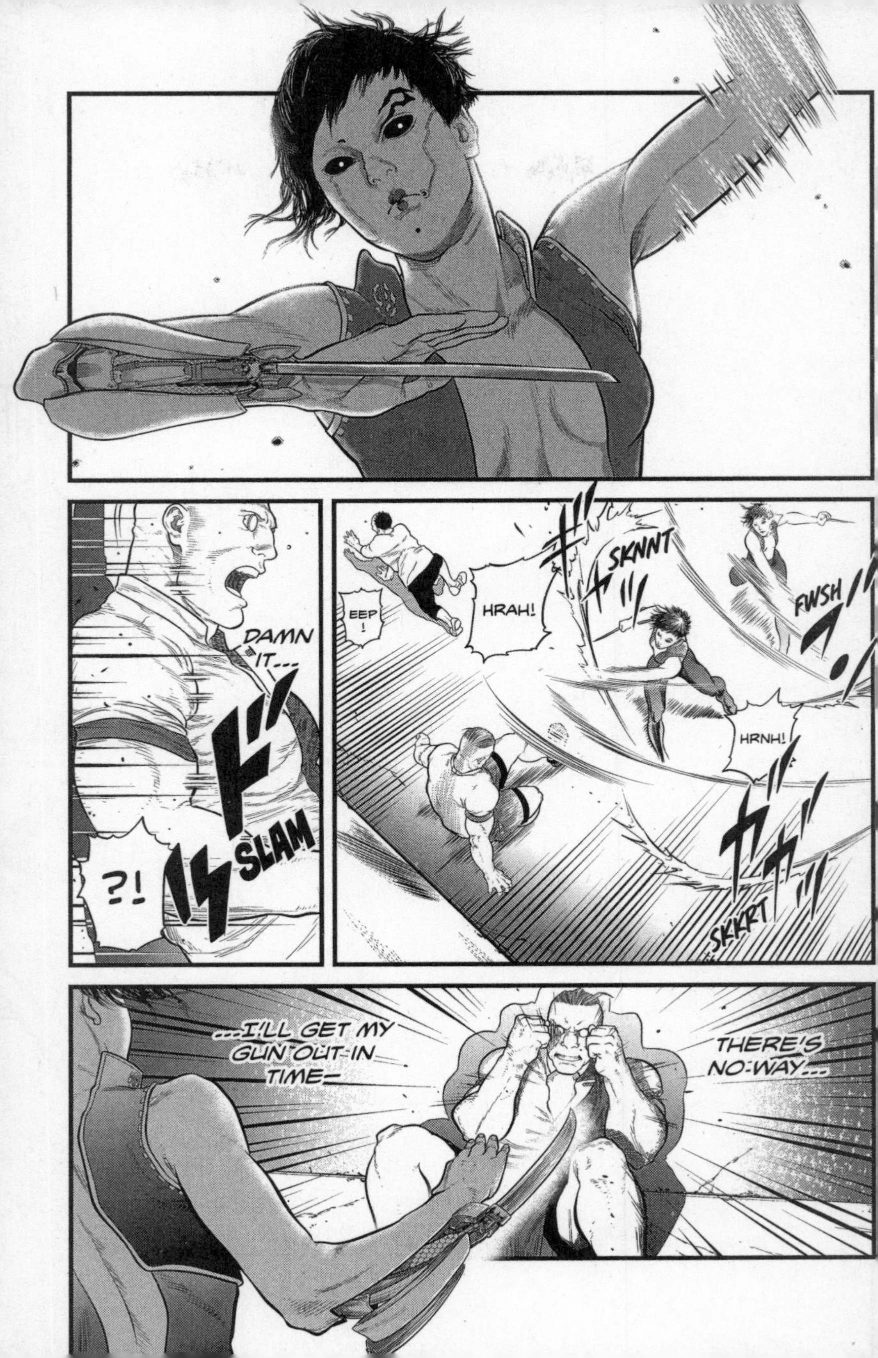
FWSH
SKNNT
HRAH!
EEP!
HRNH!
SKKRT
DAMN IT...
SLAM
?!
THERE'S NO WAY...
...I'LL GET MY GUN OUT IN TIME—

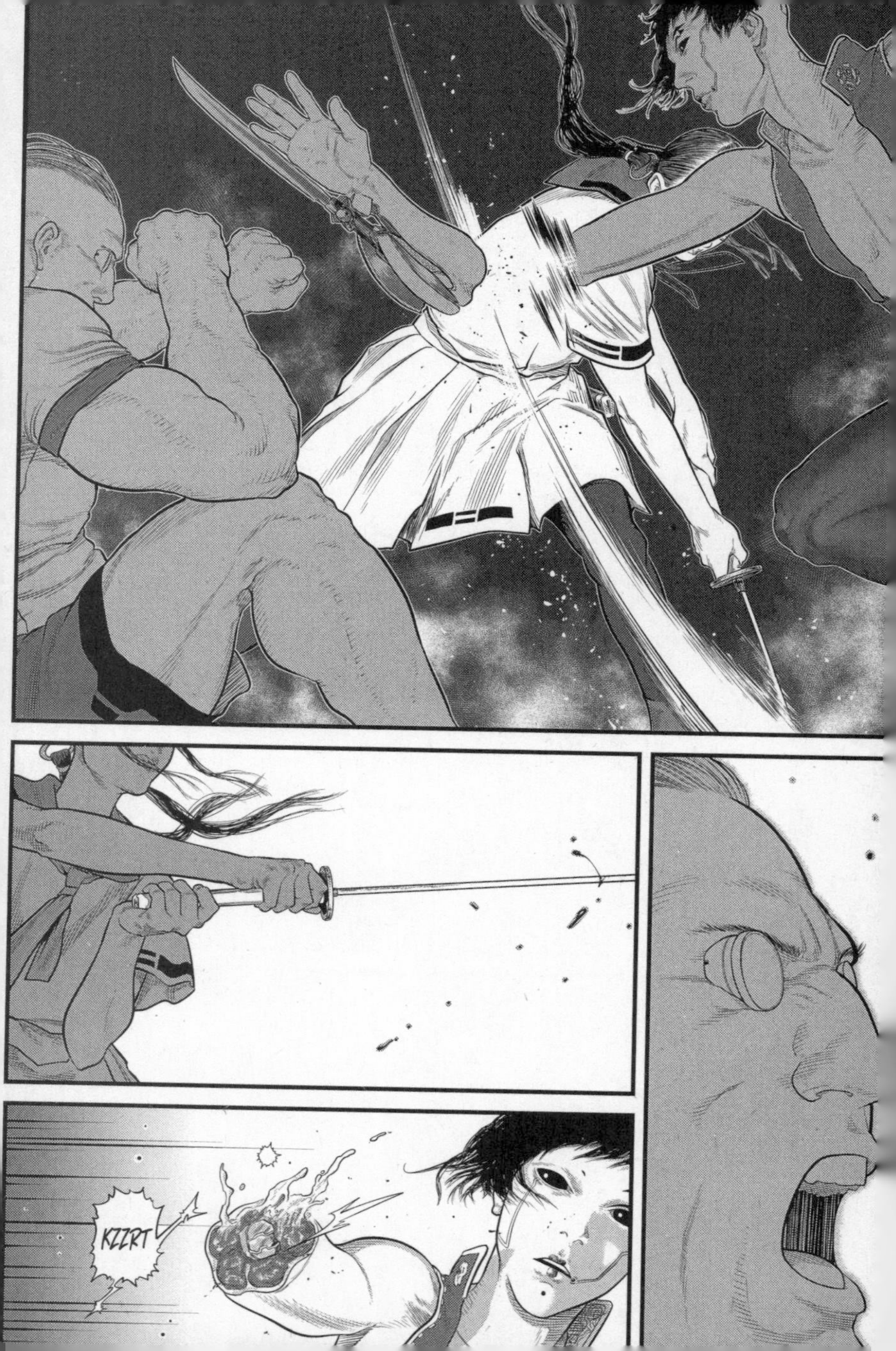
KZZRT

WHOMP

FWISH

目你

You little—

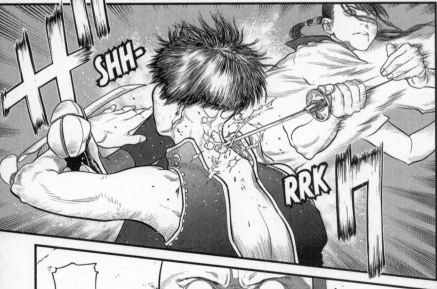

SHH-

RRK

----!!

FW-

UMP

---!

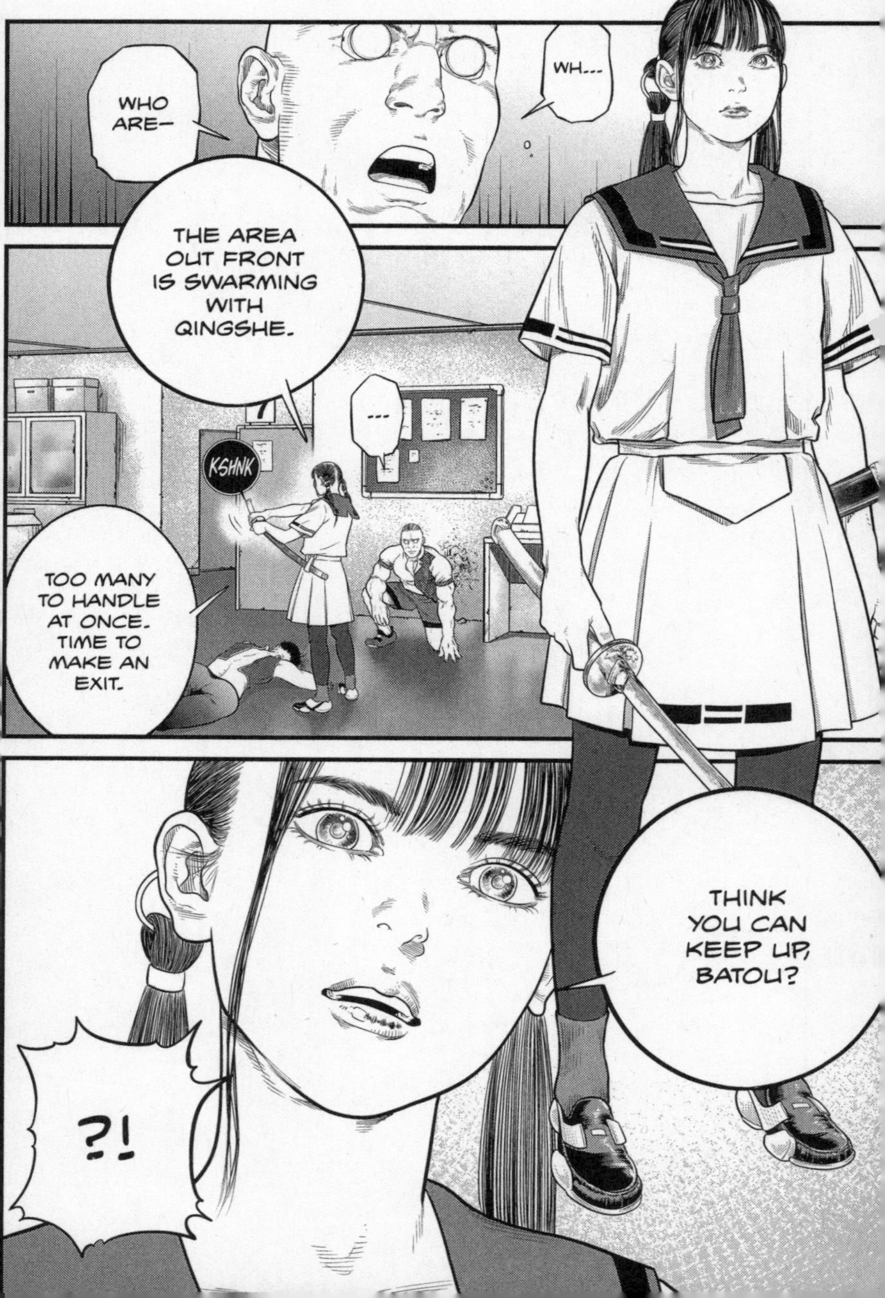

WH...
WHO ARE—
THE AREA OUT FRONT IS SWARMING WITH QINGSHE.
...
KSHNK
TOO MANY TO HANDLE AT ONCE. TIME TO MAKE AN EXIT.
THINK YOU CAN KEEP UP, BATOU?
?!

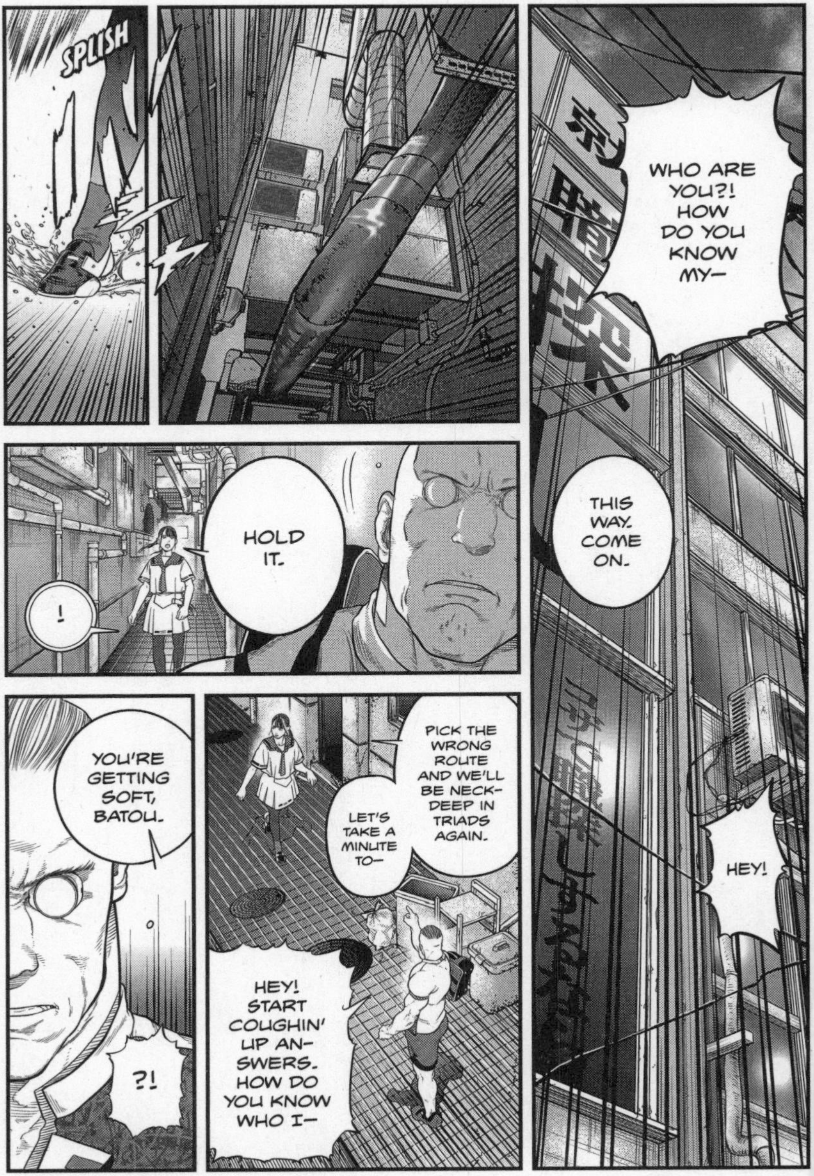
WHO ARE YOU?! HOW DO YOU KNOW MY—
THIS WAY. COME ON.
HEY!
SPLISH
HOLD IT.
!
PICK THE WRONG ROUTE AND WE'LL BE NECK-DEEP IN TRIADS AGAIN.
LET'S TAKE A MINUTE TO—
HEY! START COUGHIN' UP AN-SWERS. HOW DO YOU KNOW WHO I—
YOU'RE GETTING SOFT, BATOU.
?!

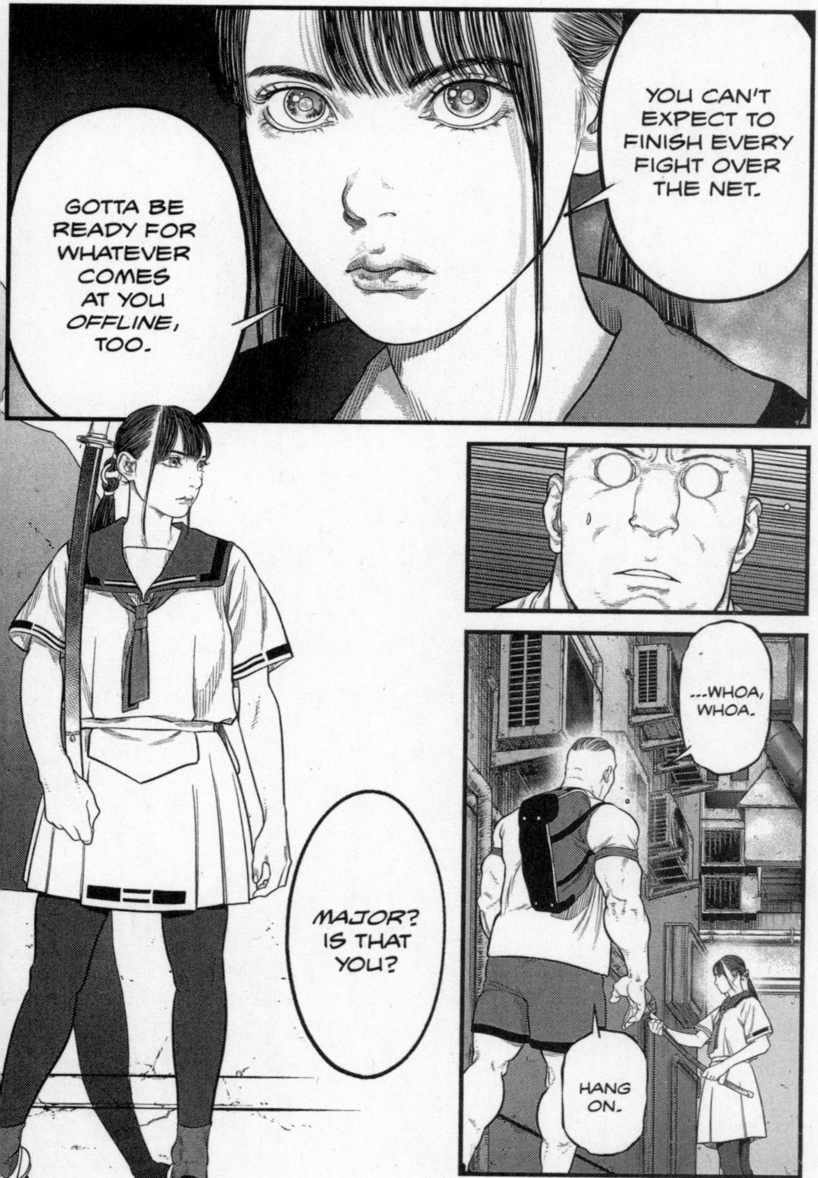
YOU CAN'T EXPECT TO FINISH EVERY FIGHT OVER THE NET.
GOTTA BE READY FOR WHATEVER COMES AT YOU *OFFLINE*, TOO.
...WHOA, WHOA.
HANG ON.
MAJOR? IS THAT YOU?

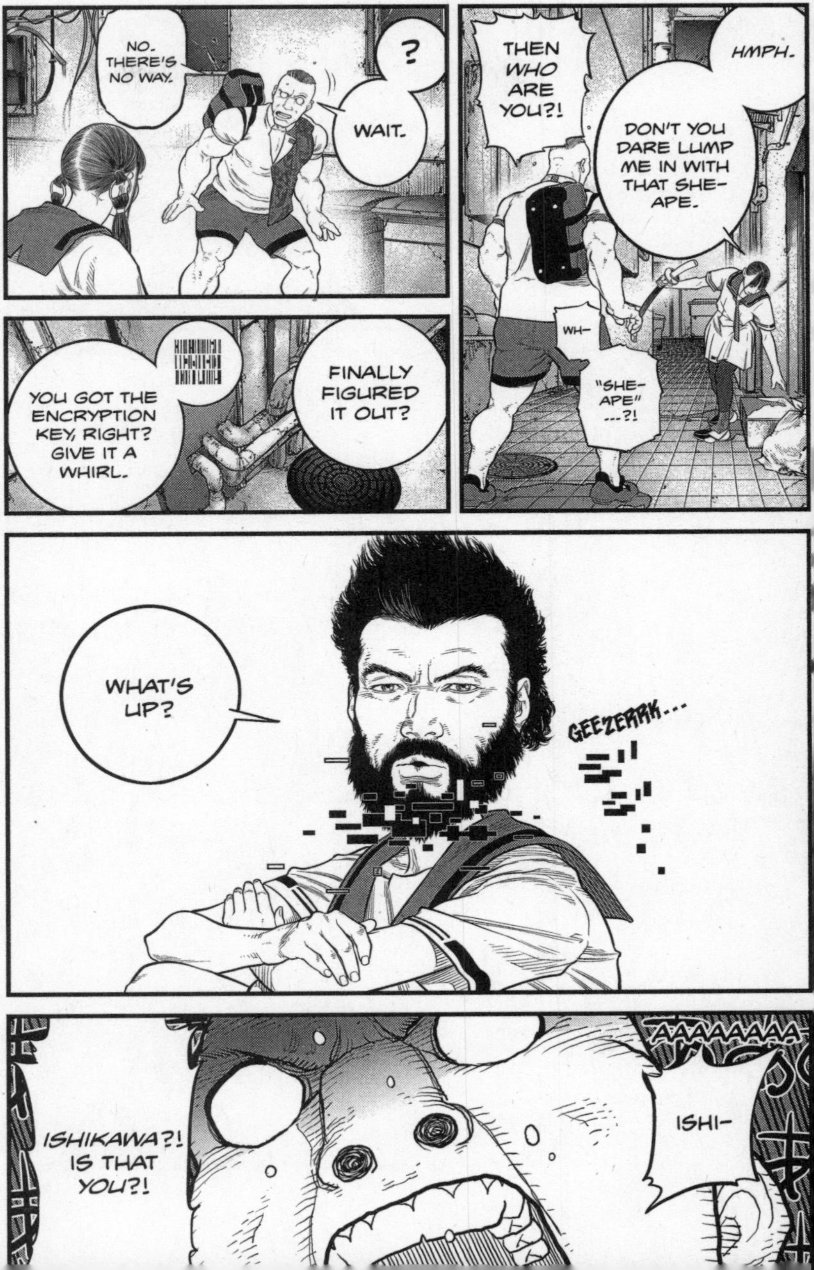
HMPH.
THEN WHO ARE YOU?!
DON'T YOU DARE LUMP ME IN WITH THAT SHE-APE.
WH-
"SHE-APE" ...?!
?
NO. THERE'S NO WAY.
WAIT.
FINALLY FIGURED IT OUT?
YOU GOT THE ENCRYPTION KEY, RIGHT? GIVE IT A WHIRL.
GEEZERRK...
WHAT'S UP?
AAAAAAAA
ISHI-
ISHIKAWA?! IS THAT YOU?!

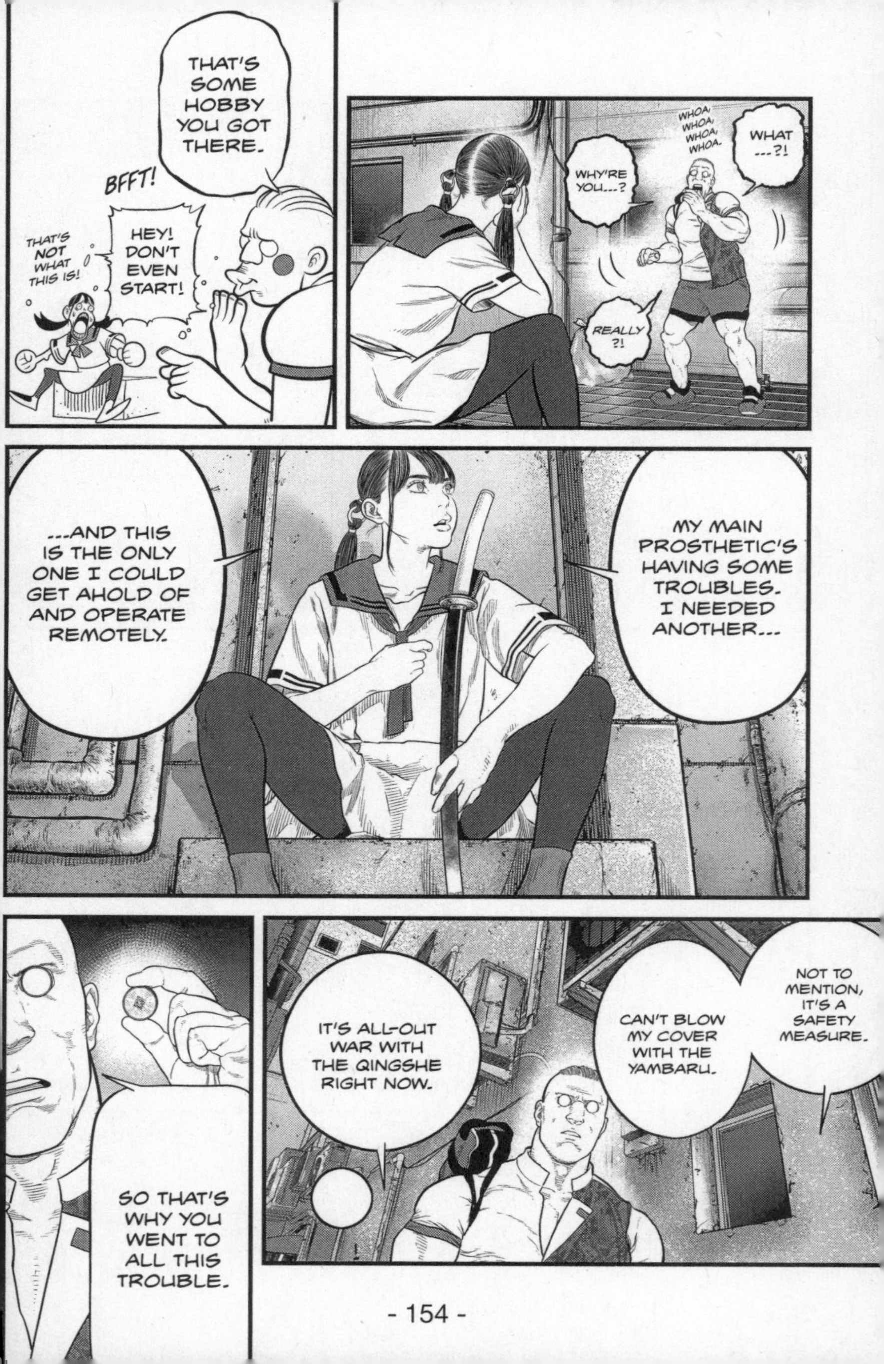
WHAT ---?!
WHOA, WHOA, WHOA, WHOA.
WHY'RE YOU---?
REALLY ?!
THAT'S SOME HOBBY YOU GOT THERE.
BFFT!
HEY! DON'T EVEN START!
THAT'S NOT WHAT THIS IS!
MY MAIN PROSTHETIC'S HAVING SOME TROUBLES. I NEEDED ANOTHER---
---AND THIS IS THE ONLY ONE I COULD GET AHOLD OF AND OPERATE REMOTELY.
NOT TO MENTION, IT'S A SAFETY MEASURE.
CAN'T BLOW MY COVER WITH THE YAMBARU.
IT'S ALL-OUT WAR WITH THE QINGSHE RIGHT NOW.
SO THAT'S WHY YOU WENT TO ALL THIS TROUBLE.

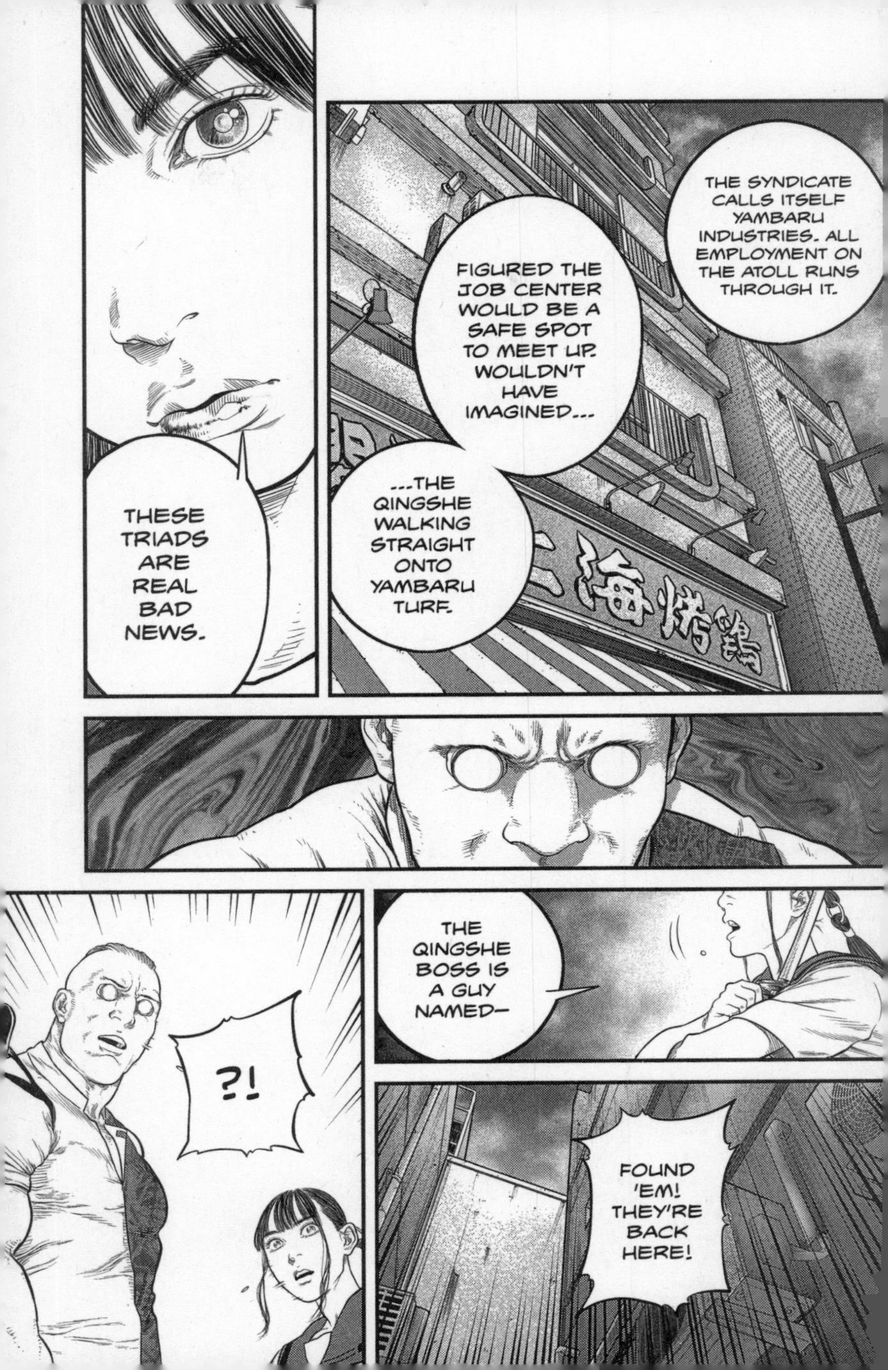
THE SYNDICATE CALLS ITSELF YAMBARU INDUSTRIES. ALL EMPLOYMENT ON THE ATOLL RUNS THROUGH IT.
FIGURED THE JOB CENTER WOULD BE A SAFE SPOT TO MEET UP. WOULDN'T HAVE IMAGINED...
...THE QINGSHE WALKING STRAIGHT ONTO YAMBARU TURF.
THESE TRIADS ARE REAL BAD NEWS.
THE QINGSHE BOSS IS A GUY NAMED—
FOUND 'EM! THEY'RE BACK HERE!
?!

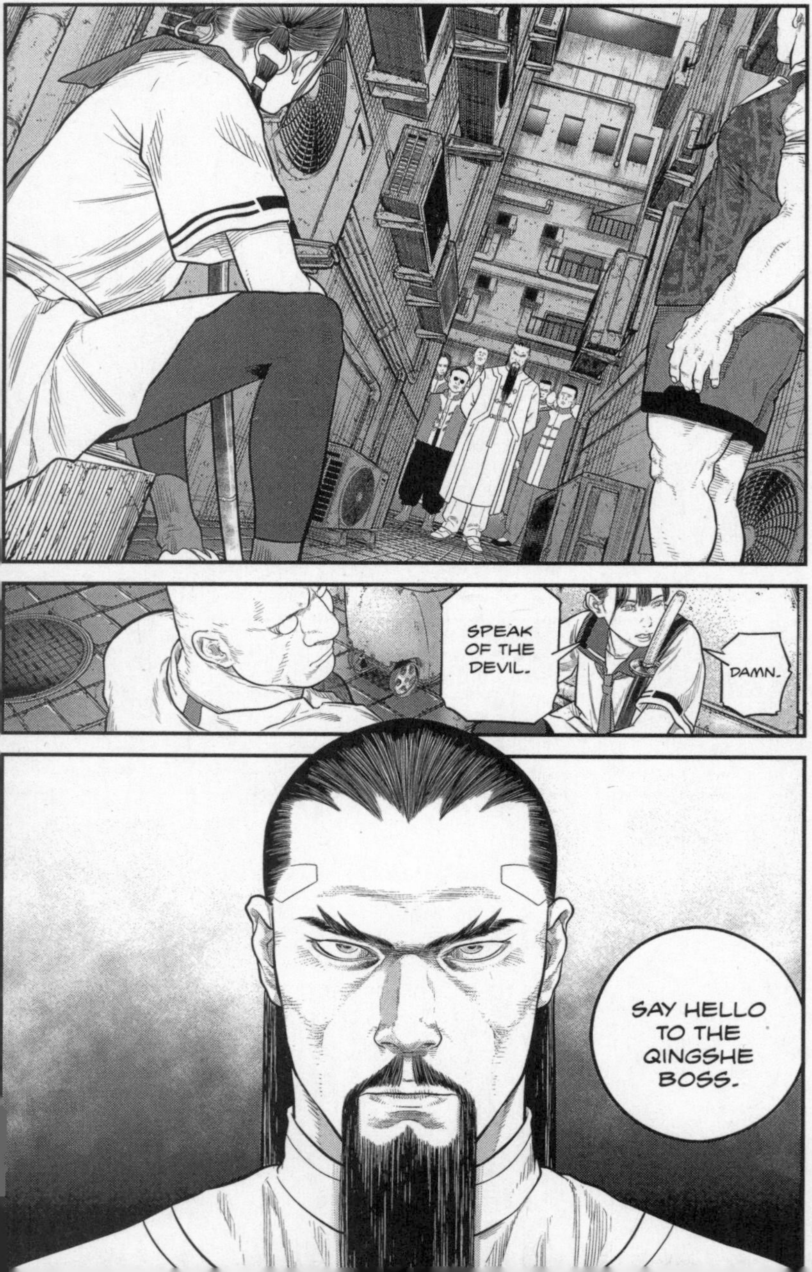
DAMN.
SPEAK OF THE DEVIL.
SAY HELLO TO THE QINGSHE BOSS.

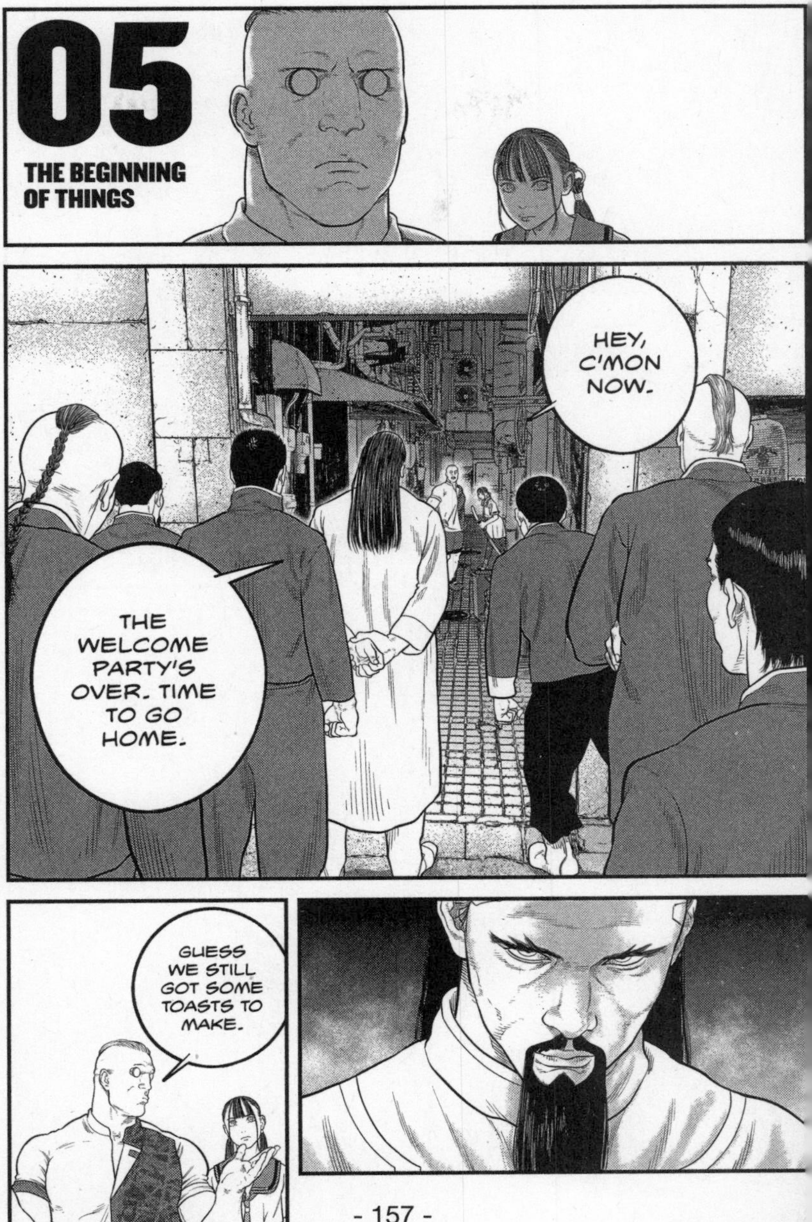
05
THE BEGINNING OF THINGS
HEY, C'MON NOW.
THE WELCOME PARTY'S OVER. TIME TO GO HOME.
GUESS WE STILL GOT SOME TOASTS TO MAKE.

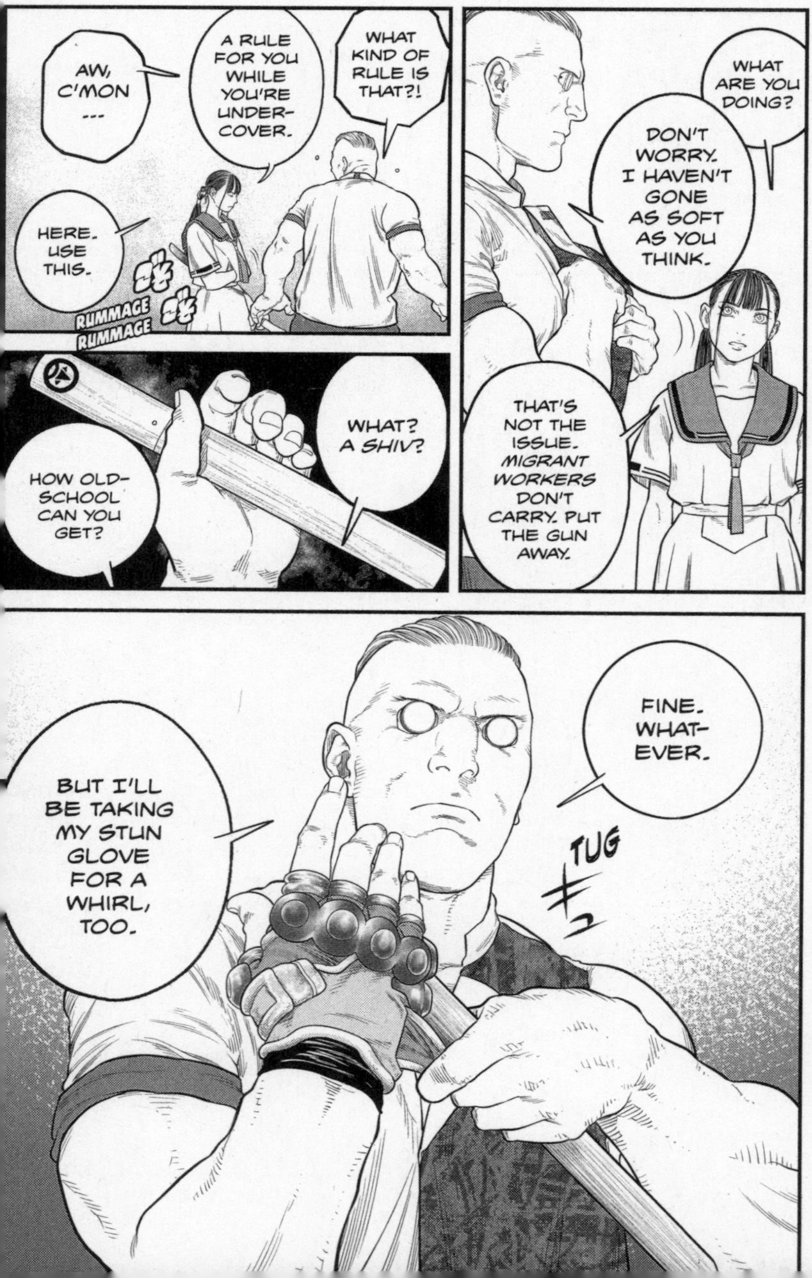
WHAT ARE YOU DOING?
DON'T WORRY. I HAVEN'T GONE AS SOFT AS YOU THINK.
THAT'S NOT THE ISSUE. *MIGRANT WORKERS* DON'T CARRY. PUT THE GUN AWAY.
WHAT KIND OF RULE IS THAT?!
A RULE FOR YOU WHILE YOU'RE UNDER-COVER.
AW, C'MON ---
HERE. USE THIS.
RUMMAGE RUMMAGE
WHAT? A *SHIV*?
HOW OLD-SCHOOL CAN YOU GET?
FINE. WHAT-EVER.
TUG
BUT I'LL BE TAKING MY STUN GLOVE FOR A WHIRL, TOO.

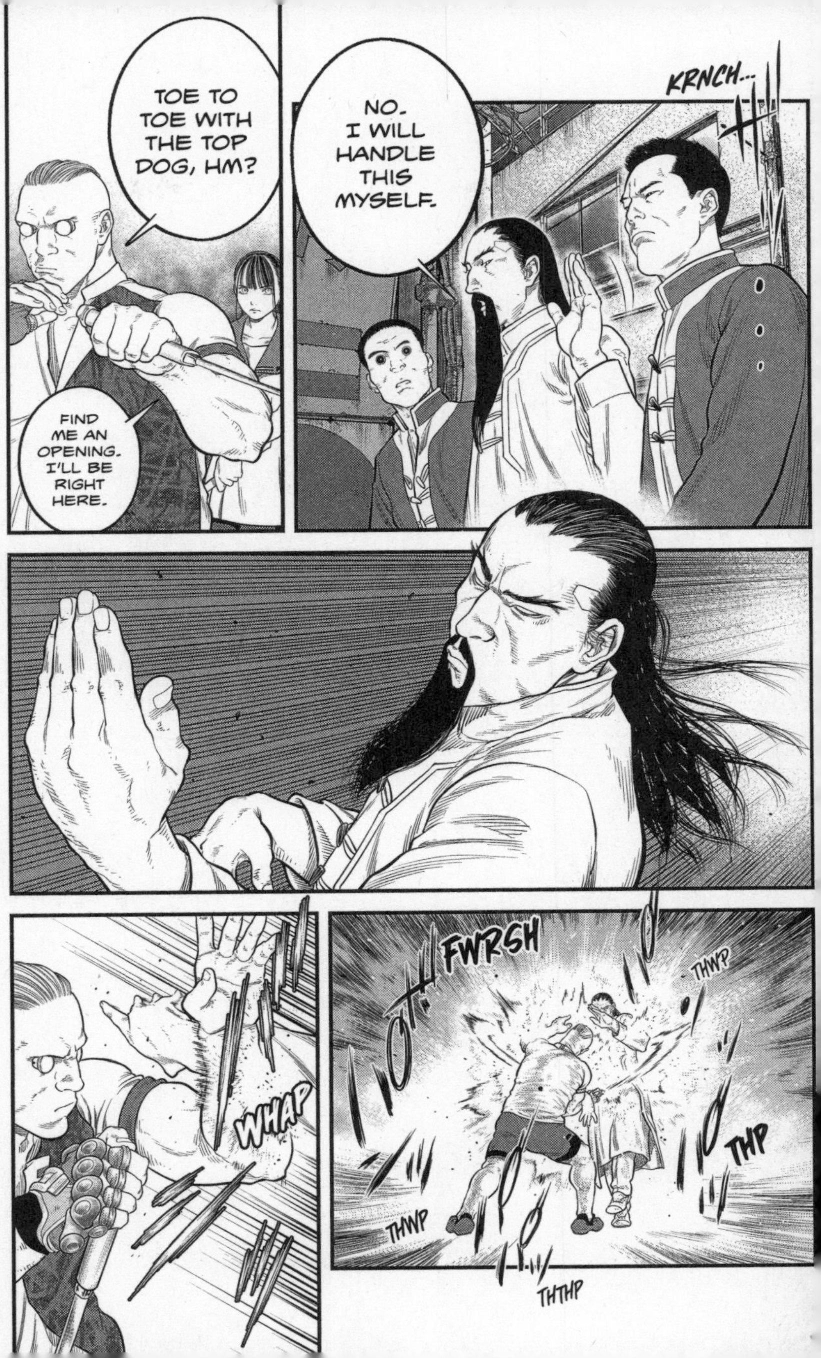
KRNCH...
NO. I WILL HANDLE THIS MYSELF.
TOE TO TOE WITH THE TOP DOG, HM?
FIND ME AN OPENING. I'LL BE RIGHT HERE.
FWRSH
THWP
THP
THWP
THTHP
WHAP

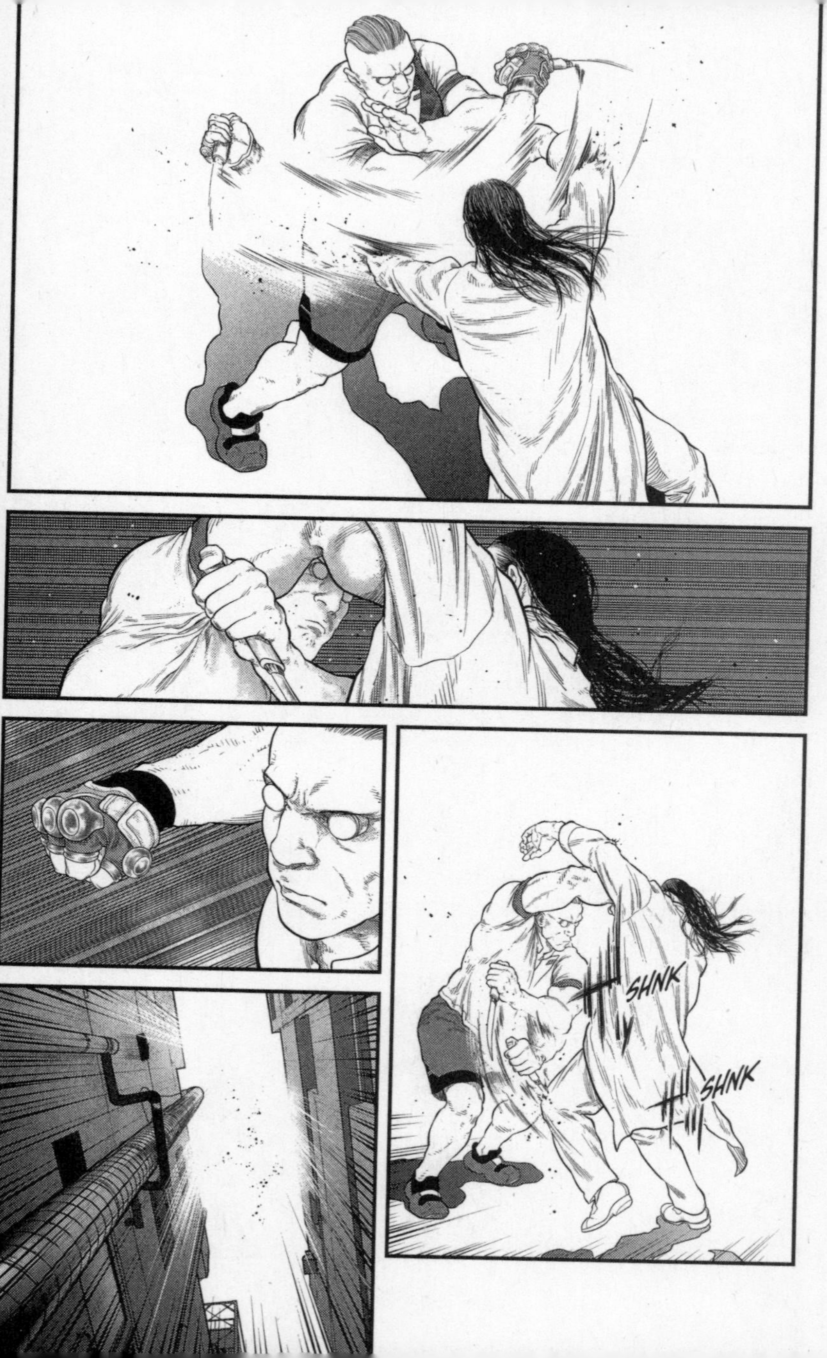
SHNK
SHNK

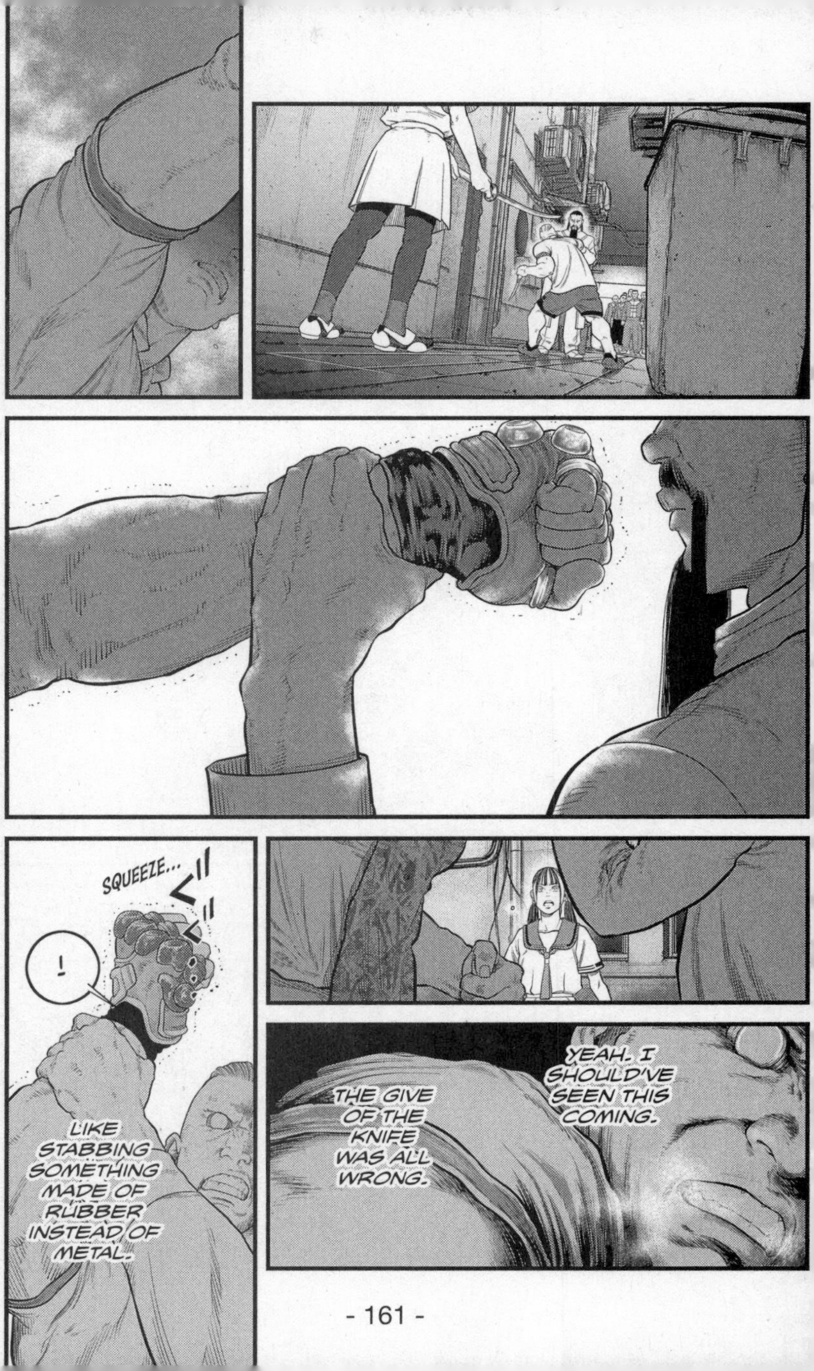
YEAH. I SHOULD'VE SEEN THIS COMING.
THE GIVE OF THE KNIFE WAS ALL WRONG.
SQUEEZE...
!
LIKE STABBING SOMETHING MADE OF RUBBER INSTEAD OF METAL.

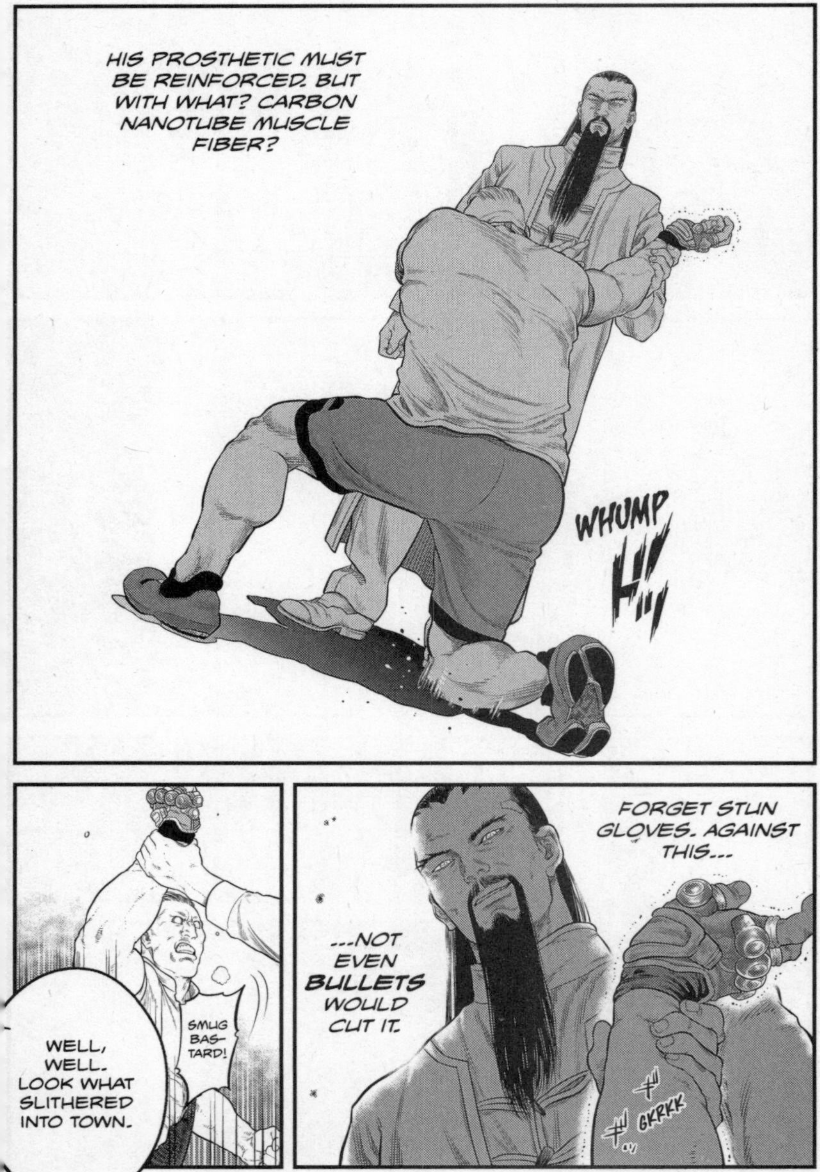
HIS PROSTHETIC MUST BE REINFORCED. BUT WITH WHAT? CARBON NANOTUBE MUSCLE FIBER?
WHUMP
FORGET STUN GLOVES. AGAINST THIS...
...NOT EVEN BULLETS WOULD CUT IT.
GKRKK
SMUG BASTARD!
WELL, WELL. LOOK WHAT SLITHERED INTO TOWN.

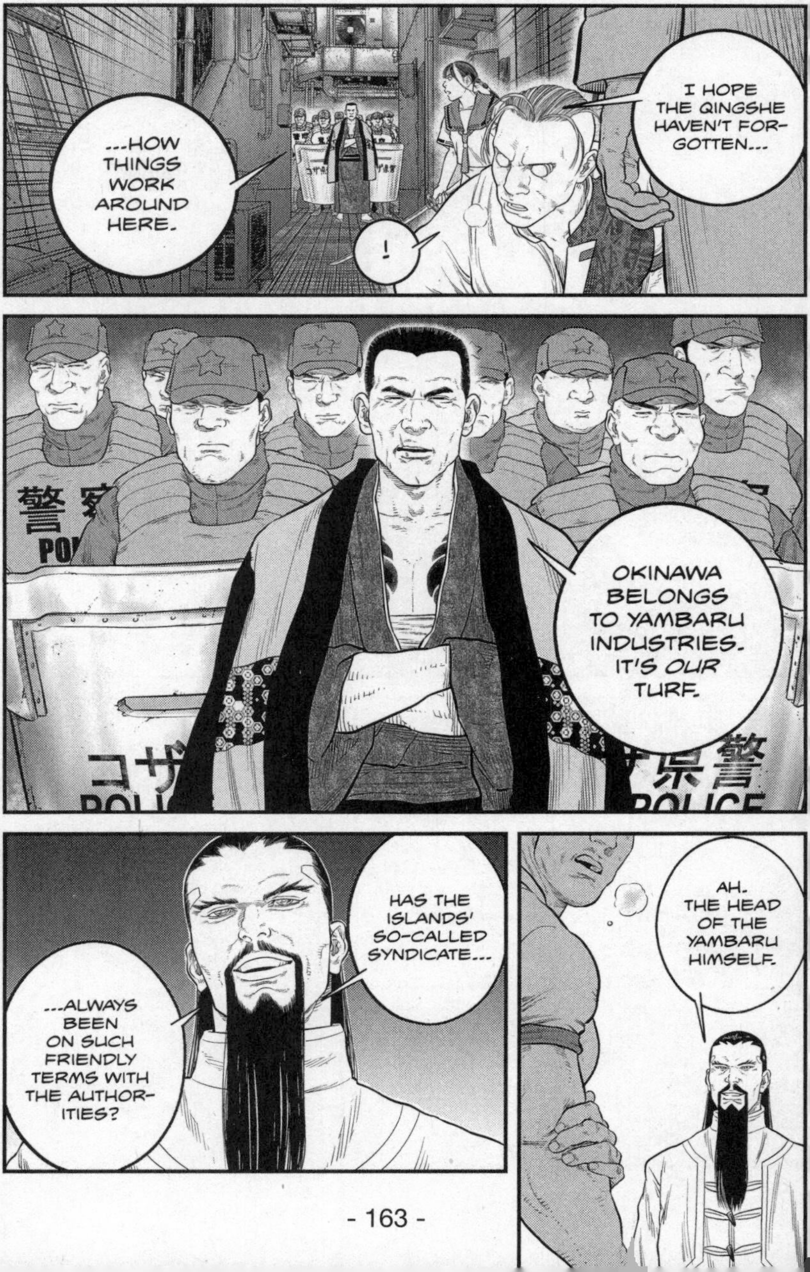
I HOPE THE QINGSHE HAVEN'T FORGOTTEN...
...HOW THINGS WORK AROUND HERE.
!
OKINAWA BELONGS TO YAMBARU INDUSTRIES. IT'S *OUR* TURF.
AH. THE HEAD OF THE YAMBARU HIMSELF.
HAS THE ISLANDS' SO-CALLED SYNDICATE...
...ALWAYS BEEN ON SUCH FRIENDLY TERMS WITH THE AUTHORITIES?

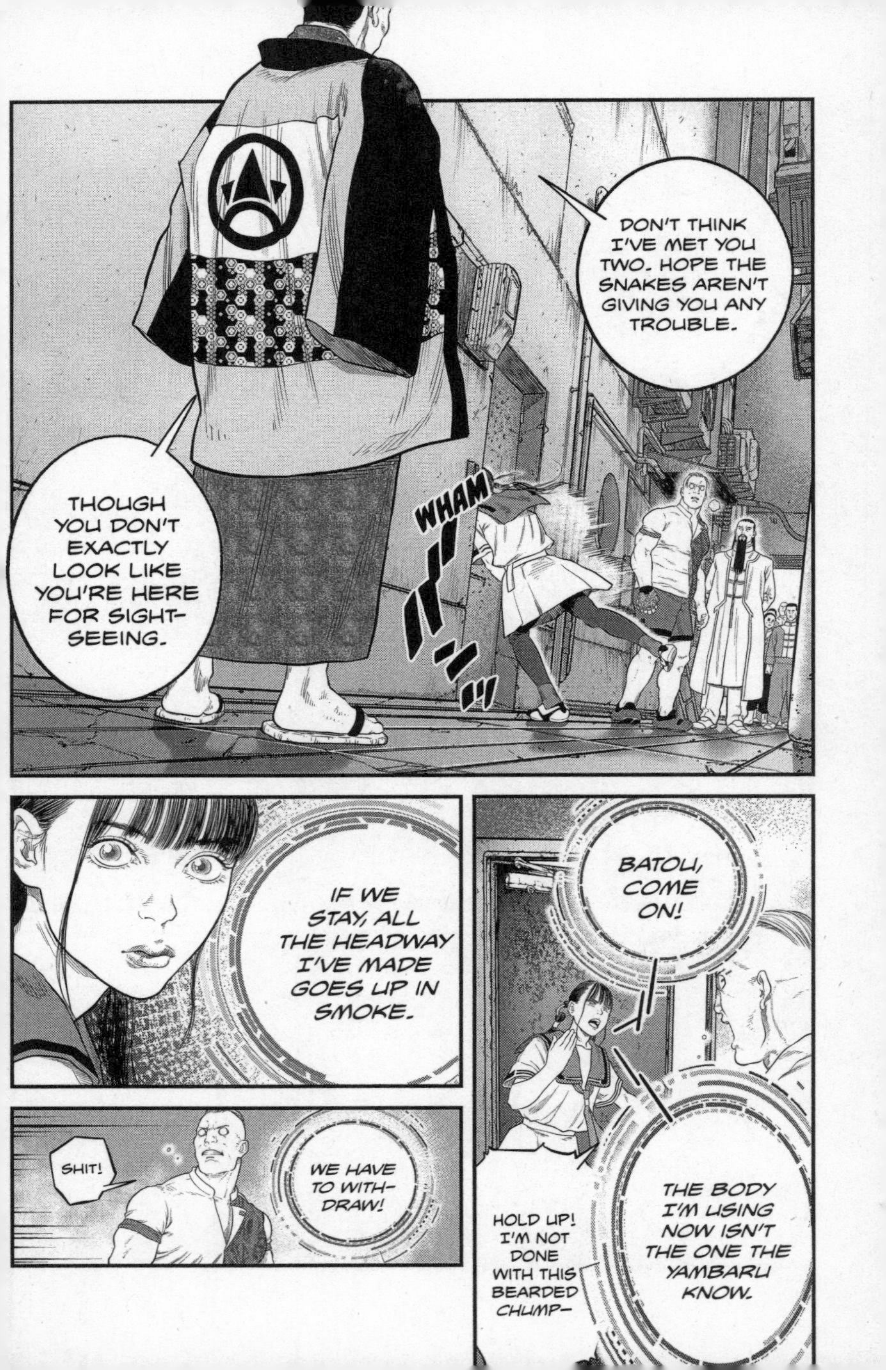
DON'T THINK I'VE MET YOU TWO. HOPE THE SNAKES AREN'T GIVING YOU ANY TROUBLE.
THOUGH YOU DON'T EXACTLY LOOK LIKE YOU'RE HERE FOR SIGHT-SEEING.
WHAM
BATOU, COME ON!
THE BODY I'M USING NOW ISN'T THE ONE THE YAMBARU KNOW.
HOLD UP! I'M NOT DONE WITH THIS BEARDED CHUMP–
IF WE STAY, ALL THE HEADWAY I'VE MADE GOES UP IN SMOKE.
WE HAVE TO WITH-DRAW!
SHIT!

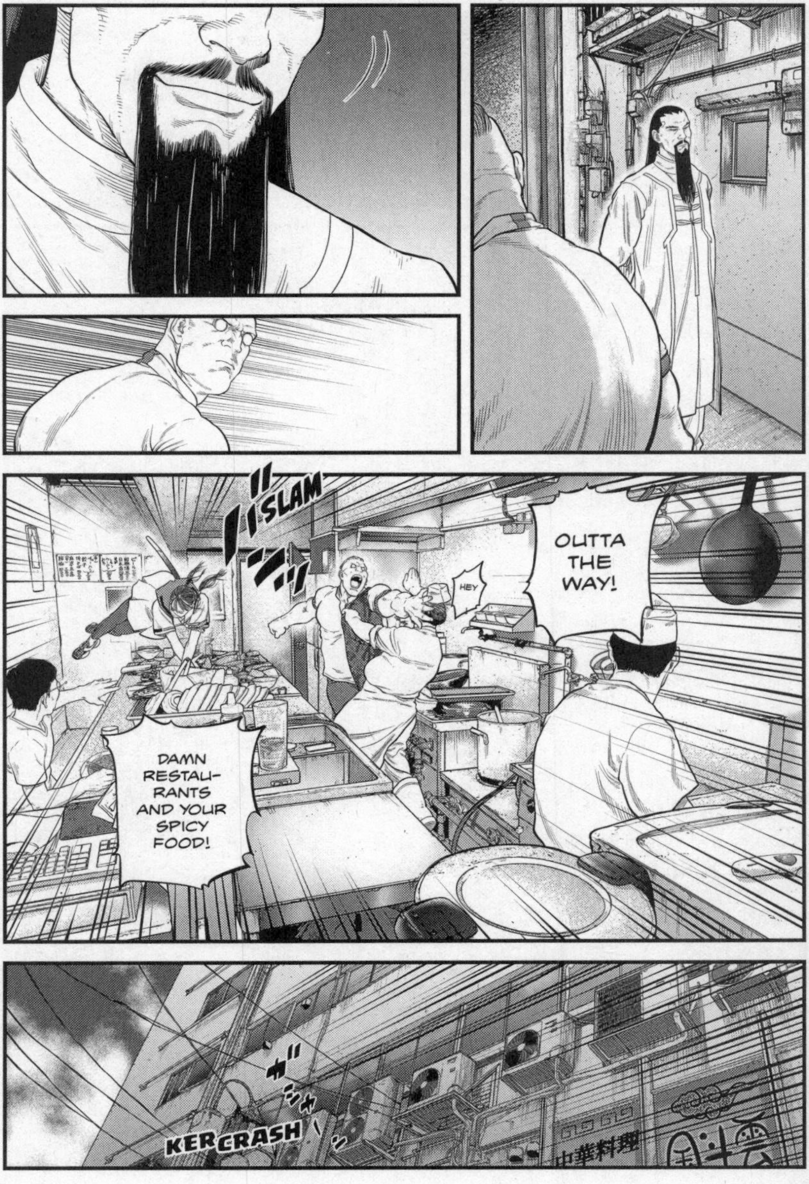
OUTTA THE WAY!
HEY
SLAM
DAMN RESTAU-RANTS AND YOUR SPICY FOOD!
中華料理
KERCRASH

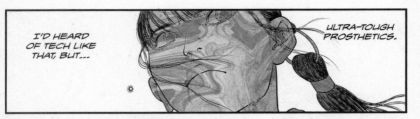

ULTRA-TOUGH PROSTHETICS.
I'D HEARD OF TECH LIKE THAT, BUT...
WHAT BROUGHT YOU DOWN HERE, ANYWAY?
I'D RATHER NOT HAVE MADE CONTACT WITH SECTION 9 WHILE I'M INCOGNITO.
I'VE ALREADY GOT MY HANDS FULL WITH THIS TURF WAR.
CHIEF'S ORDERS.

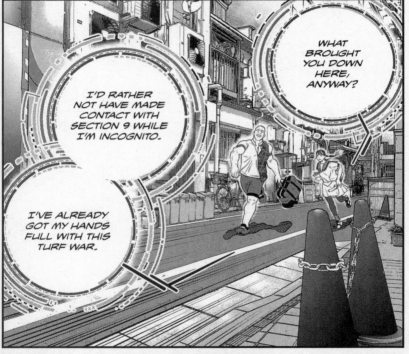

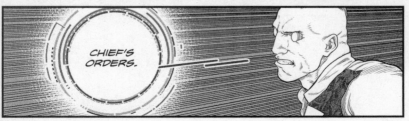

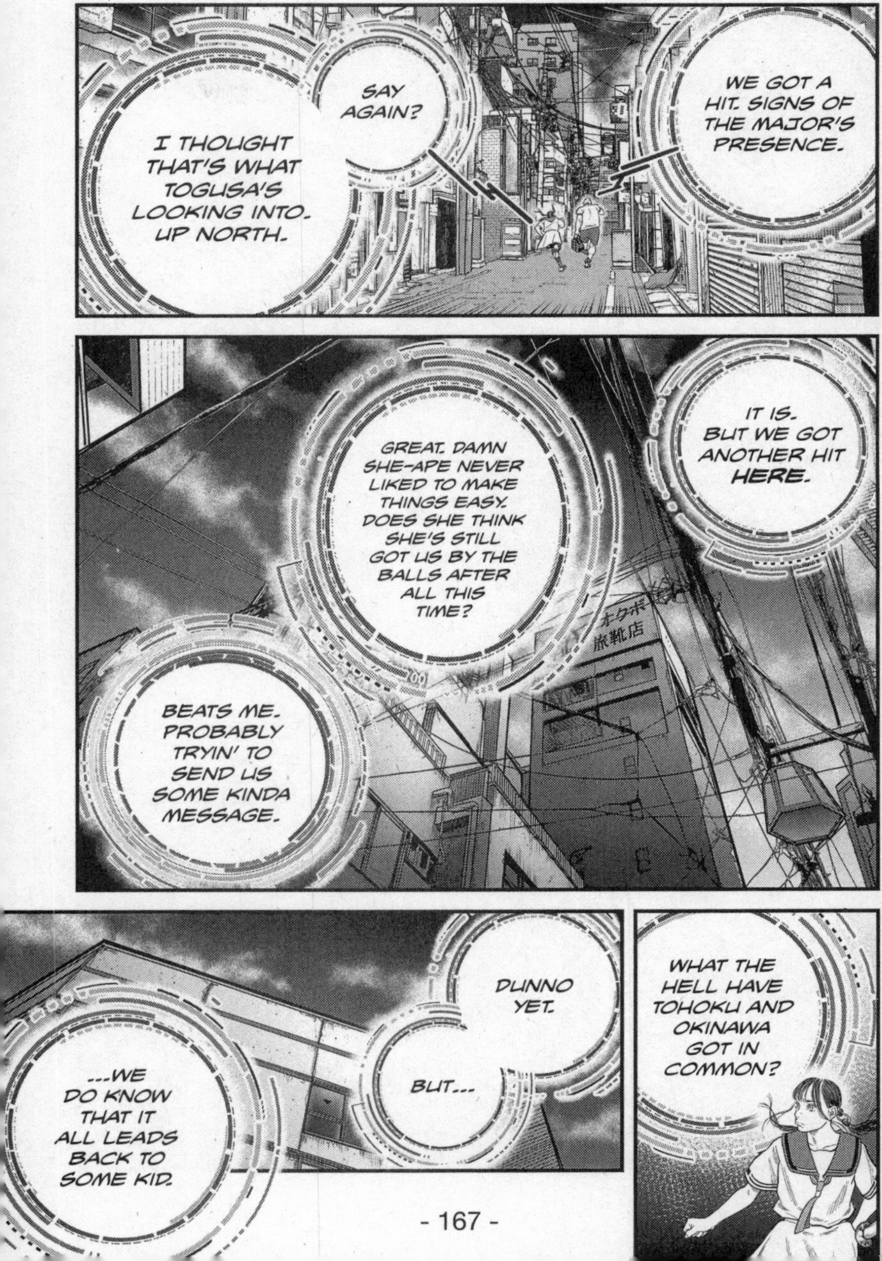
WE GOT A HIT. SIGNS OF THE MAJOR'S PRESENCE.
SAY AGAIN?
I THOUGHT THAT'S WHAT TOGUSA'S LOOKING INTO. UP NORTH.
IT IS. BUT WE GOT ANOTHER HIT **HERE.**
GREAT. DAMN SHE-APE NEVER LIKED TO MAKE THINGS EASY. DOES SHE THINK SHE'S STILL GOT US BY THE BALLS AFTER ALL THIS TIME?
BEATS ME. PROBABLY TRYIN' TO SEND US SOME KINDA MESSAGE.
WHAT THE HELL HAVE TOHOKU AND OKINAWA GOT IN COMMON?
DUNNO YET.
BUT...
...WE DO KNOW THAT IT ALL LEADS BACK TO SOME KID.

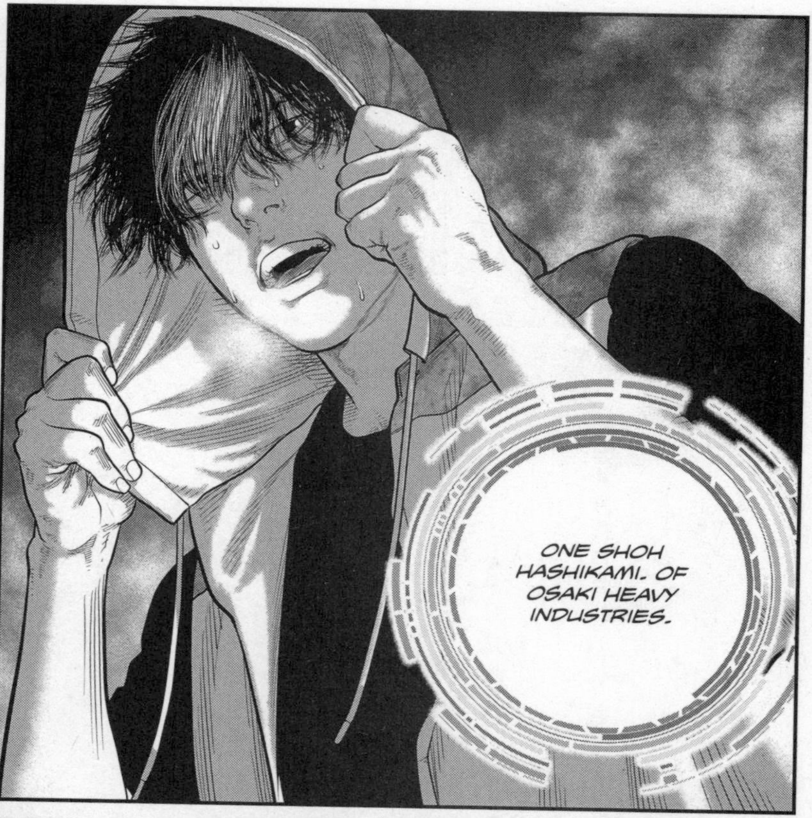
ONE SHOH HASHIKAMI. OF OSAKI HEAVY INDUSTRIES.

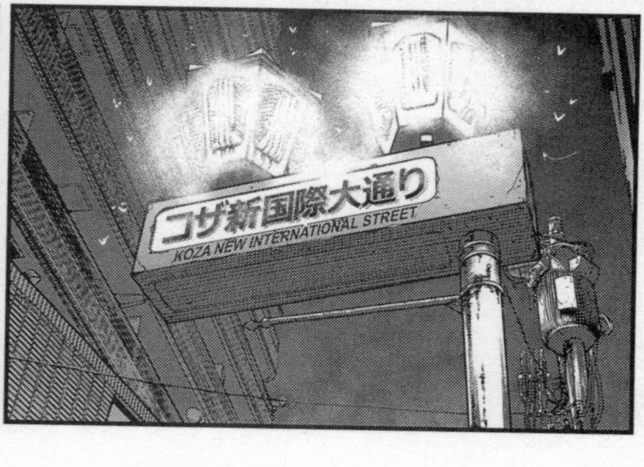
コザ新国際大通り
KOZA NEW INTERNATIONAL STREET

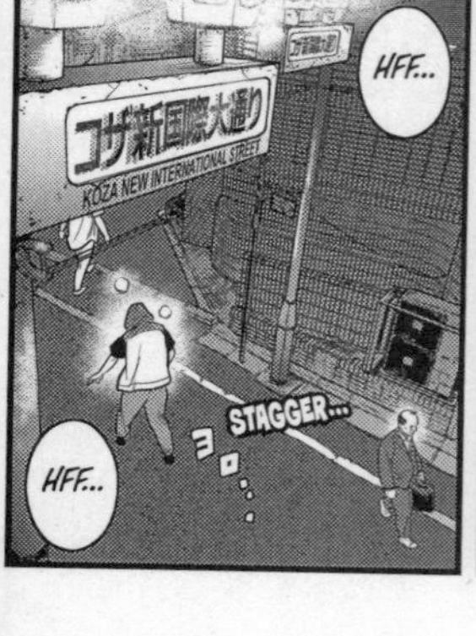
HFF...
コザ新国際大通り
KOZA NEW INTERNATIONAL STREET
STAGGER...
ヨロ...
HFF...

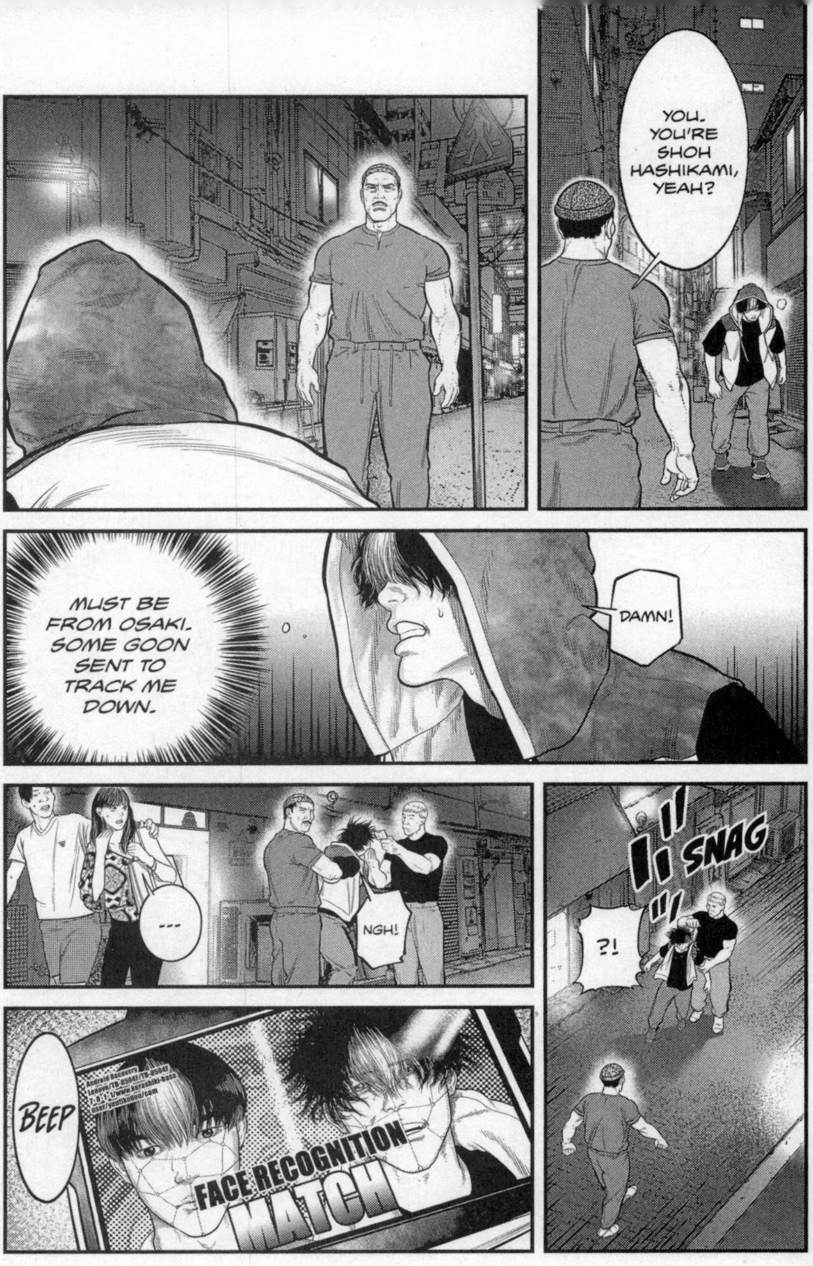
YOU. YOU'RE SHOH HASHIKAMI, YEAH?
DAMN!
MUST BE FROM OSAKI. SOME GOON SENT TO TRACK ME DOWN.
SNAG
?!
NGH!

BEEP
FACE RECOGNITION MATCH

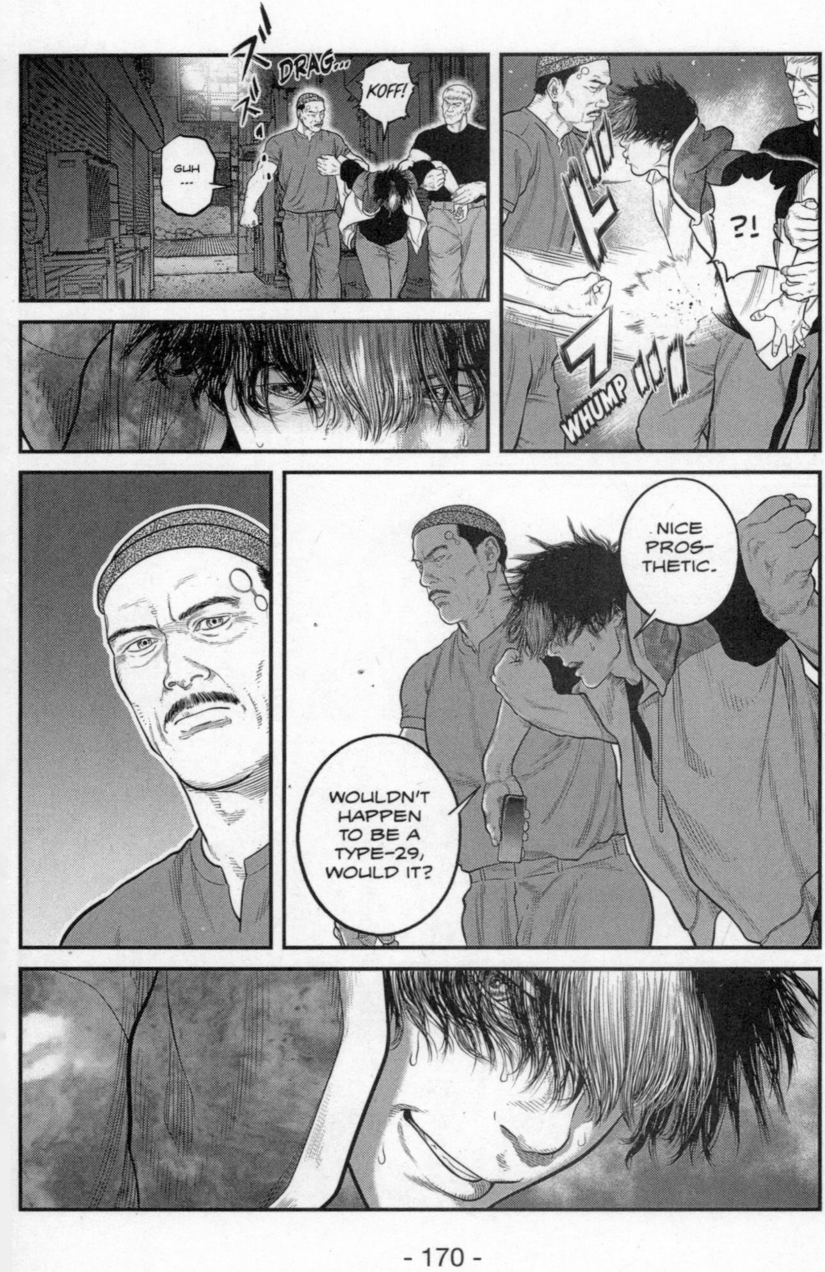
?!
WHUMP
DRAG...
KOFF!
GUH...
NICE PROSTHETIC.
WOULDN'T HAPPEN TO BE A TYPE-29, WOULD IT?

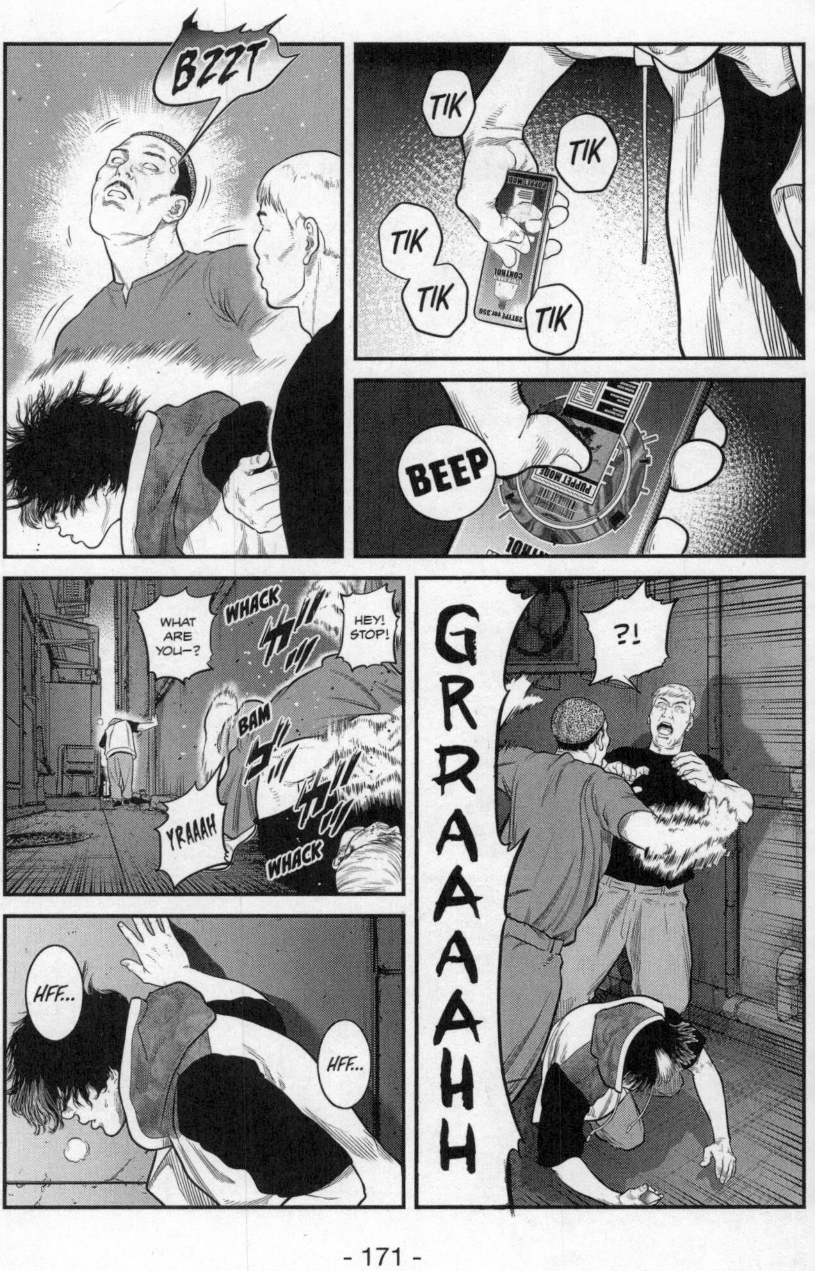

TIK
TIK
TIK
TIK
TIK
BEEP
PUPPET MODE
BZZT
GRAAAAAH
?!
HEY! STOP!
WHACK
WHAT ARE YOU–?
BAM
WHACK
YRAAAH
HFF...
HFF...

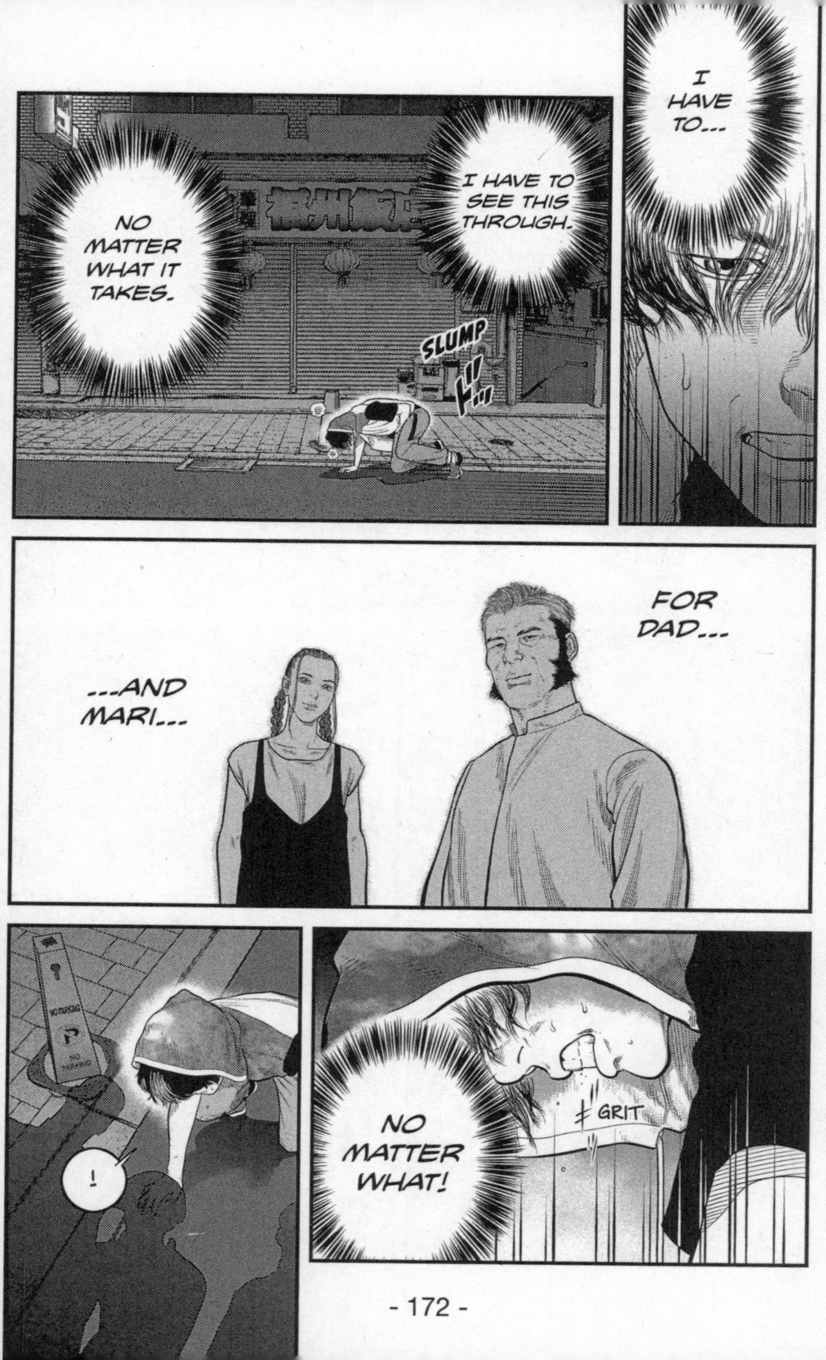
I HAVE TO...
I HAVE TO SEE THIS THROUGH.
NO MATTER WHAT IT TAKES.
SLUMP
FOR DAD...
...AND MARI...
GRIT
NO MATTER WHAT!
!

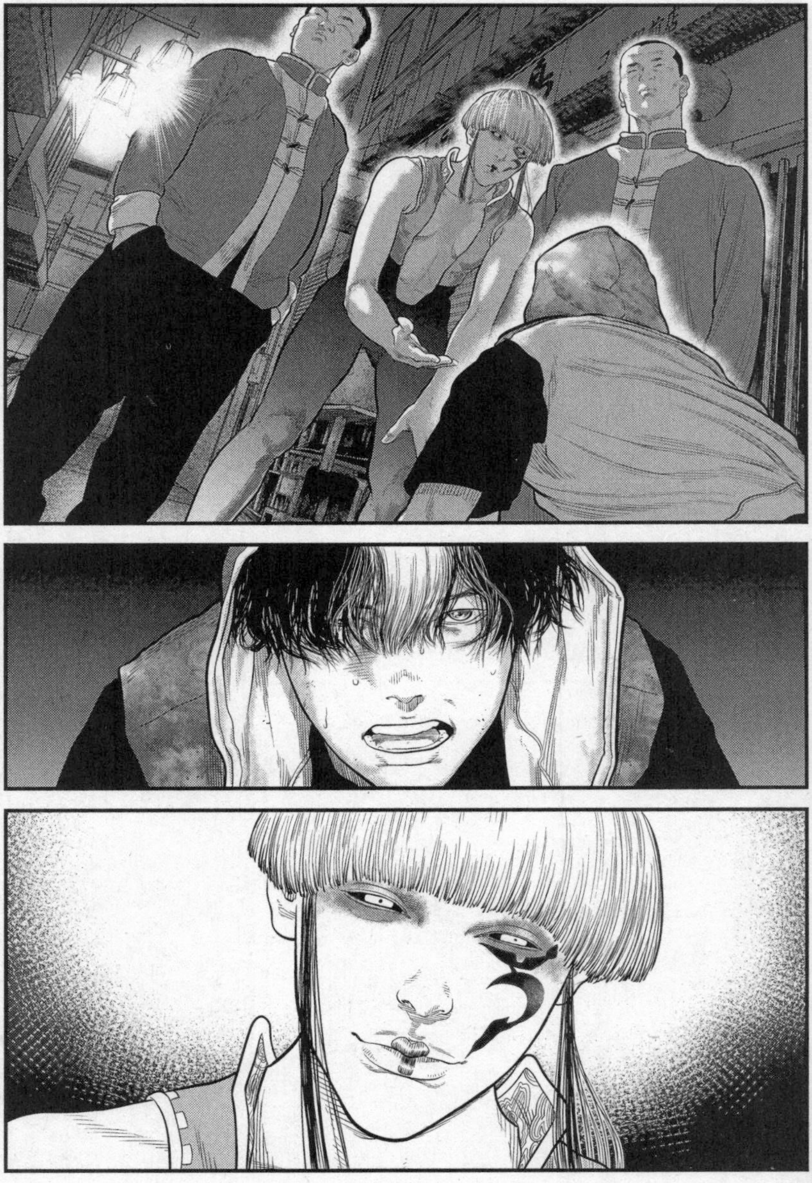

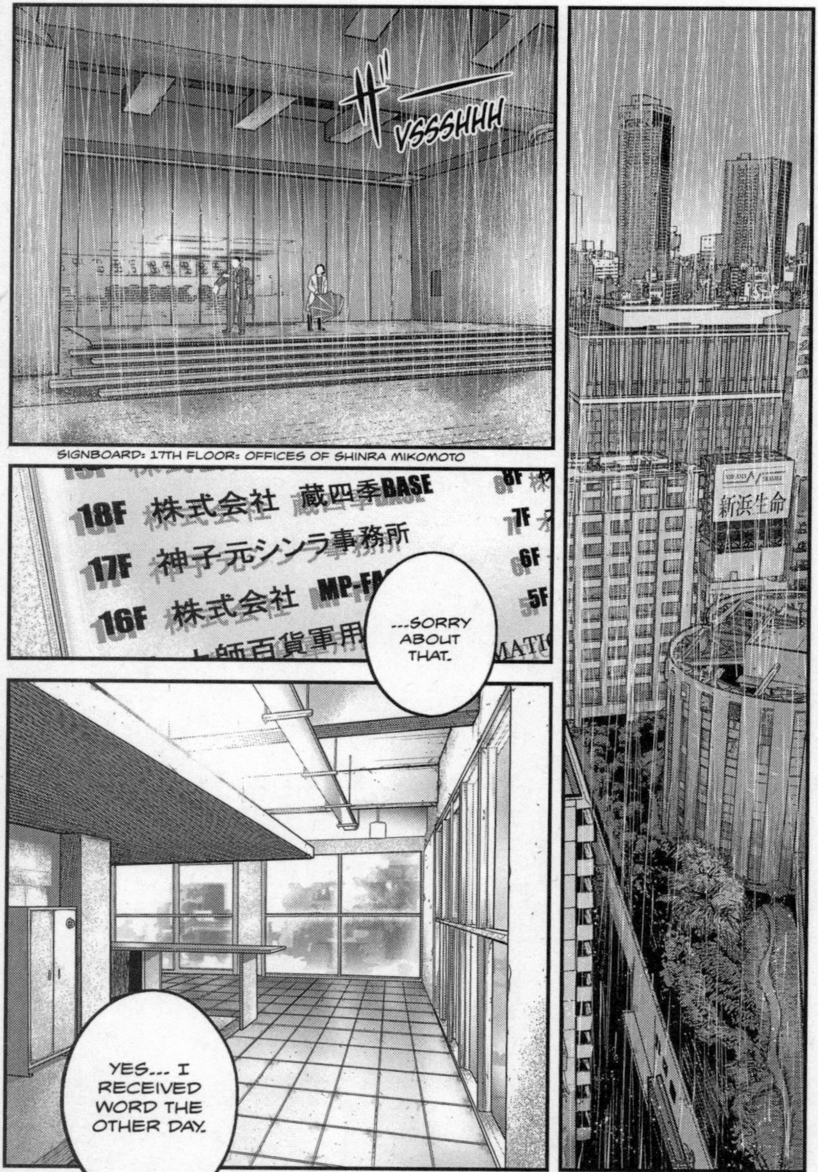
新浜生命
ザ──
VSSSHHH
SIGNBOARD: 17TH FLOOR: OFFICES OF SHINRA MIKOMOTO
18F 株式会社 蔵四季BASE
17F 神子元シンラ事務所
16F 株式会社 MP-FA
---SORRY ABOUT THAT.
YES... I RECEIVED WORD THE OTHER DAY.

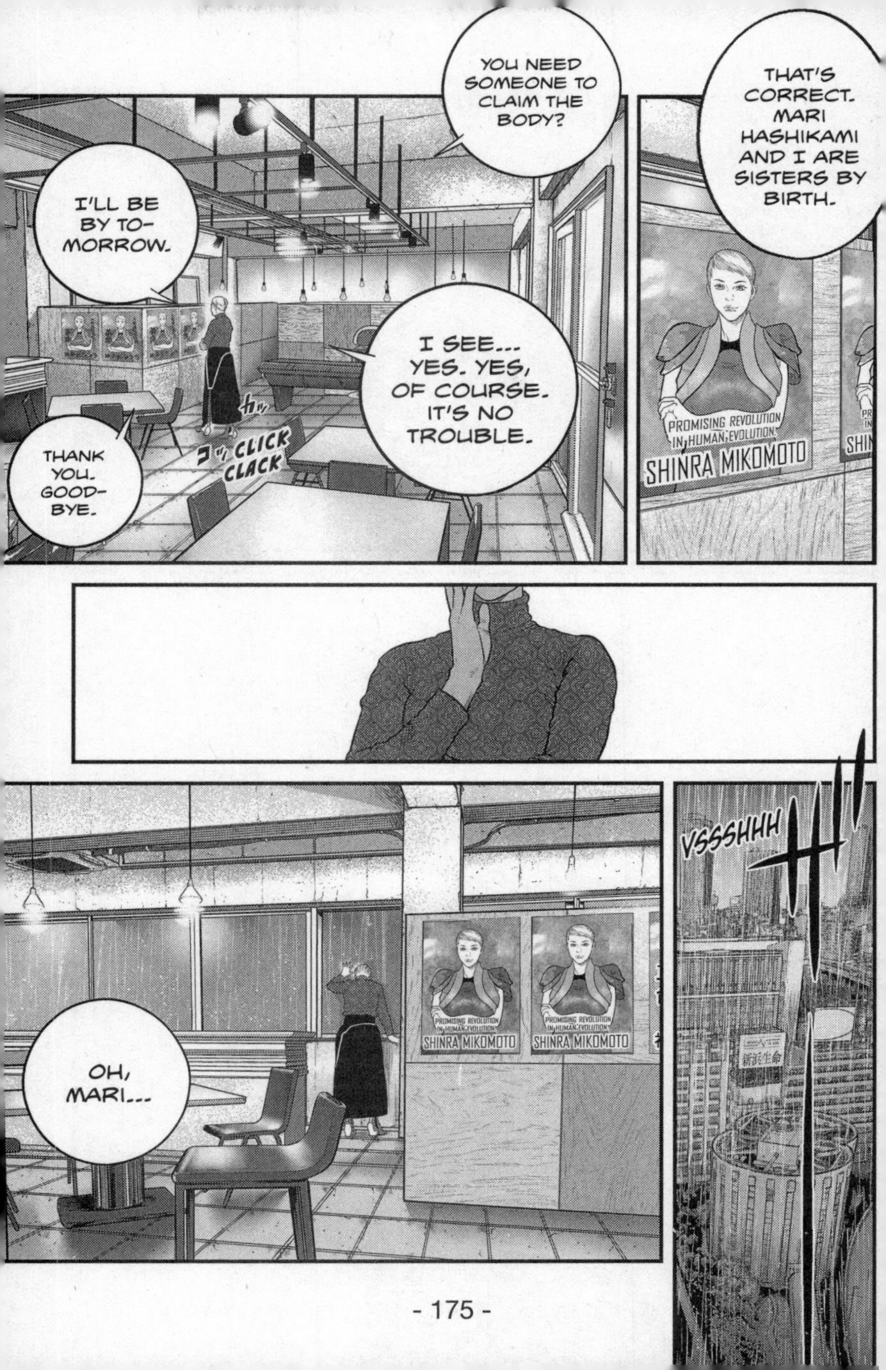
THAT'S CORRECT. MARI HASHIKAMI AND I ARE SISTERS BY BIRTH.
PROMISING REVOLUTION IN HUMAN EVOLUTION
SHINRA MIKOMOTO
YOU NEED SOMEONE TO CLAIM THE BODY?
I SEE... YES. YES, OF COURSE. IT'S NO TROUBLE.
I'LL BE BY TO-MORROW.
CLICK CLACK
THANK YOU. GOOD-BYE.
VSSSHHH
新浜生命
PROMISING REVOLUTION IN HUMAN EVOLUTION
SHINRA MIKOMOTO
PROMISING REVOLUTION IN HUMAN EVOLUTION
SHINRA MIKOMOTO
OH, MARI...

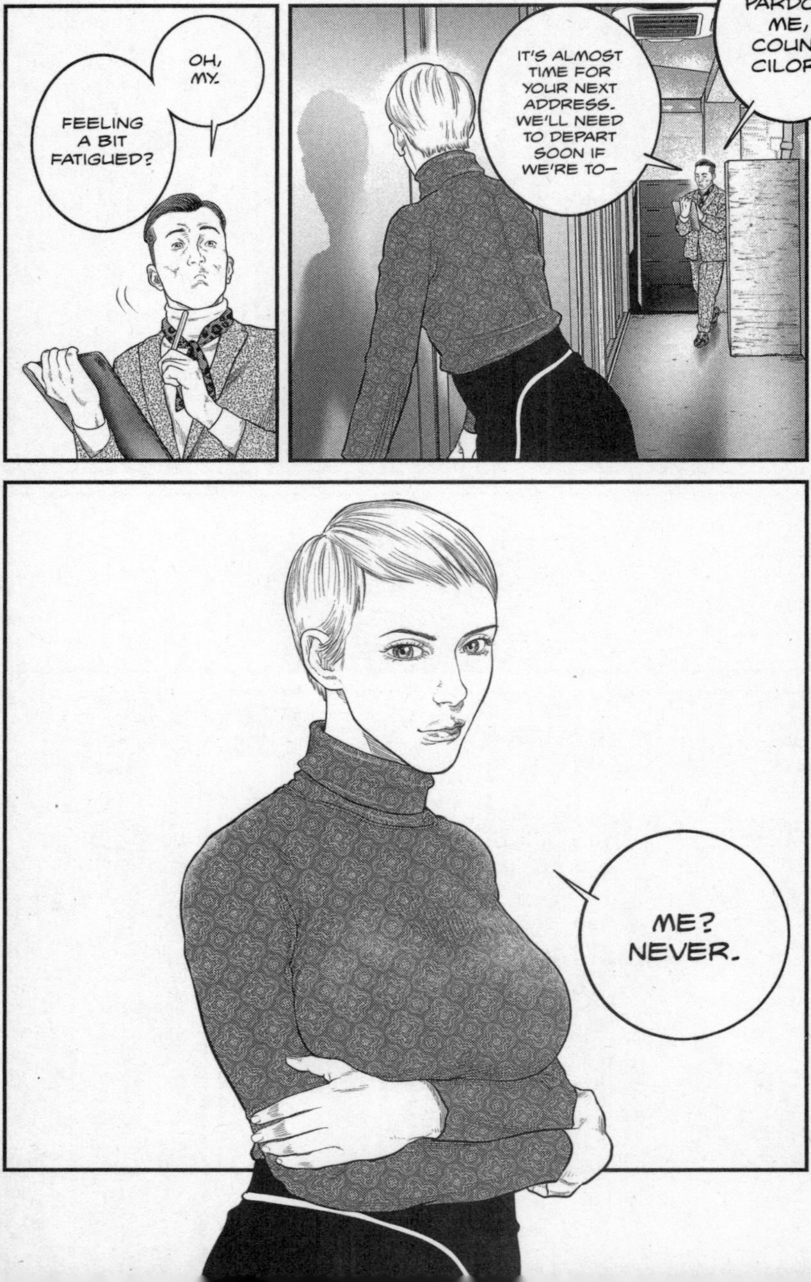
PARDON ME, COUN-CILOR.
IT'S ALMOST TIME FOR YOUR NEXT ADDRESS. WE'LL NEED TO DEPART SOON IF WE'RE TO—
OH, MY.
FEELING A BIT FATIGUED?
ME? NEVER.

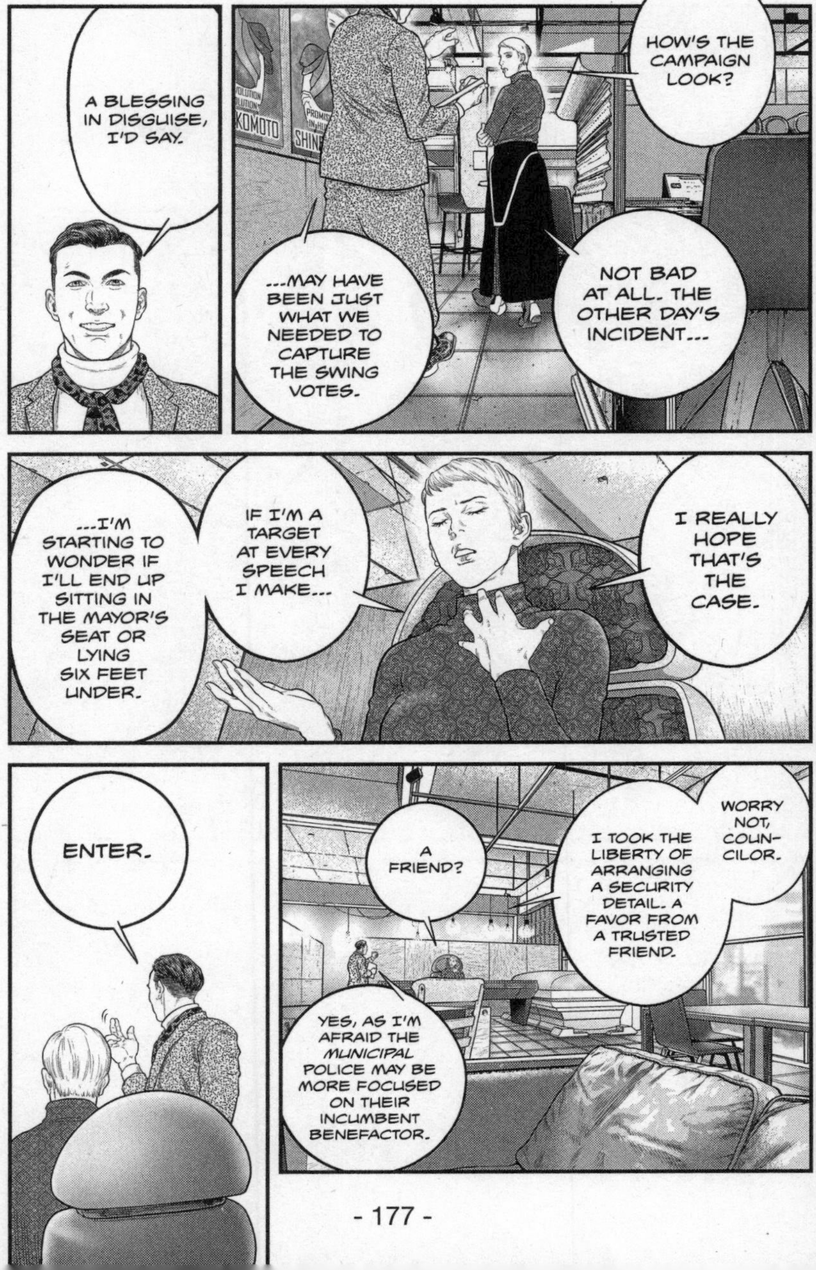
HOW'S THE CAMPAIGN LOOK?
NOT BAD AT ALL. THE OTHER DAY'S INCIDENT...
...MAY HAVE BEEN JUST WHAT WE NEEDED TO CAPTURE THE SWING VOTES.
A BLESSING IN DISGUISE, I'D SAY.
I REALLY HOPE THAT'S THE CASE.
IF I'M A TARGET AT EVERY SPEECH I MAKE...
...I'M STARTING TO WONDER IF I'LL END UP SITTING IN THE MAYOR'S SEAT OR LYING SIX FEET UNDER.
WORRY NOT, COUNCILOR.
I TOOK THE LIBERTY OF ARRANGING A SECURITY DETAIL. A FAVOR FROM A TRUSTED FRIEND.
A FRIEND?
YES, AS I'M AFRAID THE *MUNICIPAL* POLICE MAY BE MORE FOCUSED ON THEIR INCUMBENT BENEFACTOR.
ENTER.

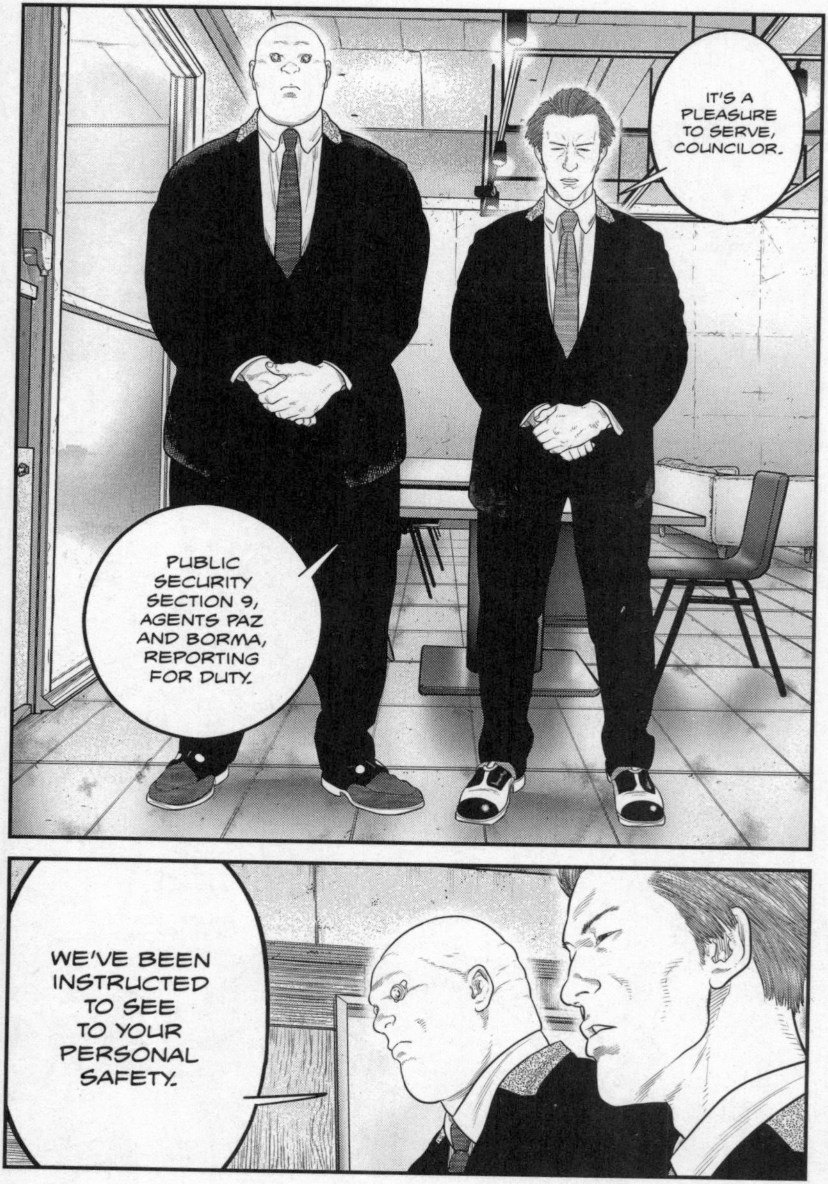
IT'S A PLEASURE TO SERVE, COUNCILOR.
PUBLIC SECURITY SECTION 9, AGENTS PAZ AND BORMA, REPORTING FOR DUTY.
WE'VE BEEN INSTRUCTED TO SEE TO YOUR PERSONAL SAFETY.

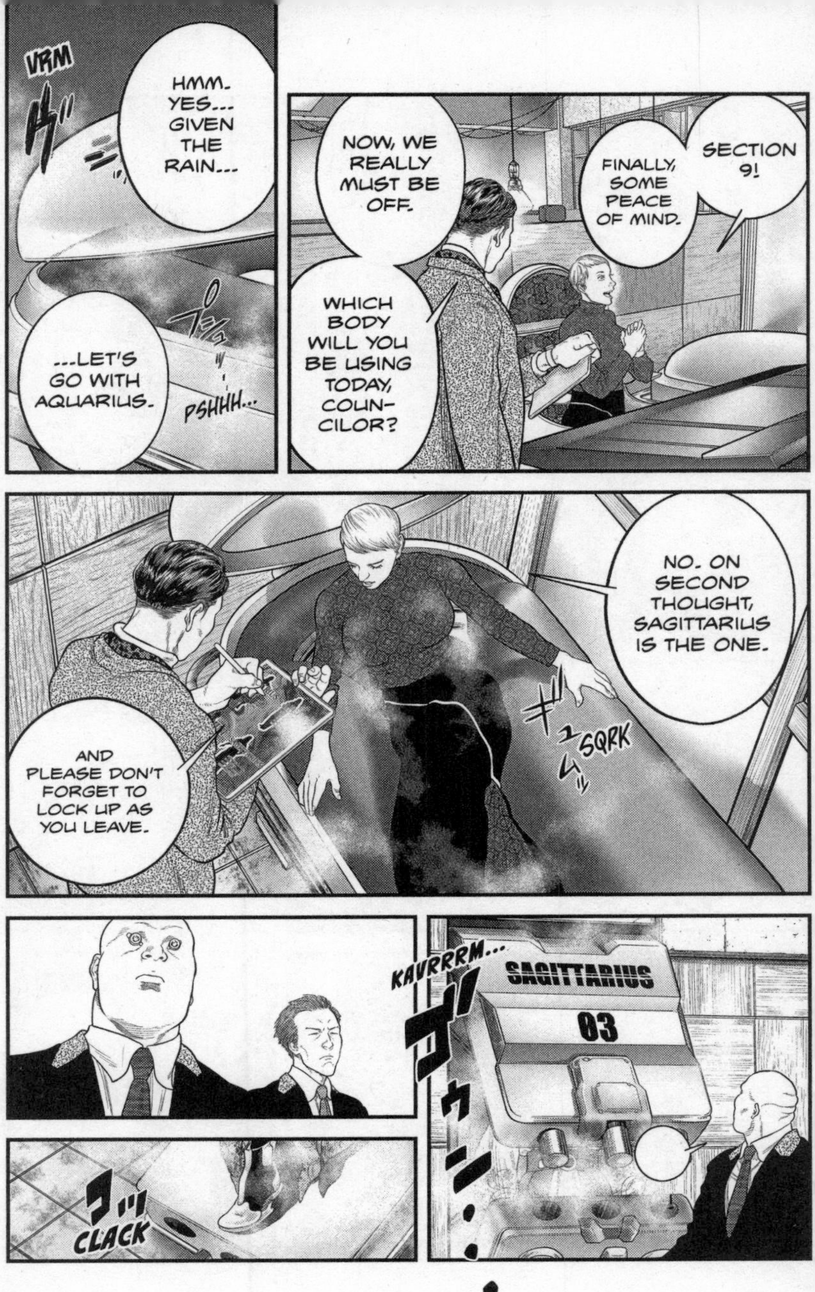
SECTION 9!
FINALLY, SOME PEACE OF MIND.
NOW, WE REALLY MUST BE OFF.
WHICH BODY WILL YOU BE USING TODAY, COUN-CILOR?
HMM. YES... GIVEN THE RAIN...
VRM
...LET'S GO WITH AQUARIUS.
PSHHH...
NO. ON SECOND THOUGHT, SAGITTARIUS IS THE ONE.
SQRK
AND PLEASE DON'T FORGET TO LOCK UP AS YOU LEAVE.
SAGITTARIUS
03
KAVRRRM...
CLACK

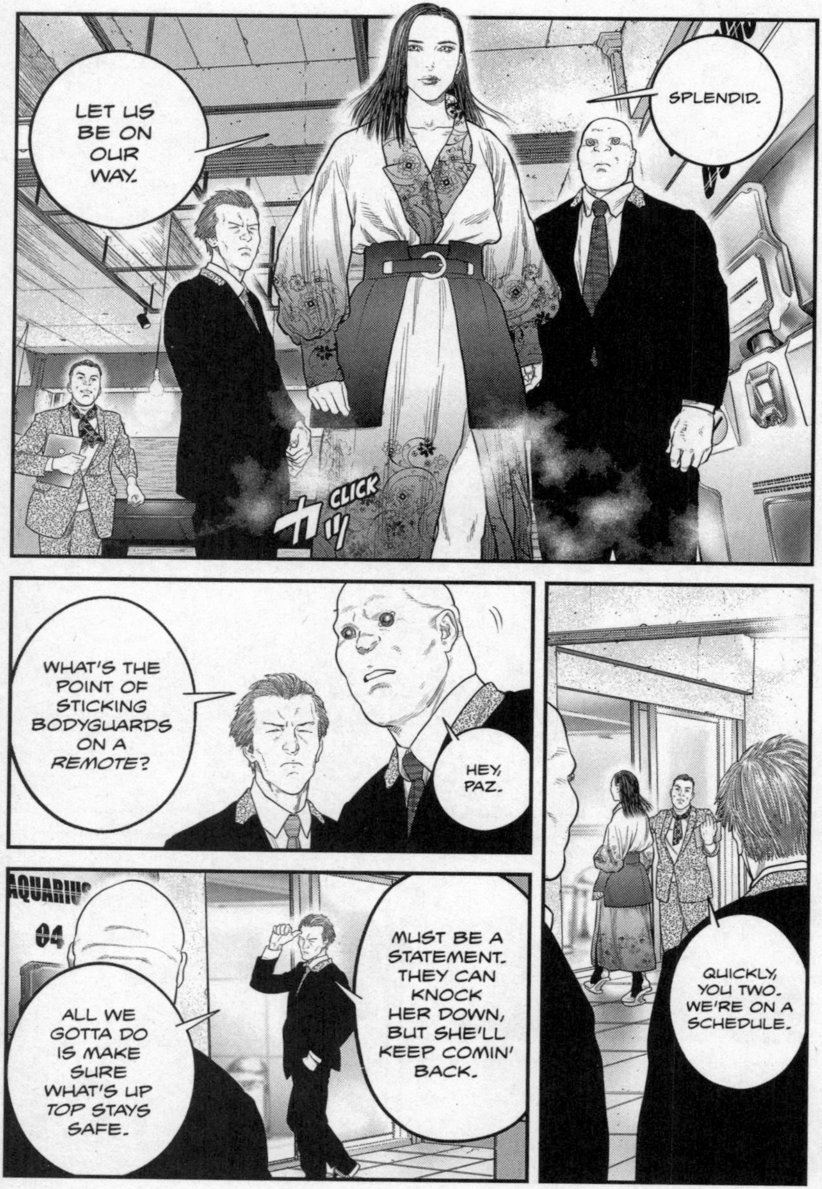
SPLENDID.
LET US BE ON OUR WAY.
CLICK
カッ
QUICKLY, YOU TWO. WE'RE ON A SCHEDULE.
HEY, PAZ.
WHAT'S THE POINT OF STICKING BODYGUARDS ON A *REMOTE*?
MUST BE A STATEMENT. THEY CAN KNOCK HER DOWN, BUT SHE'LL KEEP COMIN' BACK.
AQUARIUS
04
ALL WE GOTTA DO IS MAKE SURE WHAT'S UP *TOP* STAYS SAFE.

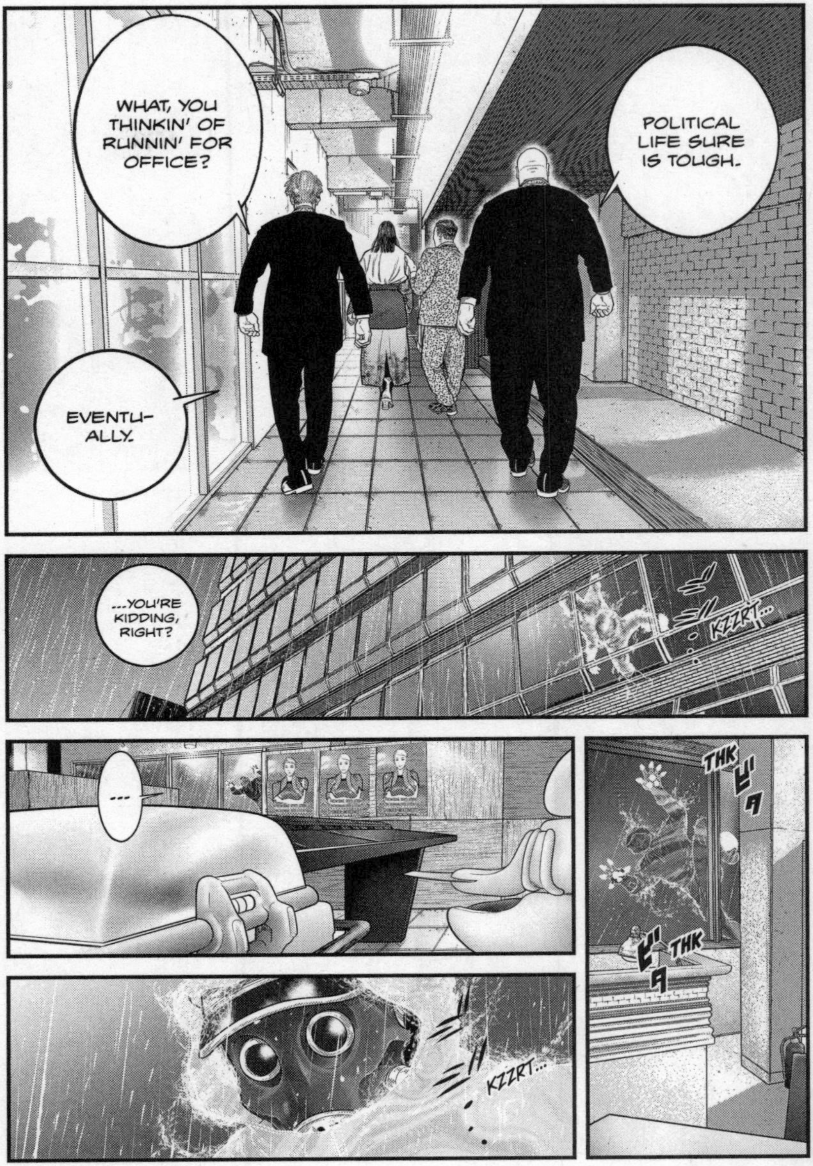

POLITICAL LIFE SURE IS TOUGH.
WHAT, YOU THINKIN' OF RUNNIN' FOR OFFICE?
EVENTU-ALLY.
KZZRT...
...YOU'RE KIDDING, RIGHT?
THK
THK
...
KZZRT...

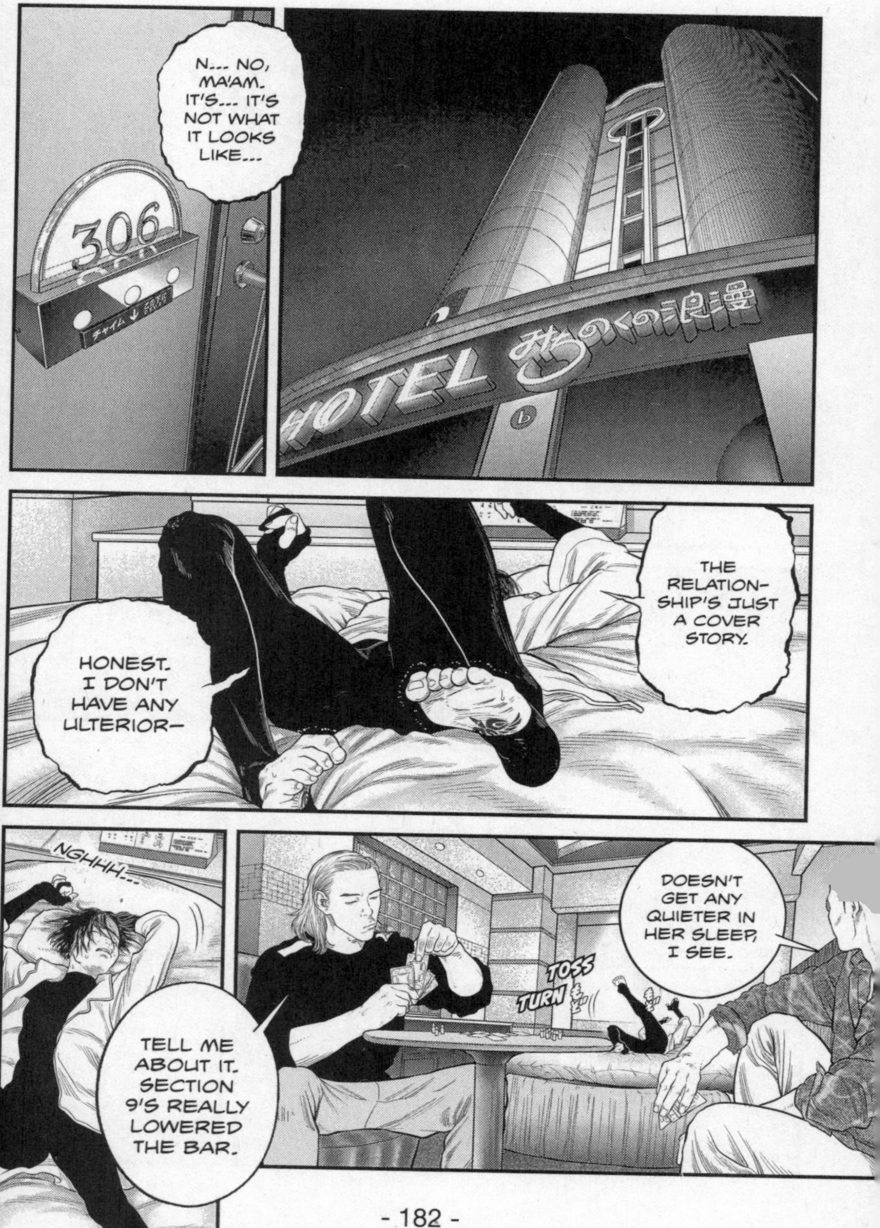
HOTEL みちのくの浪漫
306
N... NO, MA'AM. IT'S... IT'S NOT WHAT IT LOOKS LIKE...
THE RELATION-SHIP'S JUST A COVER STORY.
HONEST. I DON'T HAVE ANY ULTERIOR—
DOESN'T GET ANY QUIETER IN HER SLEEP, I SEE.
TOSS
TURN
TELL ME ABOUT IT. SECTION 9'S REALLY LOWERED THE BAR.
NGHHH...

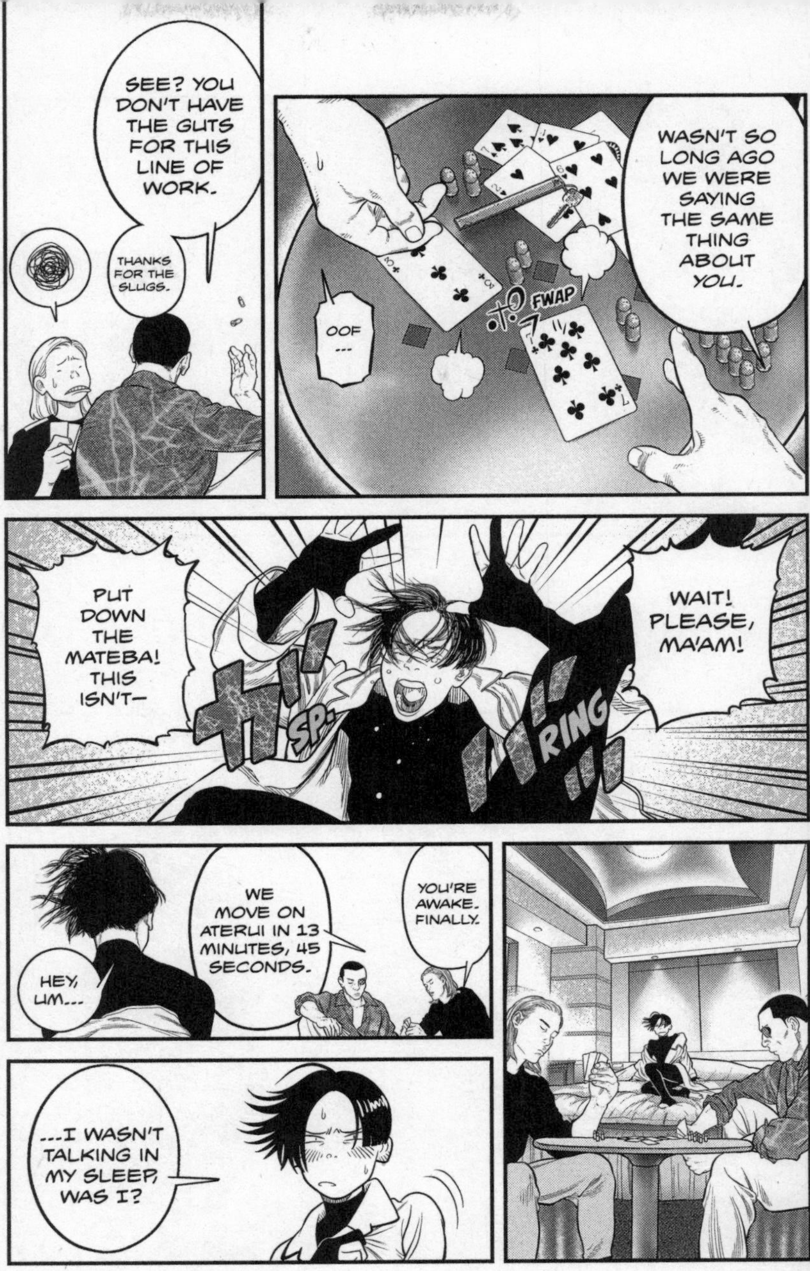
WASN'T SO LONG AGO WE WERE SAYING THE SAME THING ABOUT YOU.
FWAP
OOF ---
SEE? YOU DON'T HAVE THE GUTS FOR THIS LINE OF WORK.
THANKS FOR THE SLUGS.
WAIT! PLEASE, MA'AM!
RING
SP
PUT DOWN THE MATEBA! THIS ISN'T—
YOU'RE AWAKE. FINALLY.
WE MOVE ON ATERUI IN 13 MINUTES, 45 SECONDS.
HEY, UM---
---I WASN'T TALKING IN MY SLEEP, WAS I?

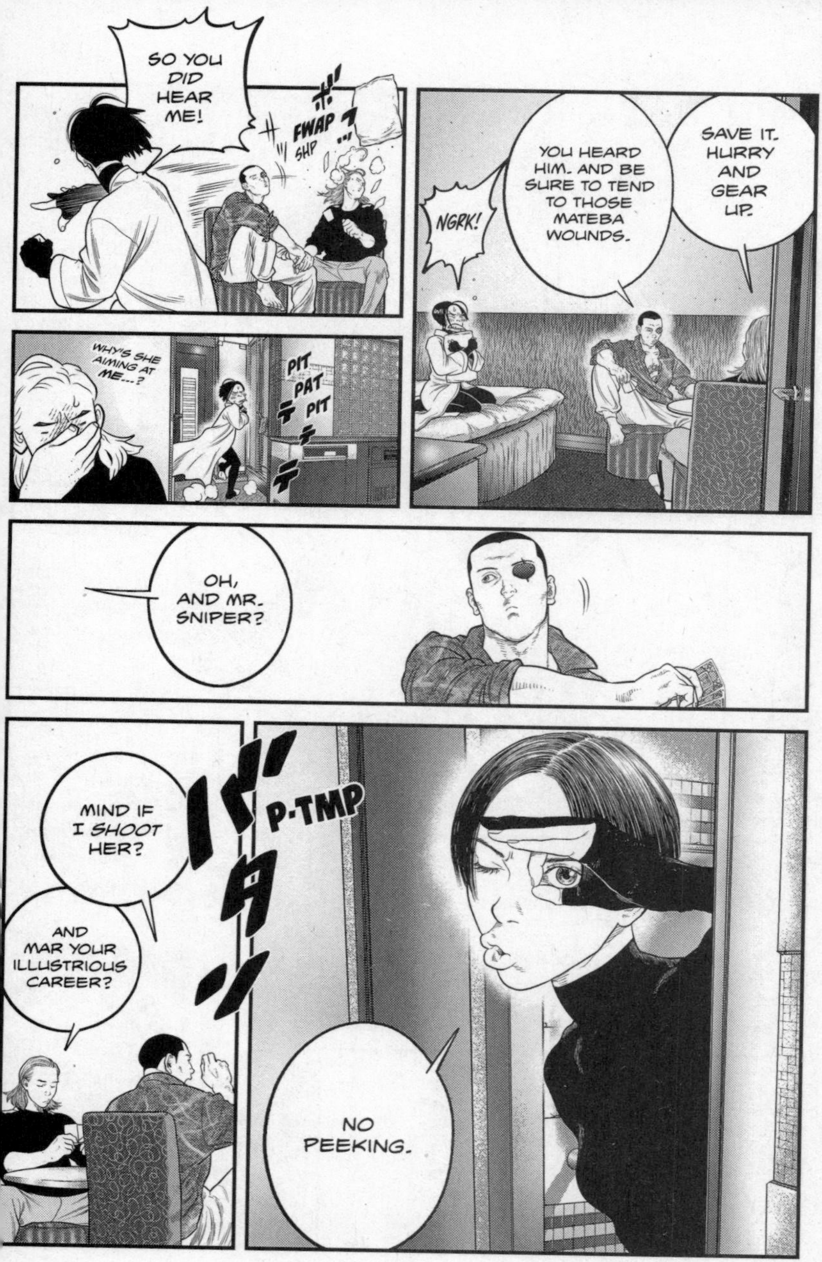
SAVE IT. HURRY AND GEAR UP.
YOU HEARD HIM. AND BE SURE TO TEND TO THOSE MATEBA WOUNDS.
NGRK!
SO YOU DID HEAR ME!
FWAP
SHP
WHY'S SHE AIMING AT ME...?
PIT
PAT
PIT
OH, AND MR. SNIPER?
P-TMP
NO PEEKING.
MIND IF I SHOOT HER?
AND MAR YOUR ILLUSTRIOUS CAREER?

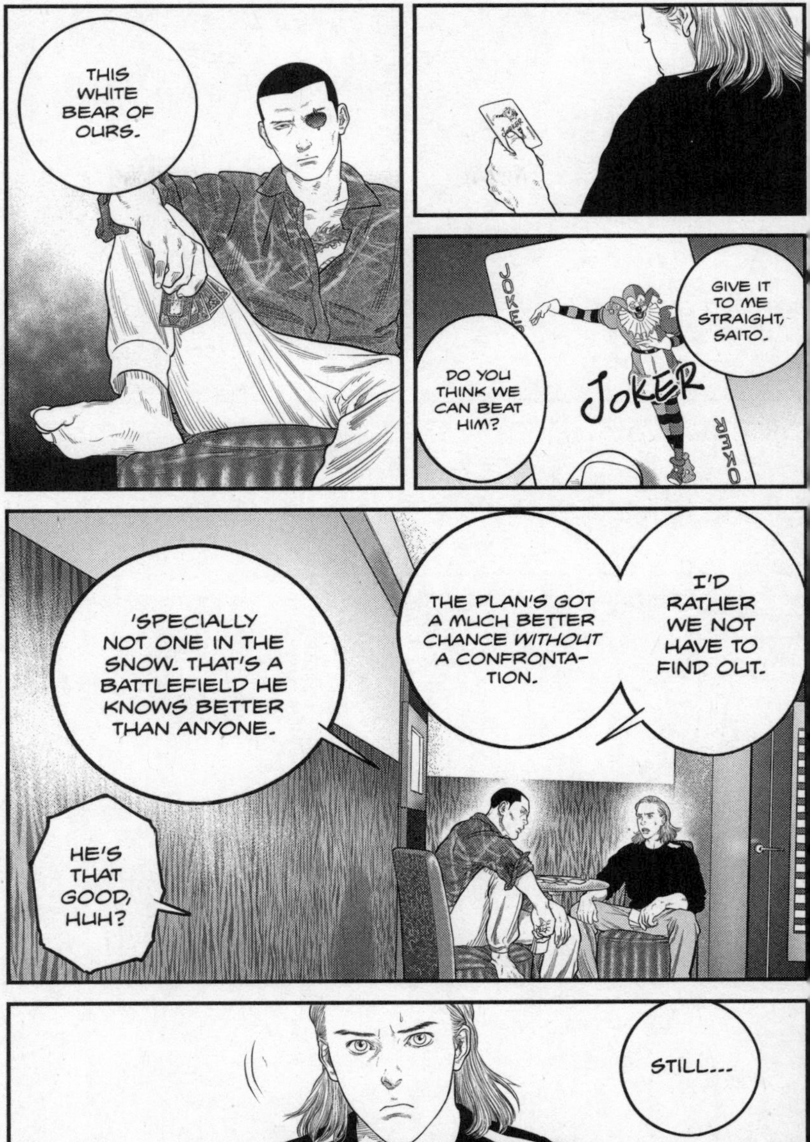
GIVE IT TO ME STRAIGHT, SAITO.
DO YOU THINK WE CAN BEAT HIM?
JOKER
THIS WHITE BEAR OF OURS.
I'D RATHER WE NOT HAVE TO FIND OUT.
THE PLAN'S GOT A MUCH BETTER CHANCE *WITHOUT* A CONFRONTATION.
'SPECIALLY NOT ONE IN THE SNOW. THAT'S A BATTLEFIELD HE KNOWS BETTER THAN ANYONE.
HE'S THAT GOOD, HUH?
STILL...

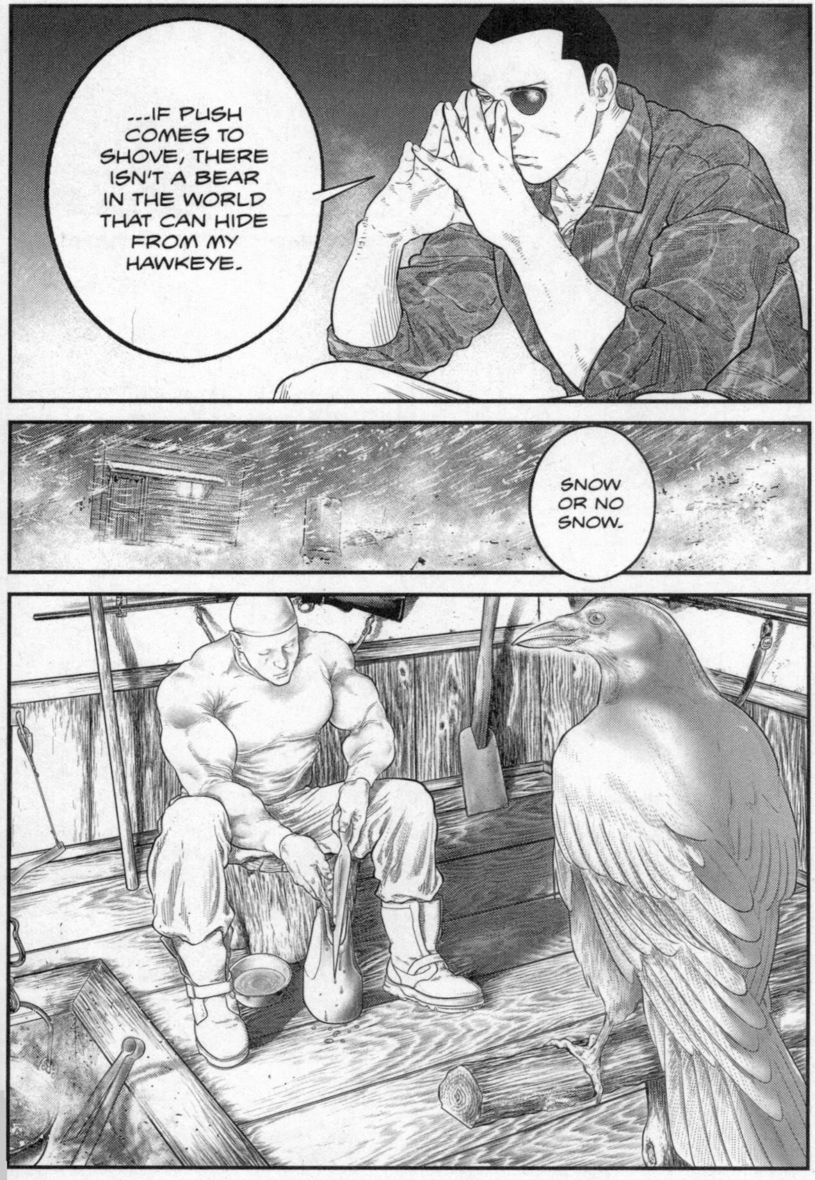
...IF PUSH COMES TO SHOVE, THERE ISN'T A BEAR IN THE WORLD THAT CAN HIDE FROM MY HAWKEYE.
SNOW OR NO SNOW.

06

NO MASTER NO LIFE

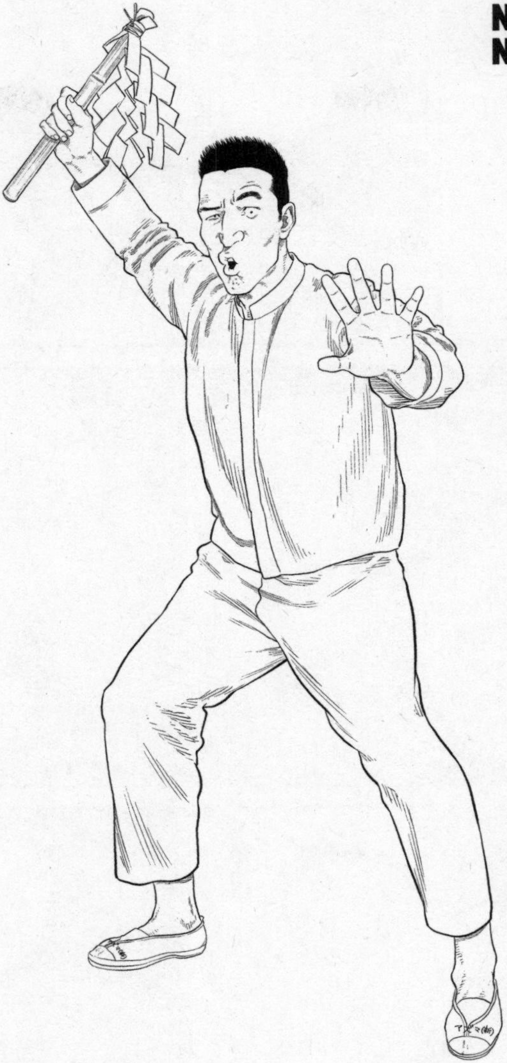

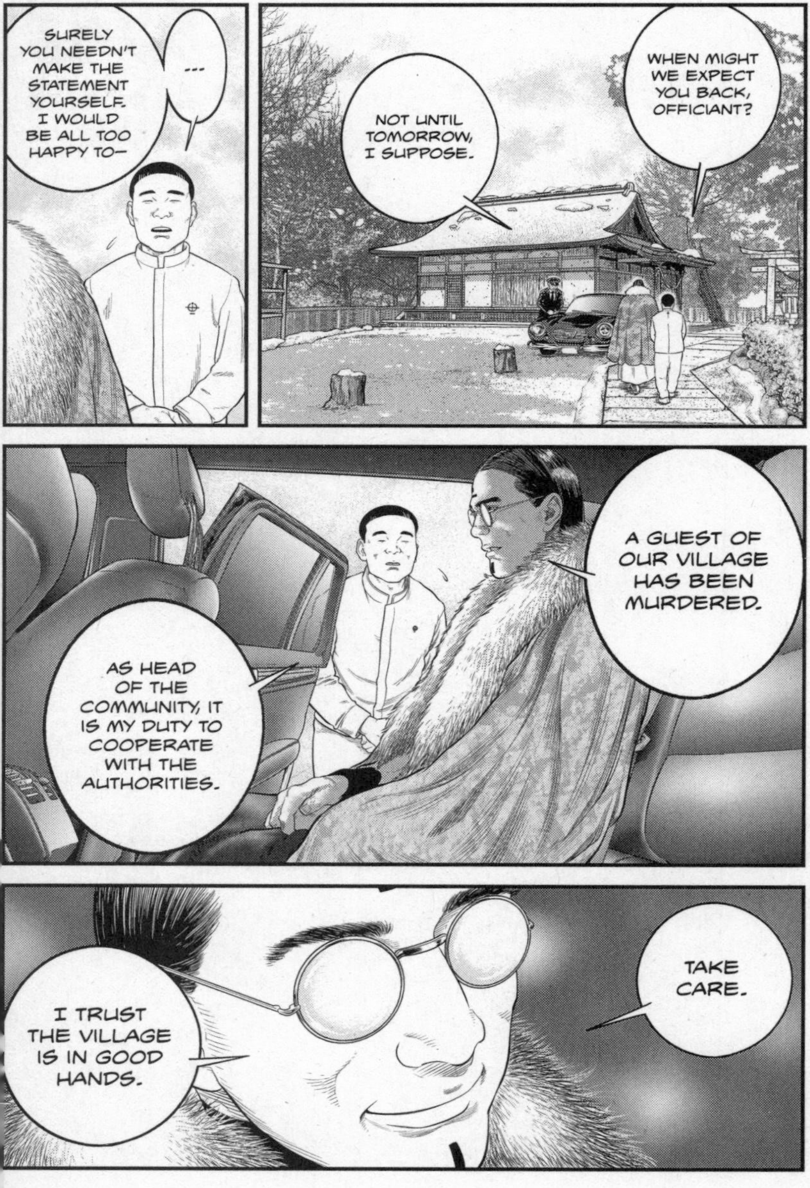
WHEN MIGHT WE EXPECT YOU BACK, OFFICIANT?
NOT UNTIL TOMORROW, I SUPPOSE.

SURELY YOU NEEDN'T MAKE THE STATEMENT YOURSELF. I WOULD BE ALL TOO HAPPY TO—
A GUEST OF OUR VILLAGE HAS BEEN MURDERED.
AS HEAD OF THE COMMUNITY, IT IS MY DUTY TO COOPERATE WITH THE AUTHORITIES.
TAKE CARE.
I TRUST THE VILLAGE IS IN GOOD HANDS.

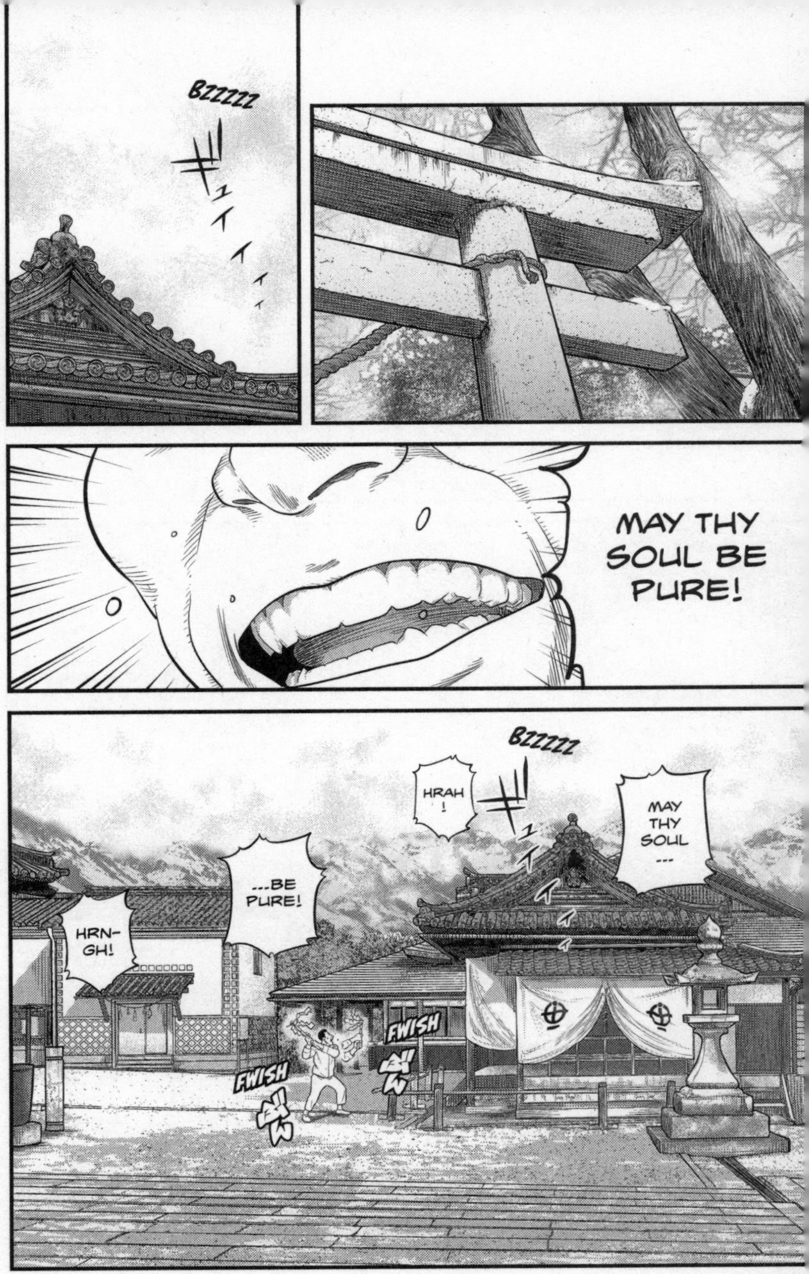
BZZZZZ
MAY THY SOUL BE PURE!
MAY THY SOUL ---
BZZZZZ
HRAH !
FWISH
...BE PURE!
FWISH
HRN-GH!

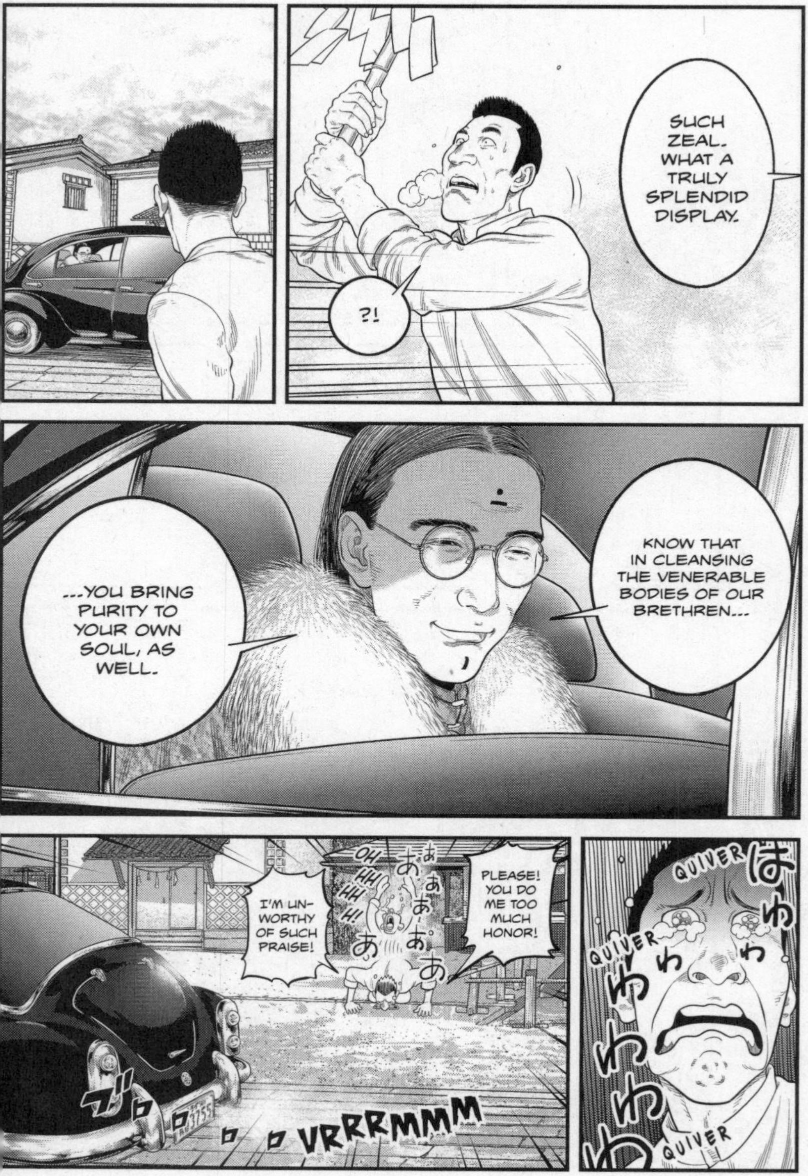
SUCH ZEAL. WHAT A TRULY SPLENDID DISPLAY.
?!
KNOW THAT IN CLEANSING THE VENERABLE BODIES OF OUR BRETHREN...
...YOU BRING PURITY TO YOUR OWN SOUL, AS WELL.
QUIVER
QUIVER
QUIVER
PLEASE! YOU DO ME TOO MUCH HONOR!
I'M UN-WORTHY OF SUCH PRAISE!
OHHHHH!
VRRRMMM

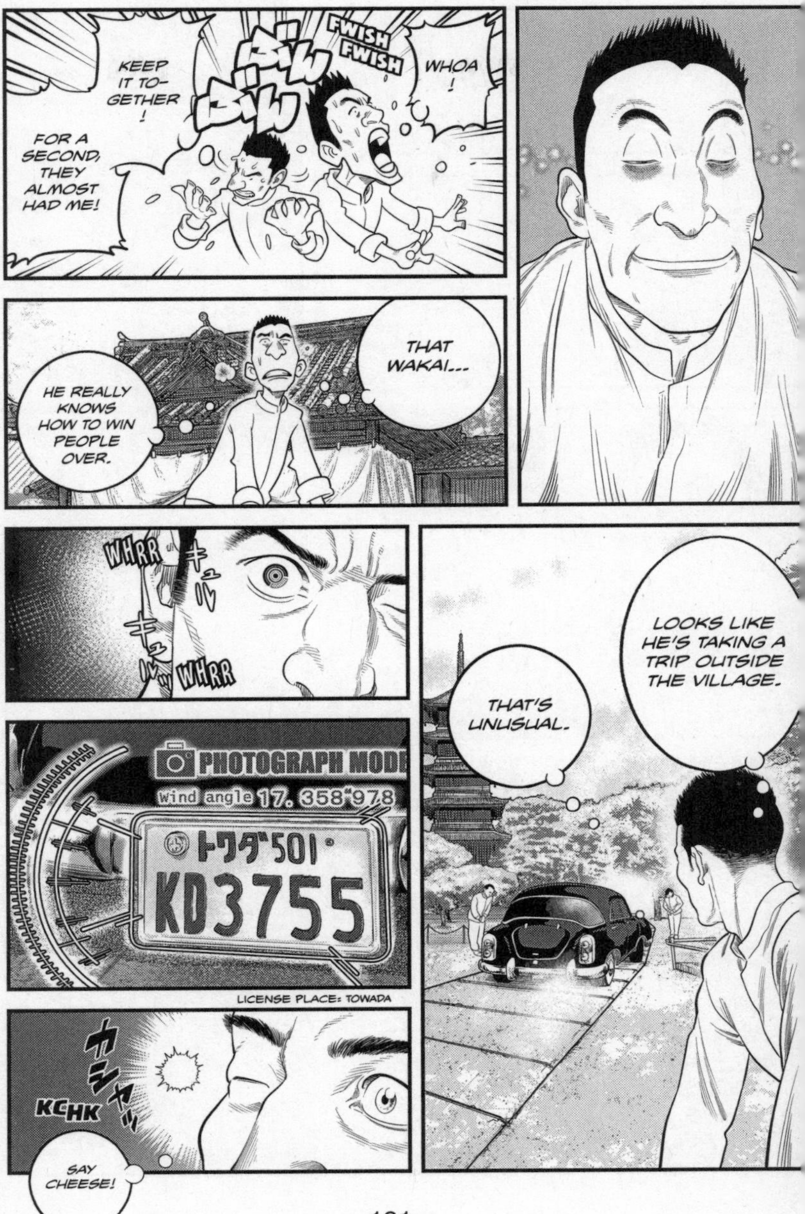
FWISH FWISH
WHOA!
KEEP IT TO-GETHER!
FOR A SECOND, THEY ALMOST HAD ME!
THAT WAKAI...
HE REALLY KNOWS HOW TO WIN PEOPLE OVER.
LOOKS LIKE HE'S TAKING A TRIP OUTSIDE THE VILLAGE.
THAT'S UNUSUAL.
WHRR
WHRR
PHOTOGRAPH MODE
Wind angle 17.358"978
トワダ501
KD3755
LICENSE PLACE: TOWADA
KCHK
SAY CHEESE!

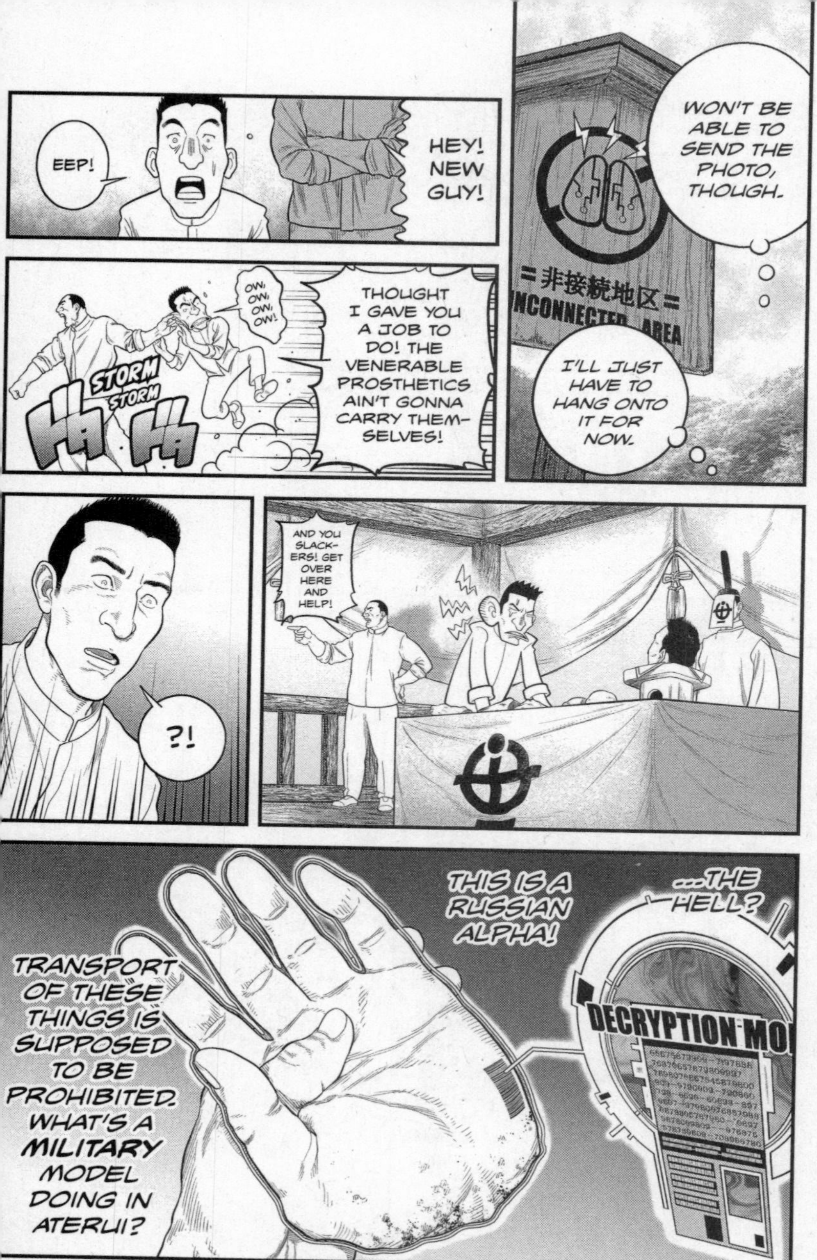
WON'T BE ABLE TO SEND THE PHOTO, THOUGH.
=非接続地区=
UNCONNECTED AREA
I'LL JUST HAVE TO HANG ONTO IT FOR NOW.
HEY! NEW GUY!
EEP!
THOUGHT I GAVE YOU A JOB TO DO! THE VENERABLE PROSTHETICS AIN'T GONNA CARRY THEMSELVES!
OW, OW, OW, OW!
STORM STORM
AND YOU SLACKERS! GET OVER HERE AND HELP!
?!
...THE HELL?
THIS IS A RUSSIAN ALPHA!
DECRYPTION MO
TRANSPORT OF THESE THINGS IS SUPPOSED TO BE PROHIBITED. WHAT'S A MILITARY MODEL DOING IN ATERUI?

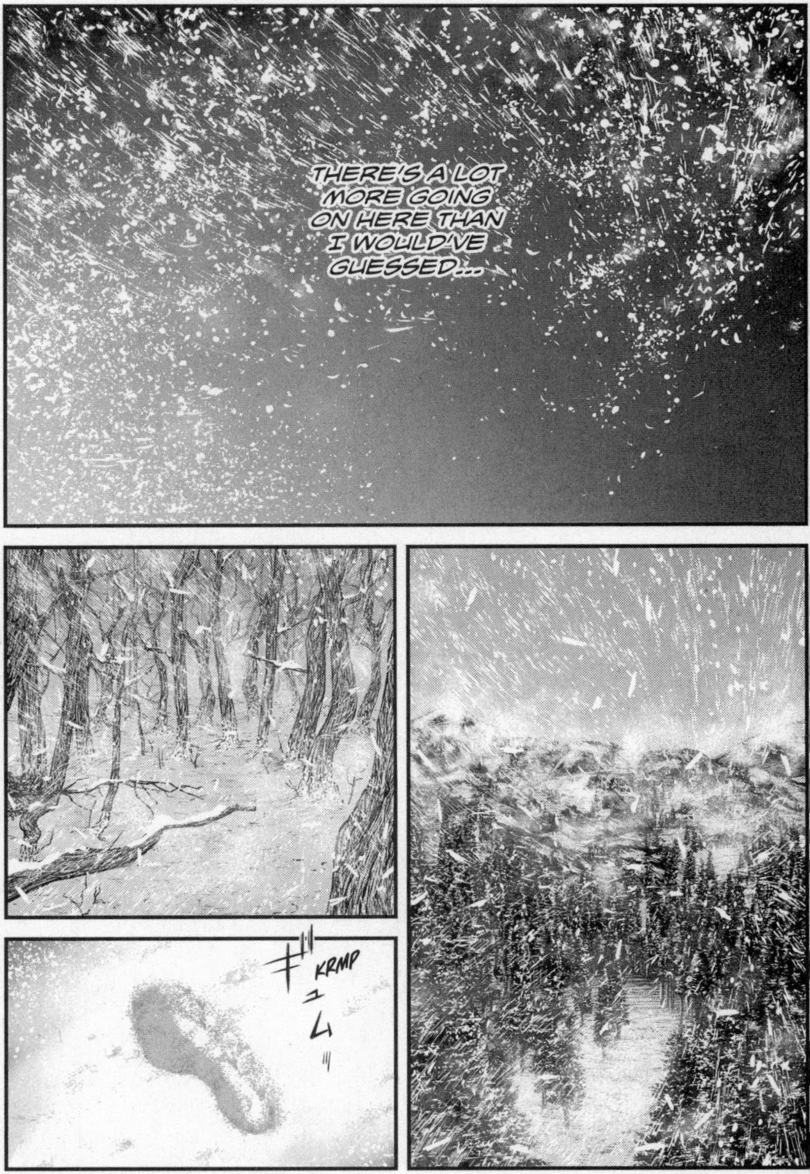
THERE'S A LOT MORE GOING ON HERE THAN I WOULD'VE GUESSED...
ギュム
KRMP

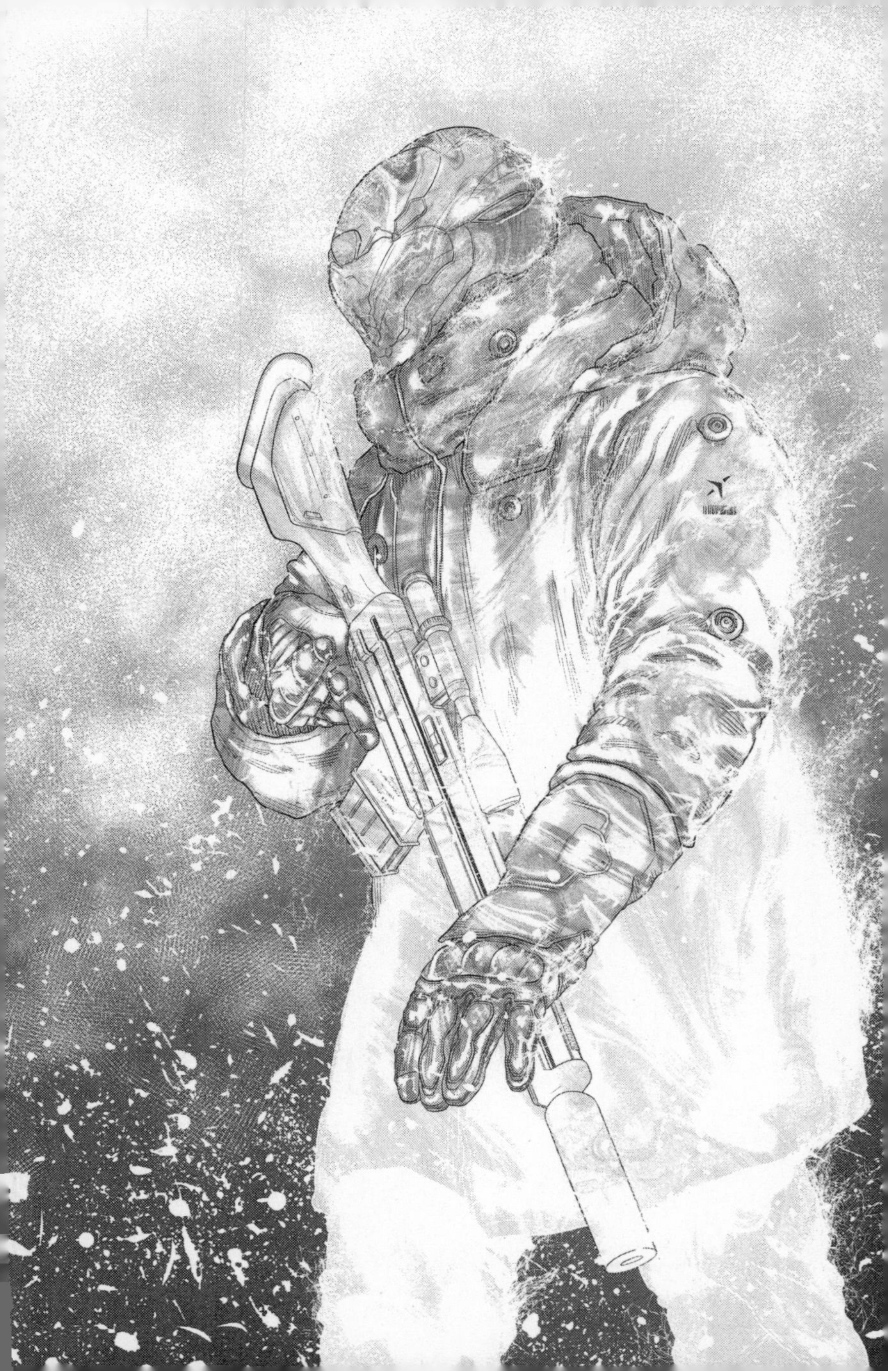

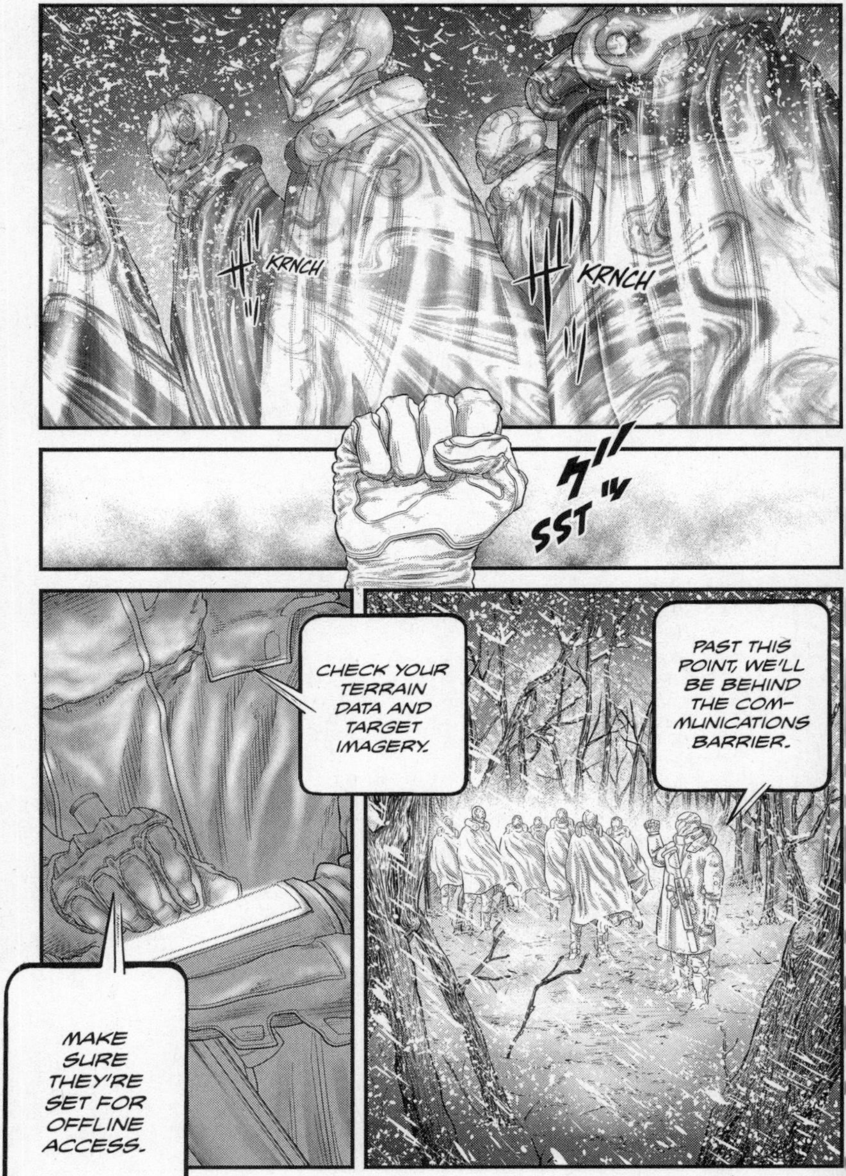
KRNCH
KRNCH
SST
PAST THIS POINT, WE'LL BE BEHIND THE COM-MUNICATIONS BARRIER.
CHECK YOUR TERRAIN DATA AND TARGET IMAGERY.
MAKE SURE THEY'RE SET FOR OFFLINE ACCESS.

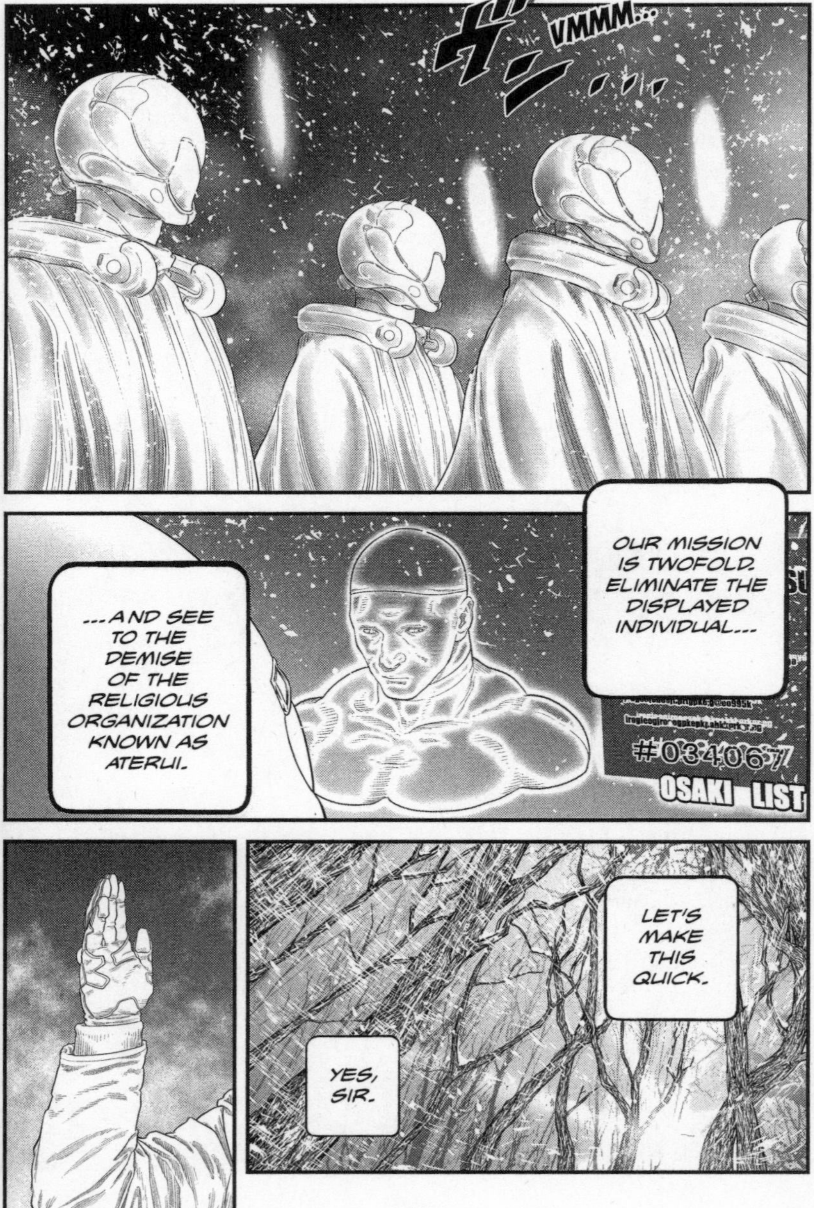
ヴン
VMMM...
OUR MISSION IS TWOFOLD. ELIMINATE THE DISPLAYED INDIVIDUAL...
#03406 7
OSAKI LIST
...AND SEE TO THE DEMISE OF THE RELIGIOUS ORGANIZATION KNOWN AS ATERUI.
LET'S MAKE THIS QUICK.
YES, SIR.

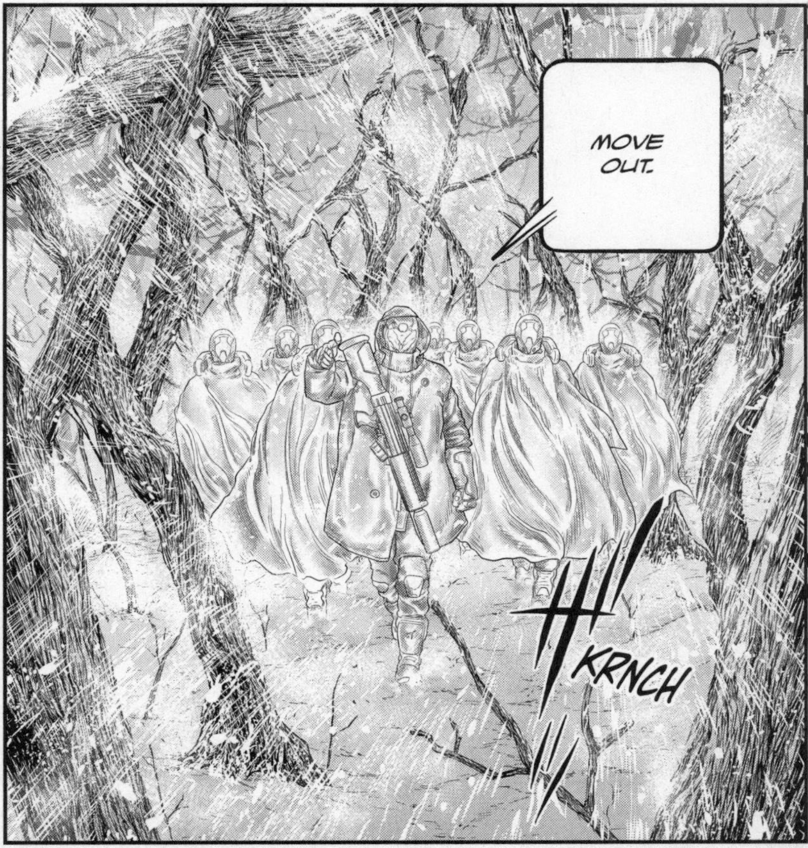
MOVE OUT.
KRNCH
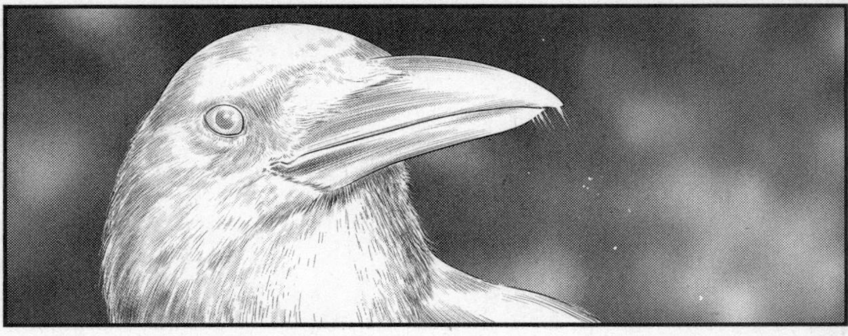

ゴリッ
SHRK
ゴリッ
SHRK

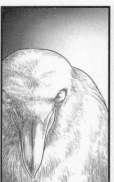

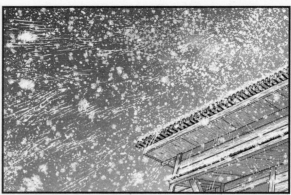

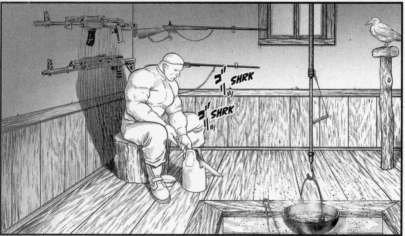

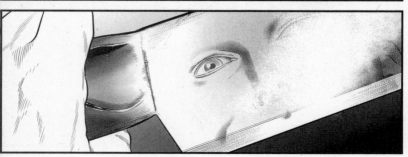

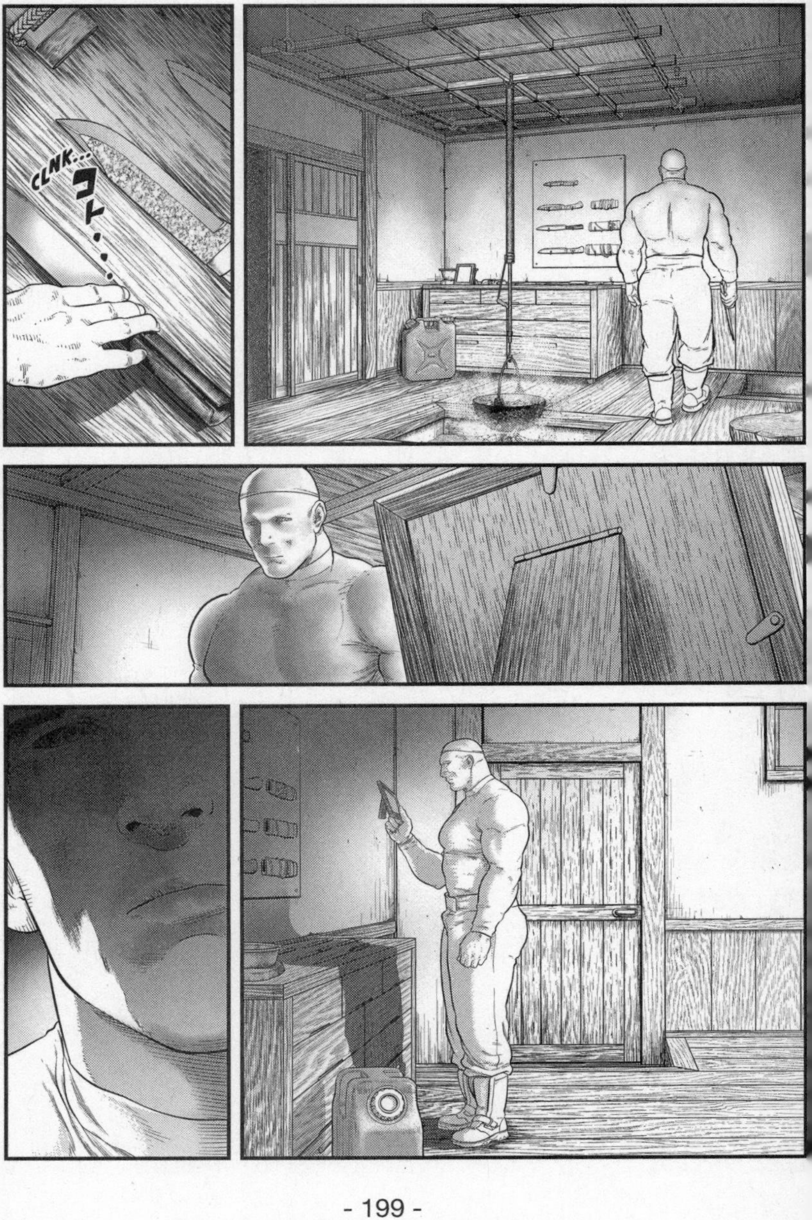
CLNK...
コト・・・

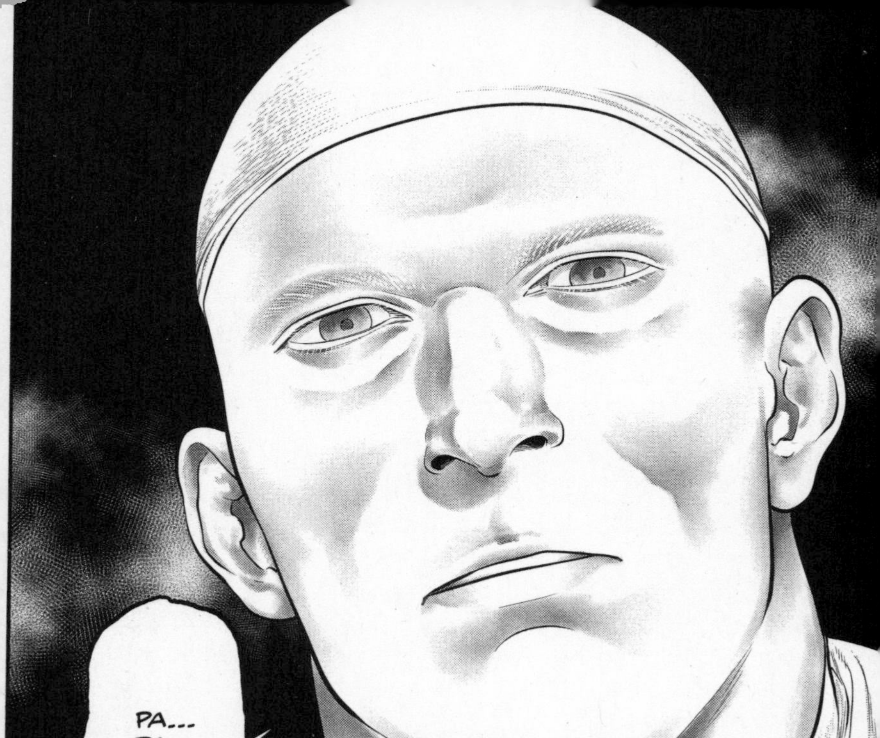
PA...
PA...
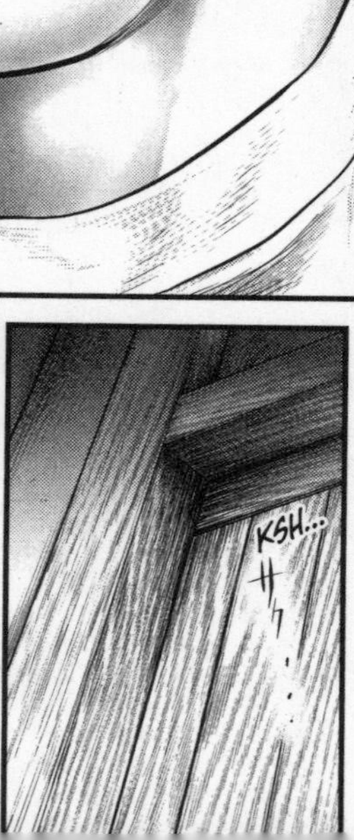
KSH...
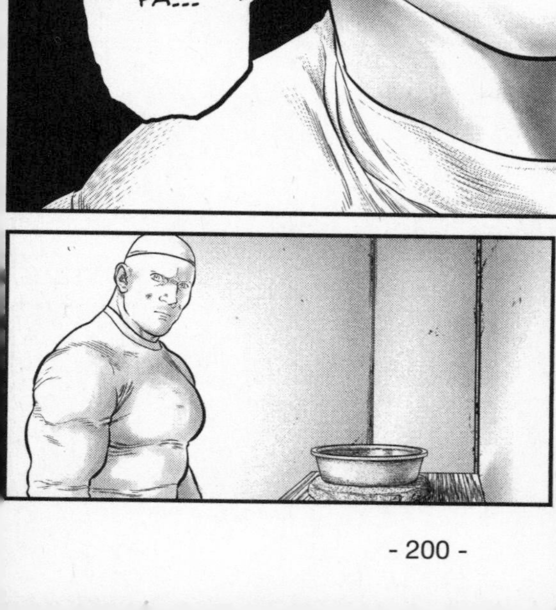

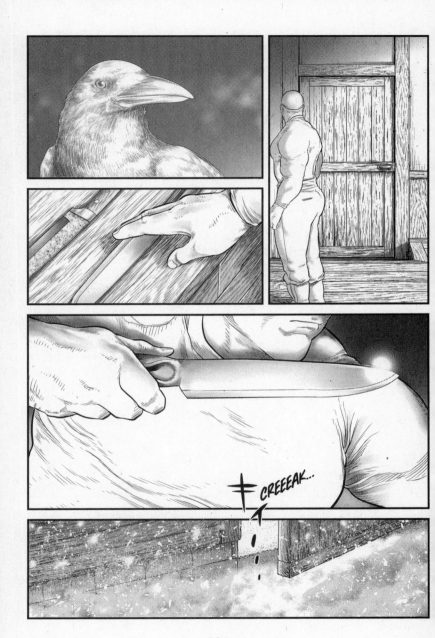

CREEEAK...

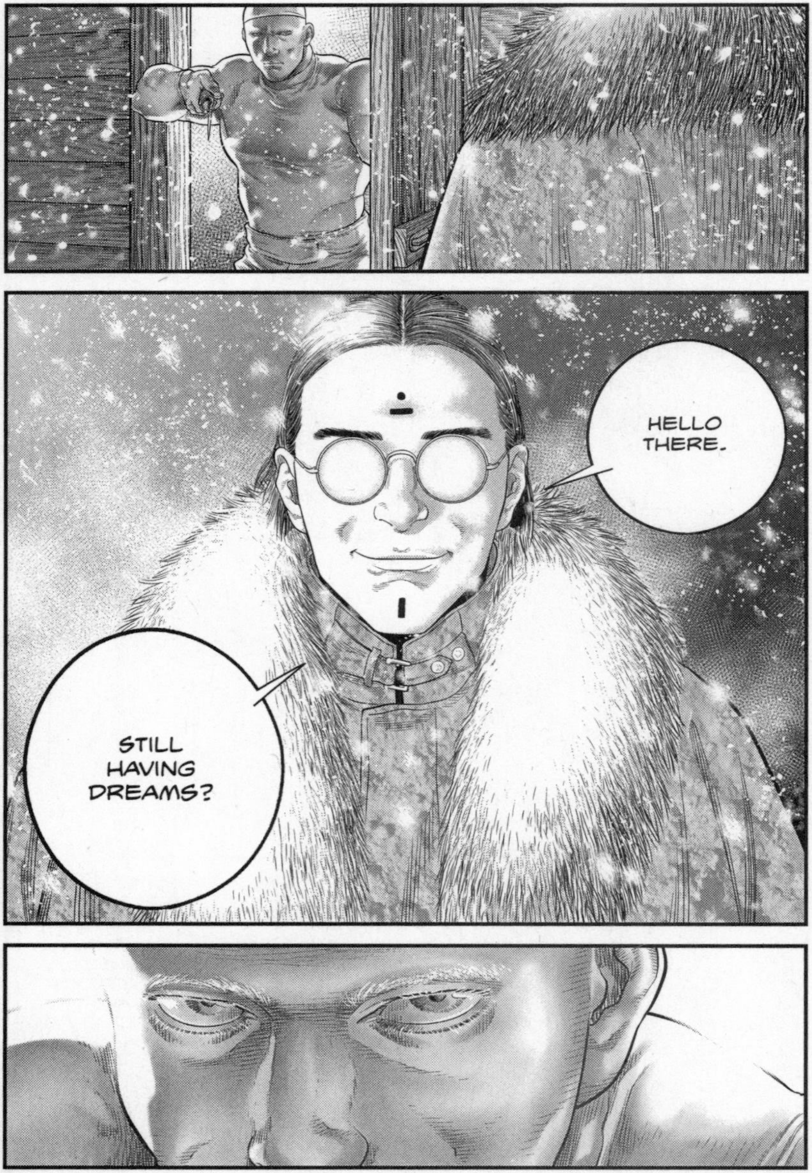
HELLO THERE.
STILL HAVING DREAMS?

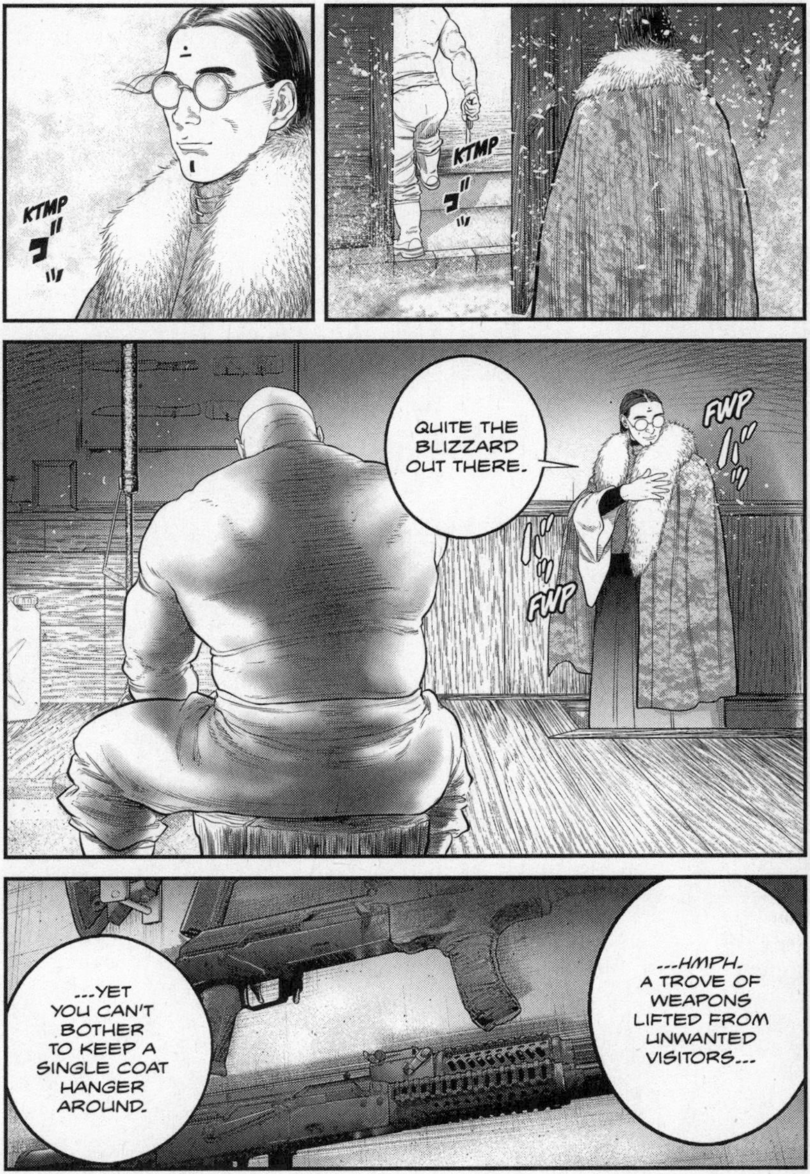
KTMP
KTMP
QUITE THE BLIZZARD OUT THERE.
FWP
FWP
---HMPH. A TROVE OF WEAPONS LIFTED FROM UNWANTED VISITORS---
---YET YOU CAN'T BOTHER TO KEEP A SINGLE COAT HANGER AROUND.

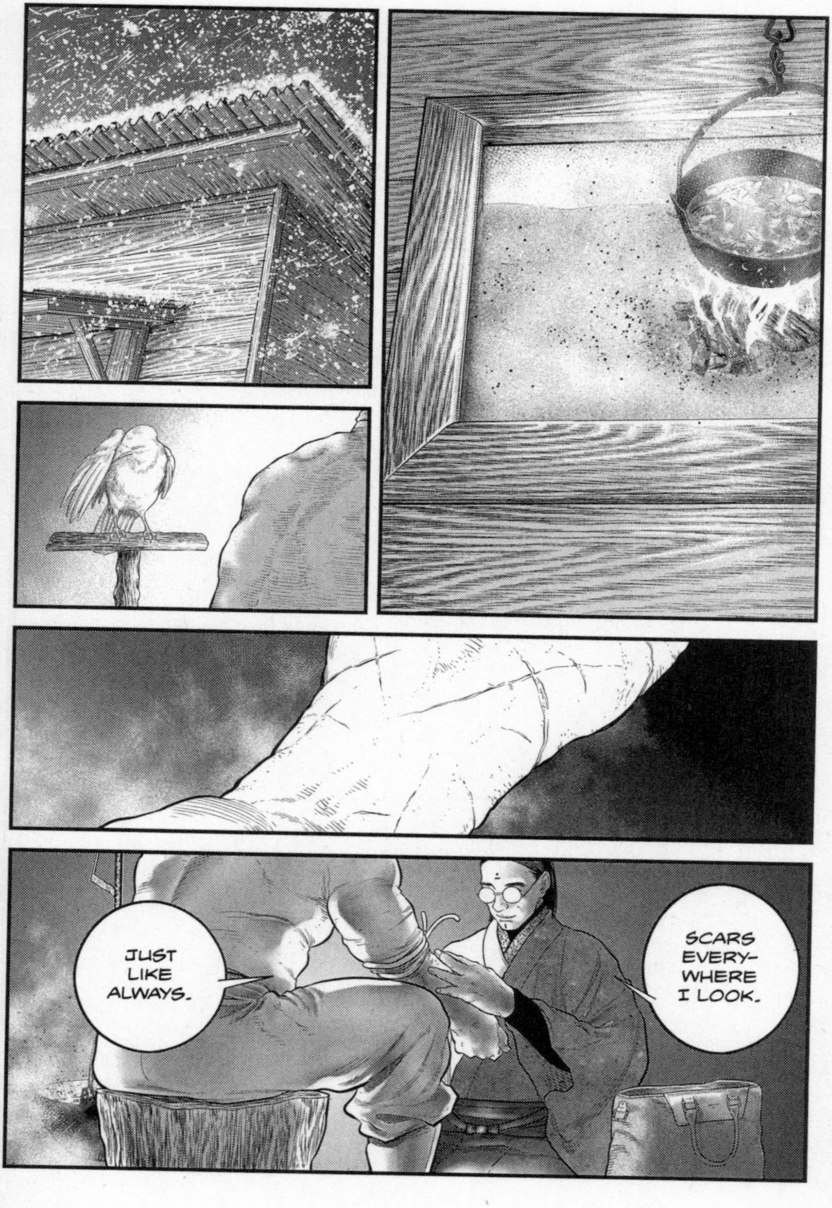
SCARS EVERY-WHERE I LOOK.
JUST LIKE ALWAYS.

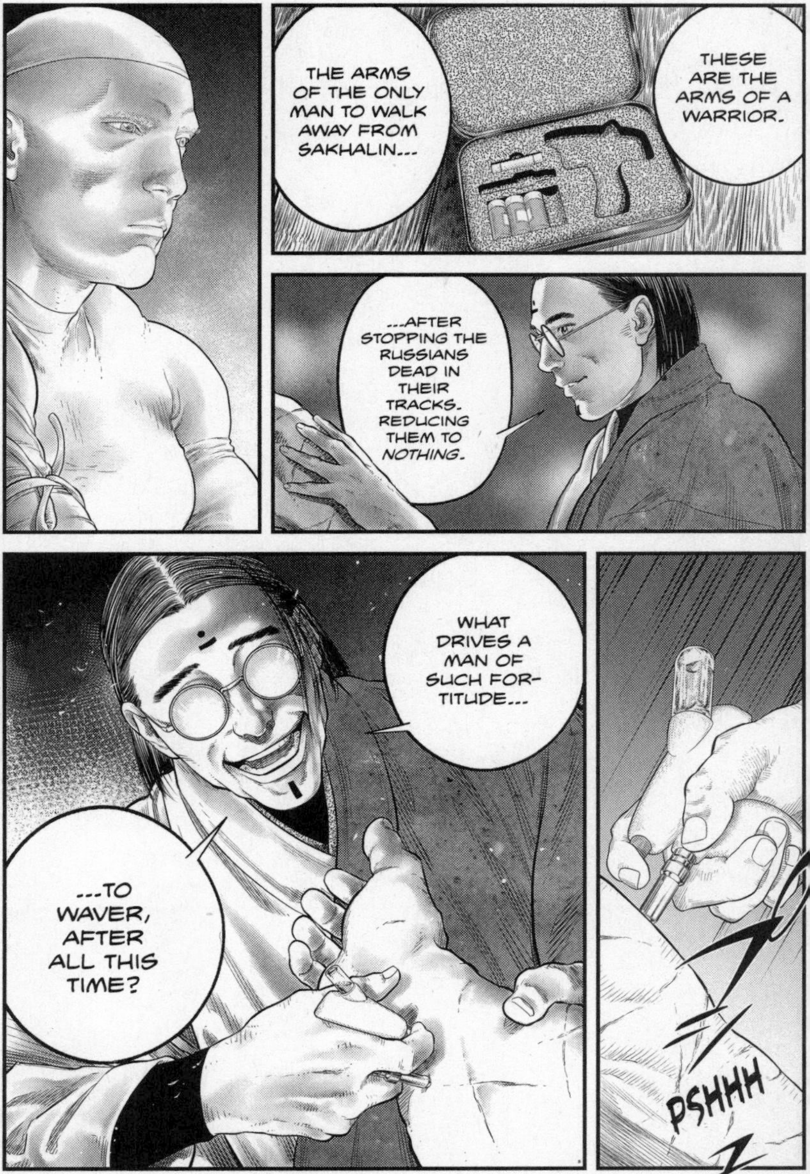
THESE ARE THE ARMS OF A WARRIOR.
THE ARMS OF THE ONLY MAN TO WALK AWAY FROM SAKHALIN...
...AFTER STOPPING THE RUSSIANS DEAD IN THEIR TRACKS. REDUCING THEM TO *NOTHING*.
PSHHH
WHAT DRIVES A MAN OF SUCH FOR-TITUDE...
...TO WAVER, AFTER ALL THIS TIME?

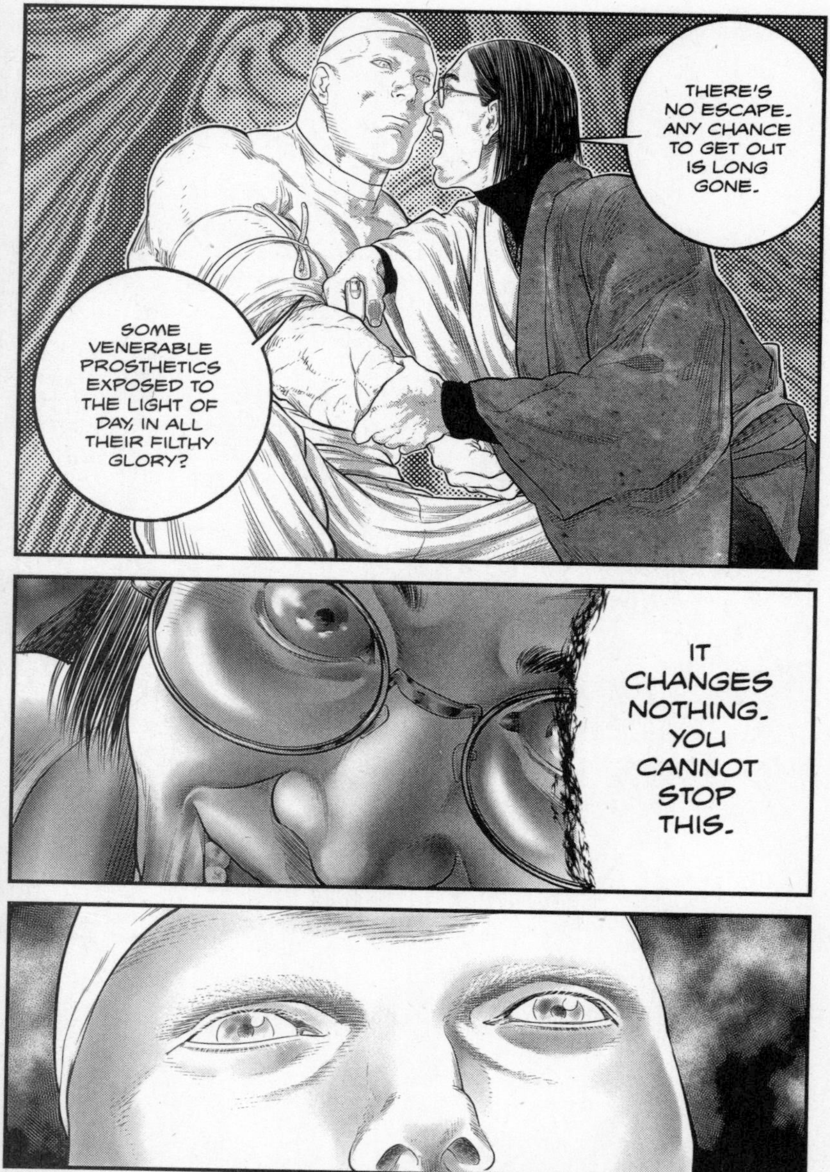
THERE'S NO ESCAPE. ANY CHANCE TO GET OUT IS LONG GONE.
SOME VENERABLE PROSTHETICS EXPOSED TO THE LIGHT OF DAY, IN ALL THEIR FILTHY GLORY?
IT CHANGES NOTHING. YOU CANNOT STOP THIS.

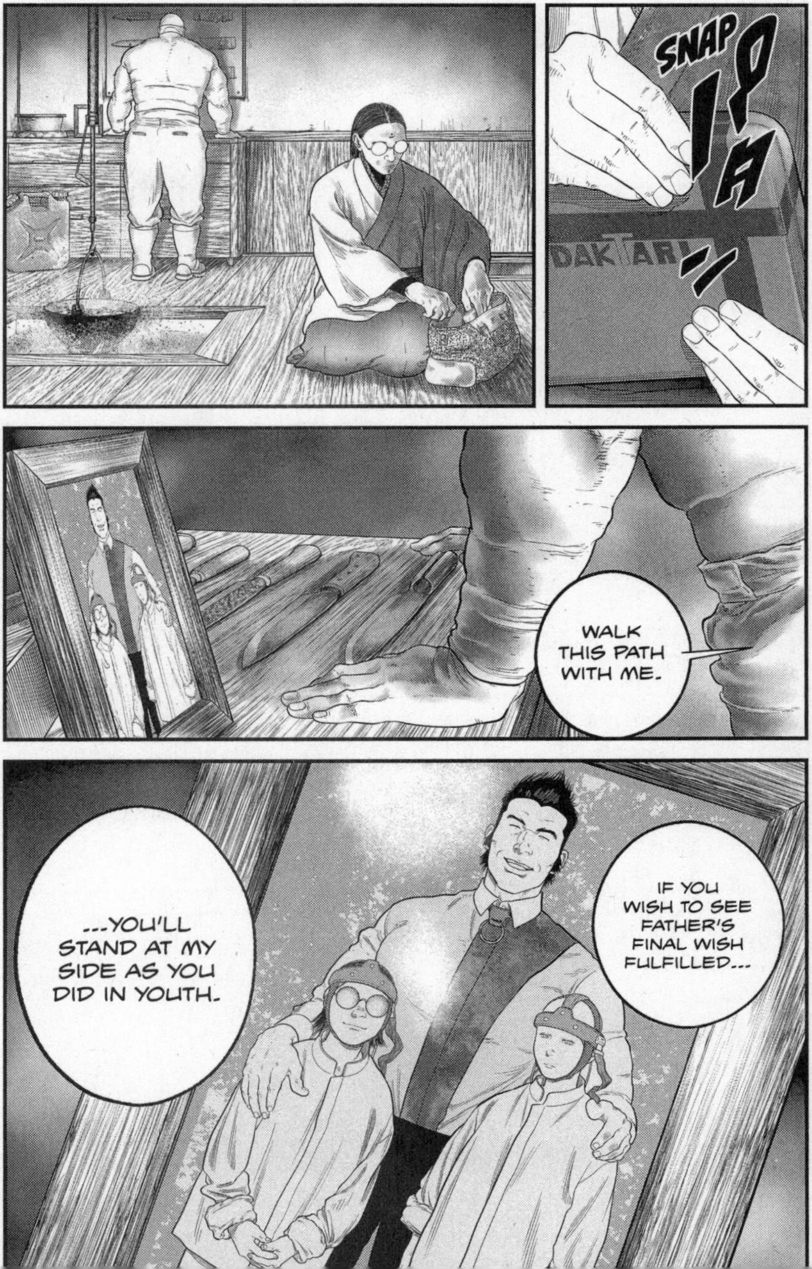
SNAP
DAKTARI
WALK THIS PATH WITH ME.
IF YOU WISH TO SEE FATHER'S FINAL WISH FULFILLED...
...YOU'LL STAND AT MY SIDE AS YOU DID IN YOUTH.

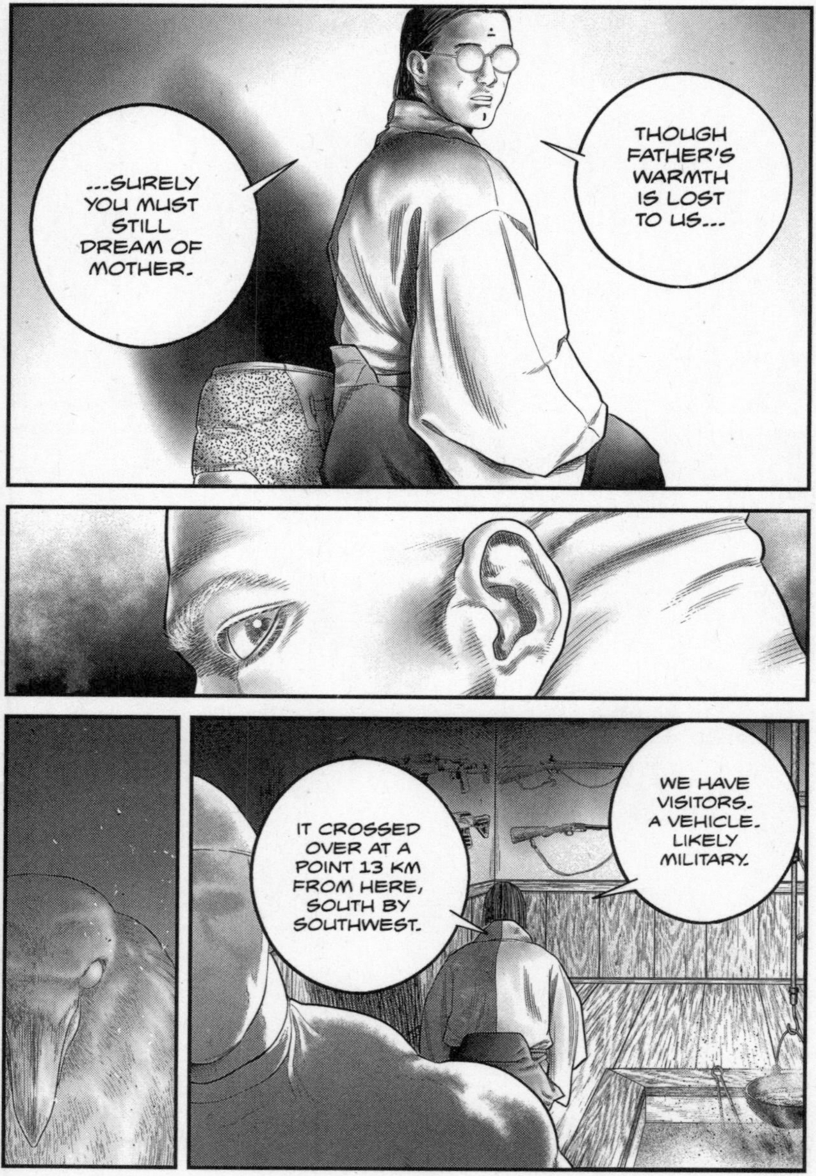
THOUGH FATHER'S WARMTH IS LOST TO US...
...SURELY YOU MUST STILL DREAM OF MOTHER.
WE HAVE VISITORS. A VEHICLE. LIKELY MILITARY.
IT CROSSED OVER AT A POINT 13 KM FROM HERE, SOUTH BY SOUTHWEST.

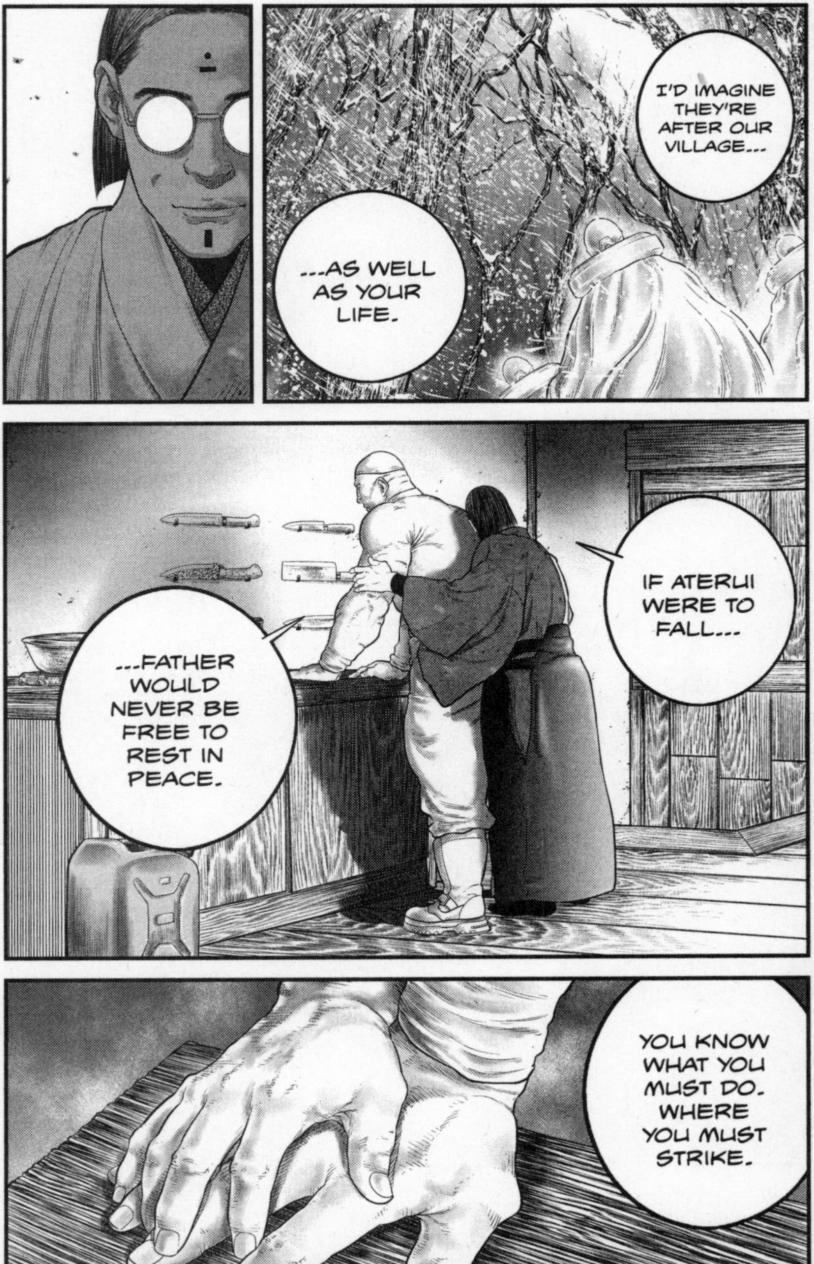
I'D IMAGINE THEY'RE AFTER OUR VILLAGE...
...AS WELL AS YOUR LIFE.
IF ATERUI WERE TO FALL...
...FATHER WOULD NEVER BE FREE TO REST IN PEACE.
YOU KNOW WHAT YOU MUST DO. WHERE YOU MUST STRIKE.

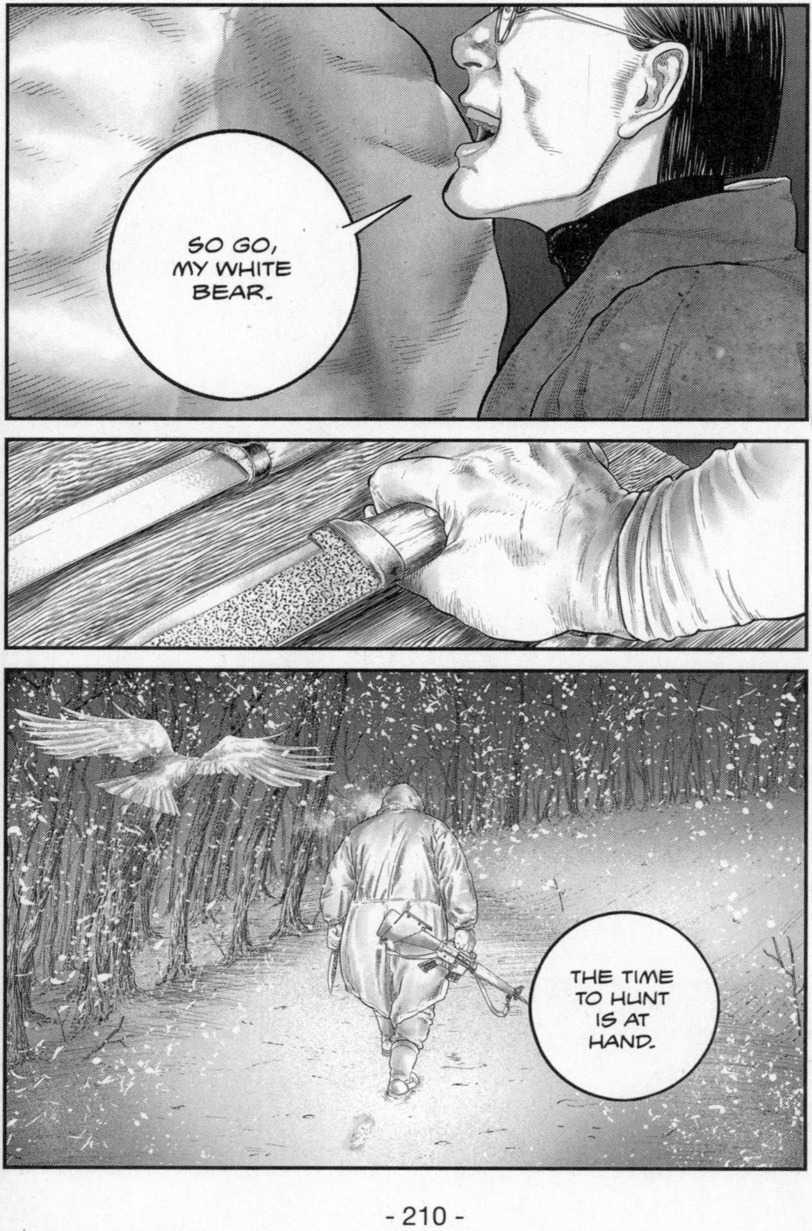
SO GO, MY WHITE BEAR.
THE TIME TO HUNT IS AT HAND.

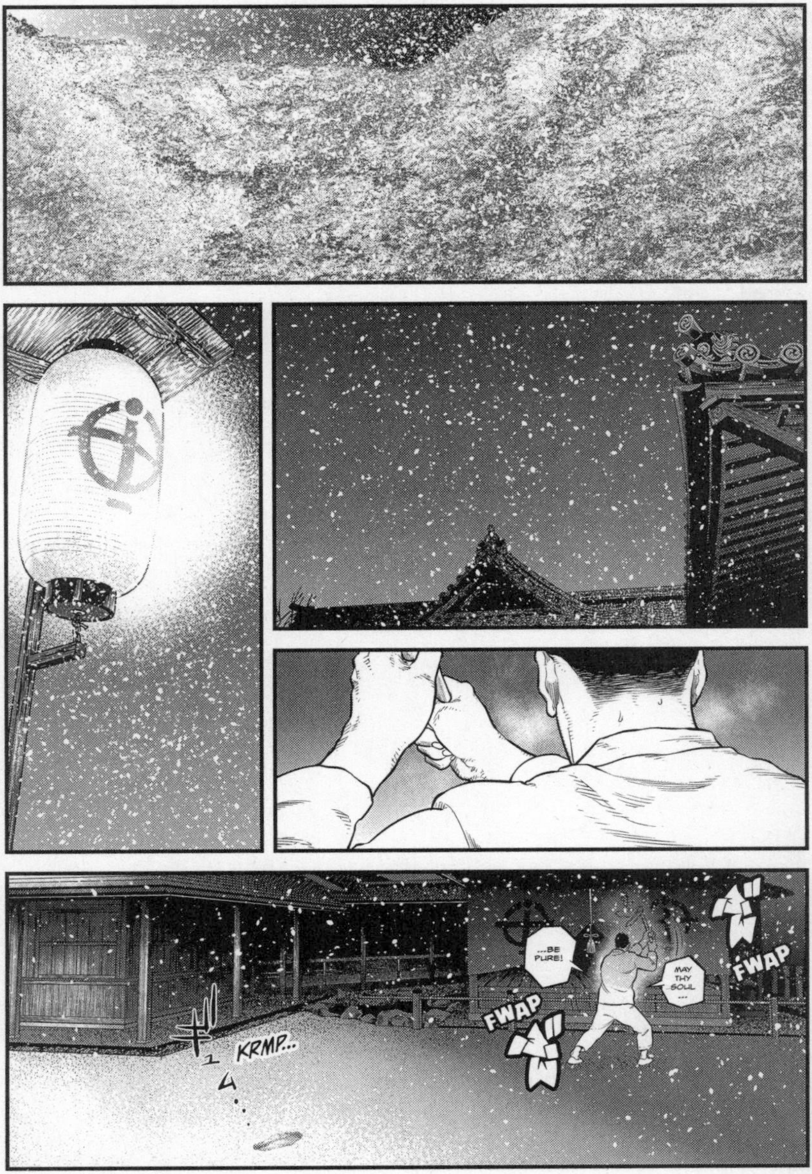
FWAP
MAY THY SOUL ...
...BE PURE!
FWAP
KRMP...

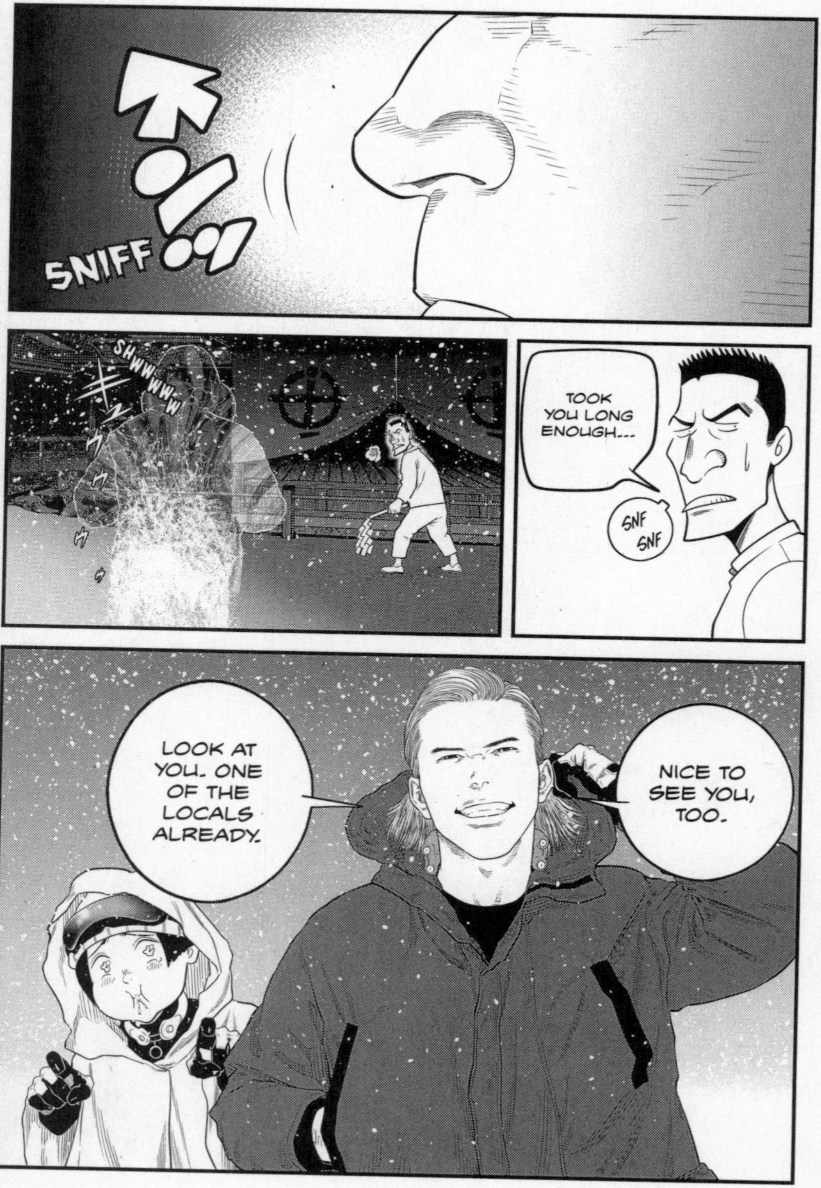
SNIFF
TOOK YOU LONG ENOUGH...
SNF SNF
SHWWWWW
NICE TO SEE YOU, TOO.
LOOK AT YOU. ONE OF THE LOCALS ALREADY.

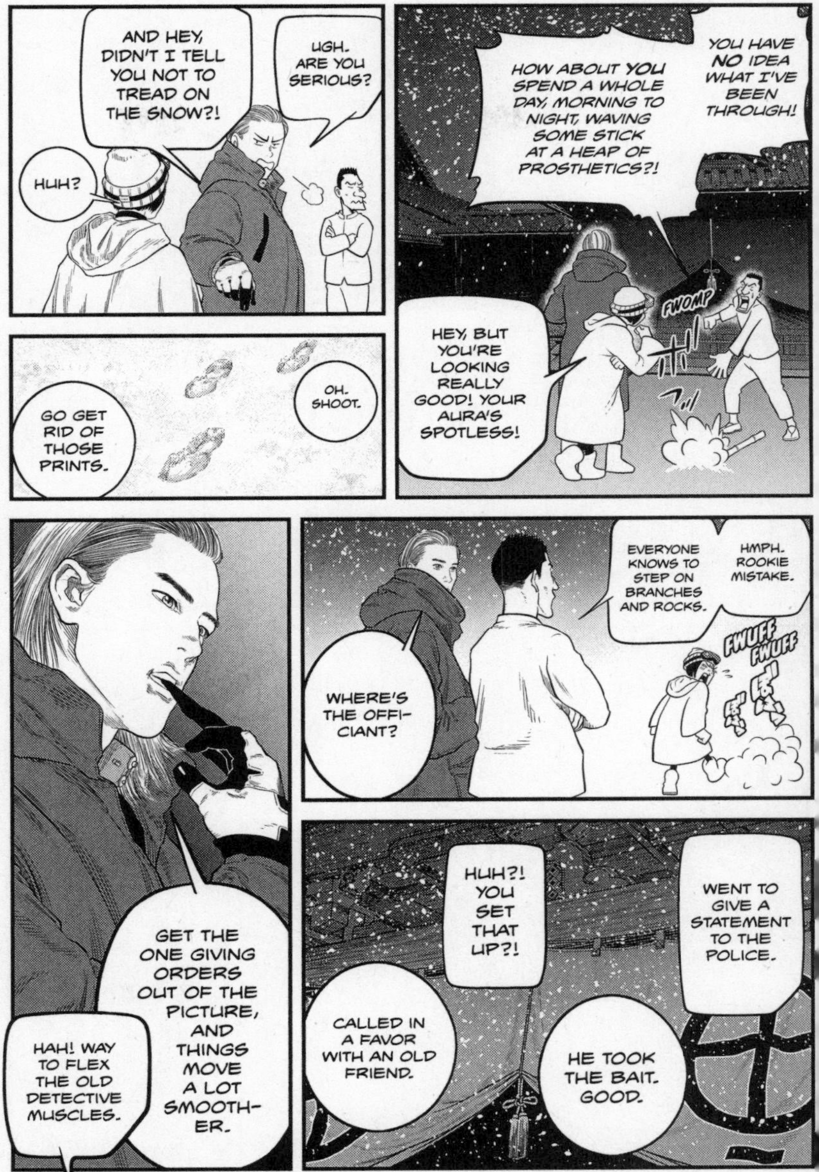
YOU HAVE NO IDEA WHAT I'VE BEEN THROUGH!
HOW ABOUT YOU SPEND A WHOLE DAY, MORNING TO NIGHT, WAVING SOME STICK AT A HEAP OF PROSTHETICS?!
FWOMP
HEY, BUT YOU'RE LOOKING REALLY GOOD! YOUR AURA'S SPOTLESS!
UGH. ARE YOU SERIOUS?
AND HEY, DIDN'T I TELL YOU NOT TO TREAD ON THE SNOW?!
HUH?
OH. SHOOT.
GO GET RID OF THOSE PRINTS.
HMPH. ROOKIE MISTAKE.
EVERYONE KNOWS TO STEP ON BRANCHES AND ROCKS.
FWUFF FWUFF
WHERE'S THE OFFICIANT?
WENT TO GIVE A STATEMENT TO THE POLICE.
HUH?! YOU SET THAT UP?!
HE TOOK THE BAIT. GOOD.
CALLED IN A FAVOR WITH AN OLD FRIEND.
GET THE ONE GIVING ORDERS OUT OF THE PICTURE, AND THINGS MOVE A LOT SMOOTHER.
HAH! WAY TO FLEX THE OLD DETECTIVE MUSCLES.

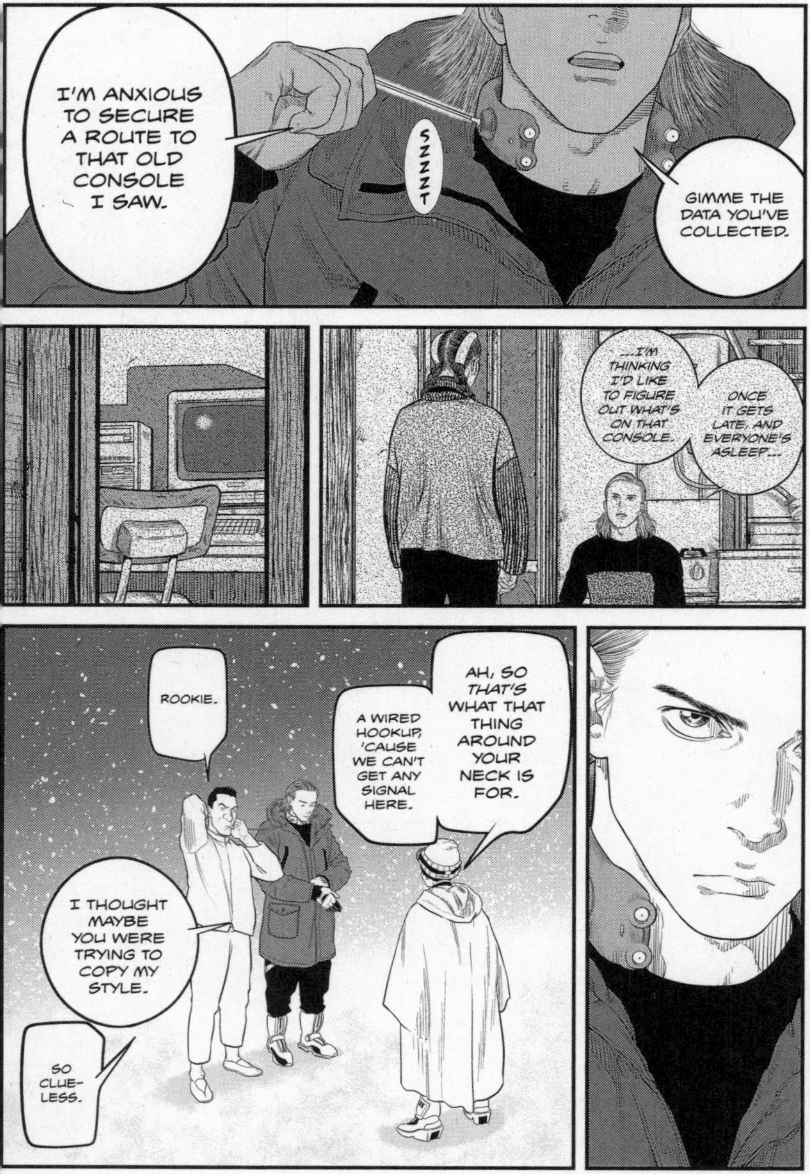
GIMME THE DATA YOU'VE COLLECTED.
SZZZT
I'M ANXIOUS TO SECURE A ROUTE TO THAT OLD CONSOLE I SAW.
...I'M THINKING I'D LIKE TO FIGURE OUT WHAT'S ON THAT CONSOLE.
ONCE IT GETS LATE, AND EVERYONE'S ASLEEP...
AH, SO THAT'S WHAT THAT THING AROUND YOUR NECK IS FOR.
A WIRED HOOKUP, 'CAUSE WE CAN'T GET ANY SIGNAL HERE.
ROOKIE.
I THOUGHT MAYBE YOU WERE TRYING TO COPY MY STYLE.
SO CLUE-LESS.

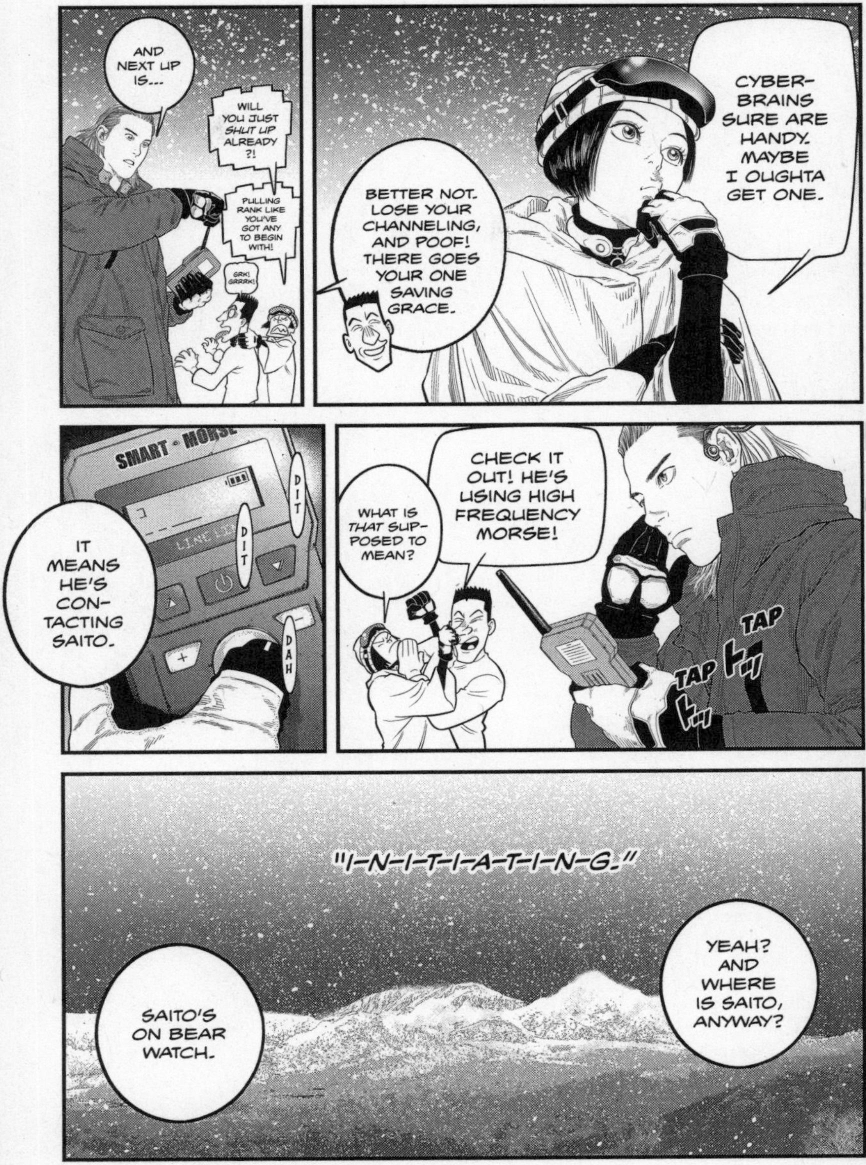
CYBER-BRAINS SURE ARE HANDY. MAYBE I OUGHTA GET ONE.
BETTER NOT. LOSE YOUR CHANNELING, AND POOF! THERE GOES YOUR ONE SAVING GRACE.
AND NEXT UP IS...
WILL YOU JUST SHUT UP ALREADY ?!
PULLING RANK LIKE YOU'VE GOT ANY TO BEGIN WITH!
GRK! GRRRK!
CHECK IT OUT! HE'S USING HIGH FREQUENCY MORSE!
WHAT IS THAT SUPPOSED TO MEAN?
TAP
TAP
SMART MORSE
DIT
DIT
DAH
IT MEANS HE'S CONTACTING SAITO.
"I-N-I-T-I-A-T-I-N-G."
YEAH? AND WHERE IS SAITO, ANYWAY?
SAITO'S ON BEAR WATCH.

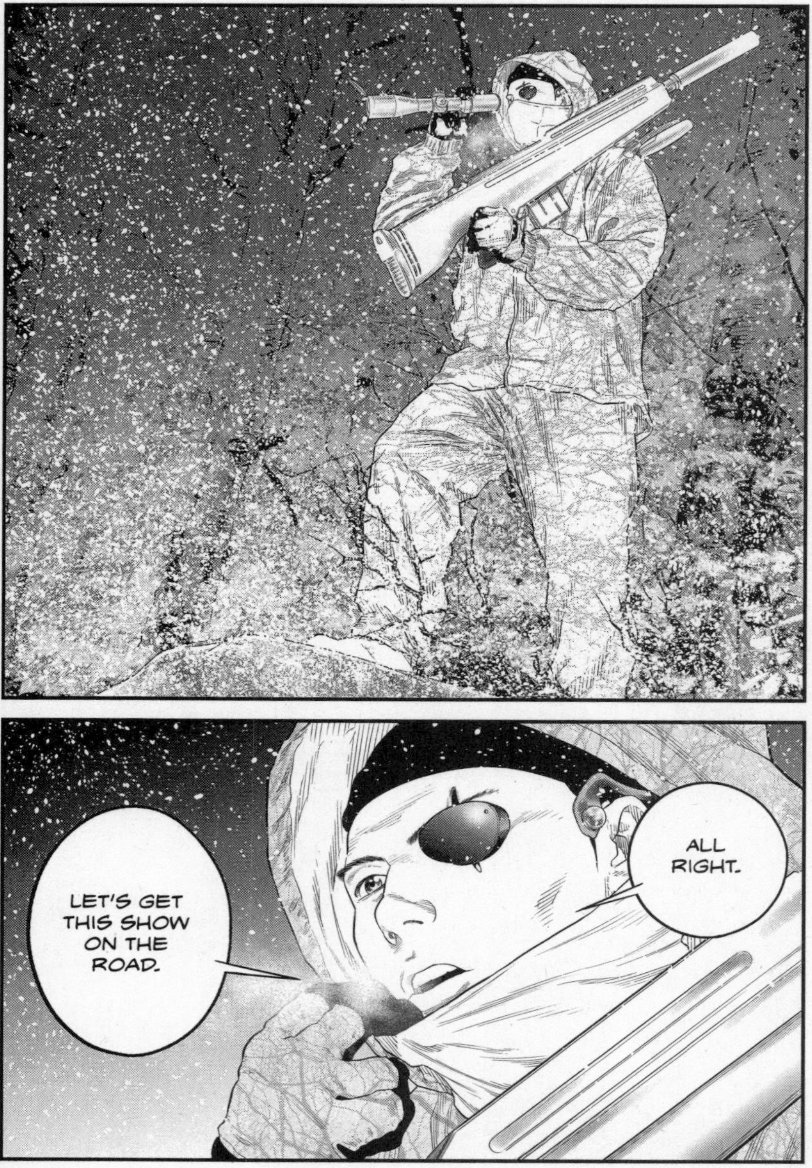
ALL RIGHT.
LET'S GET THIS SHOW ON THE ROAD.

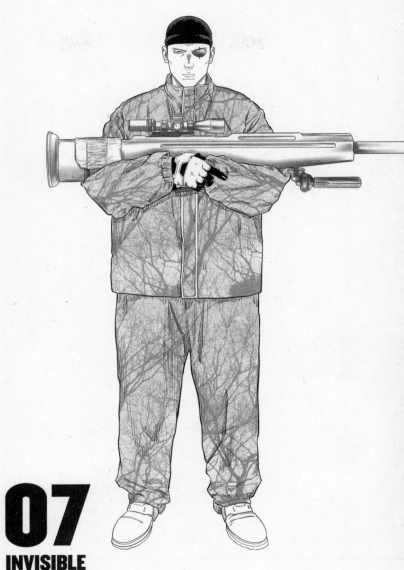

07
INVISIBLE
ENEMIES

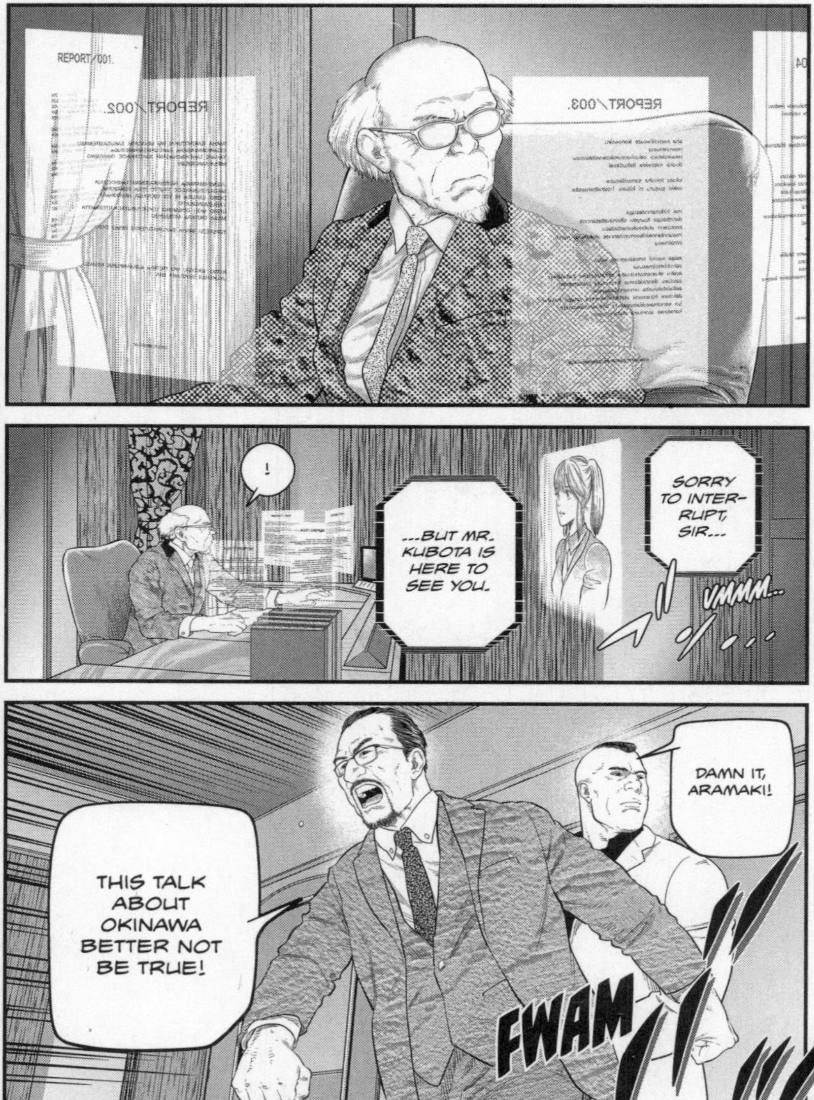
REPORT/001.
SORRY TO INTER-RUPT, SIR...
VMMM...
...BUT MR. KUBOTA IS HERE TO SEE YOU.
!
DAMN IT, ARAMAKI!
FWAM
THIS TALK ABOUT OKINAWA BETTER NOT BE TRUE!

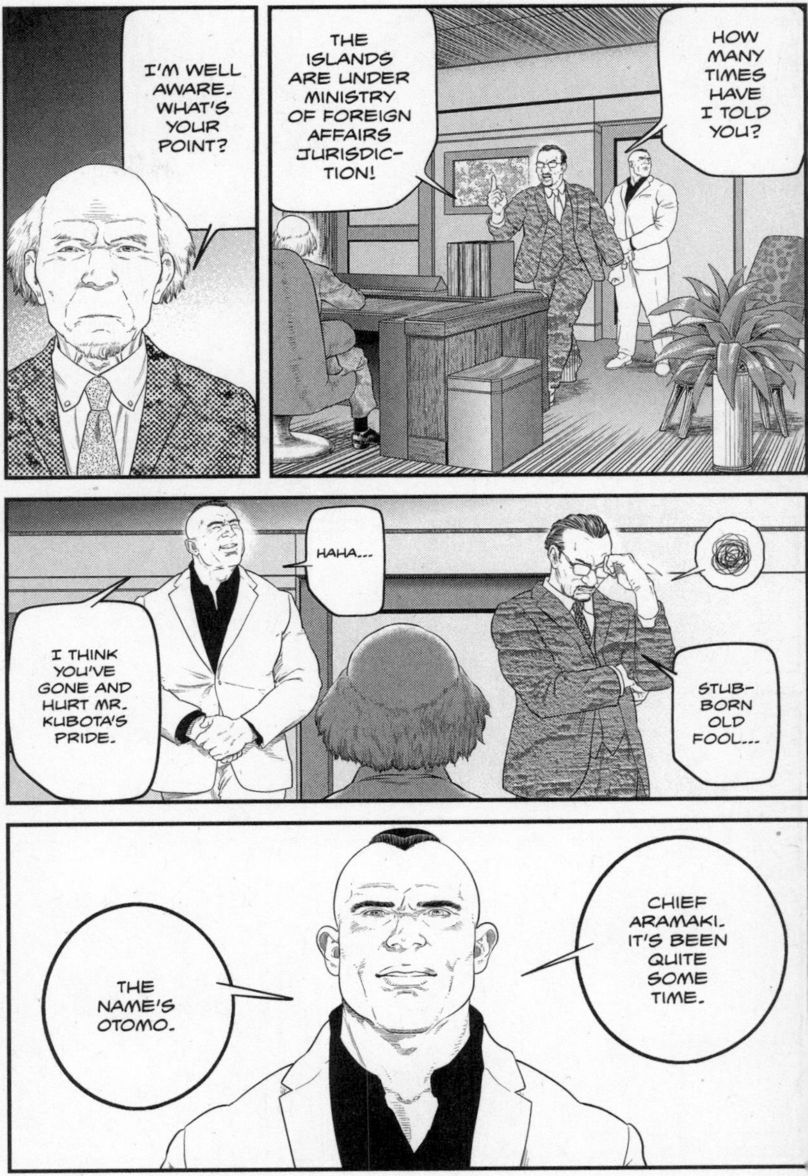
HOW MANY TIMES HAVE I TOLD YOU?
THE ISLANDS ARE UNDER MINISTRY OF FOREIGN AFFAIRS JURISDIC-TION!
I'M WELL AWARE. WHAT'S YOUR POINT?
STUB-BORN OLD FOOL...
HAHA...
I THINK YOU'VE GONE AND HURT MR. KUBOTA'S PRIDE.
CHIEF ARAMAKI. IT'S BEEN QUITE SOME TIME.
THE NAME'S OTOMO.

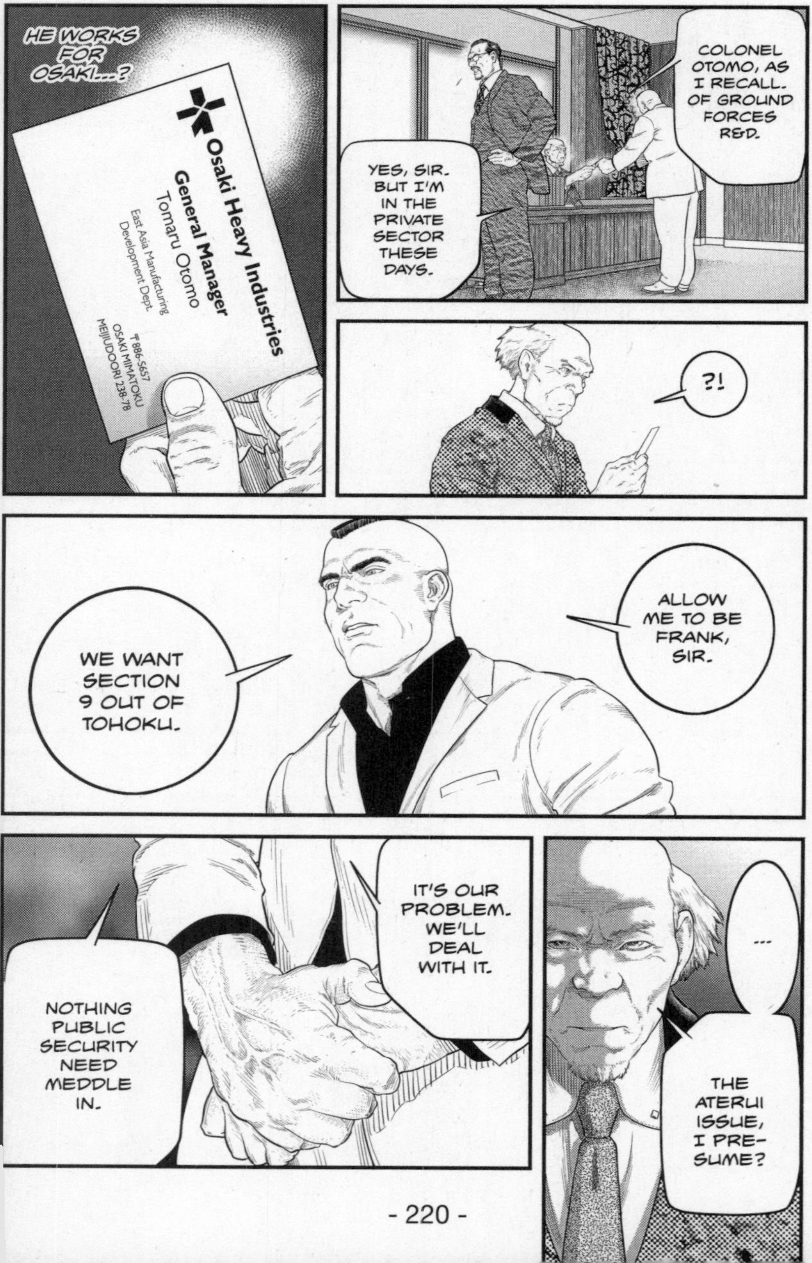
COLONEL OTOMO, AS I RECALL. OF GROUND FORCES R&D.
YES, SIR. BUT I'M IN THE PRIVATE SECTOR THESE DAYS.
?!
HE WORKS FOR OSAKI...?
Osaki Heavy Industries
General Manager
Tomaru Otomo
East Asia Manufacturing
Development Dept.
〒886-5657
OSAKI MIMATOKU
MEIJIDOORI 238-78
ALLOW ME TO BE FRANK, SIR.
WE WANT SECTION 9 OUT OF TOHOKU.
...
THE ATERUI ISSUE, I PRESUME?
IT'S OUR PROBLEM. WE'LL DEAL WITH IT.
NOTHING PUBLIC SECURITY NEED MEDDLE IN.

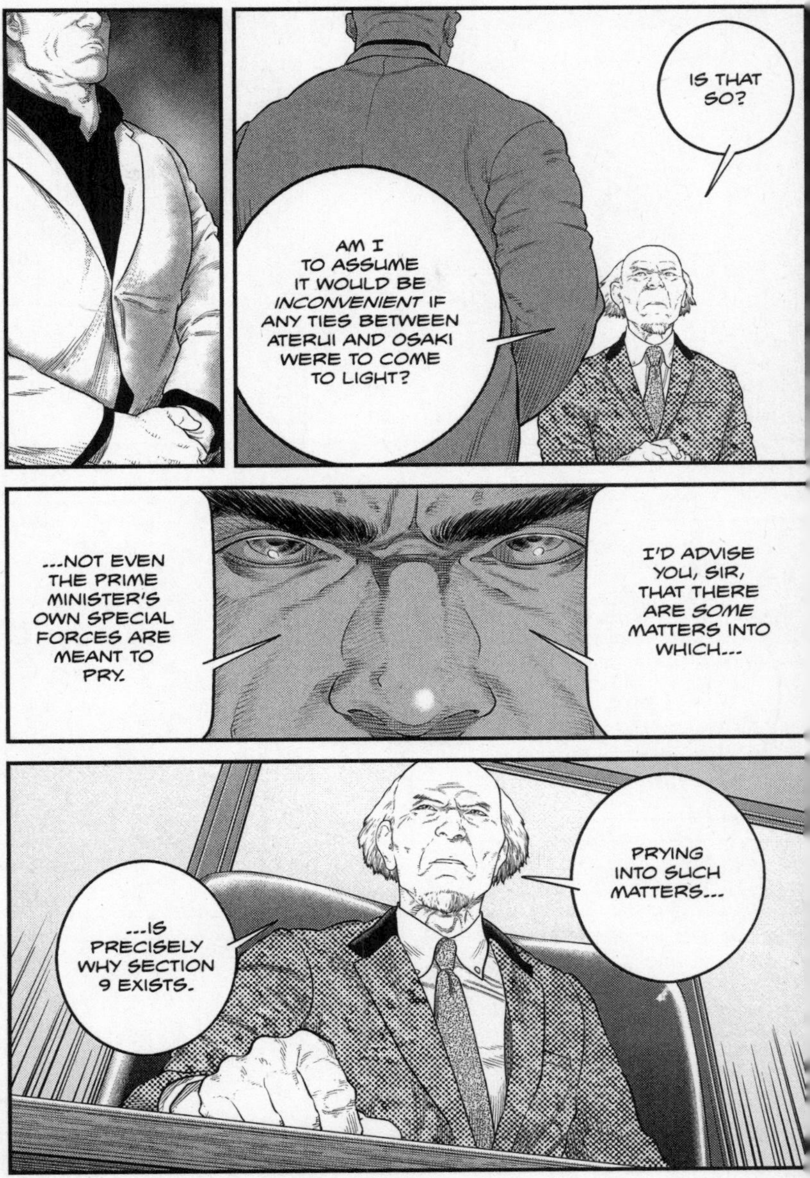
IS THAT SO?
AM I TO ASSUME IT WOULD BE *INCONVENIENT* IF ANY TIES BETWEEN ATERUI AND OSAKI WERE TO COME TO LIGHT?
I'D ADVISE YOU, SIR, THAT THERE ARE *SOME* MATTERS INTO WHICH...
...NOT EVEN THE PRIME MINISTER'S OWN SPECIAL FORCES ARE MEANT TO PRY.
PRYING INTO SUCH MATTERS...
...IS PRECISELY WHY SECTION 9 EXISTS.

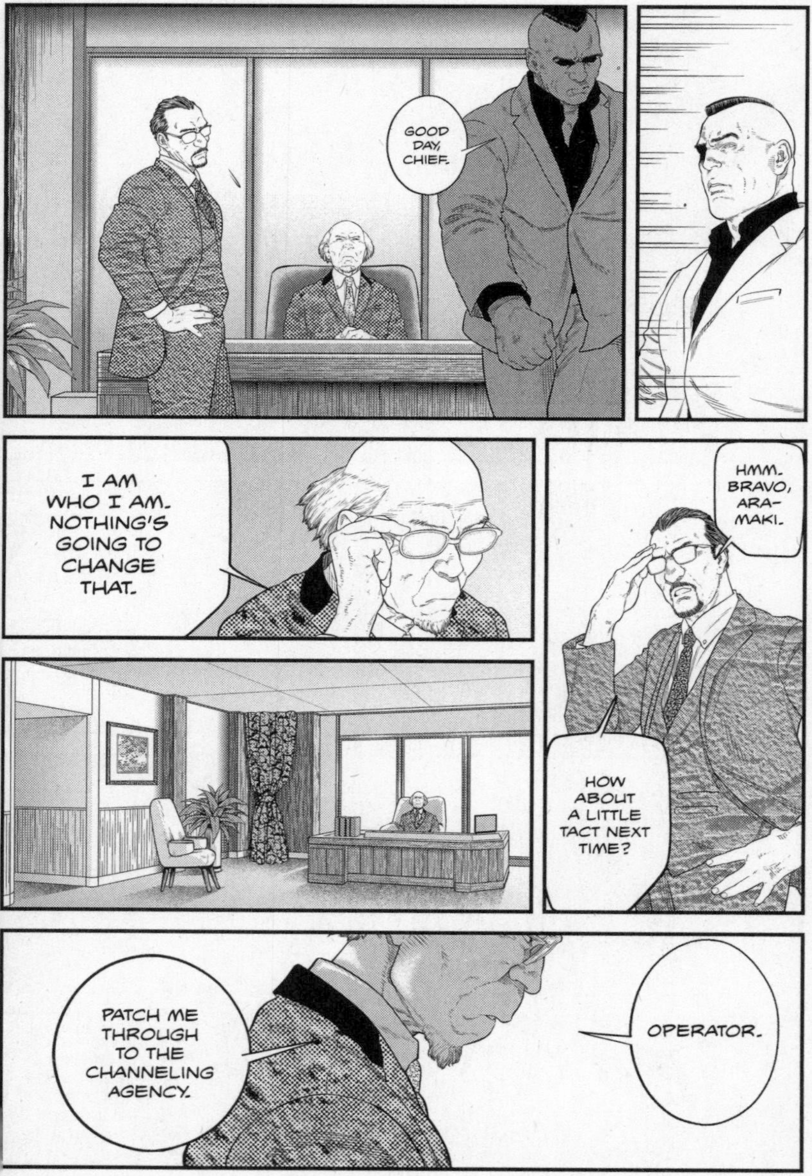
GOOD DAY, CHIEF.
HMM. BRAVO, ARA-MAKI.
HOW ABOUT A LITTLE TACT NEXT TIME?
I AM WHO I AM. NOTHING'S GOING TO CHANGE THAT.
OPERATOR.
PATCH ME THROUGH TO THE CHANNELING AGENCY.

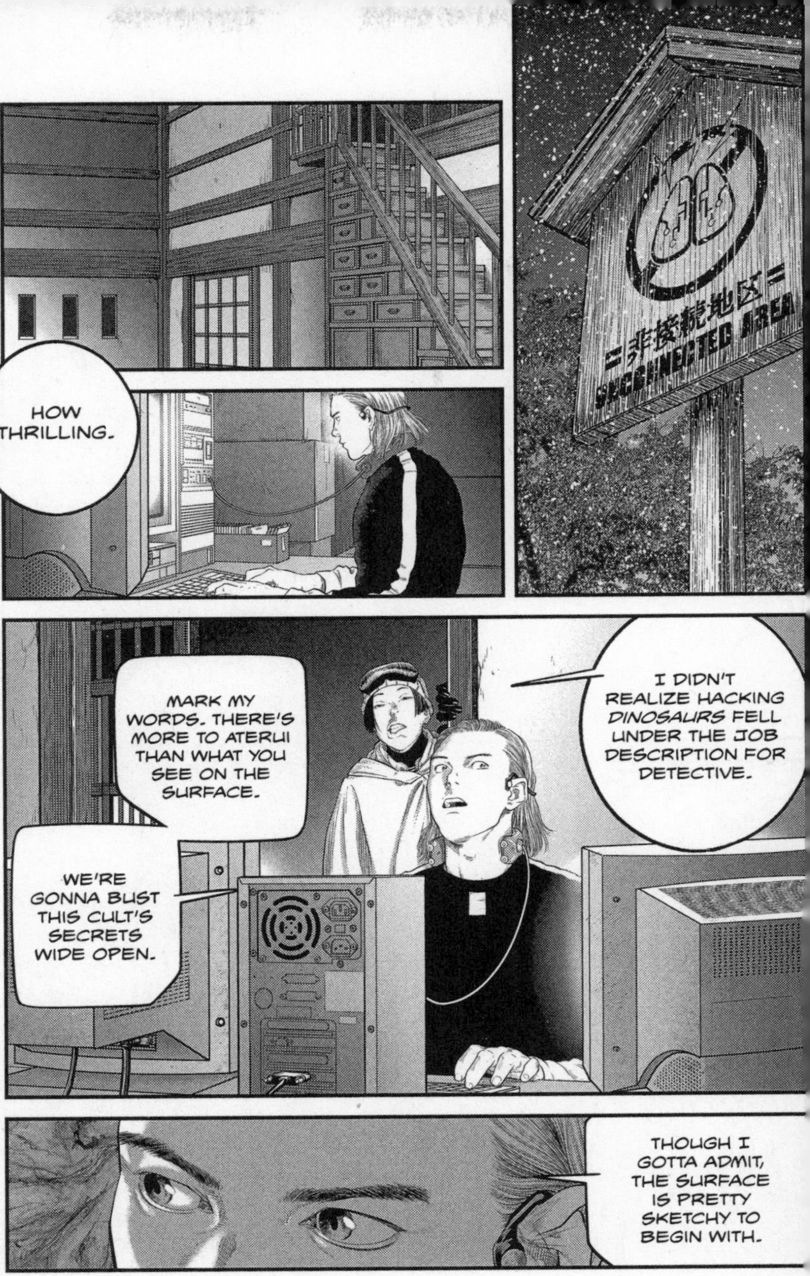
=非接続地区=
=UNCONNECTED AREA=
HOW THRILLING.
I DIDN'T REALIZE HACKING *DINOSAURS* FELL UNDER THE JOB DESCRIPTION FOR DETECTIVE.
MARK MY WORDS. THERE'S MORE TO ATERUI THAN WHAT YOU SEE ON THE SURFACE.
WE'RE GONNA BUST THIS CULT'S SECRETS WIDE OPEN.
THOUGH I GOTTA ADMIT, THE SURFACE IS PRETTY SKETCHY TO BEGIN WITH.

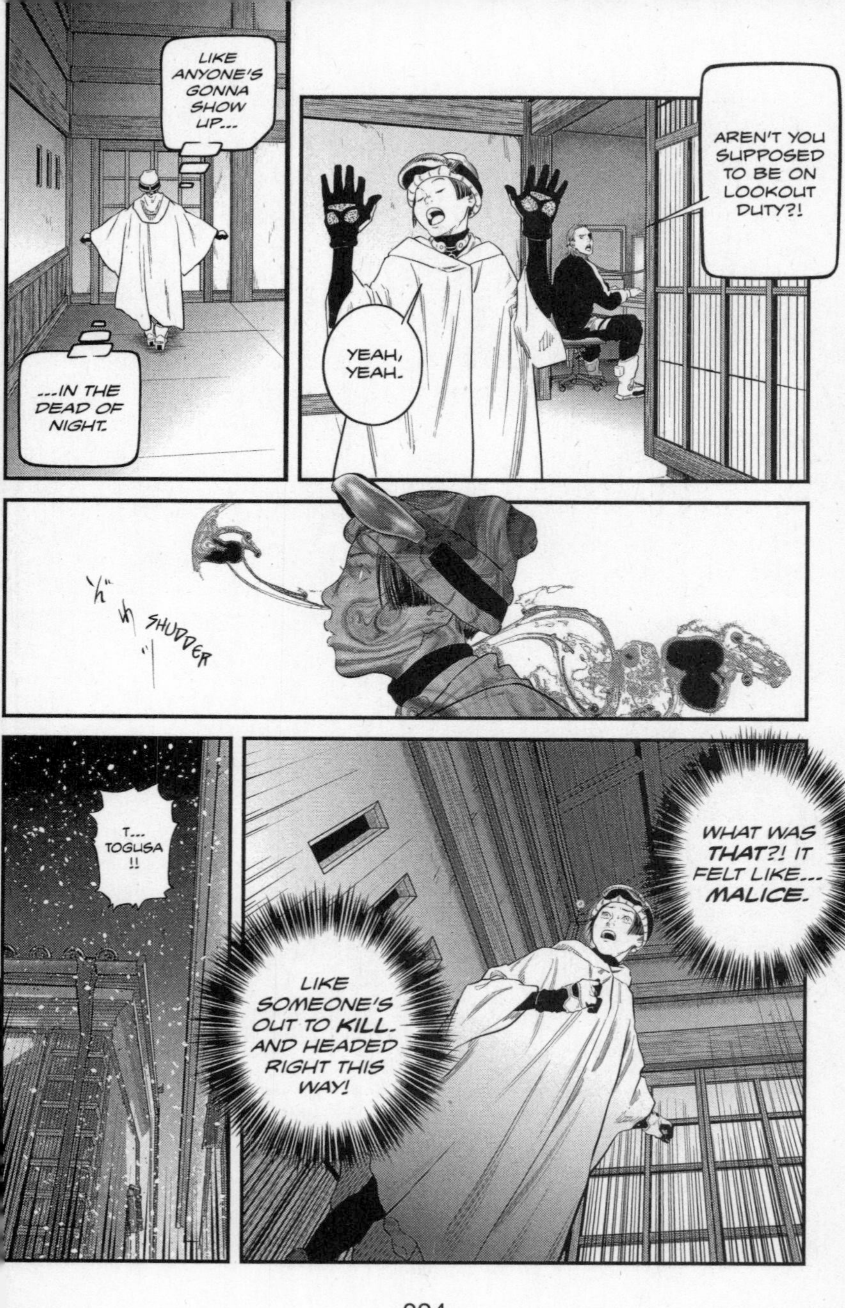
AREN'T YOU SUPPOSED TO BE ON LOOKOUT DUTY?!
YEAH, YEAH.
LIKE ANYONE'S GONNA SHOW UP...
...IN THE DEAD OF NIGHT.
SHUDDER
WHAT WAS THAT?! IT FELT LIKE... MALICE.
LIKE SOMEONE'S OUT TO KILL. AND HEADED RIGHT THIS WAY!
T... TOGUSA!!

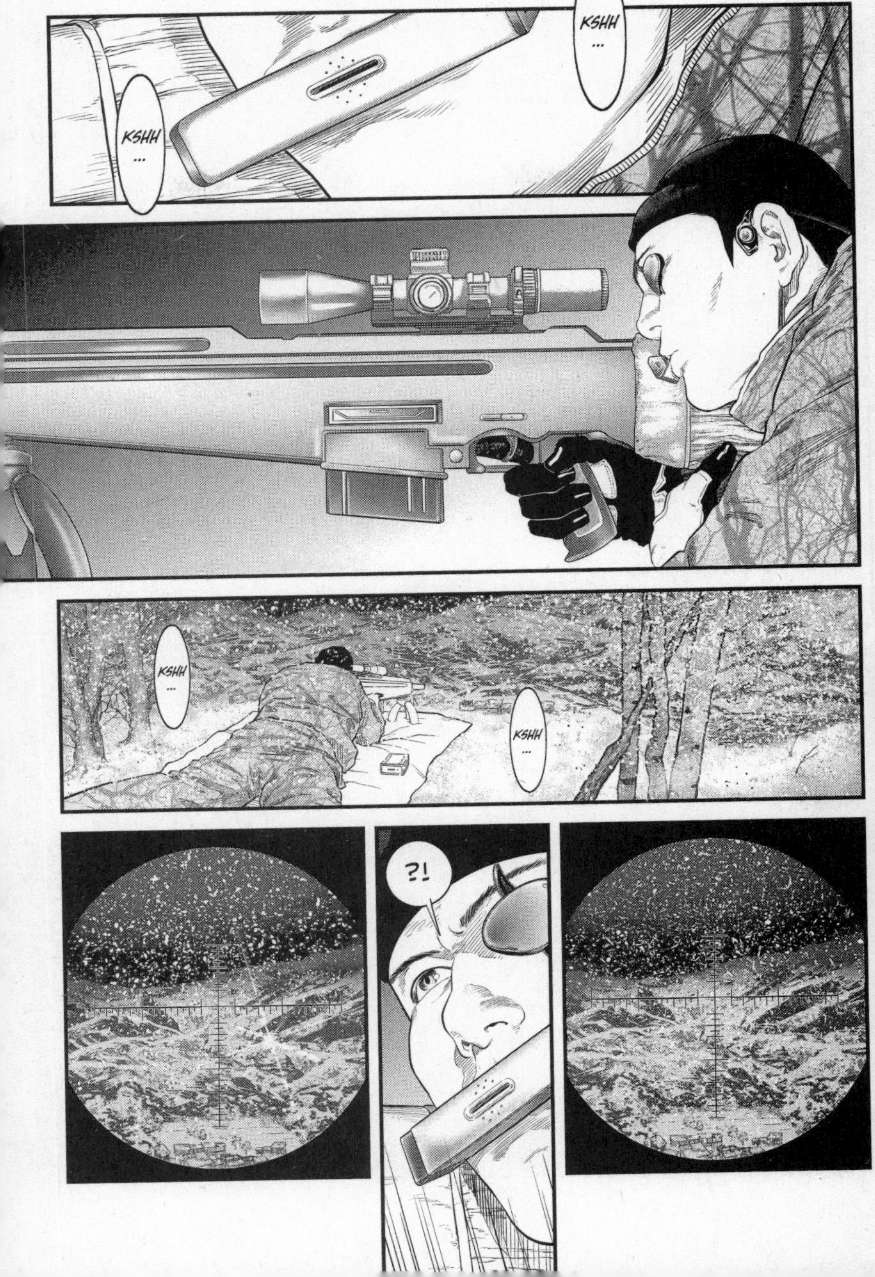
KSHH ...
KSHH ...
KSHH ...
KSHH ...
?!

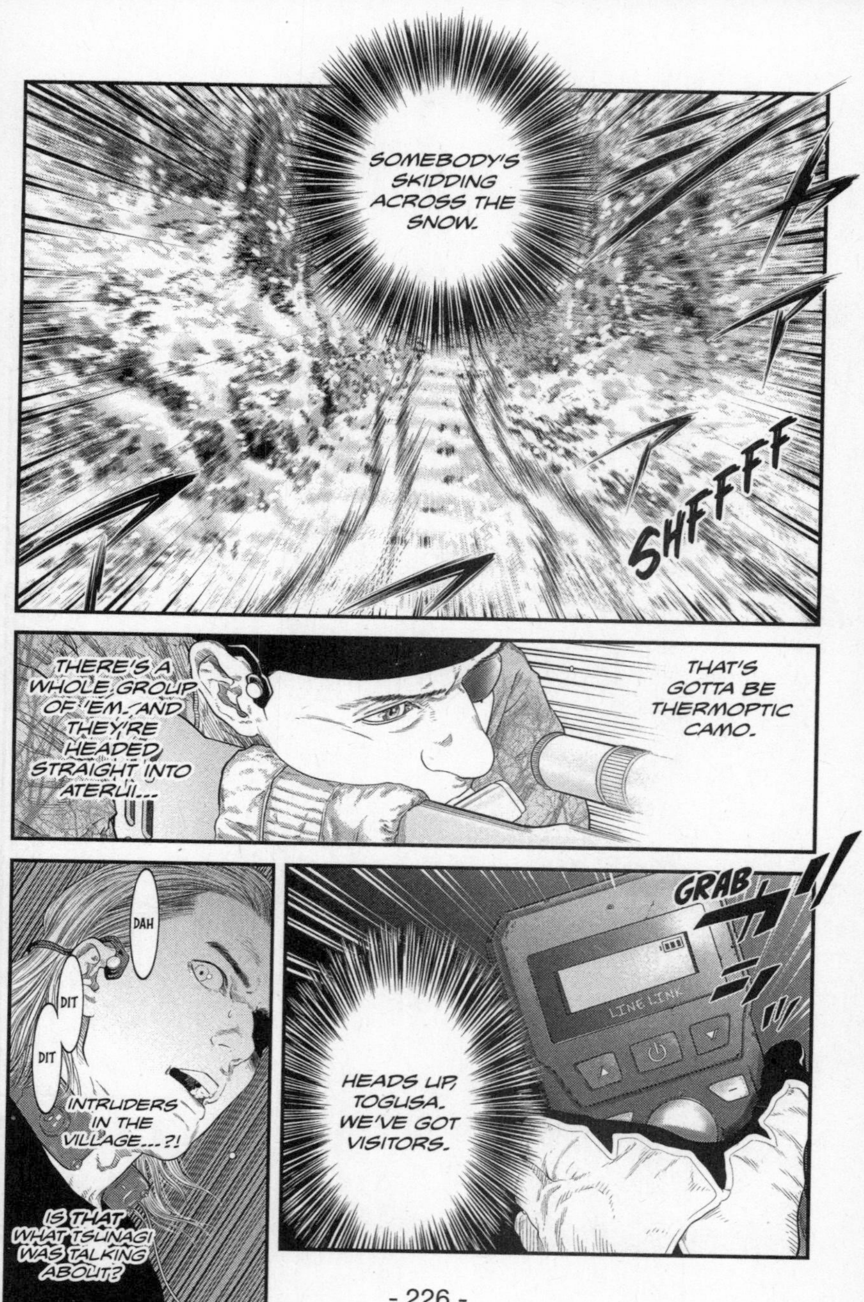
SOMEBODY'S SKIDDING ACROSS THE SNOW.
SHFFFF
THAT'S GOTTA BE THERMOPTIC CAMO.
THERE'S A WHOLE GROUP OF 'EM, AND THEY'RE HEADED STRAIGHT INTO ATERUI...
GRAB
LINE LINK
HEADS UP, TOGUSA. WE'VE GOT VISITORS.
DAH
DIT
DIT
INTRUDERS IN THE VILLAGE...?!
IS THAT WHAT TSUNAGI WAS TALKING ABOUT?

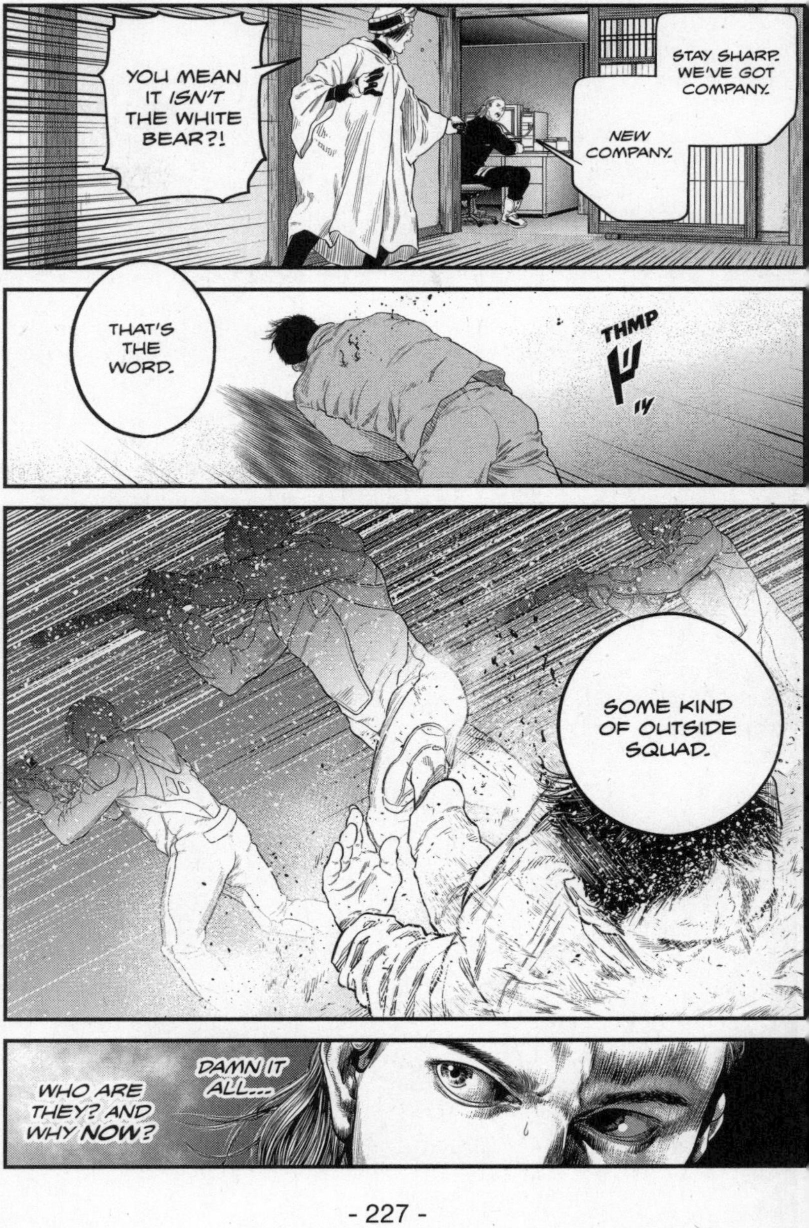
STAY SHARP. WE'VE GOT COMPANY.
NEW COMPANY.
YOU MEAN IT *ISN'T* THE WHITE BEAR?!
THMP
THAT'S THE WORD.
SOME KIND OF OUTSIDE SQUAD.
DAMN IT ALL...
WHO ARE THEY? AND WHY **NOW**?

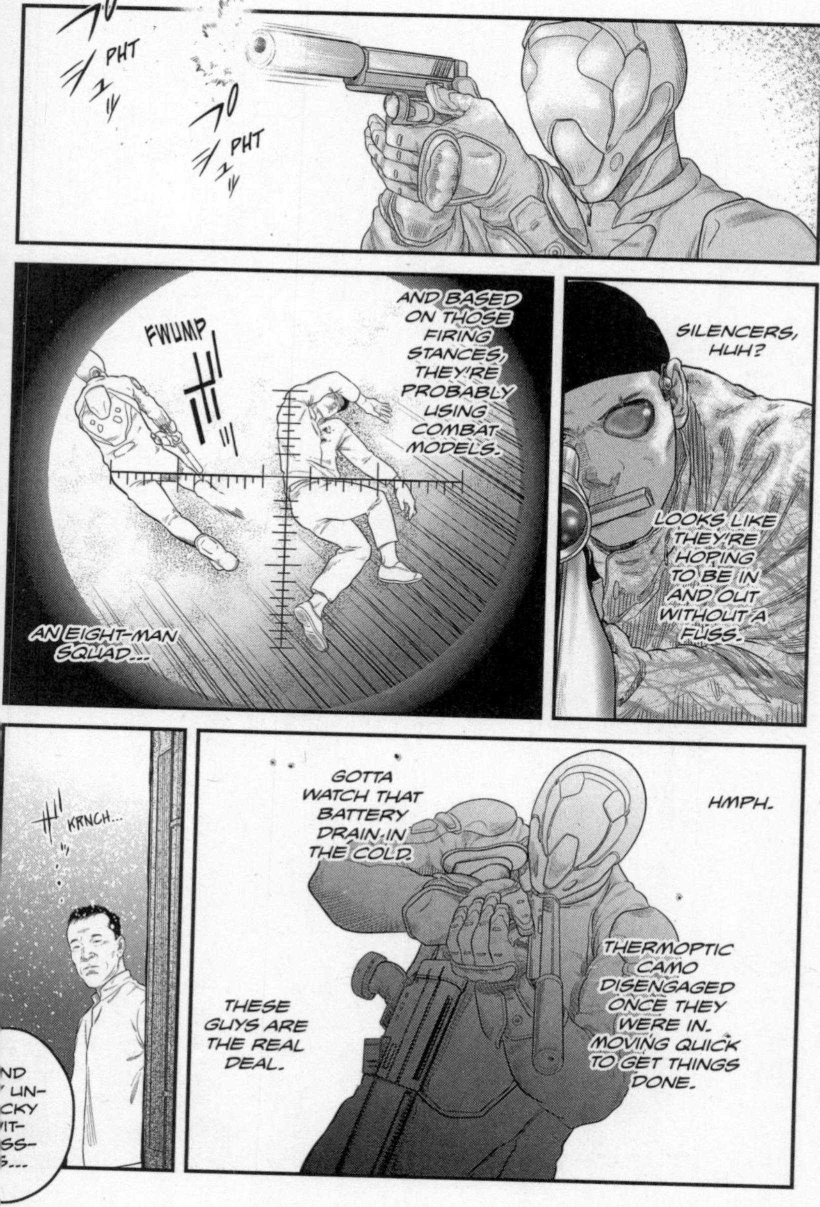
PHT
PHT
SILENCERS, HUH?
LOOKS LIKE THEY'RE HOPING TO BE IN AND OUT WITHOUT A FUSS.
AND BASED ON THOSE FIRING STANCES, THEY'RE PROBABLY USING COMBAT MODELS.
FWUMP
AN EIGHT-MAN SQUAD...
HMPH.
THERMOPTIC CAMO DISENGAGED ONCE THEY WERE IN. MOVING QUICK TO GET THINGS DONE.
GOTTA WATCH THAT BATTERY DRAIN IN THE COLD.
THESE GUYS ARE THE REAL DEAL.
KRNCH...

...ARE DEAD BEFORE THEY EVEN REALIZE WHAT THEY'VE SEEN.

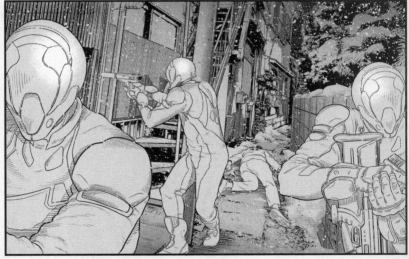

GREAT. JUST HAD TO BE HEADED IN THAT DIRECTION, HUH?

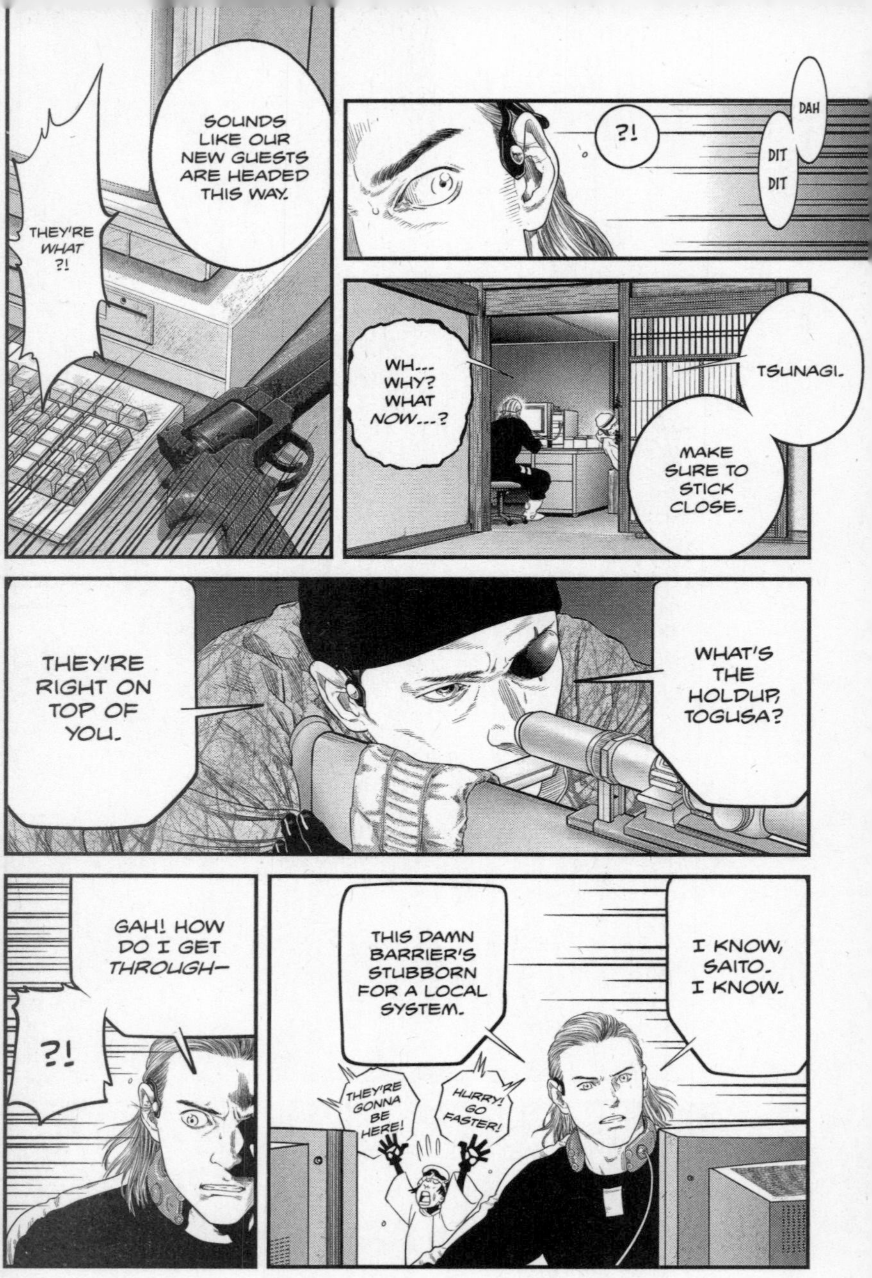
DAH
DIT DIT
?!
TSUNAGI.
MAKE SURE TO STICK CLOSE.
WH... WHY? WHAT NOW...?
SOUNDS LIKE OUR NEW GUESTS ARE HEADED THIS WAY.
THEY'RE WHAT ?!
WHAT'S THE HOLDUP, TOGUSA?
THEY'RE RIGHT ON TOP OF YOU.
I KNOW, SAITO. I KNOW.
THIS DAMN BARRIER'S STUBBORN FOR A LOCAL SYSTEM.
HURRY! GO FASTER!
THEY'RE GONNA BE HERE!
GAH! HOW DO I GET THROUGH—
?!

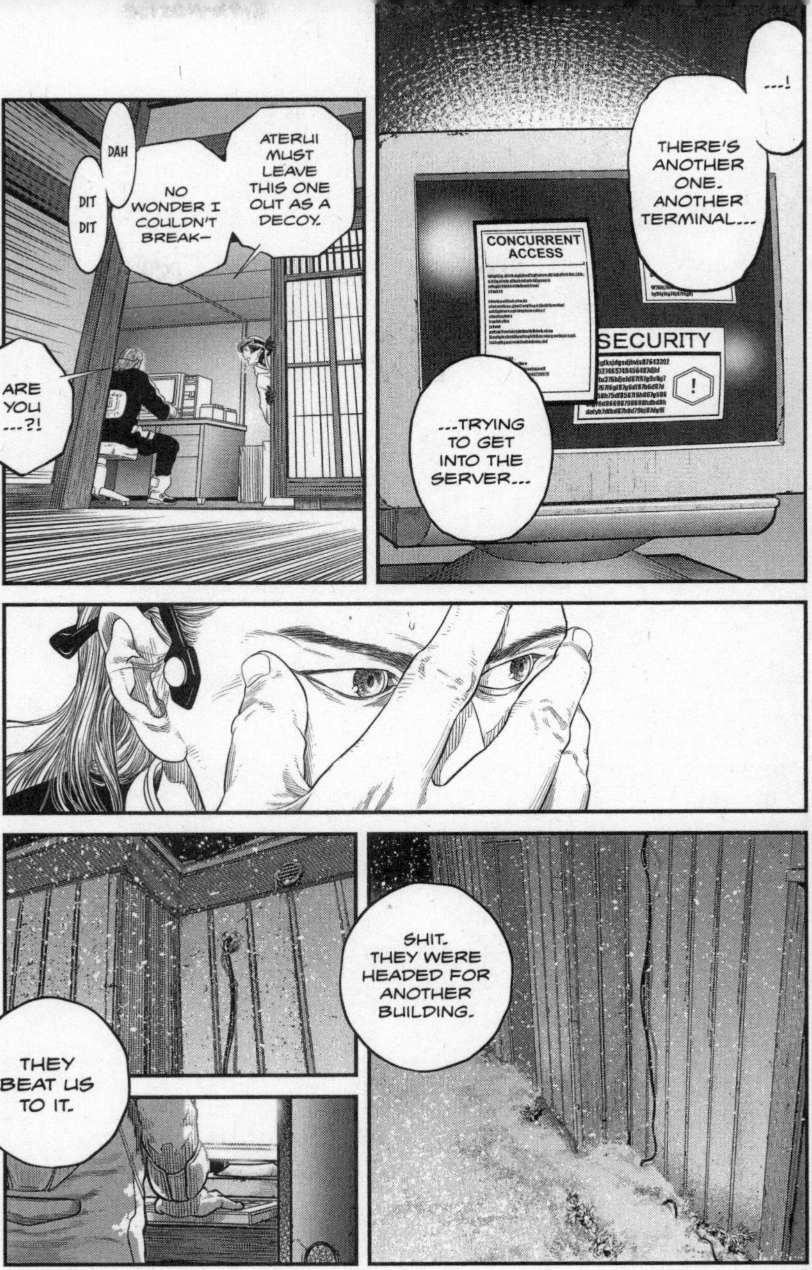
---!
THERE'S ANOTHER ONE. ANOTHER TERMINAL...
CONCURRENT ACCESS
SECURITY
...TRYING TO GET INTO THE SERVER...
ATERUI MUST LEAVE THIS ONE OUT AS A DECOY.
DAH
NO WONDER I COULDN'T BREAK—
DIT
DIT
ARE YOU ---?!
SHIT. THEY WERE HEADED FOR ANOTHER BUILDING.
THEY BEAT US TO IT.

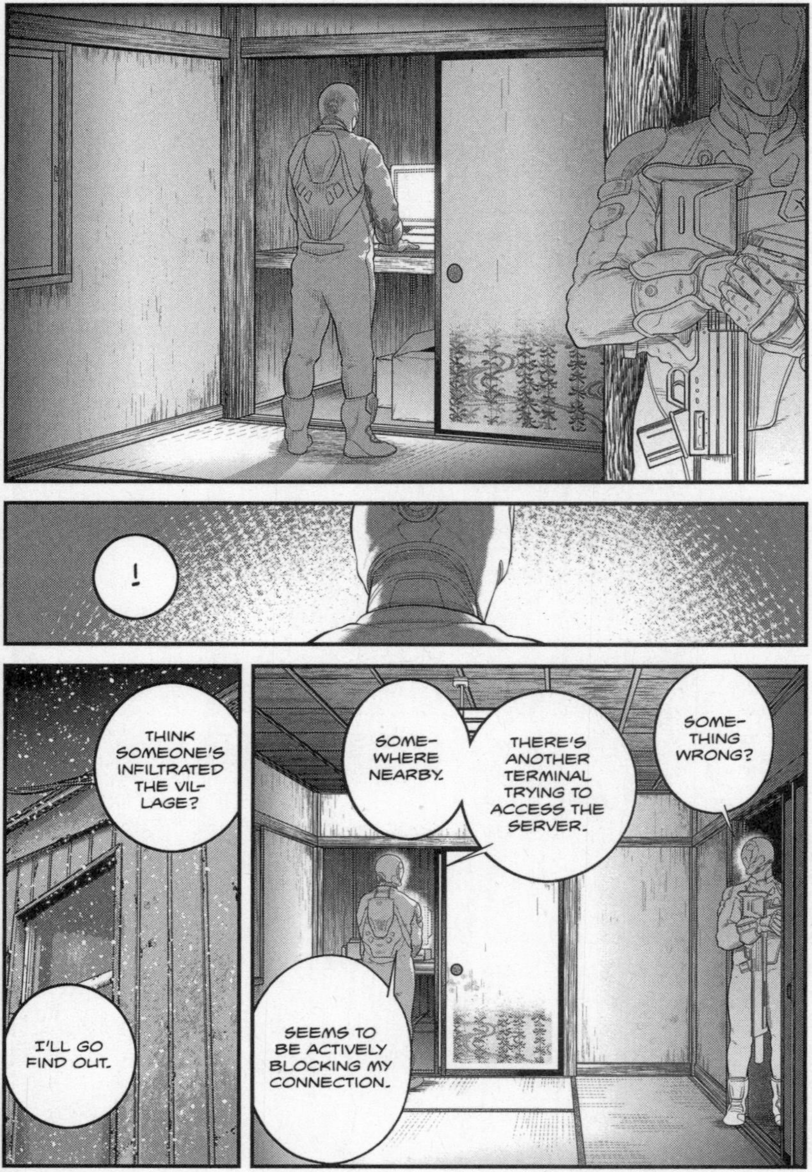
!
SOME-THING WRONG?
THERE'S ANOTHER TERMINAL TRYING TO ACCESS THE SERVER.
SOME-WHERE NEARBY.
SEEMS TO BE ACTIVELY BLOCKING MY CONNECTION.
THINK SOMEONE'S INFILTRATED THE VIL-LAGE?
I'LL GO FIND OUT.

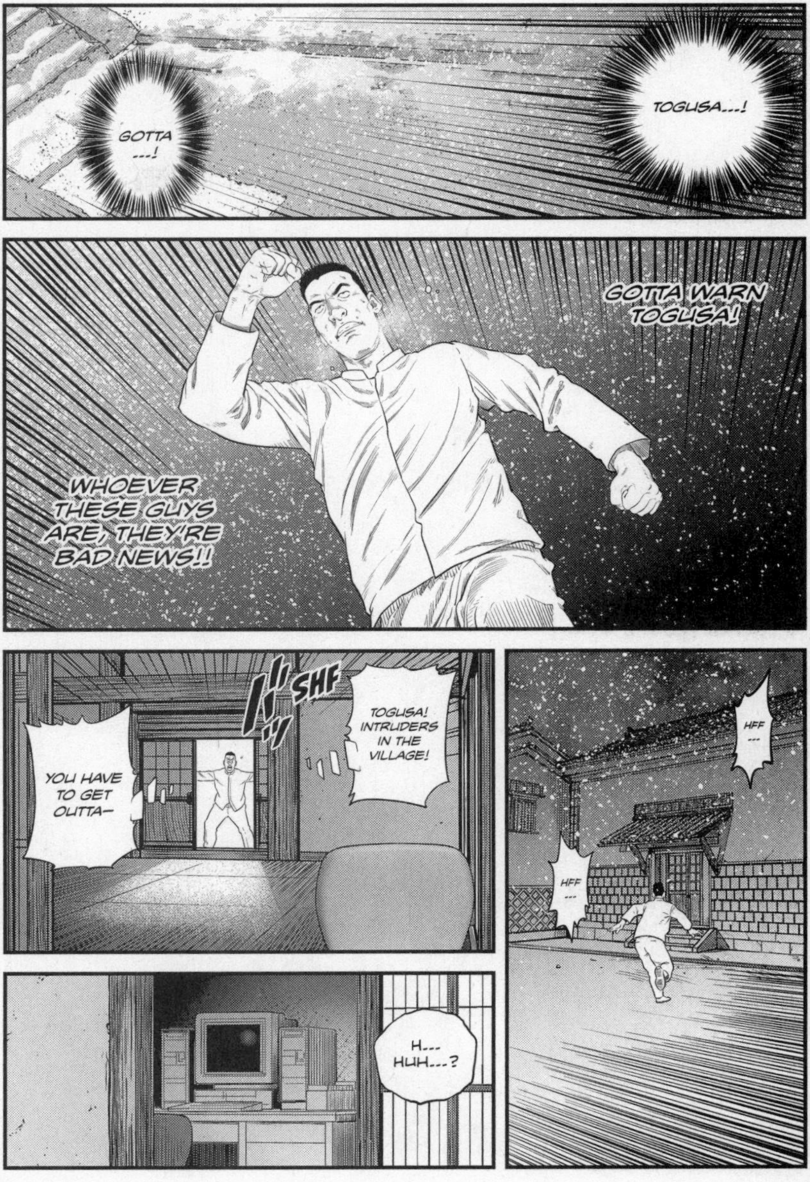

TOGUSA...!
GOTTA ...!
GOTTA WARN TOGUSA!
WHOEVER THESE GUYS ARE, THEY'RE BAD NEWS!!
HFF ...
HFF ...
SHF
TOGUSA! INTRUDERS IN THE VILLAGE!
YOU HAVE TO GET OUTTA—
H... HUH...?

HFF...
HFF...
WHERE'D THEY GO...?
SNF...
スッ...
BLAM
BLAM
?!

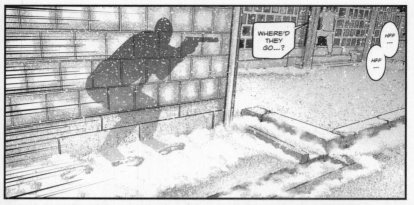

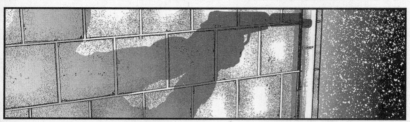

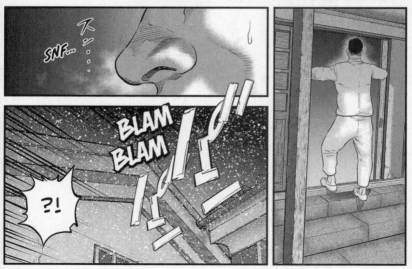

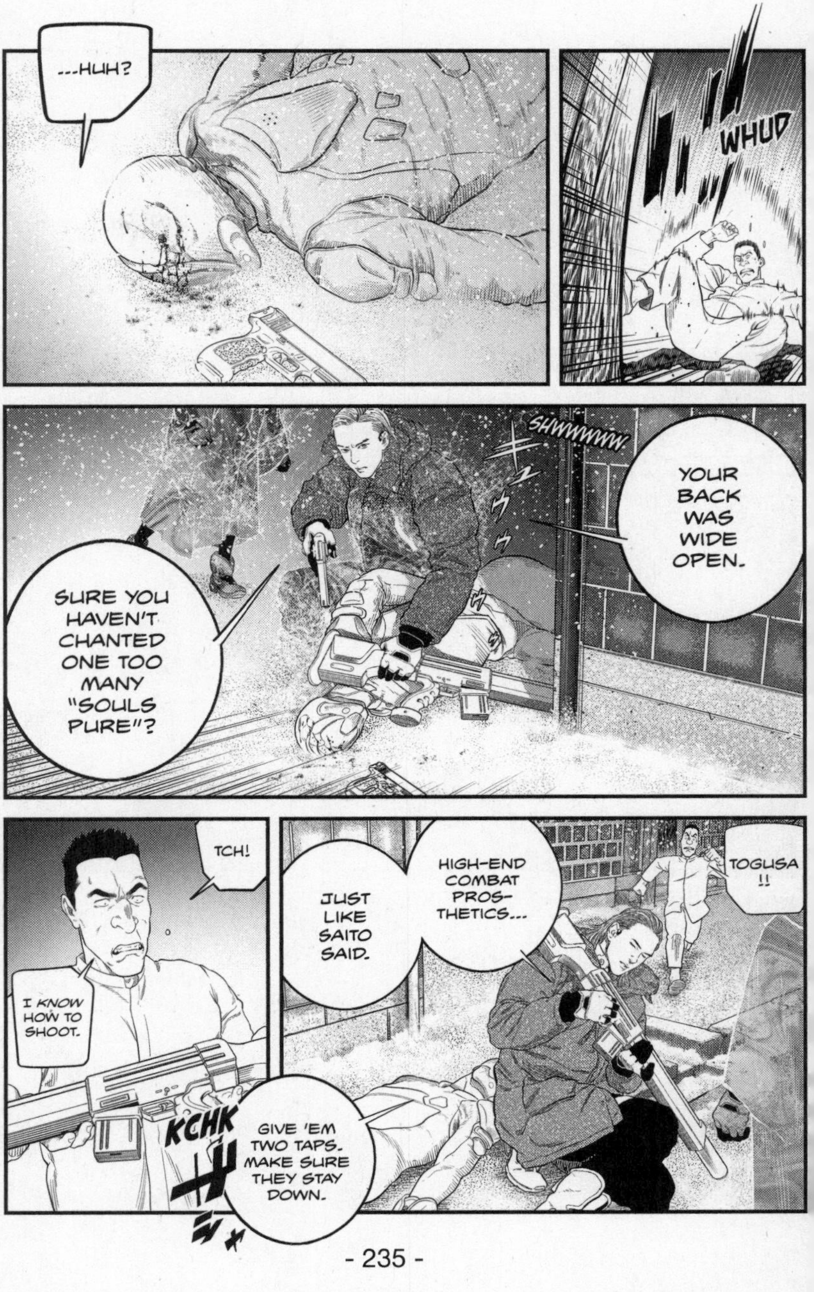
WHUD
---HUH?
YOUR BACK WAS WIDE OPEN.
SHWWWWW
SURE YOU HAVEN'T CHANTED ONE TOO MANY "SOULS PURE"?
TOGUSA !!
HIGH-END COMBAT PROS-THETICS...
JUST LIKE SAITO SAID.
TCH!
I KNOW HOW TO SHOOT.
KCHK
GIVE 'EM TWO TAPS. MAKE SURE THEY STAY DOWN.

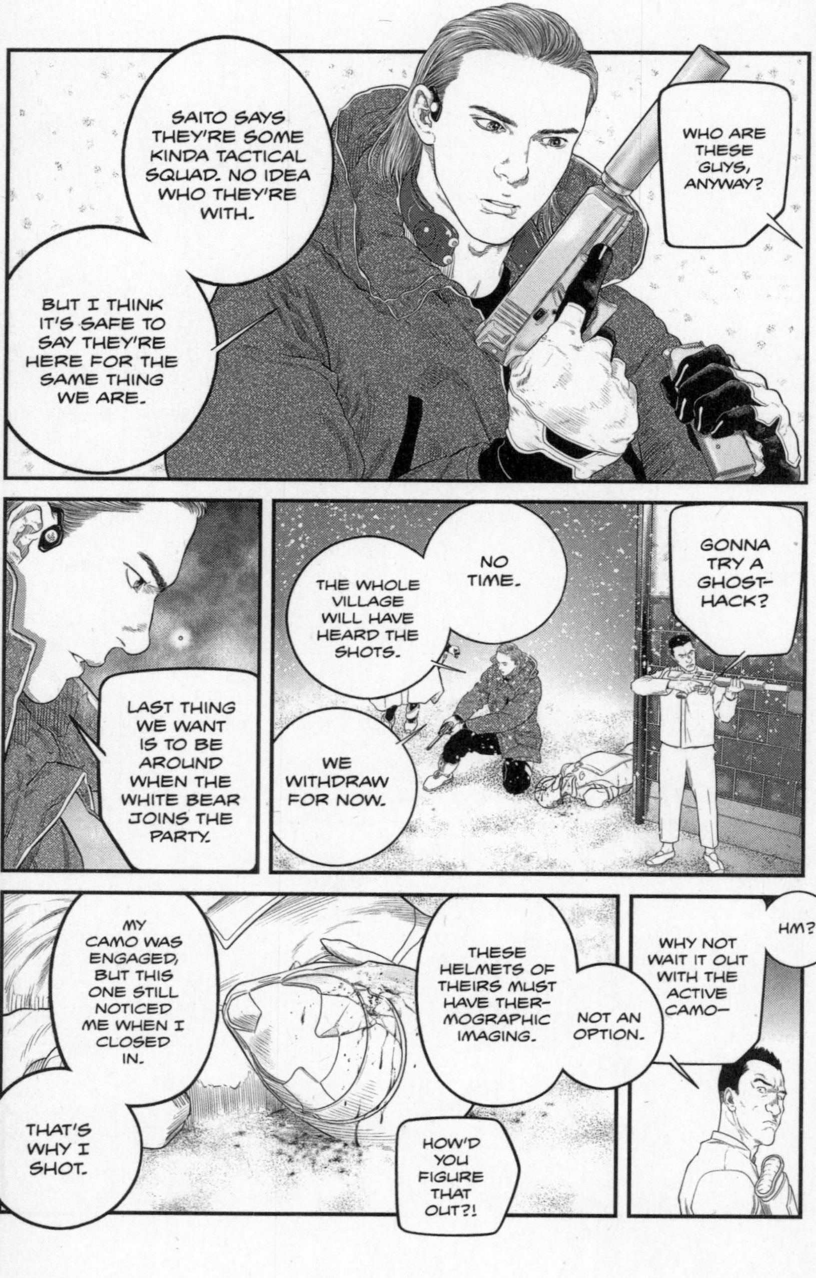
WHO ARE THESE GUYS, ANYWAY?
SAITO SAYS THEY'RE SOME KINDA TACTICAL SQUAD. NO IDEA WHO THEY'RE WITH.
BUT I THINK IT'S SAFE TO SAY THEY'RE HERE FOR THE SAME THING WE ARE.
GONNA TRY A GHOST-HACK?
NO TIME.
THE WHOLE VILLAGE WILL HAVE HEARD THE SHOTS.
WE WITHDRAW FOR NOW.
LAST THING WE WANT IS TO BE AROUND WHEN THE WHITE BEAR JOINS THE PARTY.
HM?
WHY NOT WAIT IT OUT WITH THE ACTIVE CAMO—
NOT AN OPTION.
THESE HELMETS OF THEIRS MUST HAVE THERMOGRAPHIC IMAGING.
HOW'D YOU FIGURE THAT OUT?!
MY CAMO WAS ENGAGED, BUT THIS ONE STILL NOTICED ME WHEN I CLOSED IN.
THAT'S WHY I SHOT.

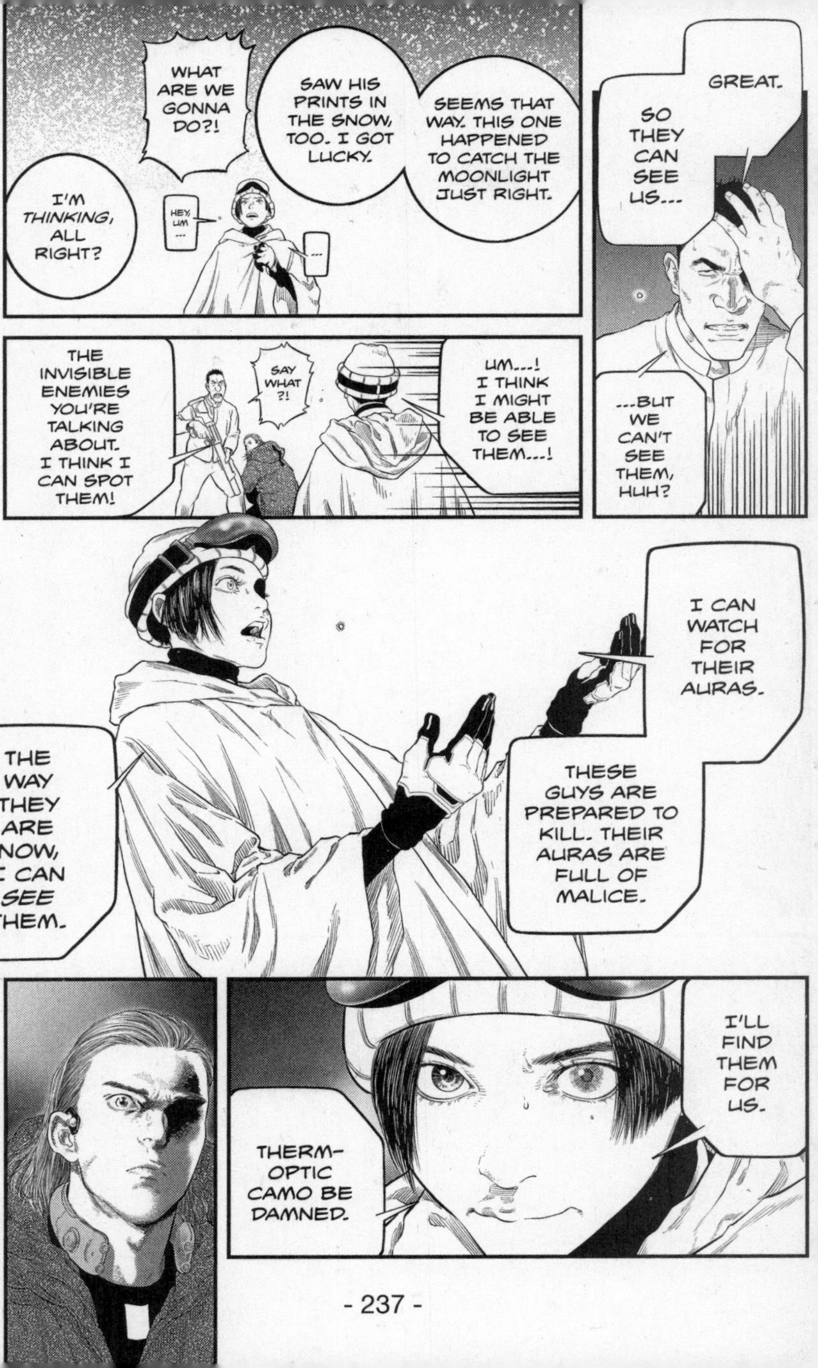
GREAT.
SO THEY CAN SEE US...
...BUT WE CAN'T SEE THEM, HUH?
SEEMS THAT WAY. THIS ONE HAPPENED TO CATCH THE MOONLIGHT JUST RIGHT.
SAW HIS PRINTS IN THE SNOW, TOO. I GOT LUCKY.
WHAT ARE WE GONNA DO?!
...
HEY, UM ...
I'M *THINKING*, ALL RIGHT?
UM...! I THINK I MIGHT BE ABLE TO SEE THEM...!
SAY WHAT ?!
THE INVISIBLE ENEMIES YOU'RE TALKING ABOUT. I THINK I CAN SPOT THEM!
I CAN WATCH FOR THEIR AURAS.
THESE GUYS ARE PREPARED TO KILL. THEIR AURAS ARE FULL OF MALICE.
THE WAY THEY ARE NOW, I CAN *SEE* THEM.
I'LL FIND THEM FOR US.
THERM-OPTIC CAMO BE DAMNED.

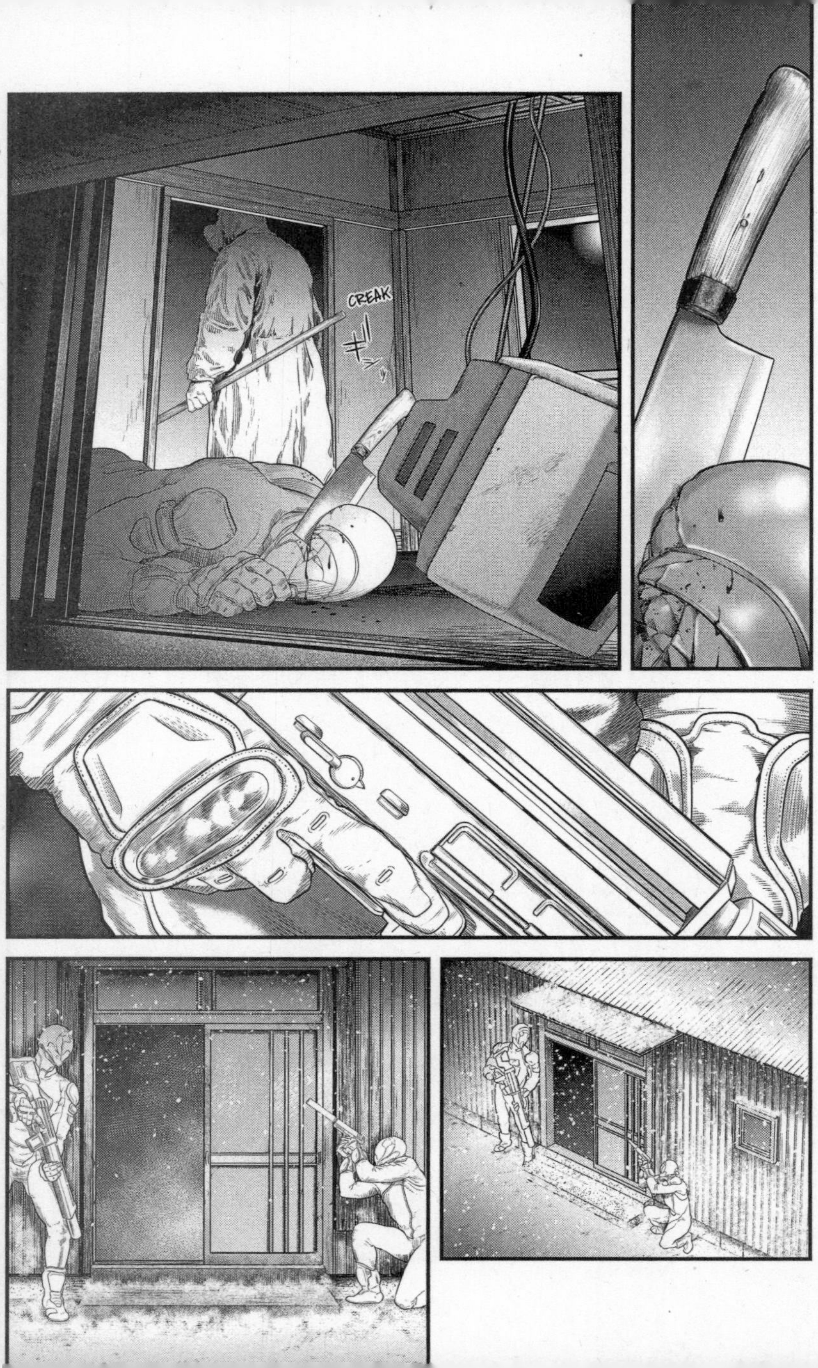
CREAK
ギシッ

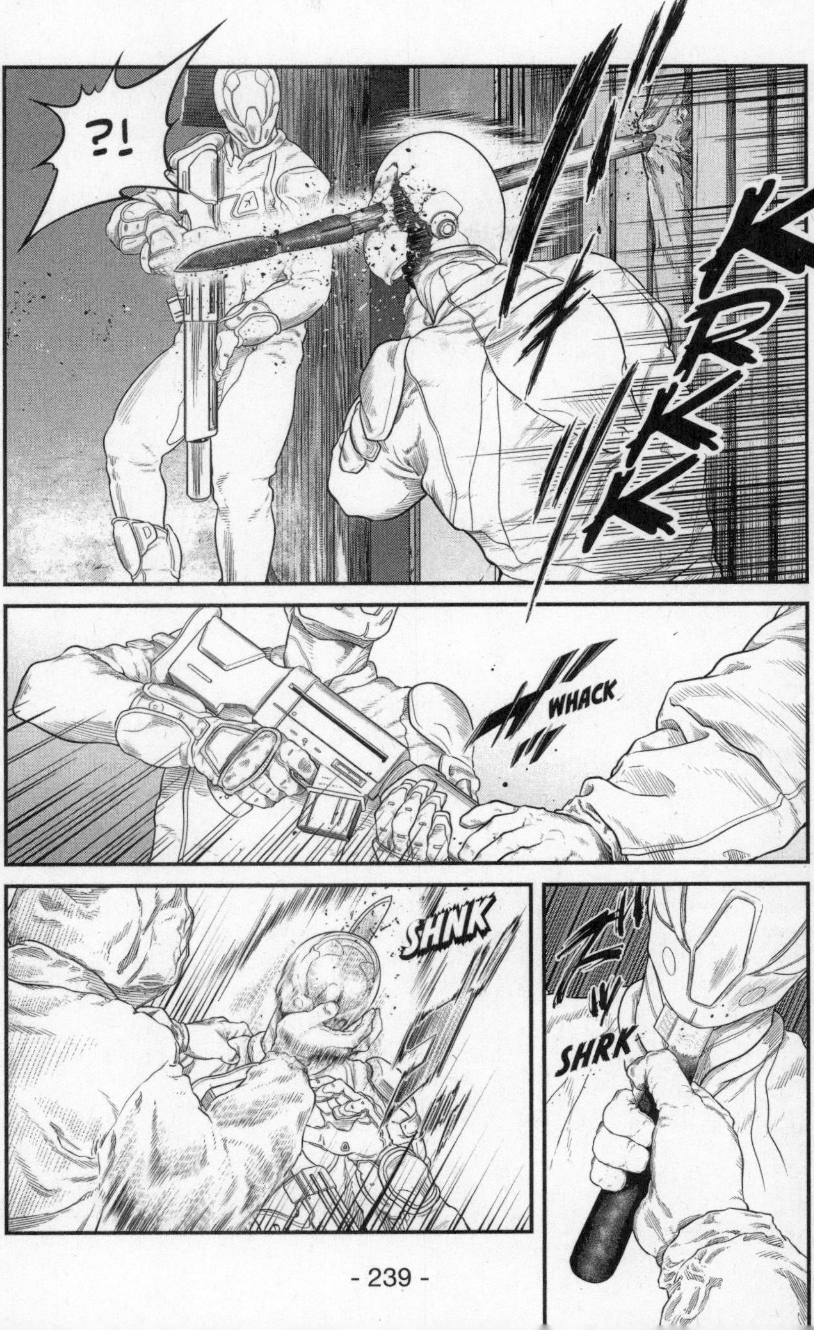
?!
KRKK
WHACK
SHRK
SHNK

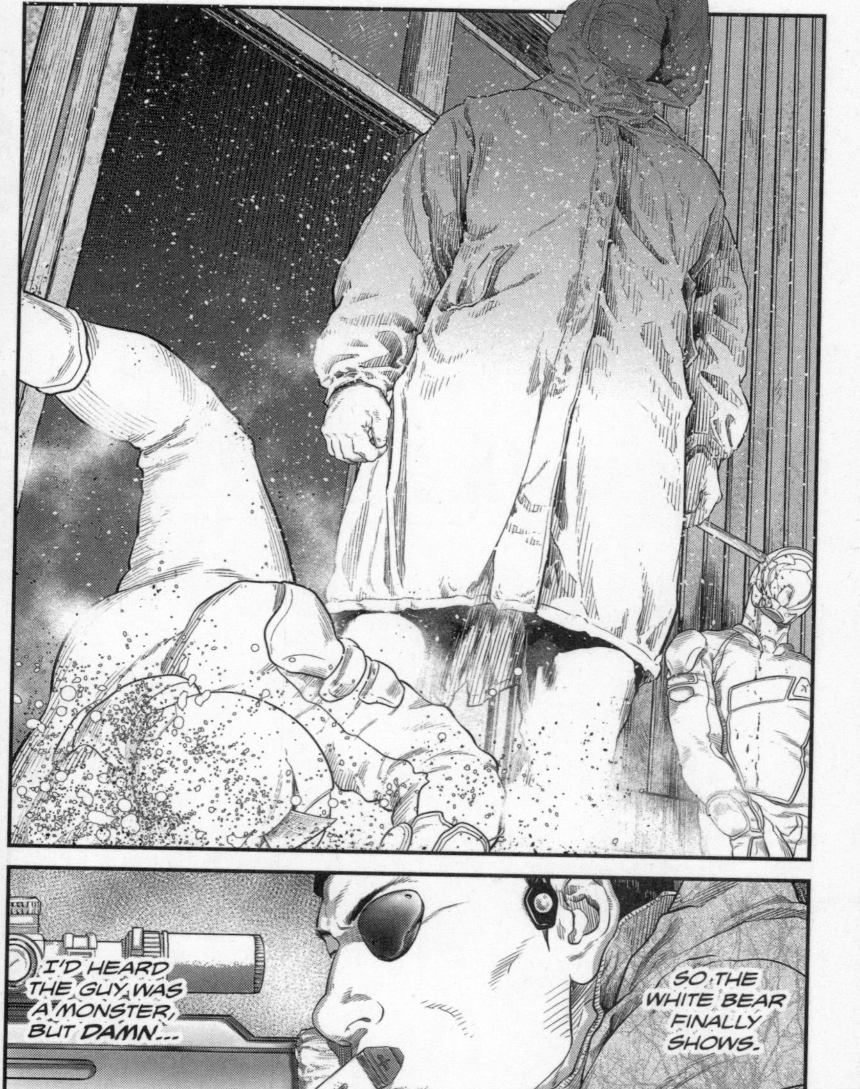
SO THE WHITE BEAR FINALLY SHOWS.
I'D HEARD THE GUY WAS A MONSTER, BUT DAMN...

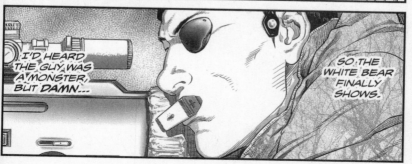

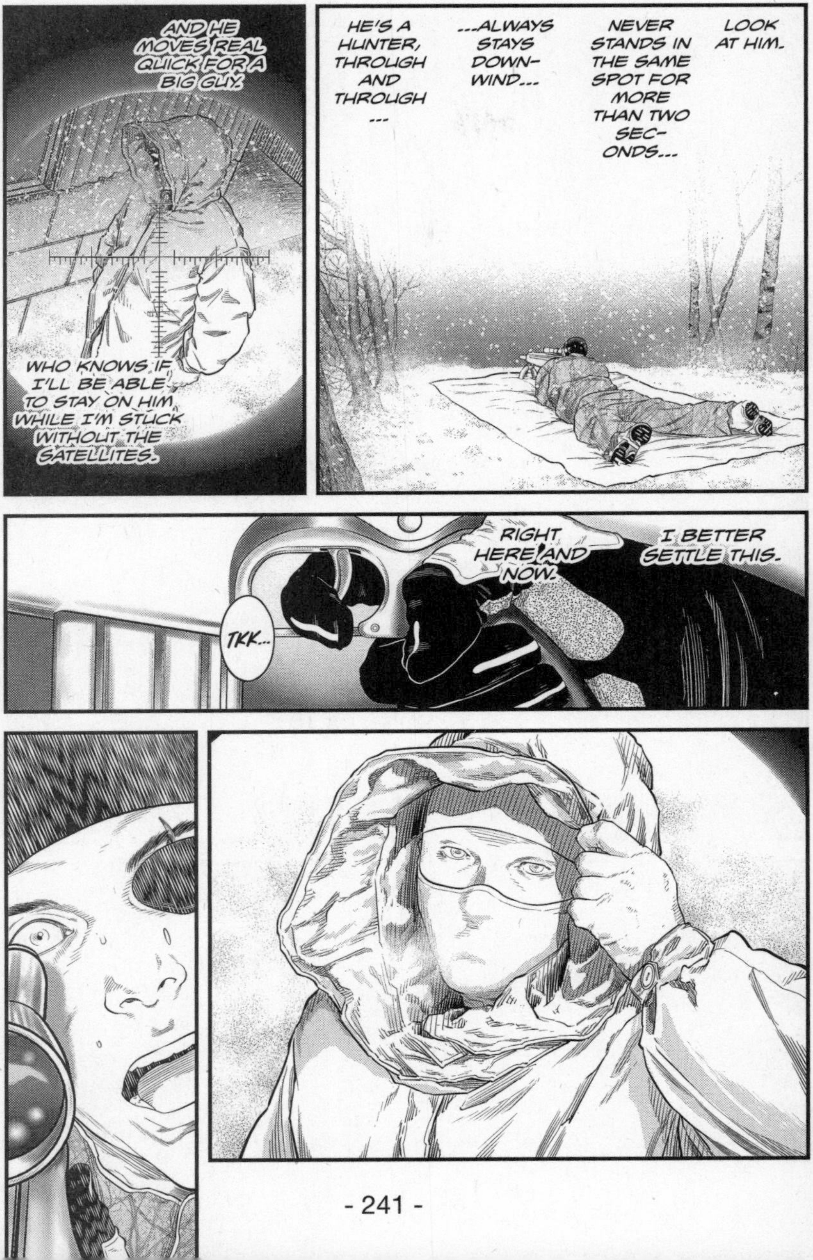
LOOK AT HIM.
NEVER STANDS IN THE SAME SPOT FOR MORE THAN TWO SEC- ONDS...
...ALWAYS STAYS DOWN- WIND...
HE'S A HUNTER, THROUGH AND THROUGH ...
AND HE MOVES REAL QUICK FOR A BIG GUY.
WHO KNOWS IF I'LL BE ABLE TO STAY ON HIM WHILE I'M STUCK WITHOUT THE SATELLITES.
I BETTER SETTLE THIS.
RIGHT HERE AND NOW.
TKK...

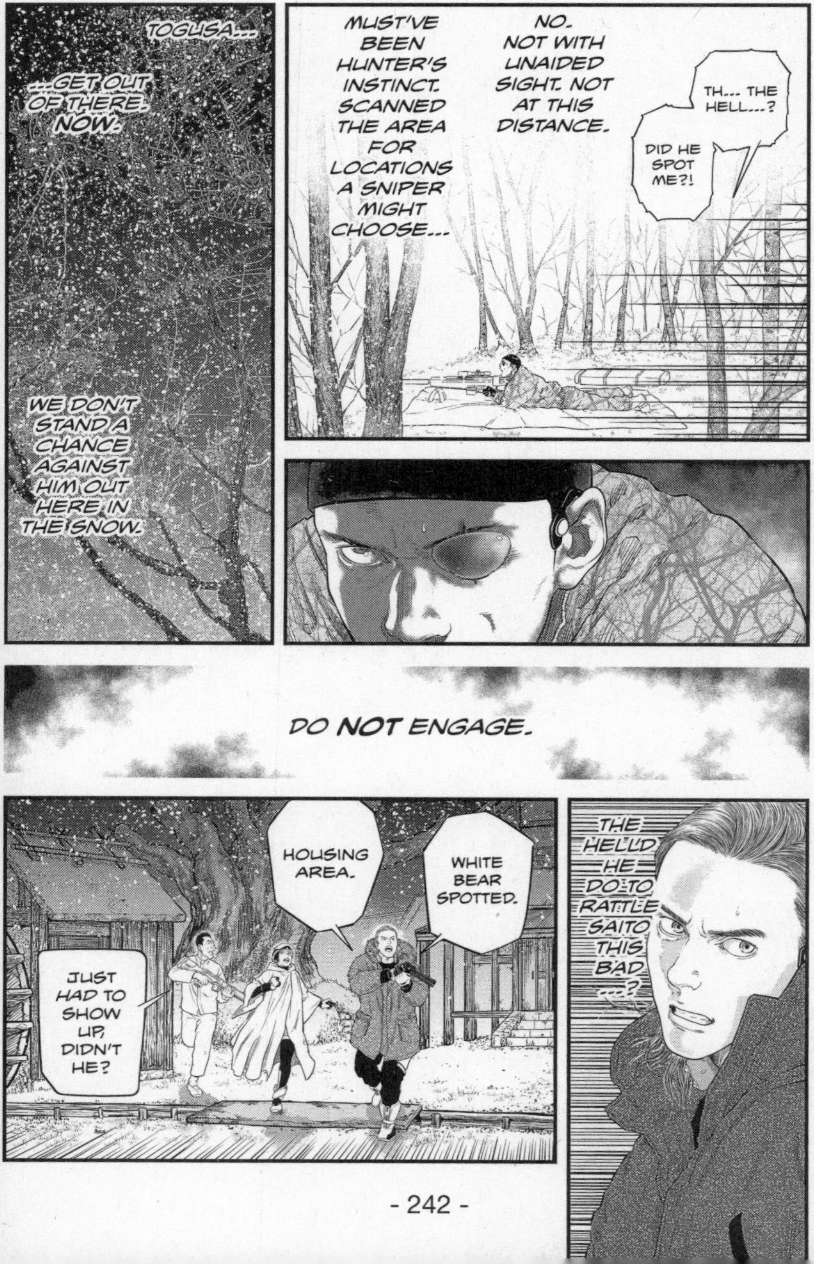
TH... THE HELL...?
DID HE SPOT ME?!
NO. NOT WITH UNAIDED SIGHT. NOT AT THIS DISTANCE.
MUST'VE BEEN HUNTER'S INSTINCT. SCANNED THE AREA FOR LOCATIONS A SNIPER MIGHT CHOOSE...
TOGUSA...
...GET OUT OF THERE. NOW.
WE DON'T STAND A CHANCE AGAINST HIM OUT HERE IN THE SNOW.
DO NOT ENGAGE.
THE HELL'D HE DO TO RATTLE SAITO THIS BAD...?
WHITE BEAR SPOTTED.
HOUSING AREA.
JUST HAD TO SHOW UP, DIDN'T HE?

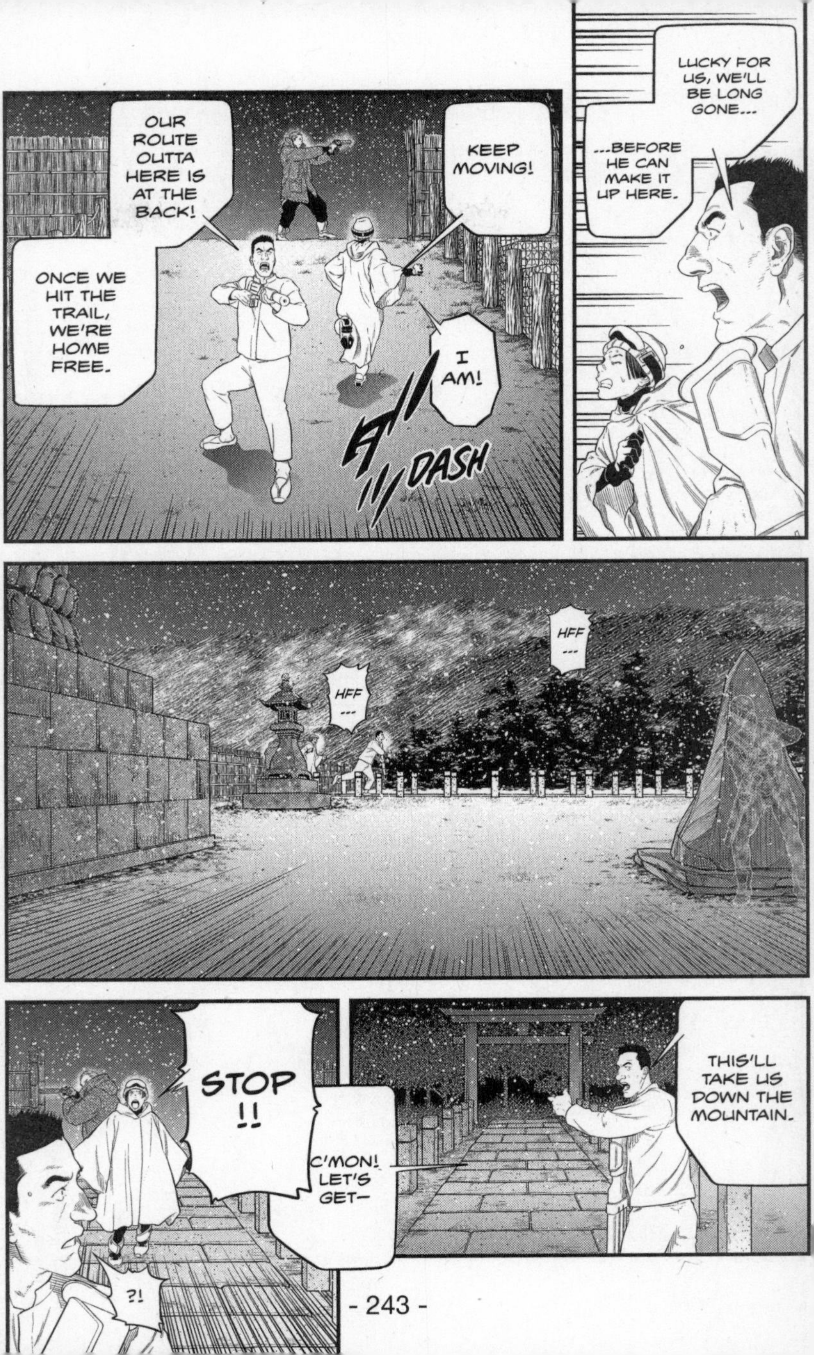
LUCKY FOR US, WE'LL BE LONG GONE...
...BEFORE HE CAN MAKE IT UP HERE.
KEEP MOVING!
OUR ROUTE OUTTA HERE IS AT THE BACK!
I AM!
ONCE WE HIT THE TRAIL, WE'RE HOME FREE.
DASH
HFF...
HFF...
THIS'LL TAKE US DOWN THE MOUNTAIN.
C'MON! LET'S GET—
STOP !!
?!

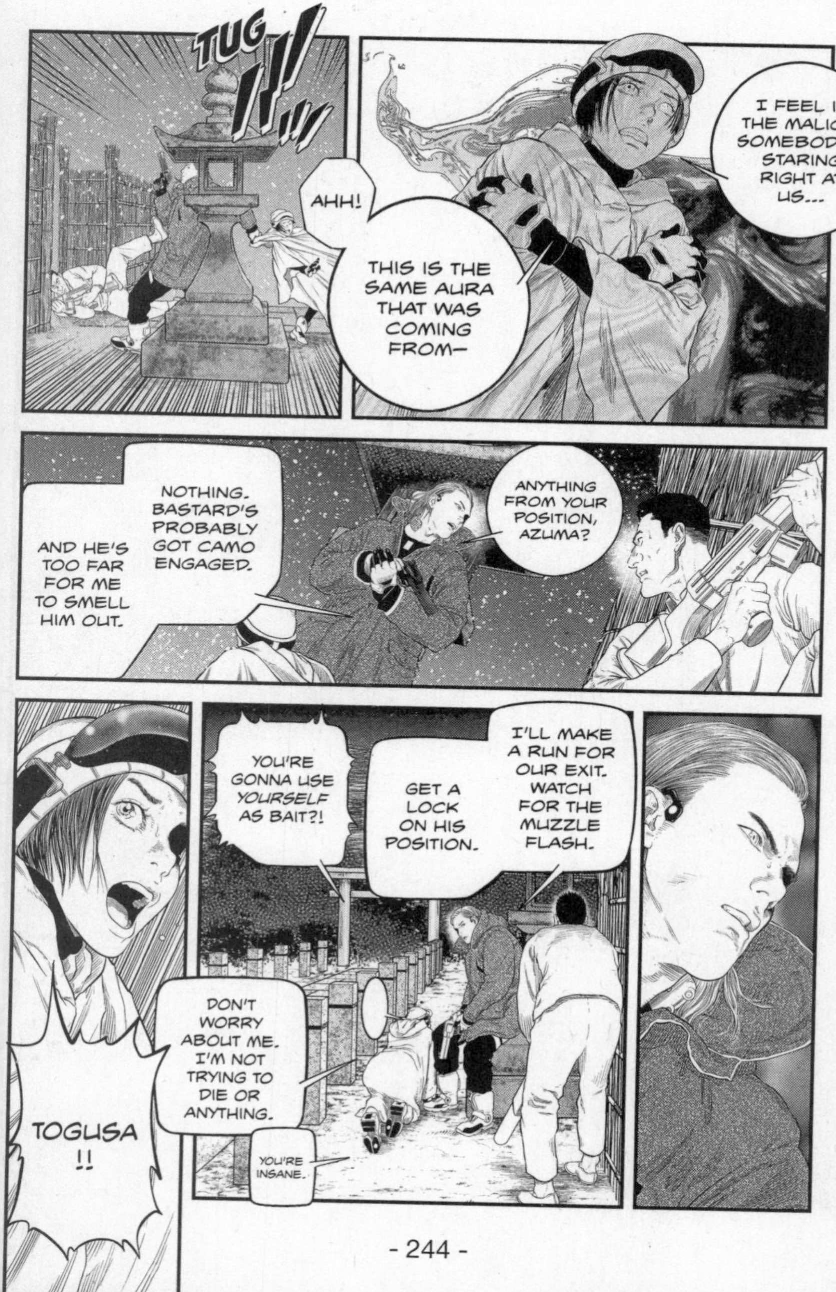

I FEEL IT. THE MALICE. SOMEBODY'S STARING RIGHT AT US...
AHH!
THIS IS THE SAME AURA THAT WAS COMING FROM—
TUG
ANYTHING FROM YOUR POSITION, AZUMA?
NOTHING. BASTARD'S PROBABLY GOT CAMO ENGAGED.
AND HE'S TOO FAR FOR ME TO SMELL HIM OUT.
I'LL MAKE A RUN FOR OUR EXIT. WATCH FOR THE MUZZLE FLASH.
GET A LOCK ON HIS POSITION.
YOU'RE GONNA USE *YOURSELF* AS BAIT?!
DON'T WORRY ABOUT ME. I'M NOT TRYING TO DIE OR ANYTHING.
YOU'RE INSANE.
TOGUSA !!

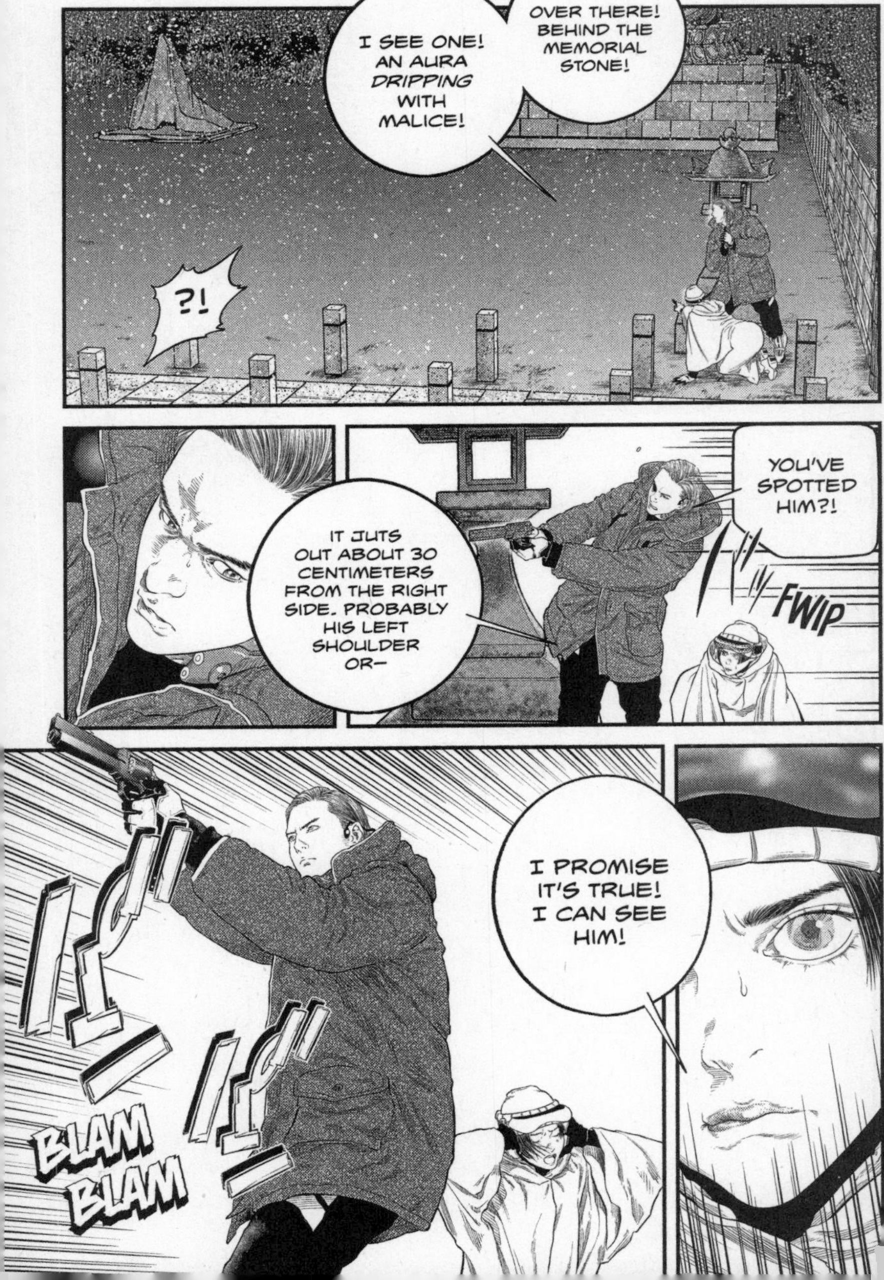
OVER THERE! BEHIND THE MEMORIAL STONE!
I SEE ONE! AN AURA *DRIPPING* WITH MALICE!
?!
YOU'VE SPOTTED HIM?!
FWIP
IT JUTS OUT ABOUT 30 CENTIMETERS FROM THE RIGHT SIDE. PROBABLY HIS LEFT SHOULDER OR—
I PROMISE IT'S TRUE! I CAN SEE HIM!
BLAM BLAM

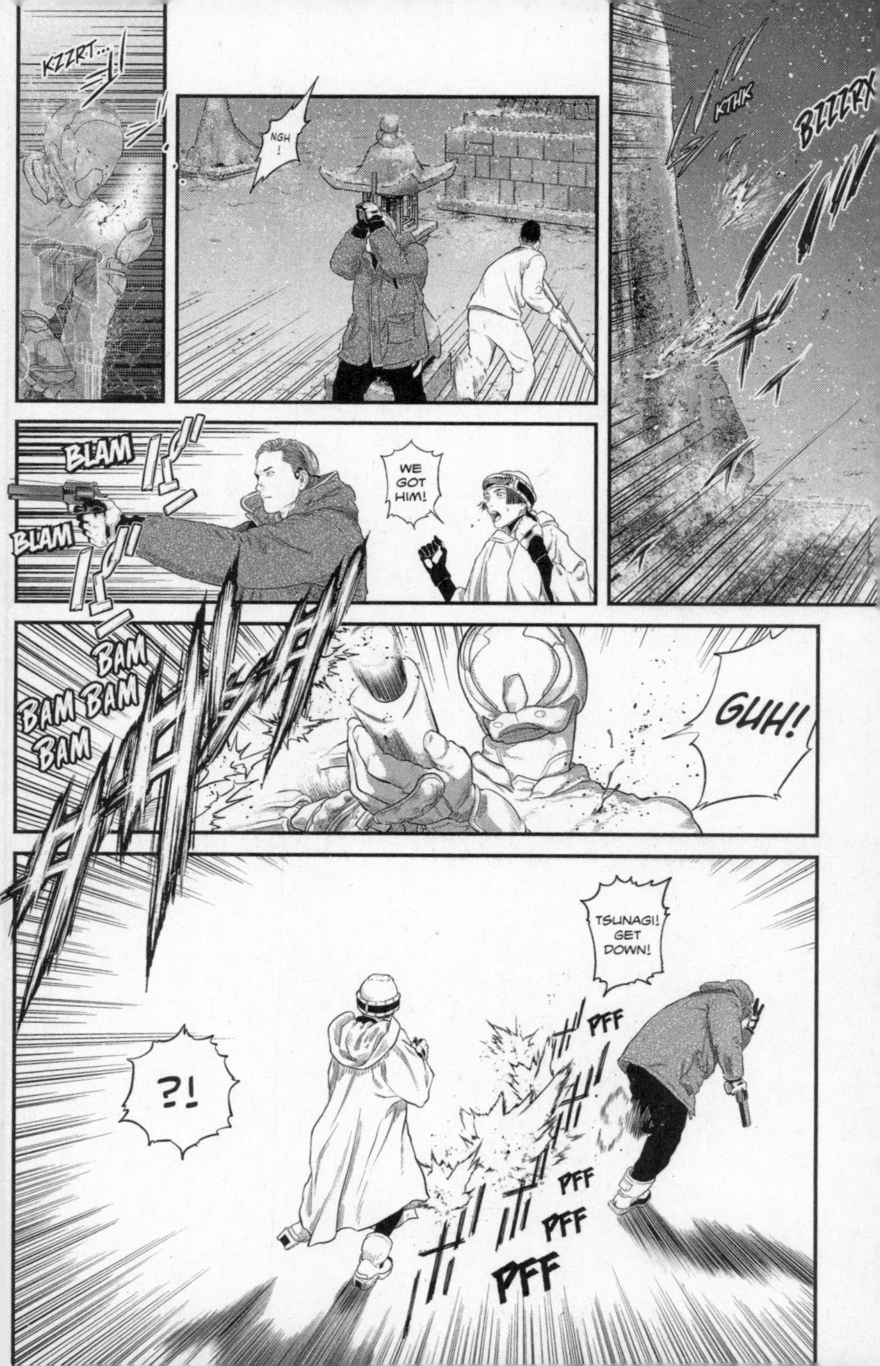
BZZZRX
KTHK
NGH!
KZZRT...
WE GOT HIM!
BLAM
BLAM
GUH!
BAM
BAM BAM
BAM
TSUNAGI! GET DOWN!
PFF
PFF
PFF
PFF
?!

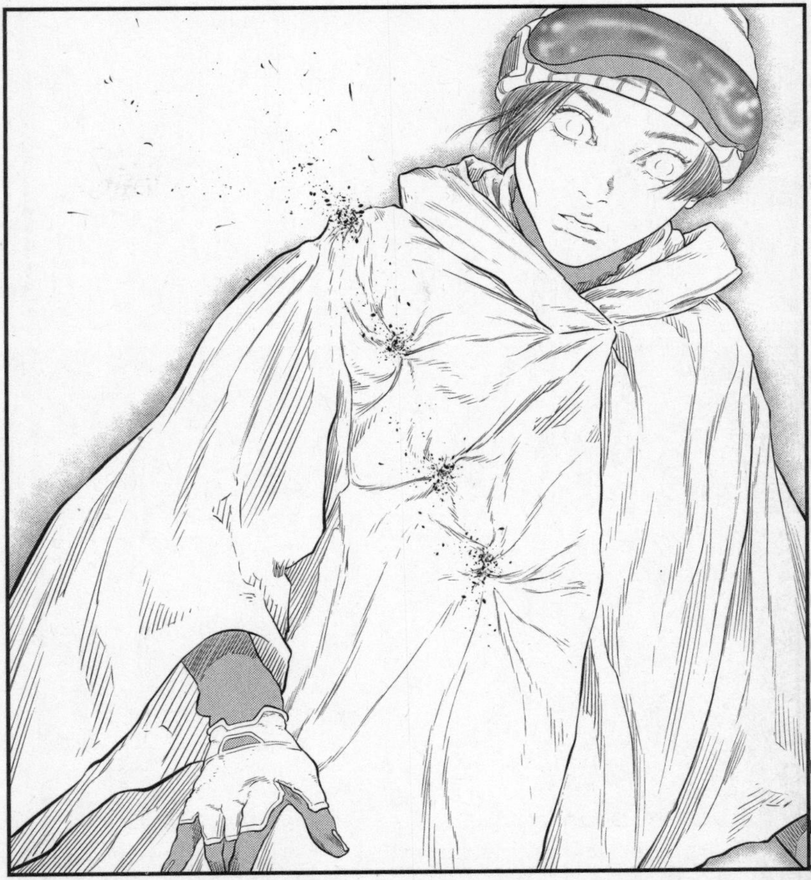
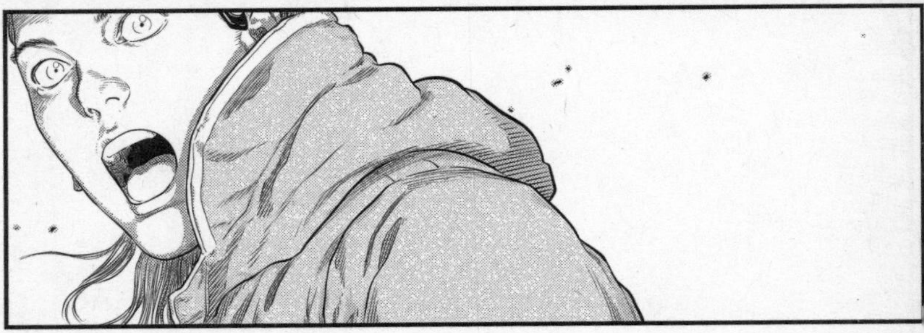

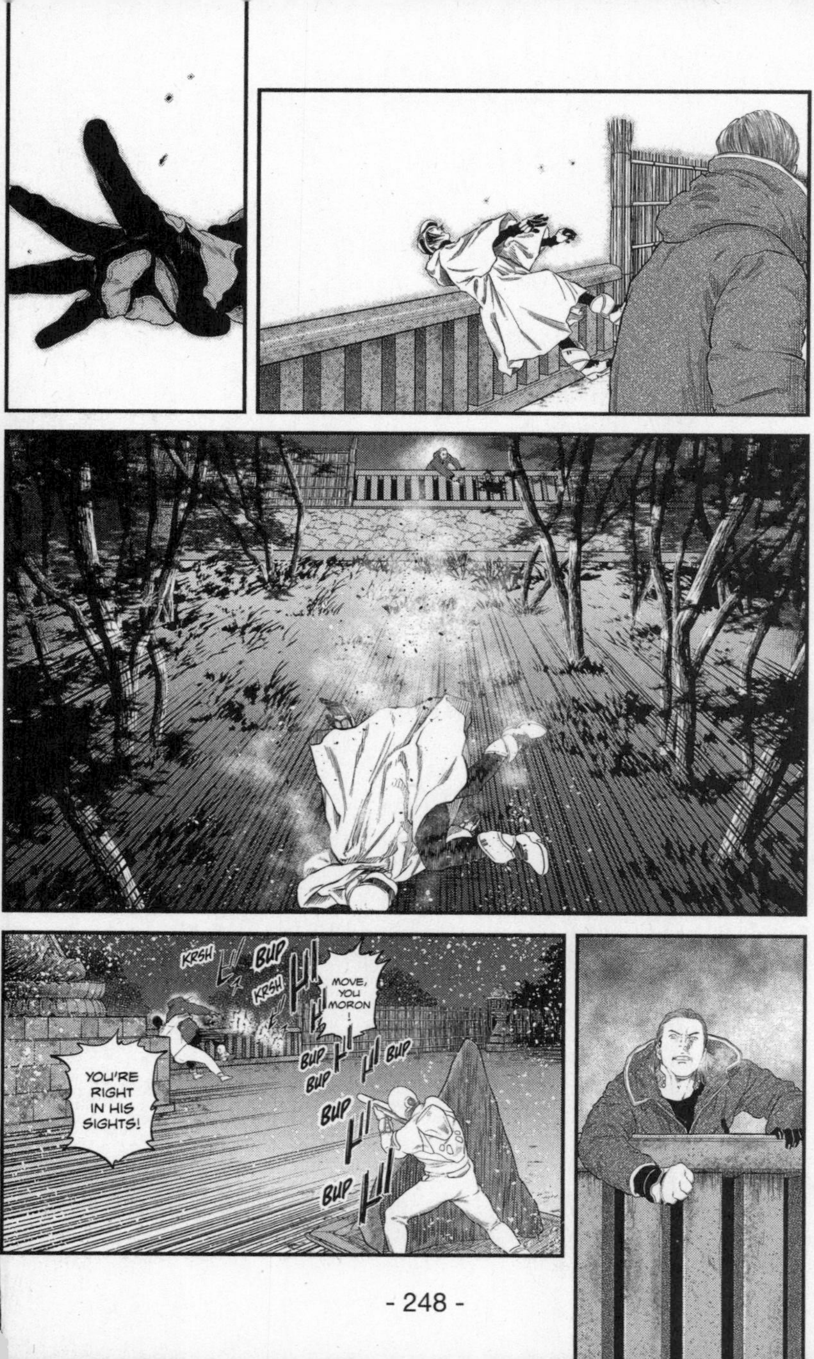
MOVE, YOU MORON!
BUP
KRSH
KRSH
BUP
BUP
BUP
YOU'RE RIGHT IN HIS SIGHTS!
BUP
BUP

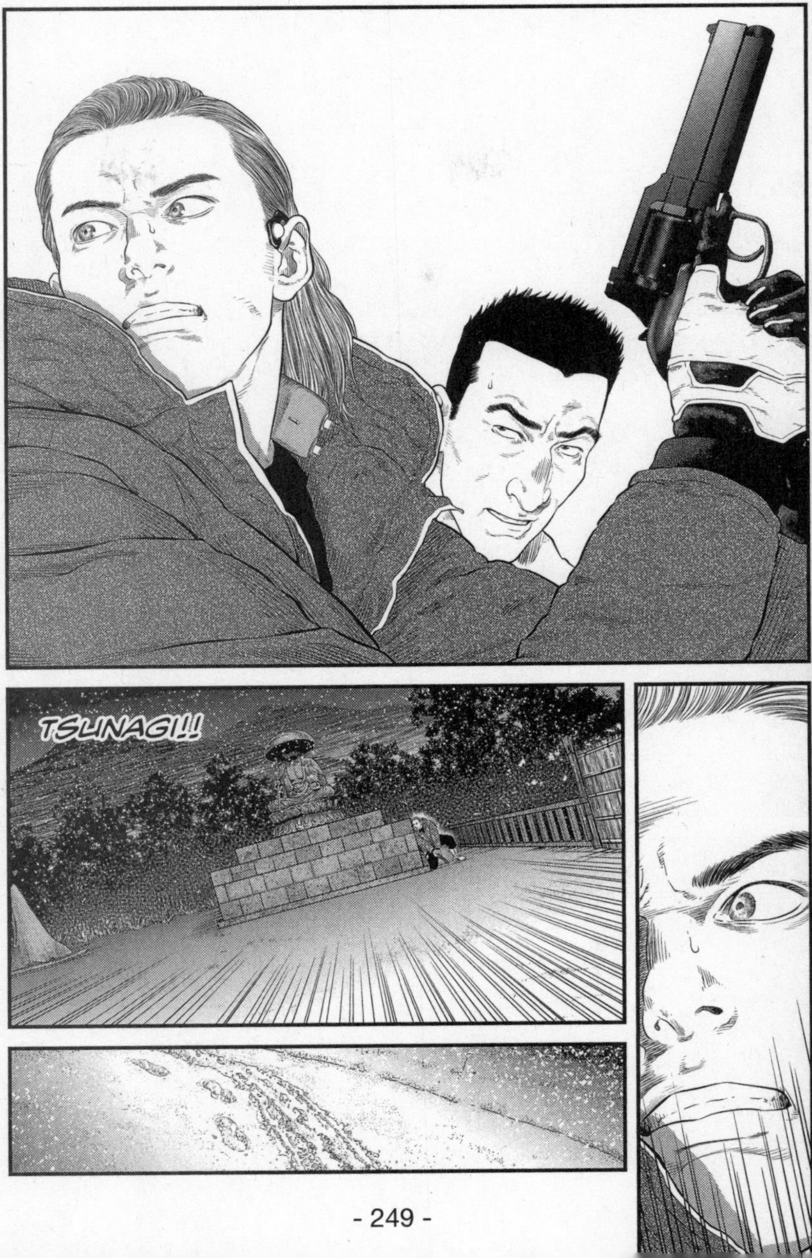
TSUNAGI!!

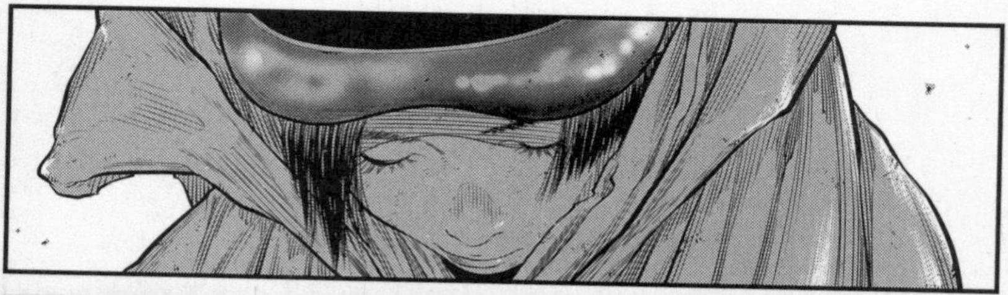

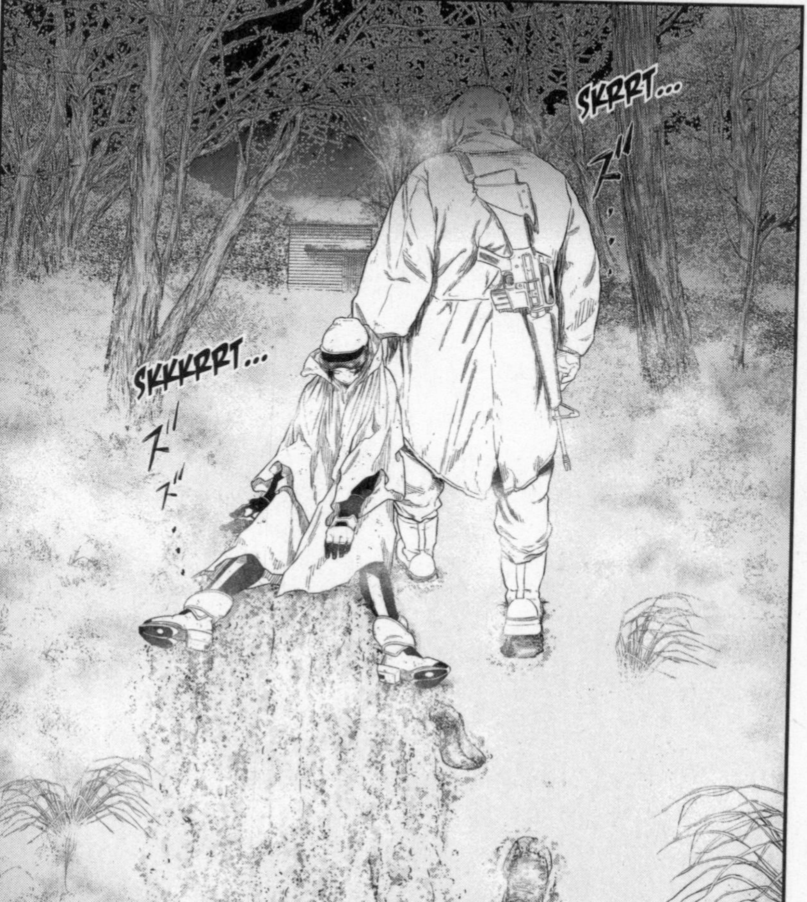
SKRRT...
SKKKRRT...

Translation Notes

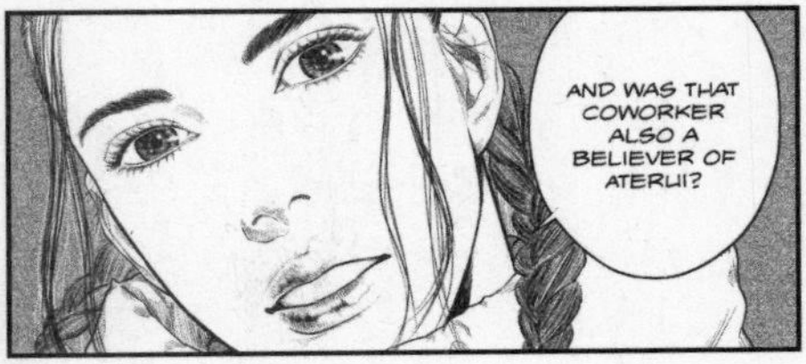
AND WAS THAT COWORKER ALSO A BELIEVER OF ATERUI?

50, Aterui

"Aterui" is the name of a famous military and political leader of the Isawa, a clan among the Emishi, who were an ethnic group based in northern Japan until the 9th century CE. They were forcibly assimilated into the Yamato imperial state during their efforts to unify the main island of what is now Japan (Honshu) during the 8th and 9th centuries CE. That clan, along with many peoples assimilated into the centralized Yamato empire from the northern, rural areas over the archipelago's history, have long been associated with mystical practices and liminal, pre-modern spaces.

57, Image on lanterns

The cross-like symbol on the lanterns is the *kanji* character for the number ten (pronounced "*ju*" or "*to*"), which is also in the first part of the name for the area in which the community is located, Towada.

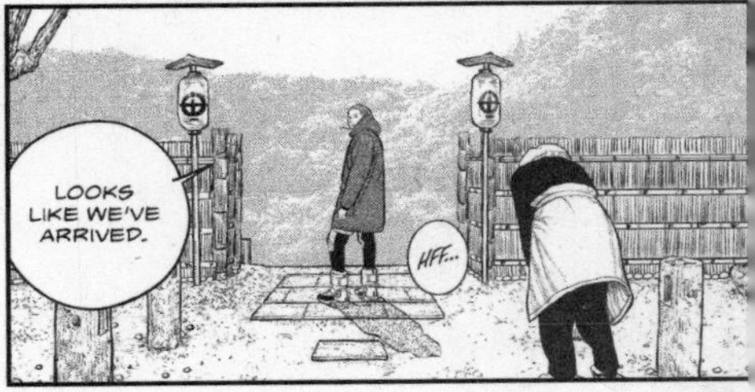
HFF...
LOOKS LIKE WE'VE ARRIVED.

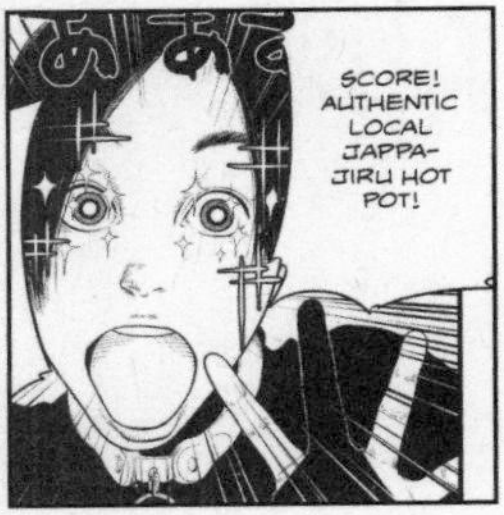
SCORE! AUTHENTIC LOCAL JAPPA-JIRU HOT POT!

68, *Jappa-jiru* hotpot

Jappa-jiru means "fish broth" in the Aomori dialect, an area in northwestern Japan.

78, Screen calligraphy

The calligraphy on the right half of the screens are lines from a Zen Buddhist priest named Getsuan (1326 - 1389), cited in a famous text called "A Mirror to the Flowers" about the form of traditional dramatic Japanese theater called *noh* by Zeami (1363 - 1443). The lines read from right to left: "Life and death come and go, we're mere puppets on a stage, and when the strings are cut, we fall in broken piles." The left half of the screens show a famous phrase from an ancient text in Buddhism, which describe Buddhas and bodhisattvas that "remove suffering and bestow bliss."

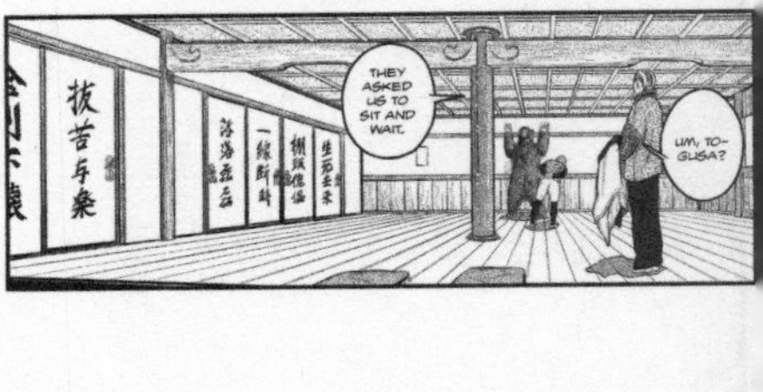
UM, TO-GUSA?
THEY ASKED US TO SIT AND WAIT.
生死去来
棚頭傀儡
一線断時
落落磊磊
抜苦与楽

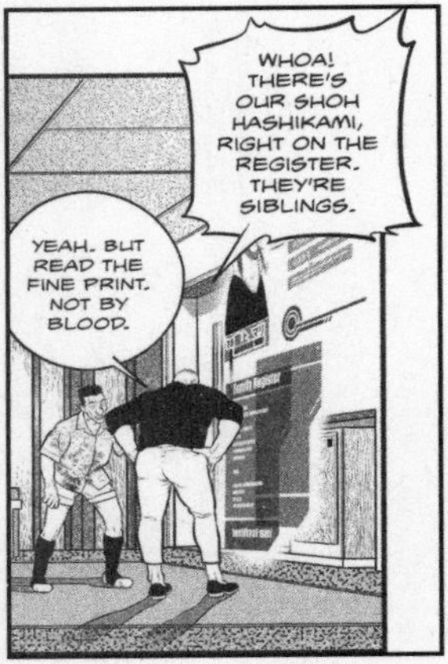
WHOA! THERE'S OUR SHOH HASHIKAMI, RIGHT ON THE REGISTER. THEY'RE SIBLINGS.
YEAH. BUT READ THE FINE PRINT. NOT BY BLOOD.

110, Family register

In Japan, an individual's legal status is registered by the government according to their family. This is called the "register system" (*koseki seido*), and each family has a "registry" with the local government, which records births, deaths, marriages, divorces and permanent residence.

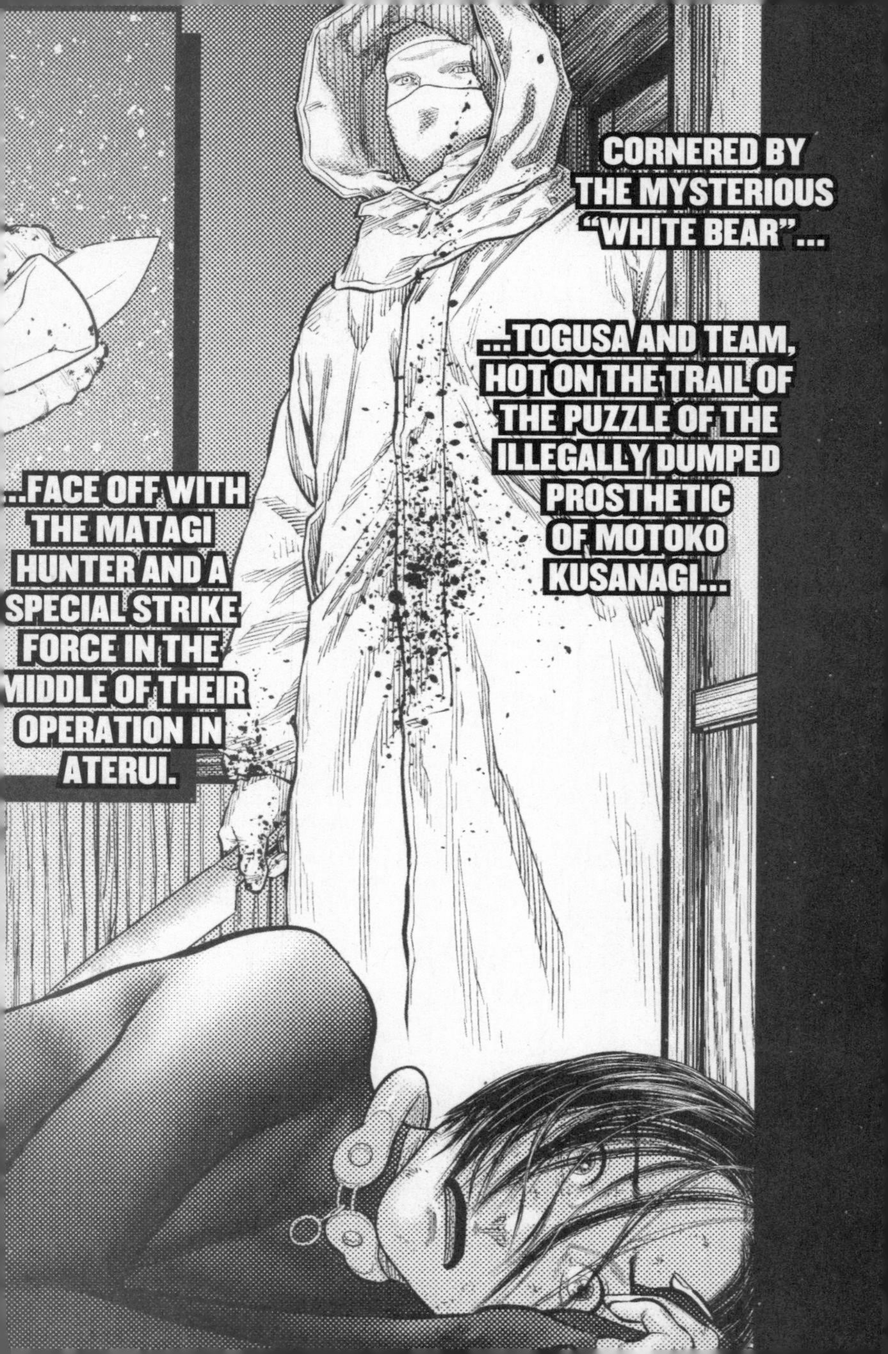
CORNERED BY THE MYSTERIOUS "WHITE BEAR"...
...TOGUSA AND TEAM, HOT ON THE TRAIL OF THE PUZZLE OF THE ILLEGALLY DUMPED PROSTHETIC OF MOTOKO KUSANAGI...
...FACE OFF WITH THE MATAGI HUNTER AND A SPECIAL STRIKE FORCE IN THE MIDDLE OF THEIR OPERATION IN ATERUI.

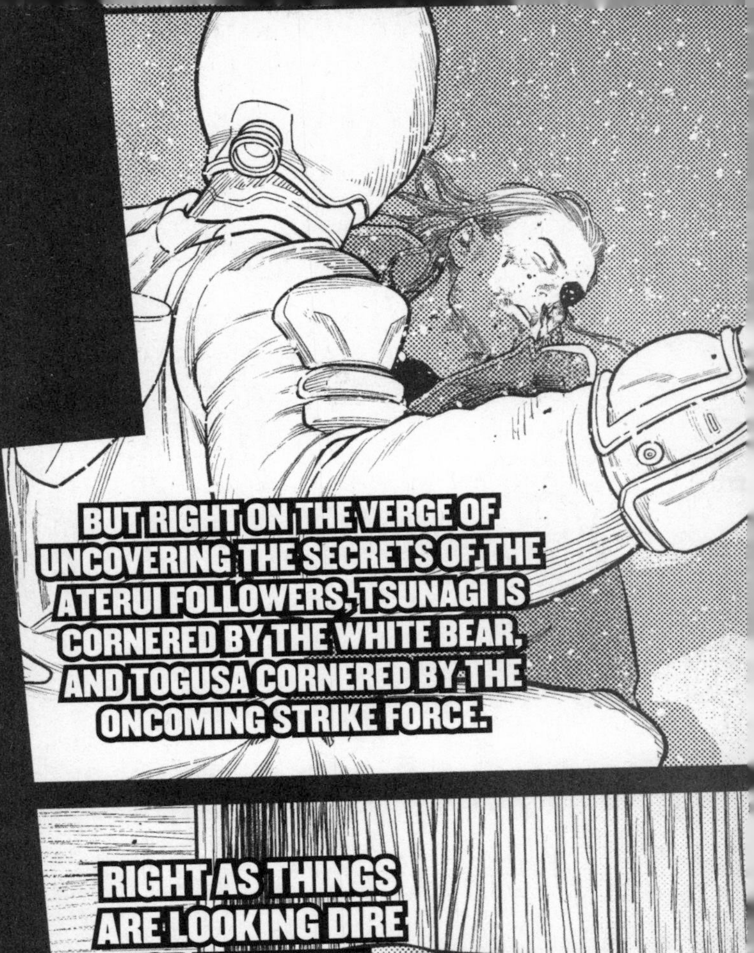
BUT RIGHT ON THE VERGE OF UNCOVERING THE SECRETS OF THE ATERUI FOLLOWERS, TSUNAGI IS CORNERED BY THE WHITE BEAR, AND TOGUSA CORNERED BY THE ONCOMING STRIKE FORCE.
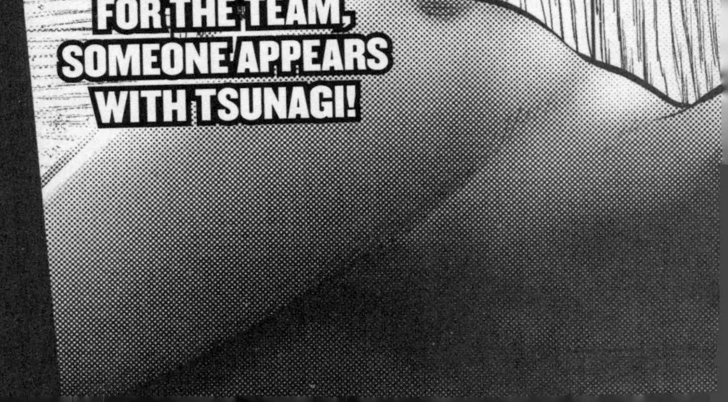
RIGHT AS THINGS ARE LOOKING DIRE FOR THE TEAM, SOMEONE APPEARS WITH TSUNAGI!

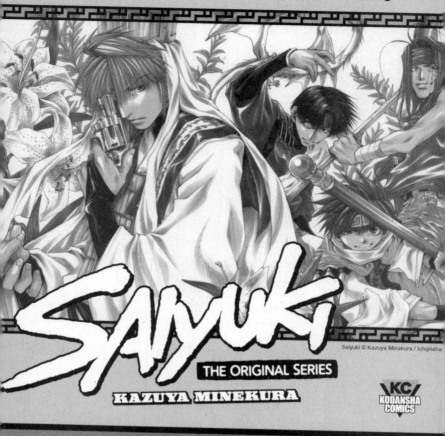

R0201721529

12/2020

A Kodansha Comics Trade Paperback Original
The Ghost in the Shell: The Human Algorithm 1 copyright © 2020 Junichi Fujisaku/Yuki Yoshimoto
© Shirow Masamune
English translation copyright © 2020 Junichi Fujisaku/Yuki Yoshimoto
© Shirow Masamune
All rights reserved.

Published in the United States by Kodansha Comics, an imprint of
Kodansha USA Publishing, LLC, New York.

Publication rights for this English edition arranged through
Kodansha Ltd., Tokyo.

First published in Japan in 2020 by Kodansha Ltd., Tokyo
as *Koukaku kidoutai: the humán algorithm*, volume 1.

ISBN 978-1-64651-177-8

Printed in the United States of America.

www.kodanshacomics.com

9 8 7 6 5 4 3 2 1
Translation: Stephen Kohler
Lettering: Paige Pumphrey
Editing: Nathaniel Gallant
Coordinator: TOYOKUNI Printing Co., Ltd
Kodansha Comics edition cover design by Phil Balsman

Publisher: Kiichiro Sugawara

Director of publishing services: Ben Applegate
Associate director of operations: Stephen Pakula
Publishing services managing editor: Noelle Webster
Assistant production manager: Emi Lotto, Angela Zurlo
Logo and character art ©Kodansha USA Publishing, LLC